Analyzing Qualitative Data

Second Edition

SAGE was founded in 1965 by Sara Miller McCune to support the dissemination of usable knowledge by publishing innovative and high-quality research and teaching content. Today, we publish over 900 journals, including those of more than 400 learned societies, more than 800 new books per year, and a growing range of library products including archives, data, case studies, reports, and video. SAGE remains majority-owned by our founder, and after Sara's lifetime will become owned by a charitable trust that secures our continued independence.

Los Angeles | London | New Delhi | Singapore | Washington DC | Melbourne

Analyzing Qualitative Data

Systematic Approaches

Second Edition

H. Russell Bernard
Arizona State University
University of Florida

Amber Wutich
Arizona State University

Gery W. Ryan
RAND Corporation

Los Angeles | London | New Delhi
Singapore | Washington DC | Melbourne

FOR INFORMATION:

SAGE Publications, Inc.
2455 Teller Road
Thousand Oaks, California 91320
E-mail: order@sagepub.com

SAGE Publications Ltd.
1 Oliver's Yard
55 City Road
London EC1Y 1SP
United Kingdom

SAGE Publications India Pvt. Ltd.
B 1/I 1 Mohan Cooperative Industrial Area
Mathura Road, New Delhi 110 044
India

SAGE Publications Asia-Pacific Pte. Ltd.
3 Church Street
#10-04 Samsung Hub
Singapore 049483

Acquisitions Editor: Leah Fargotstein
Editorial Assistant: Yvonne McDuffee
eLearning Editor: Nicole Mangona
Production Editor: Kelly DeRosa
Copy Editor: Carole Bernard
Typesetter: C&M Digitals (P) Ltd.
Proofreader: Dennis Webb
Indexer: Will Ragsdale
Cover Designer: Anupama Krishnan
Marketing Manager: Susannah Goldes

Printed in the United States of America

Library of Congress Cataloging-in-Publication Data

Names: Bernard, H. Russell (Harvey Russell), 1940- author. | Wutich, Amber, author. | Ryan, Gery Wayne, author.

Title: Analyzing qualitative data : systematic approaches / H. Russell Bernard, Arizona State University, University of Florida, Amber Wutich, Arizona State University, Gery W. Ryan, RAND Corporation.

Description: Thousand Oaks, California : SAGE, [2017] | Earlier edition: 2010. | Includes bibliographical references and index.

Identifiers: LCCN 2016000036 | ISBN 9781483344386 (pbk. : alk. paper)

Subjects: LCSH: Social sciences—Research—Methodology. | Qualitative research. | Quantitative research.

Classification: LCC H62.B438 2017 | DDC 001.4/2—dc23
LC record available at http://lccn.loc.gov/2016000036

This book is printed on acid-free paper.

SUSTAINABLE FORESTRY INITIATIVE

Certified Chain of Custody
Promoting Sustainable Forestry
www.sfiprogram.org
SFI-01268

SFI label applies to text stock

16 17 18 19 20 10 9 8 7 6 5 4 3 2 1

Brief Contents

Detailed Contents

Preface

This book is an introduction to systematic methods for analyzing qualitative data. Most qualitative data are written texts, but increasingly qualitative data include still and moving images and sound recordings of dialogs or narratives. It won't be long before qualitative data include holographic, 3-D images of people and the artifacts that people create. But that's for another edition.

We mean for this book to be useful—useful to students and colleagues who need an introduction to the range of methods available for analyzing qualitative data. There are whole texts devoted to each of the methods we discuss here—discourse analysis, grounded theory, content analysis, qualitative comparative analysis, ethnographic decision modeling, and so on. For us, the guiding principle is that, whatever our differences in epistemological principles—constructivist versus positivist, for example—or theoretical orientations—idealist versus materialist, for example—the methods that we use to collect and analyze data about human thought and human behavior belong to all of us. In the short run, methods get developed in disciplines and subdisciplines. Grounded theory was developed primarily in sociology, and qualitative comparative analysis was developed in political science, but these methods are used across the social sciences today. Cultural domain analysis and ethnographic decision modeling were developed in anthropology, but they, too, are used by scholars in many disciplines. In the long run, methods leak out across disciplines and really do belong to all of us.

Throughout the book, we use real examples from the literature in education, criminology, sociology, political sciences, and so on. You'll notice many examples from health research. This reflects our own background and also the fact that so much research on methods for analyzing qualitative data is done in the social sciences of health.

One of our reviewers emphasized that "research is not a linear process." We could not agree more. We set research up as if it were linear—first design, then data collection, then analysis, then write-up—but it's never that clean. In projects we've worked on over the years, we've redesigned things after finding out that our plans were, well, unrealistic. We've stopped collecting data to do preliminary analysis, and we've stopped analysis to collect additional, fill-in-the-holes data. And we've gone back and reanalyzed our data many, many times while writing up. When we send our research papers to a journal, anonymous reviewers often ask questions that require analyses we hadn't thought of ourselves. In short, the process of research can be messy, but that just makes it more fun, as far as we're concerned.

◆ WHAT'S IN THE BOOK?

There are two parts to this book. Part I is an overview of what we think of as the basics. Chapter 1 is about qualitative data: what they are and how they can be treated for analysis. Chapter 2 deals with how to review the literature and develop a research topic. Chapter 3 walks through solutions to a range of sampling problems. Chapter 4 covers methods for data collection. Chapter 5 is on finding themes, and is based on Ryan and Bernard's 2003 article in *Field Methods* (volume 15, pp. 85–109). Chapter 6 works through different methods for building and using codebooks. Chapter 7 is about the basics of data analysis, including data management and structure. Chapter 8 is an introduction to conceptual models.

Part II comprises 11 chapters, each treating a different method for analyzing text. Chapter 9 shows how to compare attributes of variables. This chapter will look familiar to those who have analyzed data with Excel or with a statistical package, like SPSS, SAS, Systat, Stata, and the like. That's because the process for comparing attributes of variables in a matrix is the same, whether the data are qualitative or quantitative.

Chapter 10 is an introduction to grounded theory—one of the two most widely used methods in the social sciences for analyzing text. The other is content analysis, the subject of Chapter 11.

Chapter 12 deals with schema analysis and folk models, methods that derive from psychology and linguistics. Chapter 13 focuses on narrative analysis. Chapter 14 covers two parts of the enormous field of discourse analysis—conversation analysis and performance analysis.

Chapter 15 is on the venerable method of analytic induction (based on logic) and the relatively new method of qualitative comparative analysis that derives from analytic induction.

Chapter 16 (based on Ryan and Bernard's 2006 article in *Human Organization* [volume 65, pp. 103–115]) is on ethnographic decision modeling.

Chapter 17 is about analyzing words, using simple techniques like counting and concordances.

Chapter 18 covers cultural domain analysis, including methods for collecting cognitive data (like free listing and pile sorting) and methods for analyzing those data (like multidimensional scaling and cluster analysis).

Chapter 19, on semantic network analysis, builds on Chapters 17 and 18 to show how methods like multidimensional scaling and cluster analysis can be used to analyze counts of words (or themes) extracted from texts and other qualitative data.

At the end of each chapter, there is a set of key concepts, a summary, and some hands-on exercises. Suggestions for further readings are also at the end of each chapter. These are meant as pointers to the literature, not as comprehensive reading lists for any topic. Use the Social Science Citation Index and other reference tools to find more literature on all the topics in this book. The appendix contains information on software for handling various chores in research. We've also put the appendix online so that we can update it. To access the appendix, head to https://us.sagepub.com/en-us/nam/analyzing-qualitative-data/book240717#resources. To access more resources, such as datasets, recommended readings, and video tutorials, visit study.sagepub.com/bernardaqd.

We don't have a chapter on mixed methods because we start from the idea that mixing methods is the natural order of science and always has been. So, take up any of the methods here and mix them all you want.

WHAT'S NEW IN THIS EDITION? ◆

Every chapter now has an extended summary, hands-on exercises, and a list of key concepts—**which are bolded when they are first introduced**.

Chapter 1, the Introduction, is updated and contains new text and examples. It also adds live behavior as a sixth kind of qualitative data.

Chapter 2, on literature review, is new to the book. The chapter focuses on choosing research topics that rely at least partly on qualitative data.

Chapters 3 and 4 now form a new section on research design. Chapter 3 on sampling (which was Chapter 17 in the last edition) has been updated to reflect the fast-growing literature on nonprobability sampling in qualitative research. Chapter 4, on data collection, has many new and updated examples.

Chapter 5 (Finding Themes) is updated to include information on automated coding and other forms of theme identification.

Chapter 6 (Codebooks and Coding) includes new text on deductive and inductive approaches to code development. It also has new information about how to manage codebooks in large, collaborative projects.

Chapters 7 (Introduction to Data Analysis), 8 (Conceptual Models), and 9 (Comparing Attributes of Variables) have been updated but remain largely unchanged.

Chapter 10, on grounded theory, has updated examples.

Chapter 11, on content analysis, has more on content dictionaries and on the history of automated content analysis. There is new information on distinguishing research questions and hypotheses. Some older examples have been removed.

Chapters 12 (Schema Analysis), 13 (Narrative Analysis), 14 (Discourse Analysis), 15 (Analytic Induction and Qualitative Comparative Analysis), and 16 (Ethnographic Decision Models) have been updated with new examples. Some text has been moved or replaced.

Chapter 17 (KWIC Analysis and Word Counts) has a new section on word clouds. The old section on semantic network analysis has been expanded and is now a stand-alone chapter (Chapter 19).

Chapter 18 (Cultural Domain Analysis) has been expanded to include discussions of data management, similarity matrices, multidimensional scaling, and hierarchical clustering. It also has new tables and figures.

Chapter 19 (Semantic Network Analysis) is a new chapter in this edition. It builds on material on semantic network analysis from the first edition's chapter on word-based analysis. In this edition, it also covers network analysis, how to count similarity, Jaccard's coefficient of similarity, and semantic network analyses of themes and codes. There is a new extended example covering thematic semantic network analysis.

Acknowledgments

This book comes out of courses we've taught at the University of Florida (Russ and Amber), the University of Missouri (Gery), the Pardee RAND Graduate School in Policy Analysis (Gery), Arizona State University (Amber), and the National Science Foundation's summer institutes on research design and research methods in cultural anthropology (Russ, Gery, and Amber). The summer institutes began in 1987, and we have been privileged to work with colleagues whose skills in teaching methods are an enduring source of inspiration: Stephen Borgatti, Jeffrey Johnson, Pertti Pelto, and Susan Weller. We are especially grateful to Clarence Gravlee, Elizabeth Krause, Melissa Beresford, and Sarah Szurek, who continue to teach us about the methods in this book.

Gery thanks his family for their support and patience as he worked on this project. He thanks the Robert Wood Johnson Clinical Scholars, his colleagues at RAND, and the students at the Pardee RAND Graduate School in Policy Analysis, who presented him with an array of research problems and trusted him to apply and improve new techniques for collecting and analyzing qualitative data, and he thanks David Kennedy, Hank Green, Homero Martínez, Thomas Weisner, and Gail Zellman for pushing him to new levels of methodological rigor and creativity.

Amber thanks her wonderful students—especially the students of the NSF summer programs and of ASU's Culture Health and Environment Lab. The ASU Lab has been the playground where she, alongside her colleague Alexandra Brewis, has had the fun of working with the techniques we cover in this book. Amber also thanks her family—Alexandro, Matteo, and Luis—for all the fun times at home.

Russ thanks the many students and colleagues—far too many to name—who have helped him learn to talk about research methods. Two of his closest colleagues, Thomas Schweizer and Peter Killworth, are no longer around to hear his thanks, but that neither absolves his debt nor diminishes his gratitude to them. Russ's biggest debt is for a lifetime of support by his family—his life partner, Carole, and their children, Elyssa and Sharyn—and now a third generation who get to watch how books are actually written.

Finally, our thanks to everyone in editorial and production who worked on this book. C. Deborah Laughton signed the first edition of this book while she was at SAGE and worked with us to refine our ideas and focus our writing. Vicki Knight at

SAGE was our editor for this edition and was a joy to work with. She found the kind of reviewers that authors really, really want—critical and helpful at the same time—and guided us through the revisions. Leah Fargotstein took over just as we were finishing this edition. Our production editor for this edition was Kelly DeRosa. Carole Bernard (Russ's wife) was the copyeditor for this book. She did yet again what she has done for hundreds of authors over the years, saving us from so many infelicities. Book authors will all know what we mean. Authors of research papers can just look at the bibliography for this book, imagine what it takes to clean it up—and then multiply by ten.

H. Russell Bernard
Gainesville, FL

Gery W. Ryan
Santa Monica, CA

Amber Wutich
Tempe, AZ

SAGE Publishing would like to thank the following reviewers:

Kadir Demir, Georgia State University

Marianne M. Sarkis, Clark University

Patricia Wright, University of Arkansas

James A. Bernauer, Robert Morris University

Christos Makrigeorgis, Walden University

David M. Tack, Minnesota State University Moorhead

About the Authors

H. Russell Bernard (PhD, University of Illinois, 1968) is Professor Emeritus at the University of Florida and Director of the Institute for Social Science Research at Arizona State University. Bernard has done research in Greece, Mexico, and the United States and has taught at universities in the United States, Japan, and Germany. His areas of research include technology and social change, language death, and social network analysis. Since 1987, Bernard has participated in summer courses, sponsored by the U.S. National Science Foundation, on research methods and research design. He is former editor of *Human Organization* and the *American Anthropologist* and is the current editor of *Field Methods*. Bernard's books include *Research Methods in Anthropology* (5th ed., AltaMira, 2011), *Social Research Methods* (2d ed., SAGE, 2012), and *Native Ethnography*, with Jesús Salinas Pedraza (SAGE, 1989). Bernard was the 2003 recipient of the Franz Boas Award from the American Anthropological Association and is a member of the National Academy of Sciences.

Amber Wutich (PhD, University of Florida, 2006) is Director of the Center for Global Health and a member of the faculty of the School of Human Evolution and Social Change at Arizona State University. Wutich has done ethnographic research in Bolivia, Paraguay, Mexico, and the United States. She also directs the Global Ethnohydrology Study, a long-term, transdisciplinary, multi-country study of water knowledge and management across cultures. Wutich's areas of research include resource insecurity, cultural norms, and stigma. Since 2006, Wutich has taught summer courses, sponsored by the U.S. National Science Foundation, on text analysis and research design. She is the associate editor of *Field Methods* and has been published widely, including articles in *Social Science & Medicine*, *Human Ecology*, *Ecological Economics*, and *Current Anthropology*. In 2013, Wutich was named Carnegie CASE Arizona Professor of the Year.

Gery W. Ryan (PhD, University of Florida, 1995) is a Senior Behavioral Scientist at the RAND Corporation and Assistant Dean for Academic Affairs at the Pardee RAND Graduate School in Policy Analysis. Ryan's research focuses on social factors in mental and physical health, and includes studies on HIV/AIDS, depression, serious mental illness, childhood diarrhea and acute respiratory illnesses, obesity, and complementary and alternative medicine. He has worked extensively in Latin America and Africa on health-related issues and helped redesign and implement a large-scale education reform in Qatar. As a methodologist, Ryan has published widely on the application of systematic methods to qualitative research. Over the last 20 years, he has run workshops sponsored by NSF, NIH, CDC, and WHO on qualitative research methods and has taught these methods at UCLA, Pardee RAND, and the University of Missouri.

CHAPTER **1**

INTRODUCTION TO TEXT

Qualitative Data Analysis

INTRODUCTION: WHAT IS QUALITATIVE DATA ANALYSIS? ◆

Because of a quirk in the English language, the phrase "qualitative data analysis" is mischievously ambiguous. It can mean "**the analysis of qualitative data**" or it can mean "**the qualitative analysis of data**." The confusion can be eliminated by clearly distinguishing between data and analysis. Figure 1.1 lays out the possibilities.

Cell A is the **qualitative analysis of qualitative data**. When ecologists pore over satellite images of the Earth's surface; when astronomers listen to recordings of sounds

Figure 1.1 Key Qualitative and Quantitative Distinctions

Analysis	Data	
	Qualitative (Texts)	Quantitative (Ordinal/Ratio Scale)
Qualitative	A	B
	Interpretive text studies (e.g., Hermeneutics, Grounded Theory, Phenomenology)	Search for and presentation of meaning in results of quantitative processing
Quantitative	C	D
	Turning words into numbers (e.g., Classic Content Analysis, Word Counts, Free Lists, Pile Sorts, etc.)	Statistical and mathematical analysis of numeric data

SOURCE: Adapted from: Bernard, H. Russell. 1996. Qualitative data, quantitative analysis. *Cultural Anthropology Methods Journal* 8[1]:9–11.

from other galaxies; and when medical researchers listen to heart beats they are all looking for regularities in qualitative data. "Looking for regularities" is analysis. It's the quintessential qualitative act, and it's common to all traditions of scholarship, across the humanities and the sciences.

In the social sciences, interpretive studies of texts, like transcriptions of interviews, are of this kind (Cell A). Investigators focus on and name themes in texts. They tell the story, as they see it, of how the themes are related to one another and how characteristics of the speaker or speakers account for the existence of certain themes and the absence of others. Researchers may deconstruct a text, look for hidden subtexts, and try to let their audience know—using the power of good rhetoric—the deeper meaning or the multiple meanings in it.

For many scholars, the phrase "qualitative data analysis" refers exclusively to Cell A, but for us, and for everyone in the **mixed-methods movement**, it also includes Cell C, the **quantitative analysis of qualitative data** (see Box 1.1).

Box 1.1

The Mixed-Methods Movement?

In fact, the unselfconscious mixing of qualitative and quantitative data and qualitative and quantitative analysis is the natural order of all science. When Galileo first trained his then-brand-new telescope on the moon, he noticed what he called lighter and darker areas. The large dark spots had, Galileo said, been seen from time immemorial and so he said "These

I shall call the 'large' or 'ancient' spots." He also wrote that the moon was "not smooth, uniform, and precisely spherical" as commonly believed, but "uneven, rough, and full of cavities and prominences," much like the Earth. No more qualitative description was ever penned (Galileo Galilei 1610:3).

Social scientists of the 19th and early 20th centuries combined qualitative and quantitative data in their research—see Florence Nightingale's great work (1871) on training midwives and the monumental ethnography of Middletown (Muncie, Indiana), by Robert and Helen Lynd (1929). In 1957, Martin Trow wrote "let us be done with the arguments of 'participant observation' versus interviewing" and get on with using the methods that are best suited to the job. A generation later, Reichardt and Cook (1979:19) argued that there was "no reason to choose between qualitative and quantitative methods."

And still another generation later, the mixed-methods movement today inherits this noble pedigree. The term "mixed methods" itself, however, only showed up in the *Social Science Citation Index* in 1993. Today, there are over 5,000 hits on that term, with over 70% of them since 2010. There is a *Journal of Mixed Methods Research* (mmr.sagepub.com), several textbooks on mixed methods research (Creswell and Plano Clark 2011; Greene 2007; Hesse-Biber 2010; Morse and Niehaus 2009), and a handbook of mixed-methods research (Tashakkori and Teddlie 2010). Now *that's* a movement.

Cell C involves turning words, images, sounds, or objects into numbers and then using statistical and numerical tools to analyze those numbers (Boyatzis 1998). Scholars in communications, for example, regularly tag television ads from various countries to test for differences in how sex roles are portrayed across the world (Furnham and Mak 1999; Paek et al. 2011). Political scientists code the speeches of candidates for president to detect appeals to various constituencies (Calfano and Djupe 2009). They may even code the facial expressions of political candidates to test whether those expressions affect how potential voters feel about those candidates (Weaver et al. 2015) (see Box 1.2).

Box 1.2

Quantitative Testing of Hypotheses Using Qualitative Data

Are adolescents who express a strong desire to "fit in" with their peers more likely to start smoking than are adolescents who express a strong streak of independence? This can be tested by interviewing adolescents about reasons for smoking or not smoking, coding the texts for themes (like independence or being concerned about looking good to peers), and then doing statistical analysis to test relations among the themes. This is the basis for classical content analysis—about which, much more in Chapter 11.

Cell D refers to the **quantitative analysis of quantitative data**. Closed-ended questions in surveys, for example, produce quantitative data directly—that is, they are collected initially as numbers, not as text or other qualitative data. National censuses produce numerical data about people's ages, education, income, family size, and so on. Organizations, from businesses to charities to zoos, produce gobs and gobs of numerical data, too—about the socioeconomic characteristics of people who use their products or services, about how often they have to replace managers, about how much time secretaries spend on the phone and on email, and on and on. When qualitative data are turned into numbers (Cell C), the work of analysis is indistinguishable from the work done in Cell D.

Cell B is the **qualitative analysis of quantitative data**. It's what quantitative analysts do after they get through doing the work in Cells C and D, and it involves the search for, and the presentation of, meaning in the results of quantitative data processing. Cell B includes everything from the finding of regularities in a scatter plot to the interpretation of meaning and substantive significance of statistical tests. Without the work in Cell B, Cell D studies are sterile and vacuous.

Increasingly, Cell B involves turning quantitative data into still or moving images—qualitative data—to make the quantitative data easier to analyze. When you see a weather forecaster on television standing in front of a multicolor, moving picture of temperature and precipitation, that image is produced from millions of numbers transmitted from a satellite. Techniques—like multidimensional scaling—for visualizing very complex numerical data are easily available today for social scientists. More on this in Chapters 7, 18, and 19.

◆ WHAT ARE DATA AND WHAT MAKES THEM QUALITATIVE?

Data—qualitative and quantitative alike—are **reductions of our experience** (Bernard et al. 1986). Electrons and DNA are things. With a little help from some instruments, we can look at electrons and DNA and we can record what we see. Whatever we choose to record about things like these—their shape, their size, their weight, their speed—are data. If we record numbers, we get quantitative data; and if we record sounds, words, or pictures, we get qualitative data.

In the social sciences, we are interested in people's behavior, thoughts, emotions, and artifacts (the physical residue of people's thoughts, emotions, and behavior) and the environmental conditions in which people behave, think, feel, and make things.

When we reduce our experience of those things to numbers, the result is quantitative data. And when we reduce people's thoughts, behaviors, emotions, artifacts, and environments to sounds, words, or pictures, the result is qualitative data.

We create data by chunking experience into recordable units. Consider three researchers observing children at play in a schoolyard or playground. One of them watches the children and writes up field notes on what she saw. Another records the frequency of particular behaviors using a checklist. The third uses a video camera to record the children playing. The phenomena of interest—the behavior, the words, the laughter, and the crying of children on a playground—are ephemera, disappearing as they happen. The records of the phenomena—the notes, the checklist, the video recording—remain for us to analyze and understand. Data are the **archeological record of experience**.

Some qualitative data are produced on purpose—we interview people and transcribe their words; we put children together in a room full of toys and videotape or take notes about what they do—but most of the record about human thought and behavior comes to us as naturally occurring qualitative data. The paintings produced during the first hundred years of the Italian Renaissance; the television ads that aired last week in Mexico that contained images of old people; the articles in the *Wall Street Journal* over the last 20 years that contain the phrase "corporate culture"; the diaries of U.S. Civil War soldiers; and the blogs of today's soldiers around the world are all naturally occurring, qualitative data.

The images and texts on Facebook and Twitter and the millions of blogs produced every day across the world are all qualitative data. Those data are being used by researchers to investigate questions such as presentation of self (Chen 2010; Escobar and Roman 2011), how fans engage with sports teams and artists (Bennett 2012; Stavros et al. 2014), and how brands become trusted (Habibi et al. 2014). Making sense of Big Data from social media is a big industry today, and Big Data isn't just for numbers anymore.

Across the sciences, from anthropology to zoology, from sociology to physics, data—all data, qualitative and quantitative—are selections of what's available. Satellites don't record everything going on below them any more than observers of human behavior record everything they see. People—real human beings—decide to measure some things and not others. These decisions are not random. They are sometimes based on unadulterated scientific curiosity, and they are sometimes based on what's fundable. They are sometimes motivated by humanitarian instincts and sometimes by greed.

This does not invalidate the effort to produce data. It does, however, remind us that there is a human component to science, just as there is in art, or government, or commerce.

ABOUT NUMBERS AND WORDS ♦

Every reader of this book is aware of the long-standing debate in the social sciences about the relative merits of quantitative versus qualitative data. **The qual–quant**

debate reflects principled stands by those who identify with the **positivist tradition in the social sciences** and those who identify with the **humanist tradition**.

These principled discussions on matters of **epistemology**—how we know things at all—have a noble tradition dating to the famous dictum of the Greek philosopher, **Protagoras** (485–410 BCE) that "**man is the measure of all things**"—meaning that truth is not absolute but is decided by individual human judgment—and to the Roman poet, **Titus Lucretius's** (94–49 BCE) insistence on the **material nature of all things**, including the mind. (**Further Reading**: the qualitative–quantitative issue)

In the social and behavioral sciences, the humanist position has been historically at odds with the philosophy of knowledge represented by science. In psychology, most *research* is in the positivistic tradition, while much *clinical work* is in the humanist tradition because, as its practitioners cogently point out, it works. In sociology, there is a growing tradition of interpretive research, but most sociology is done from the positivist perspective. In cultural anthropology, most *data collection* is done by field-workers—which makes cultural anthropology thoroughly empirical—but much of the *data analysis* is done in the humanist tradition.

Notice in the last paragraph our use of phrases like "positivist perspective," and "humanist tradition." Not once did we say that "research in X is mostly quantitative" or that "research in Y is mostly qualitative." We never use the distinction between quantitative and qualitative as cover for talking about the difference between science and humanism. Lots of scientists do their work without numbers; and many scientists whose work is highly quantitative consider themselves to be morally committed humanists.

Numbers do not make an inquiry scientific (searching the Bible for statistical evidence to support the subjugation of women doesn't turn the enterprise into science), and the use of qualitative data does not diminish the scientific credibility of any piece of research.

Scholars in the physical and biological sciences wonder what all the fuss is about. They already know how powerful qualitative data are. Satellite images inform geology, meteorology, astronomy, ecology, archeology, and oceanography. Images from electron microscopes inform chemistry, molecular biology, and physiology. Lengthy narratives dictated into a tape recorder by observers inform students of volcanoes, hurricanes, gorillas, and crime scenes.

♦ RESEARCH GOALS

There are **four main objectives in qualitative research**. The questions associated with each are shown in Table 1.1.

Table 1.1 Goals of Qualitative Research

General Aim	Type	Questions
1. Exploration		What kinds of things are present here?
		How are these things related to one another?
2. Description		Are there natural groups of things here?
	Case	What does a case look like?
	Group	What does a set of cases look like?
		Is a particular kind of thing (A) present or not?
		How much of that kind of thing (A) is there?
	Cultural	What does the culture look like?
3. Comparison	Case	How is case X different from case Y?
	Group	How is a group of Xs different from a group of Ys?
4. Testing models	Case	To what degree does a particular case conform to the proposed model?
	Group	To what degree does a group of cases conform to the proposed model?

1. Exploration

At this early stage, the goal is to discover themes and patterns and to build initial models of how complex systems work—that is, how themes are related to one another. Whether we're talking about astronomers scanning the night sky in search of new comets and asteroids, or grounded theorists studying how people experience illness, exploring means following leads and hunches, taking a step forward and then backtracking, uncovering what's there, experiencing the phenomenon we're studying, and identifying both its unique features and the features it shares with other phenomena.

2. Description

Every field of science depends vitally on good description. Long before the physics of avian flight were worked out, people watched and recorded as faithfully as possible just how birds managed not to fall out of the sky. Every new comet and asteroid that's discovered is described in the scientific literature, as is every new bug and plant and disease.

Descriptions can be qualitative or quantitative, or both, and detailed case studies—with their listings of typical features, idiosyncrasies, and exceptions—are used widely in the teaching of law, medicine, and management. Ethnographic field notes are typically filled with individual case studies.

How much detail should you shoot for in a good description? When you're collecting data, you should get as much as possible. You can always back off on the level of precision later, when you write up your findings. It may be enough in your write-up to say something like "Cambodian refugees comprise the largest ethnic group in this neighborhood." But if you need to know the percentage of each ethnic group in the neighborhood, then you'd better collect that data from the start by asking every refugee what his or her ethnicity (or language, or country of origin) is. You can always generalize from specifics, but you can never go the other way.

In describing cultural beliefs and practices, we focus on what people share and what they don't share. Here again, it pays to get as much as possible from the start—and for the same reason: You can only generalize if you have the specifics.

3. Comparison

Qualitative comparison involves identifying features that individuals or groups share and don't share. In the 1930s, Wayne Dennis, a psychologist, collected observational data on 41 Navajo and Hopi babies and on a similar group of white American babies in a study of child-rearing practices. Here's a thoroughly qualitative, comparative statement from his study: "Whereas some American infants are bottle-fed almost from the beginning and many are breast fed but a short time, all Hopi infants are breast fed, none are weaned under one year of age and many are not weaned before two years" (Dennis 1940:307).

Quantitative comparison involves testing whether (and how much) measurements of variables track each other. Does the weight of children between the ages of 10 and 16 vary with their height? If so, how closely do the two variables (height and weight) track each other? Does the tracking vary by ethnic group? By family income?

Just as with description, it pays to collect specific data and not rush to generalize.

4. Testing Models

This is where we test hypotheses against observations. We can do this with only qualitative data, with only quantitative data, or with both. Here is Wayne Dennis again:

American infants are usually placed on a rigid time schedule of feedings with an interval of several hours between feedings [and are] . . . often expected to cry for a period before being fed. The Hopi infant, on the other hand, is nursed as soon as he cries, and consequently nurses frequently and cries very little. (Dennis 1940:307)

Dennis has tested his hypothesis—without reporting a single number—about the relationship between crying and feeding in American and Hopi society and he has drawn a strong conclusion. In fact, he was testing a much, much larger model, or set of hypotheses, about the care of infants. After reporting on Hopi, Navajo, and white American practices for carrying, feeding, and toilet training of infants, Dennis says that: "Beginning roughly at one year of age the patterns of the infant begin to vary in accordance with the culture of the group" as children begin to learn a language and to imitate their parents' distinctly cultural behavior. Dennis concludes that: "This corroborates the view that the characteristics of infancy are universal and that culture overlays or modifies a more basic substratum of behavior" (1940:316).

Many projects involve all four of these activities—**exploration, description, comparison, and model testing**. Some scholars rely on qualitative data for exploration and discovery and rely on quantitative data for testing models. Increasingly, though, research across the social sciences relies on a balanced, commonsensical mix of both kinds of data.

KINDS OF QUALITATIVE DATA ◆

Qualitative data come to us in five forms: (1) **physical objects**; (2) **still images**; (3) **sounds**; (4) **moving images**; and, of course (5) **texts** (see Box 1.3).

Box 1.3

Live Behavior, Tastes, and Smells

Live behavior can be considered a kind of qualitative data. Like physical artifacts, still images, video, sounds, and text, live behavior comes to us whole and can be studied qualitatively or quantitatively. Judges of gymnastics or figure skating or diving evaluate behavioral events qualitatively. Then, they boil down their qualitative analysis into a single proxy number (from 1 to 10).

(Continued)

(Continued)

Much of the research done on live behavior starts with a search for nameable patterns (themes), followed by coding of the behavior stream and analysis of the codes. This is really the same exercise as coding artifacts or texts. The qualitative study of the data (the naming of themes) allows us to tag the data and look for patterns.

Live behavior has to be observed in order to be recorded, but since much of it is impossible to observe directly, most research on behavior is actually based on **reported behavior** or on videos.

Interestingly, until recently, there has been no way to collect data outside the laboratory on taste or smell. The only easily accessible olfactory and gustatory data we have come from our memories. Wine aficionados have developed an elaborate vocabulary about tastes and smells—a vocabulary that turns memory into exchangeable information. We know how important taste and smell are to people—try talking about ethnicity in the United States without referring to burritos and lasagnas and bagels and mousakas and pirogis. Kern et al. (2014), however, are developing easy-to-use tools for collecting olfactory data in the field, and we expect this to create opportunities for research.

Table 1.2 shows the **five kinds of qualitative data**, broken down by size and accessibility. Material objects range from personal trinkets to grass huts to vast remains of ancient cities. Videos can be 30-second commercials or three-hour epic pictures. Still images range from stick figures drawn by children to magazine covers to the work of graffiti artists on the walls of a city.

Texts can be single-word answers to questions, the complete works of Shakespeare, or transcribed narratives from ethnographic interviews. Data from public sources are more accessible than are data from private ones.

1. Physical Objects

For archeologists who study preliterate societies—societies that flourished prior to written communication—physical remains may be the only data available. The study of material culture, however, is not limited to societies of the distant past. Beginning in the late 15th century, the Age of Discovery in Europe produced an enormous market for material objects from societies around the world, and by the late 19th century, anthropologists in Germany, Britain, and the United States were avid collectors of artifacts for public museums.

Today, museums are repositories of data about ancient cultures and about everyday life in modern societies across the world. They provide us with a living record of

Table 1.2 Kinds of Qualitative Data Based on Form, Size, and Accessibility

	Small		Large	
	Accessibility			
Form	Public	Private	Public	Private
Physical Objects	Park sculptures, street signs, pottery shards, store merchandise	Personal jewelry, pill bottles, blood samples	Archaeological ruins, buildings, houses, universities, skyscrapers	Household garbage, clothing
Still Images	Magazine ads, cave art, billboards, web pages, paintings hung in museums	Doodles, line sketches, family portraits, patient X-rays	Large detailed murals, art exhibits	Family albums, art portfolios, CAT scans
Sounds	Jingles, radio ads, intercom announcements, messages you hear while on hold	Memo dictation, answering machine messages, elevator conversations	Political speeches, sports play-by-plays, music albums, focus group tape recordings	Oral histories, demo sound-tracks, in-depth conversations, clinical interviews
Moving Images: Video	TV ads, news footage, sitcoms	Home-movie clips	Full-length movies, documentaries, television programs	Long video recordings of family reunions and special events, like weddings
Texts	Epitaphs, obituaries, personal ads, political buttons, parking tickets	Thank-you letters, shopping lists, short responses to interview questions, emails	Books, manuals, religious tomes, court transcripts, congressional record, newspapers	Diaries, detailed correspondence, private chat-room discussions

the diversity of human religious, political, and economic activity, and social scientists from many disciplines continue to study human interaction with material objects.

Researchers in marketing and consumer behavior, of course, are vitally interested in material culture (D. Miller 1987). Students of the world's religions collect and analyze icons and talismans (Handloff 1982; McColl 1982). Education researchers study the consumer habits of students (Pedrozo 2011).

Anthropologists have long used material possessions as indicators of status, prestige, and wealth in a community (DeWalt 1979). Ryan (1995), for example, found that the presence or absence of certain material objects—things like toilets, televisions, cars, corn mills, lamps—in the homes of African villagers predicted the kind of medical treatment that people sought. (**Further Reading**: material culture and museums)

2. Still Images

For art historians, media and communication specialists, and those who study popular culture, images, both still and moving, are a standard form of data. As early as 1919, Alfred Kroeber analyzed pictures in American and French fashion magazines and found "an underlying pulsation in the width of civilized women's skirts, which is symmetrical and extends in its up and down beat over a full century; and an analogous rhythm in skirt length, but with a period of only about a third the duration" (Kroeber 1919:257).

Since then, there have been hundreds of social science studies using still images as basic data. These data include greeting cards (Bridges 1993; West 2010), comic strips (Yasumoto and LaRossa 2010), pictures in ads (Goffman 1979), photographs (Drazin and Frolich 2007), and images from photo-sharing web sites (Stepchenkova and Zhan 2013).

Malkin et al. (1999) analyzed the covers of 12 popular women's magazines (*Ladies Home Journal, Cosmopolitan*, etc.) and nine popular men's magazines (*Esquire, Sports Illustrated*, etc.). The culturally patterned messages are clear: Men are enjoined to expand their knowledge, hobbies, and activities, while women are enjoined to improve their life by losing weight and doing other things to change their appearance. (**Further Reading**: analyzing still images)

3. Sounds

Audio data—electrical representations of sounds—include recordings of things like music, narratives, jokes, speeches, radio programs, and interviews. We're not talking here about the substantive content of these data. If you record and transcribe doctors and patients during examinations or husbands and wives during counseling sessions or pupils and teachers in classrooms, you create a set of texts. You can analyze those texts for their thematic content (we'll talk about this in Chapters 5 and 6), but important parts of these interactions can be found only in their **prosodic features**—tone of voice, pitch, cadence, rhythm, and so on.

In a classic study, Labov and Waletzky (1997) used recorded narratives to understand differences in class and ethnic markers of black and white American speech. Joel Sherzer (1994) compared a recorded, two-hour traditional chant by Chief Olopinikwa of the San Blas Kuna Indians in Panama, with a phonetic transcription of the event. The transcription left out the chanted utterances of the responding chief (usually something like "so it is"), which was key to understanding the verse structure of the chant.

This may seem like an exotic example, but it really isn't. It's just an example from a language that's exotic to speakers of English of something that goes on in all story-telling, in all languages: The use of prosodic features convey meaning in human speech. If you want to pursue this kind of linguistic analysis of discourse, see Wennerstrom (2001a). (**Further Reading**: prosody and narrative)

4. Moving Images: Video

Moving images, or what we call video in the rest of this book, combines the power of images and sounds through time. Scholars in film studies, sociologists, political scientists, and researchers in gender and media studies have become expert in analyzing video documents such as films, television programs and commercials, political ads, and even home-made movies.

Cowan and O'Brian (1990), for example, studied 474 cases of "victims" in slasher movies. Surviving as a female slasher victim, it turns out, is strongly associated with the absence of sexual behavior and with being less physically attractive than nonsurviving women. The male nonsurvivors were cynical, egotistical, and dictatorial. Cowan and O'Brien conclude that, in slasher films, sexually pure women survive and that "unmitigated masculinity" ends in death (1990:195).

The Third International Mathematics and Science Study, or TIMSS, was a massive study of how math and science were taught in the 1990s in 41 countries around the world. One part of the TIMSS effort was the intensive study of instructional practices and lesson content in three countries, Japan, Germany, and the United States. Researchers studied videotapes of eighth-grade classrooms in the three countries and found very different teaching styles.

In the United States and Germany, students spent nearly all their time practicing routine procedures to learn math. In Japan, students spent less than half their time on this kind of learning and a lot of time figuring out new solutions to standard problems—an effort that stimulates conceptual, rather than rote, thinking about mathematics (Jacobs et al. 2007; Stigler et al. 1999:vii). (**Further Reading**: analyzing video)

5. Texts

By far the largest trove of qualitative data are the mountains of written texts that have been produced over the centuries. Scholars from across the social and behavioral sciences—humanists and positivists alike—have analyzed newspaper articles, novels, congressional reports, brochures published by hate groups, personal want ads, court records, diaries, email messages, personal web-pages, blogs, and so on.

Most of this book is about analyzing this kind of qualitative data, but almost everything we have to say about finding themes, coding themes, and analyzing text can be applied as easily to objects, images, and sounds as they can to words.

Key Concepts in This Chapter

analysis of qualitative data
qualitative analysis of data
qualitative analysis of
    qualitative data
mixed-methods
    movement
quantitative analysis of
    qualitative data
quantitative analysis of
    quantitative data
qualitative analysis of
    quantitative data
reductions of our
    experience

archeological record of
    experience
the qual–quant debate
positivist tradition in the
    social sciences
humanist tradition in the
    social sciences
epistemology
Protagoras' dictum that
    "man is the measure of
    all things"
Lucretius's observation
    about the material
    nature of all things

four main objectives
    in qualitative
    research
exploration, description,
    comparison, model
    testing
physical objects, still
    images, sounds, moving
    images, text
reported behavior
five kinds of qualitative
    data
prosodic features

Summary

- The phrase "qualitative data analysis" can mean "the analysis of qualitative data" or "the qualitative analysis of data."

  o Since data and analysis can be either qualitative or quantitative, there are four possibilities: qualitative analysis of qualitative data; qualitative analysis of quantitative data; quantitative analysis of qualitative data; and quantitative analysis of quantitative data.

- Looking for regularities is analysis. Regularities can be detected in either qualitative or quantitative data.
- The phrase "mixed methods" is barely 25 years old, but all sciences rely on qualitative and quantitative data and on qualitative and quantitative analysis.
- Data are reductions of experience.

  o When we reduce our experience or observations of things to numbers, the result is quantitative data. When we reduce our experience of things to words or images, the result is qualtitative data.

  o Most of the record about human thought and behavior comes to us as naturally occurring qualitative data

- All data, qualitative and quantitative, are selections of what's available and are constructed by researchers to address specific questions.

  o People make those selections. This subjective component does not invalidate the effort to produce data. It reminds us that there is a human component to science, just as there is in art, or government, or commerce.

- The qual–quant debate reflects principled stands by those who identify with the positivist, or scientific tradition in the social sciences, and humanist tradition, dating to the Roman poet, Lucretius (94–49 BCE) and the Greek philosopher, Protagoras (485–410 BCE), respectively.

  o The distinction between quantitative and qualitative is not the same as the difference between science and humanism. Much of science is based on qualitative data and qualitative analysis, and many scientists whose work is highly quantitative consider themselves to be humanists.

- There are four main objectives in qualitative research: exploration, description, comparison, and testing of models.

  o At the start of a research project, a lot of detail in data collection is desirable. You can always generalize from specifics, but you can never go the other way.

- Qualitative data come to us in five forms: physical objects, still images, sounds, moving images, and written words.

  o These five kinds of qualitative data are distinguished by size and accessibility (public vs. private).

Further Reading

The qual–quant problem. Allwood (2012), Bryman (1984, 1988), Hanson (2008), Howe (1988), Guba and Lincoln (1994), King et al. (1994), Rossi (1994), Sandelowski et al. (2012), Tashakkori and Teddlie (1998).

Material culture and museums. Some examples of the role of museums and their artifacts in shaping culture include Coombes (1994), Hilden and Huhndorf (1999), and Taylor (1995).

Modern material culture. See the *Journal of Material Culture*, the *Journal of Social Archaeology*, and the *Journal of Consumer Culture*. See Dant (2005, 2006) for an overview. On clothing and fashion, see Crane and Bovone (2006). See Haldrup and Larsen (2007) on the importance of material objects in the study of tourism. For example, Holly and Cordy (2007) analyze the detritus left by visitors to gravesites as a way to document behavior (like vandalism, magic, legend tripping, and partying) that would be difficult to observe directly without long-term, participant observation research. On culture and consumption, see McCracken (1988, 2005).

On material culture as a reflection of gender roles, see Chatterjee (2007). See Cavanaugh (2007) on how the production of a particular kind of food became a symbol for a town in Italy. See Öztürkmen (2003) for how material artifacts are used in the creation of nostalgic narratives about the past.

Analyzing still images. Work on using still images as data include Ball and Smith (1992), Capello (2005), Clark and Zimmer (2001), Gardner (1990), Lawson and Wardle (2013), Rendon and Guerda (2012), Táboas-Pais and Rey-Cao (2013), and Wondergem and Friedlmeier (2012).

Prosody and narrative. Examples of research on prosodic features of narrative include Attardo et al. (2011), Lawson (2012), Pickering et al. (2009), and Wennerstrom (2001b).

Analyzing video. There is a very large literature on the use of film, video, and still images as qualitative data. Major works covering all of these media include Chaplin (1994), Collier and Collier (1986 [1967]), El Guindi (2004), Harper (2012), Hockings (2003), and van Leeuwen and Jewitt (2001). Some recent studies based on analyzing video include DeCuir-Gunby et al. (2012), Henry and Fetters (2012), and Lomax et al. (2011). See also the journals *Visual Studies*, *Visual Anthropology*, and *Visual Anthropology Review*.

Visit the online resource site at study.sagepub.com/bernardaqd to access engaging and helpful digital content, like video tutorials on working with MAXQDA, presentation slides, MAXQDA keyboard shortcuts, datasets, stop list, and recommended readings.

CHAPTER 2

CHOOSING A TOPIC AND SEARCHING THE LITERATURE

INTRODUCTION

This chapter and the next two are about some of the things that go on *before* you start collecting data. First, you need a research topic or question. Next, you need to get current with the literature on your topic. That's all in this chapter. Then, you need a

research design: (1) a plan for collecting data to answer your research questions or test hypotheses and (2) a plan for selecting the actual thing (people, texts, whatever) that you're going to study. Those topics are covered in Chapters 3 and 4.

♦ EXPLORATORY AND CONFIRMATORY RESEARCH

There are two kinds of research: exploratory, or inductive research, and confirmatory, or deductive research. Exploratory research is what you do early in any research process. It's appropriate when you're starting out and are trying to understand a research topic. Data collection and theme identification are especially important stages in exploratory research, as shown in Figure 2.1, because they tend to generate lots of new ideas. Exploratory research often ends with the positing of hypotheses or research questions. Here's an example of a hypothesis, derived from inductive work:

Based on ethnography and open-ended interviews and on a review of the relevant literature, it looks like girls show greater enthusiasm than boys do for reading by the time they are in first grade.

Any hypothesis can be phrased as a research question, and vice versa. Here's the same hypothesis, phrased as a research question.

Do boys or girls in the first grade show greater enthusiasm for reading?

Confirmatory research is what you do when you already have a firm idea of the concepts you want to explore and how they are related to each other. Confirmatory research often begins by testing hypotheses derived from exploratory research. Code definition and intercoder reliability testing are especially important stages in confirmatory research, as shown in Figure 2.1, because this is when researchers develop instruments to test their hypotheses.

There is nothing particularly qualitative or quantitative about either inductive or deductive research, as Figure 2.2 demonstrates. Qualitative and quantitative methods

Figure 2.1 The Research Process for Text Analysis

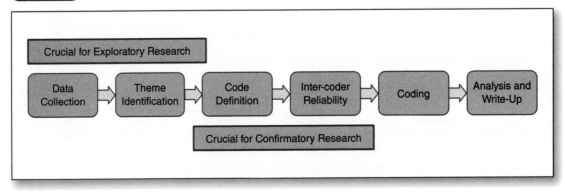

Figure 2.2 Methods for Text Analysis Arranged Along a Continuum From Exploratory to Confirmatory Approaches

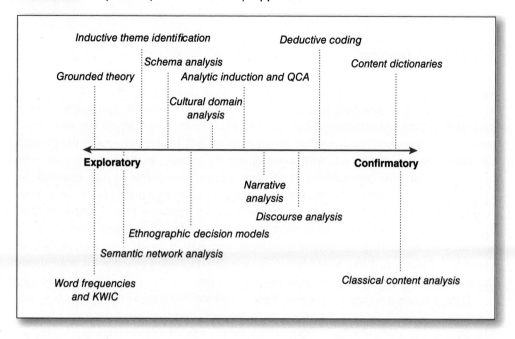

for text analysis run all along the exploratory-to-confirmatory continuum. After all, the derivation *and* the testing of research questions can be based on either qualitative or quantitative data—or on both. This is how all science works.

FOUR QUESTIONS TO ASK ♦ ABOUT RESEARCH QUESTIONS

There are four questions to ask yourself about any research question you are thinking about pursuing.

1. Does this topic really interest me?

2. Is this a problem that is amenable to empirical inquiry?

3. Do I have the resources I need to investigate this topic at the level of detail that I need to be confident about results? Do I have the resources to study *this population* at *this particular research site?* To use *this particular data collection method?*

4. Will my research question, or the methods I want to use, or the population I want to study involve unresolvable ethical problems?

These questions apply to research populations, research sites, and research methods. Answer these questions honestly (at least to yourself) and you will save yourself a lot of grief.

1. Personal Interest

The first thing to ask about any potential research question is: Am I really excited about this? A lot of research gets done by accident. (1) Someone you know—like a professor in your department—has a grant to study how politicians in the state legislature make decisions. She has funds for an assistant and invites you to join the project. (2) You have a part-time job with a social service agency in the same city as your university. Your boss has a friend at another agency who needs to hire someone to evaluate a new program they are running to support farmer's markets in the area. Your boss recommends you for the job. (3) One summer, between your sophomore and junior years in college, you study Swahili in Kenya. While there, you meet a young woman who is studying to become a midwife. You stay in touch. One day, on Skype, you tell her that you'd like to study her now well-established practice for your thesis in medical sociology. She invites you and off you go.

There's nothing wrong with any of these scenarios—as long as the project is something you feel good about. We've seen many students doing research for term projects, MA theses, and even doctoral dissertations simply out of convenience and with no enthusiasm for the topic. If you aren't interested in a research question, don't bother with it. If others are so sure that it's a dynamite topic of great theoretical significance, let *them* study it.

The same goes for research populations. It's really hard to spend several weeks to a year in a place, observing and interviewing people, if you aren't interested in the lives of the people you're studying. Some nursing researchers enjoy working in the maternity ward, while others are drawn to pediatric oncology. The maternity ward is filled with children being born, and the oncology ward with children who are facing death. Which of these is an attractive environment to *you?* Federal prisons and Wall Street banking firms are both complex organizations, but they are very, very different kinds of places to spend time in. Which of these is more attractive to *you?*

There is no right or wrong answer here; just be honest with yourself and you'll do better work. Accessibility of a research site or the availability of funds for the conduct of a study are pluses, but by themselves they're not enough to make good research happen.

2. Empirical Versus Nonempirical Questions

If you're really excited about a research topic, then the next question is: Is this a topic that can be studied empirically—by means of observation—or is it a topic that requires nonempirical methods? Consider this question: Are there references in the Old and New Testaments that are derogatory to women? This is an **empirical question**. You can answer it by looking through the corpus of data (the Judeo-Christian Bible) and coding for instances of statements that are derogatory to women.

But consider this question: Does the Old Testament offer support for unequal pay for women today? This question cannot be answered empirically. Whether a majority of people in Seattle like Rachmaninoff's music more than they like Tschaikovsky's is an empirical question. Whether the music of one or the other is *better*, is not. The extent to which mildly autistic children are mainstreamed in Grades K–6 in the 14,000 school districts in the United States is an empirical question. Whether it *should* be done at all, is not. The number of crimes prevented by surveillance cameras in London is an empirical question. Whether the crime-fighting goals of the surveillance is worth the loss of privacy is not.

Whether or not a study can be done by collecting and analyzing data empirically depends first on the nature of the question being asked and *then* on the methods used. It is important not to confuse *empirical* with *numerical*. Some empirical questions obviously require numerical data to answer. What is the average age at death for men and women in Sri Lanka and how does that compare with the figures for Japan? How many women die of breast cancer in the United States each year? What is the average annual salary for soccer players in the United Kingdom?

In contrast, first-pass descriptions of processes (preparing for surgery, putting on makeup, setting the table for Thanksgiving), or of events (weddings, football games, art shows), or of systems of nomenclature (kinds of trucks, ways to avoid getting AIDS) all require words, not numbers. Dorothy Holland and Debra Skinner (1987) asked some university women to list the "kinds of guys" there are. They got a list of words like "creep," "hunk," "nerd," "jerk," "sweetie pie," and so on. Then they asked some women, for each kind: "Is this someone you'd like to date?" The yes–no answers are nominal—that is, qualitative—measurement.

We'll deal with how to analyze this kind of qualitative data in Chapters 9 and 19.

3. Resources

The next question to ask is whether adequate resources are available for you to conduct your study. There are four major kinds of resources: (1) time, (2) money, (3) people, and (4) skills. What may be adequate for some projects may be inadequate for others. Be totally honest with yourself about this issue, too.

Time

Some social research projects can be completed in just a few days, while others take years. It takes a year or more to do an ethnographic study of a culture that is very different from your own, but a lot of focused ethnography can be done much more quickly. Gwendolyn Dordick (1996) spent three months studying a homeless shelter for 700 men in New York City. She visited the shelter four times a week for three hours or more each time, and spent four days at the shelter from morning until lights-out at 10 p.m. This was enough time for her to understand a great deal about life in the shelter, including how a group of just 15 men had coalesced into a ruling elite and how some men had formed faux marriages (that could, but did not necessarily, involve sex) to protect themselves and their few possessions from violence and thievery.

If you are doing research for a term project, it makes no sense to select a topic that requires two semesters' work.

Money

Many things come under the umbrella of money. Equipment is essentially a money issue, as is salary or subsistence for you and other persons involved in the research. Funds for assistants, supplies, and travel all have to be calculated before you can actually conduct a major research project. If you haven't got the resources to use the right methods for your project, then either pick another project or lower the level of detail or precision that you can live with.

Suppose your research requires comparing the responses in face-to-face interviews of people in two panels of 30 people each. Do you have the resources to conduct this study? If you don't, can you accomplish your research goals by using telephone interviews? If not, can you accomplish them by cutting out the comparison and running the more expensive interviews on just one group or on panels of 20 people each? Don't launch any research project unless you know you have the resources to complete the task.

People

"People" includes you and others involved in the research as well as those whom you are studying.

Will the research require that you interview elite members of the society you are studying—like medical malpractice lawyers, plastic surgeons, Lutheran priests, ambulance paramedics? Do you have access to these groups? How about hard-to-find people, like men who have sex with men? Will you be able to gain their cooperation? Or will they tell you to get lost or, even worse, provide you with perfunctory or even false answers to your questions? Better not do the study in the first place than wind up with useless data.

Skills

Does the research require using multiple coders of interviews and testing the coders for interrater reliability? If it does, do you have that skill? Or are you prepared to acquire it?

Does the research require that you speak Haitian Creole? If so, are you willing to put in the time and effort to learn that language? If the research can be done with interpreters, are competent people available at a cost that you can handle?

4. Ethics of Social Research

It would be convenient if we could just give you a list of criteria against which you could measure the "ethicalness" of every research idea you ever come up with. Unfortunately, it's not so simple. During World War II, many social scientists worked for what would today be called the Department of Defense and they were applauded as patriots for lending their expertise to the war effort. Twenty-five years later, during the Vietnam War, social scientists who worked for the Department of Defense were excoriated.

During the recent wars in Iraq and Afghanistan, social scientists participated in U.S. military programs for studying local culture in battle zones. This produced intense debate about the proper role, if any, of social scientists in military and intelligence operations (McFate 2005; Price 2011; Rohde 2007). (**Further Reading**: social science in the military and in intelligence)

Just because times and ethics seem to change, however, does not mean that any-thing goes. Don't get trapped into nihilistic relativism. Cultural relativism (the unassail-able fact that people's ideas about what is good and beautiful are shaped by their culture) is a great antidote for overdeveloped ethnocentrism. But, as Merrilee Salmon makes clear (1997), ethical relativism (that all ethical systems are equally good since they are all cultural products) is something else entirely.

Can you imagine defending the human rights violations of Nazi Germany as just another expression of the richness of culture? Would you feel comfortable defending, on the basis of cultural relativism, the so-called ethnic cleansing in the 1990s of Bosnians and Kosovar Albanians by Serbs in the former Yugoslavia? Or of Native Americans by immigrant Europeans in the 19th century?

There is no value-free science. All research carries potential risks—to you and to the people you study. Should social scientists do social marketing for a state lottery, knowing that poor people will be squandering their meager resources on false hopes of sudden riches? Or is social marketing only for getting people to use condoms and to stop teens from binge drinking?

Some percentage of the variation in earning power in the United States may be predictable from (*not* caused by) darkness of skin color. A study that shows this con-clusively might be useful evidence in the fight against racism. It might also be used by racists to do further damage in our society. Should you participate in that study?

There is no answer to this dilemma. Above all, be honest with yourself. Ask your-self: Is this ethical? If *your own, personal* answer is "no," then skip it; find another topic. There are plenty of interesting research questions that won't put you into a moral bind. (**Further Reading**: ethical issues in social science)

◆ THE ROLE OF THEORY IN SOCIAL RESEARCH

All research is specific. Whether you conduct ethnographic or questionnaire research, do content analysis or run an experiment, the first thing you do is *describe a process* or *investigate a relation* among some variables in a population. Description is essential, but to get from description to theory is a big leap. It involves asking: "What causes the phenomenon to exist in the first place?" and "What does this phenomenon cause?" Theory, then, is about explaining and predicting things.

It may seem odd to talk about theory in a textbook on research methods, but you can't design research until you choose a research question, and research questions depend crucially on theory. A good way to understand what theory is about is to pick a phenomenon that begs to be explained and to look at competing explanations for it. See which explanation you like best. Do that for a few phenomena and you'll quickly discover which paradigm you identify with. That will make it easier to pick research problems and to develop hypotheses that you can go off and test.

Here is an example of something that begs to be explained: Everywhere in the world, there is a very small chance that children will be killed or maimed by their parents. However, the chance that a child is killed by a parent is much higher if a child has one or more nonbiological parents than if the child has two biological parents (Daly and Wilson 1988, 1998; Lightcap et al. 1982). This "Cinderella effect," as it's known, means that those evil-step-parent folktales are based on more than fantasy. Or are they? A lot depends on the paradigm you start with.

Alternative Paradigms for Building Theories

One explanation is that this it's biological—in the genes, as it were. Male gorillas are known to kill off the offspring of new females they bring into their harem. Humans, the reasoning goes, have a bit of that instinct in them, too. They fight the impulse, and culture usually trumps biology, but over millions of cases, biology is bound to come out sometimes. This is an explanation based on assumptions from **evolutionary theory**. (There are several varieties of this, which you'll see under the label of **evolutionary psychology**, or **evolutionary anthropology**, or **human behavioral ecology**, or **sociobiology**.)

Another explanation is that it's cultural. Yes, it's more common for children to be killed by nonbiological than by biological parents, but this kind of mayhem is more common in some cultures than in others. Also, the deaths of some children at the hand of their biological parents may go unnoticed and unreported simply because we don't expect that, while the deaths of children at the hands of nonbiological parents get more notice simply because we're on the lookout for it (Crume et al. 2002).

And, although killing children is rare everywhere, in some cultures mothers are more likely to kill their children; in other cultures, fathers are more likely to be the culprits. This is because women and men learn different gender roles in different societies. So, the theory goes, we have to look at cultural differences for a true explanation of the phenomenon.

This is called an **idealist** (or **ideational**) **theory** because it is based on what people think—on their ideas.

Yet another explanation is that, when adult men and women bring children to a second marriage, they know that their assets are going to be diluted by the claims the spouse's children have on those assets—immediate claims and claims of inheritance. This leads some of those people to harm their spouse's children from the former marriage. In a few cases, this causes death.

This is a **materialist theory**, as is the idea that women who have children from a previous marriage may, on average, be forced to marry men who carry a higher risk of being abusive.

Sociobiology, idealism, and materialism are **theoretical paradigms** or **theoretical perspectives**. They contain a few basic *rules for finding theories* that explain observed events. Sociobiology stresses the primacy of evolutionary, biological features of humans as the basis for human behavior. Idealism stresses the importance of internal states—attitudes, preferences, ideas, beliefs, values—as the basis for human behavior. And materialism stresses structural and infrastructural forces—like the economy, the technology of production and reproduction, demography, and environmental conditions—as causes of human behavior.

When you want to explain a specific phenomenon, you apply the principles of your favorite paradigm and come up with a specific explanation—a theory.

Why do women everywhere in the world tend to have nurturing roles? If you think that biology rules here, then you'll be inclined to support evolutionary theories about other phenomena as well. If you think economic and political forces cause values and behavior, then you'll be inclined to apply the materialist perspective in your search for explanations in general. If you think that culture—people's values—is of paramount importance, then you'll tend to apply the idealist perspective to come up with explanations.

The different paradigms are not so much in competition as they are complementary, for different **levels of analysis**. The evolutionary explanation for the battering of nonbiological children is appealing for *aggregate*, evolutionary phenomena—the big, big picture. An evolutionary explanation addresses the question: What is the reproductive advantage of this behavior happening at all?

We know that the behavior of hurting or killing step-children is not inevitable, so an evolutionary explanation can't account for why some step-parents hurt their children and others don't. A materialist explanation is more productive for addressing that question. Some step-parents who bring a lot of resources to a second marriage become personally frustrated by the possibility of having their wealth raided and diluted by their new spouse's children. The reaction would be strongest for step-parents who have competing obligations to support their biological children who are living with yet another family. These frustrations will cause *some* people to become violent, but not others.

But the materialist explanation doesn't tell us why a *particular* step-parent is supportive or unsupportive of his or her nonbiological children. At this level of analysis, we need a processual and psychological explanation, one that takes into account the particular historical facts of the case. We might theorize that step-parents who bring a lot of resources to a second marriage become personally frustrated by the possibility of having their wealth raided and diluted by their new spouse's children. Maybe the step-parent has competing obligations to biological children who are now with yet another family. Perhaps these frustrations cause some people to become violent.

Draw two conclusions from this discussion of paradigms and theory: (1) different paradigms produce different answers to the same question; and (2) a lot of really interesting questions may have answers that are generated from several paradigms.

◆ CHOOSING A RESEARCH QUESTION

There is no list of research topics, but Table 2.1 offers some guidelines.

We've divided research topics into classes, based on relations among five kinds of variables.

I. **Internal states**. These include attitudes, beliefs, preferences, values, and perceptions.

II. **External states**. These include characteristics of people, such as age, wealth, health status, height, weight, gender, birth order, longevity, whether they have a twin sibling, and so on. Many external states, like longevity, health status, and weight, can be either independent variables or dependent variables. That is, they can predict other things (obesity predicts the probability of certain illnesses, like diabetes) or they can be the things predicted (low socioeconomic status of parents predicts obesity in children).

III. **Behavior**. This covers what people eat, who they communicate with, how much they work and play—in short, everything that people do and much of what social scientists are interested in understanding.

IV. **Artifacts**. This includes all the physical residue from human behavior—radioactive waste, tomato slicers, sneakers, arrowheads, computer disks, Viagra, skyscrapers—everything.

Table 2.1 Types of Studies Based on Interactions Among Classes of Variables

	I Internal States	II External States	III Behavior		IV Artifacts	V Environment
			Reported	Observed		
I Internal States	I	II	IIIa	IIIb	IV	V
II External States		VI	VIIa	VIIb	VIII	IX
IIIa Reported Behavior			Xa	Xb	XIa	XIIa
IIIb Observed Behavior				Xc	XIb	XIIb
IV Artifacts					XIII	XIV
V Environment						XV

SOURCE: H. R. Bernard and G. W. Ryan. 2012. *Social Research Methods: Qualitative and Quantitative Approaches, Second Edition*. Thousand Oaks, CA: Sage Publications.

V. **Environment**. This includes characteristics of the physical, biological, and social environments in which people live. Some physical characteristics you'll see in the literature include whether children in school work at individual desks or in small groups; whether people live in a high-rise apartment or in a rural hamlet; the number of sunny (or rainy) days per year; and so on. Living under a democratic versus an authoritarian régime or working in an organization that tolerates or does not tolerate sexual harassment are examples of social environments that have consequences for what people think and how they behave (see Box 2.1).

Box 2.1

Biological Variables

A sixth kind of variable comprises biological indicators, like blood pressure and body mass index. We won't cover this kind of variable here, but biocultural research—the interaction among biological, cultural, and environmental factors in shaping human thought and human behavior—is a rapidly growing field in the social sciences. As one example, see Jones et al. (2012) on cultural differences in how women experience menopause.

Category (3) includes both **reported behavior** and **actual behavior**. A great deal of research has shown that about a third to a half of everything people report about their behavior is not true (Bernard et al. 1984). If you ask children what they eat or how much they exercise, they'll tell you, but their report may have no useful resemblance to what they actually eat or how much they actually exercise (R. K. Johnson et al. 1996). If you ask people how many times a year they go to church, you're likely to get data that do not reflect actual behavior (Hadaway and Marler 2005; Rossi and Scappini 2014).

Some of the difference between what people say they do and what they do is the result of out-and-out lying. Most of the difference, though, is because people can't hang on to the level of detail about their behavior that is called for when they are confronted by social scientists asking them how often they go to church, or eat beef, or whatever. What people *think* about their behavior may be precisely what you're interested in, but that's a different matter.

Most social research focuses on internal states and on reported behavior. But the study of humanity can be much richer, once you get the hang of putting together these five kinds of variables and conjuring up potential relations. Here are examples of real studies, done either entirely with qualitative data or with mixed qualitative and quantitative data, for the cells in Table 2.1.

Cell I: The interaction of internal states, like perceptions, attitudes, beliefs, values, and moods.

Women who have traditional views about taking their husband's name at marriage (one internal state) are more collectivist in their orientation (another internal state), while women who reject the traditionalist view are more individualist in their orientation (Hamilton et al. 2011).

Cell II: The interaction of internal states (perceptions, beliefs, moods, etc.) and external states (age, completed education, health status, organizational conditions).

Women who had their first child after 40 years of age through in vitro fertilization (an external characteristic) did not understand how quickly fertility declines with age (an internal state) (MacDougall et al. 2013). College men and women (variation in gender) differ on their expectations (an internal state) of viewing pornography with their partners when they are in a committed relationship (Olmstead et al. 2013).

Cell IIIa: The interaction between *reported* behavior and internal states.

The relation between self-reported fluency in English (reported behavior) in a French high-tech company and language performance anxiety (an internal state) (Neely 2013).

Cell IIIb: The interaction between *observed* behavior and internal states.

Ideas about a good death (an internal state) and behavior, like having a living will, moving into a retirement home, and buying a burial plot (behaviors), among Japanese Americans (Hattori and Ishida 2012).

Cell IV: The interaction of material artifacts and internal states.

The effects on Holocaust Museum staff in Washington, D.C., of working with the physical reminders of the Holocaust (McCarroll et al. 1995).

How young children in New Zealand learn gender roles from pictures in early school readers (Jackson and Gee 2005).

Cell V: The interaction of social and physical environmental factors and internal states.

How tourists in popular places, like Florence, Italy, cope with crowding (Popp 2011).

Cell VI: How the interaction among external states relates to outcomes (i.e., other external states), like longevity or financial success.

A short interval between pregnancies is related to pre-term birth. How counseling and appropriate health care can facilitate optimal pregnancy spacing and reduce the possibility of a pre-term birth (Hogue et al. 2011).

Cell VIIa: The relation between external states and *reported* behavior.

Early career firefighters (rookies) report being unwilling to voice concerns during risky situations, but they become more confident and more forceful about voicing their concerns as they mature in the field (Lewis et al. 2011).

Cell VIIb: The relation between external states and *observed* behavior.

Ethnicity of clientele, gender of bartender, and other factors associated with smoking in bars, despite laws against smoking (Moore et al. 2009).

Cell VIII: The relation of material artifacts and external states.

Business commuters, students, and unemployed differ systematically in what they consider their most important material possessions (Dittmar 1994).

Cell IX: The relation of external states and environmental conditions.

Differences in how mothers talk about their twin children predict behavioral differences in those children. Over time, less warmth expressed by mothers toward one twin produces more antisocial behavior in that twin (Caspi et al. 2004).

Cell Xa: The relation between behaviors, as *reported* by people to researchers.

Do behaviors in youth establish a pattern for behaviors in adulthood? Men at two club scenes in Philadelphia report on various masculinity behaviors in their youth and currently, including the commission of crimes, playing sports, consuming alcohol, and the like (Anderson et al. 2009).

Cell Xb: The relation between reported and observed behavior.

People exaggerate by a factor of 3 their exposure to TV news stories, compared to direct measures of their exposure (Prior 2009).

Cell Xc: The relation between behaviors, as *observed* by researchers.

People in assisted living facilities engage in a variety of behaviors during meals, including making conversation, sharing, giving/getting assistance, humoring, showing appreciation and affection, and rebuffing/ignoring/excluding. Some behaviors, like giving assistance and appreciation, occur in regular sequence (Curle and Keller 2010).

Cell XIa: The relation of reported behavior to specific physical artifacts.

People who are employed view prized possessions as symbols of their own personal history, while people who are unemployed see prized possessions as having utilitarian value (Dittmar 1991).

Cell XIb: The relation of observed behavior to specific physical artifacts.

Content analysis of top-grossing films from 1950 to 2006 shows that the portrayal of tobacco use declined proportionate to the actual decline of smoking in the population (Jamieson and Romer 2010).

Cell XIIa: The relation of reported behavior to factors in the social or physical environment.

In Shanghai, introducing safe-sex practices among female sex workers was easier to accomplish in small venues where people know and trust each other than in large ones. Women in small venues encouraged each other to either use condoms or not accept clients (Chen et al. 2012).

Cell XIIb: The relation of observed behavior to factors in the social or physical environment.

The influence of environmental factors (one-way vs. two-way traffic, the presence or absence of a specific pedestrian signal, number of lanes in a road, and so on) on pedestrians obeying a traffic signal in Montreal (Cambon de Lavalette et al. 2009).

Cell XIII: The association of physical artifacts to one another.

Comparing the favorite possessions of urban Indians (in India) and Indian immigrants to the United States to see whether certain sets of possessions remain meaningful among immigrants (Mehta and Belk 1991).

Cell XIV: The association of artifacts and their environment.

Tourists have to decide where and how to place their souvenirs when they return home (Peters 2011).

Cell XV: How features of the social and physical environment interact and affect human behavioral and cognitive outcomes.

In Ontario, Canada, the overall quality of life (a social environmental variable) is related to physical conditions (like green space) and social conditions (like crime and safety) (Eby et al. 2012).

THE LITERATURE SEARCH ◆

Once you have an idea for a research question, the next thing to do is get current on the literature about that topic. You need to make a heroic effort to uncover all the sources related to any research topic. Fortunately, heroic efforts are pretty easy these days, what with all the **documentation resources** available for scouring the literature.

All you need is a few key references to get started. If you know the name of just one author whose work *should* be cited by anyone working in a particular field, you can find out who cited that author and where. In other words, you can search the literature *forward* in time; this means that older bibliographies are never out of date.

For example, anyone writing on the test-score achievement gap between white and minority students is probably going to cite an article by Spencer Kagan and G. Lawrence Zahn (1975). Anyone writing about urban gangs in the United States is likely to cite William Foote Whyte's book, *Street Corner Society* (1981 [1943]) or Gerald Suttles's book *The Social Order of the Slum* (1968). Anyone writing on the pros and cons of single-sex schools is likely to cite Cornelius Riordan's (1990) book, *Girls and Boys in School: Together or Separate?* (see Box 2.2)

Box 2.2

Tips for Searching Online Databases

1. Get the spelling right. Some databases have intelligent spell checkers (if you type in "bilingaul education" they'll ask if you really meant "bilingual education"), but many don't. If you ask for references on "apropriate technology" and the database comes back, incongruously, with "nothing found," check the spelling with your word processor's spell check or with an online dictionary.

2. If there are two or more ways to spell a word, then search with all spellings. Use both Koran and Qur'an (and several other spelling variants) in your searches; behavior and behaviour; Chanukah and Hanukah (and several other spelling variants); Rom and Roma (both are used to refer to Gypsies); Thessaloniki and Salonika; Mumbai and Bombay; Beijing and Peking; and so on.

3. Use wildcards liberally. Search for "behav* measur*" rather than "behavior measurement." That way, you'll capture "behaviour measurement," "behavioral measurement," "behavioral measures," and so on.

◆ DATABASES FOR SEARCHING THE LITERATURE

The most popular database is Google Scholar (scholar.google.com). It's easy to use and it's free. Don't stop there, though. If your library subscribes to other major databases, get to know them really well.

The *Thompson Reuters Web of Knowledge* contains the *Science Citation Index*, the *Social Sciences Citation Index*, and the *Arts and Humanities Citation Index*. This set of indexes, available at most university libraries and in many small college libraries, covers over 12,000 journals, including over 3,000 in the social sciences. The title, author, journal, year, and page numbers for every article goes into the database, along with the email address of the corresponding author, when it's available. This is a real plus.

The *Social Science Citation Index* alone indexes about 150,000 articles a year. That's only a good-sized fraction of the social science papers published in the world each year, but consider: the *authors* of those articles read—and cited—about 3 *million* citations to references to the literature. That's 3 million citations every year, for decades. The Social Science Citation Index is a treasure.

Other Documentation Databases

Besides Google Scholar and the citation indexes, some important resources for social scientists are: Annual Reviews, ERIC, NTIS and FDsys, PubMed, PsycINFO, Sociological Abstracts, the ProQuest Dissertations and Theses Database, LEXISNEXIS, and OCLC.

The **Annual Review** volumes in psychology, anthropology, sociology, public health, political science, and others are a treasure. Authors who are invited to publish in these volumes are experts in their fields; they have digested a lot of information and have packaged it in a way that gets you right into the middle of a topic in a hurry.

ERIC is a federally funded product of the Educational Resources Information Center and is available free at http://www.eric.ed.gov/. It covers literature since 1966 of interest to researchers in education, but many of the nearly 1,200 journals in the database are of interest to all social scientists. The ERIC database includes a lot of grey literature—government reports and reports from private foundations and industries that contain useful information but can be tough to find.

NTIS, the National Technical Information Service, indexes and abstracts federally funded research reports in all areas of science. It's available free at http://www.ntis .gov/. Anyone who has a contract for research with a U.S. government agency generally produces a series of technical reports on the work they do. The NTIS has technical reports from voter registration surveys, from consumer behavior surveys, from focus groups on attitudes about unprotected sex, from evaluations of new designs for low-cost housing, from laboratory experiments on how much people might be willing to pay for gasoline, from natural experiments to test how long people can stay in a submerged submarine without going crazy—if the federal government has funded it under contract, there's probably a technical report of it.

It used to be that reports on government contracts were filed and then shelved, never to be heard from again. But with the NTIS database, the public can now easily locate all that information.

Agencies of the U.S. government publish a vast array of reports and data on housing, the elderly, alcohol and drug abuse, violence against women, Native American health, prisons, and hundreds of other topics. These reports are available through **FDsys**, the Federal Digital System at http://www.gpo.gov/fdsys/.

PubMed is a product of the National Library of Medicine (National Institutes of Health) and is available free at http://www.ncbi.nlm.nih.gov/pubmed/. This database covers about 5,600 journals in the medical sciences, including the medical social sciences. It contained over 24 million citations in 2015 and is continually updated. Ask PubMed for articles on "high-risk" and "sexual behavior" and "adolescents" and it returns a list of over 1,700 items going back to 1973.

PsycINFO is a product of the American Psychological Association. The Jurassic version of this database goes back to the early 1800s. It indexes and abstracts about 2,500 journals in the behavioral and social sciences and contains about 4 million records, with 4,000 records added every week.

Sociological Abstracts, a product of ProQuest, indexes and abstracts about 1,800 journals dating from 1952, with excellent coverage of research methods, the sociology of language, occupations and professions, health, family violence, poverty, and social control. It covers the sociology of knowledge and the sociology of science as well as the sociology of the arts, religion, and education.

The **ProQuest Dissertations and Theses Database** provides full text for dissertations dating from 1997 and abstracts for dissertations dating from 1980. Much of the best and most up-to-date research is done by graduate students. If your institution subscribes to this database, be sure to check it out when you do the background reading for your own project.

LEXISNEXIS began in 1973 as a way to help lawyers find information on cases. Today, the database contains the searchable text of over 5 billion documents from some 40,000 sources, including the major English-language newspapers in the world, law cases, transcripts of U.S. congressional hearings, and publications and reports of the U.S. Congress. (The congressional database is a product of ProQuest and is incorporated in the LexisNexis database.)

OCLC (Online Computer Library Center) is the world's largest library database. Over 71,000 libraries across the world catalog their holdings, in 479 languages, in OCLC's catalog, called WorldCat. If you find a book or a journal article in the SSCI or PsycINFO, and the like, and your library doesn't have it, then OCLC will tell you which library *does* have it. The **Interlibrary Loan** system depends on OCLC. In addition, OCLC publishes a database called ArticleFirst. This leviathan, which is updated daily, covers 16,000 journals in all fields, including many in the social sciences.

Key Concepts in This Chapter

research design
empirical questions
evolutionary theory
evolutionary
  psychology
evolutionary
  anthropology
human behavioral
  ecology
sociobiology
idealist or ideational
  theory
materialist theory

theoretical paradigms
  or theoretical
  perspectives
levels of analysis
internal states
external states
behavior
artifacts
environment
reported behavior
actual behavior
documentation
  resources

Annual Review
ERIC
NTIS
PubMed
PsycINFO
Sociological
  Abstracts
ProQuest Dissertations
  and the Theses
  Database
LEXISNEXIS
OCLC
Interlibrary Loan

Summary

- Before you start collecting data, you need a research question and a research design. Research design is covered in Chapters 3 and 4.
- Researchers choose their problems for many reasons, including personal interest, availability of research funds, contractual obligations, and to build sound explanations for social and behavioral phenomena.
- Ask four questions about any research question you are thinking about pursuing: Does this topic really interest me? Can this question be investigated empirically? Are the resources available to investigate this topic? Does the research involve unresolvable ethical problems?

  o Whether or not a study can done by collecting and analyzing data empirically depends first on the nature of the question being asked and *then* on the methods used. Empirical should not be confused with numerical.
  o There are four major kinds of resources: time, money, people, and skills.

- The ethics dilemma in social research is profound. The operational test of whether a particular piece of research is ethical is whether social norms tolerate it.

  o This relativistic position, however, does not encourage absolute moral judgments. Ultimately, the choice is left to researchers, and the researchers are responsible for the consequences of their actions.

- There are different approaches, or paradigms, to theory building in the social sciences. These paradigms guide us to search for different *kinds* of answers—biological, ideational, and material—to the same question.

  o The three main paradigms for explanation are idealism, materialism, and sociobiology.

- There is no list of research topics, but there are some guidelines.

  o We can divide research topics into classes, based on relations among five kinds of variables: internal states (values, emotions, opinions, etc.), external states (ages, gender, etc.), behavior (both observed and reported), artifacts (buildings, clothes, etc.), and the environment (social, biological, and physical). Working in an organization that tolerates or does not tolerate sexual harassment is an example of a social environment that has consequences for what people think and how they behave.

- All research projects begin with a literature search. The bibliographic tools available today make it much easier than in the past to cover the literature thoroughly.

  o The Social Science Citation Index, ERIC, NTIS and FDsys, PubMed, Sociological Abstracts, LEXISNEXIS, and OCLC are some of the documentation resources available.

Exercises

1. Building a database of references for a research topic of your choice is the best way to learn how to use the bibliographic tools in your college library. Choose any topic you like and try to make the literature search exhaustive. This is a great way to learn about narrowing down your research *interests* into manageable research *problems*.

   If you're interested in gender differences, for example, the initial search for the string "gender differences" in the Social Science Citation Index returns about 55,000 items between 1973 and 2013. Better focus it more. Asking for "gender differences" and "mate choice" returns about 50 items, with the earliest at 1993. Asking for "gender differences" and "STEM" returns about 300 items, beginning with 1990.

2. Use Table 2.1 to think up some research problems. Think about how you would operationalize the variables for each study you think up. Scour the documentation resources and see if you can find any studies on the research problems you come up with.

Box 3.1

On Units of Analysis

One of the first things to do in any research project is decide on the unit of analysis. In a case study, there is one unit of analysis—the school, the hospital, the police squad, the sports team, the community, the church, the nation. Most social research is about a collection of things—usually, people, but many other things can be the units of analysis. You can study a collection of court cases, building permits, countries, companies, hospitals, school districts, editorials, folktales, song lyrics, personal ads, or blog posts.

Both components of research design are about increasing the **validity** of research—that is, increasing the likelihood that your study has really answered the question that motivated it. If your colleagues believe that whatever you learned in a study of some units of analysis is likely to be true *about those units of analysis*, then your work has **internal validity**. This depends crucially on measurement—how you collect your data. If your colleagues believe that whatever you learned in a study of some units of analysis is likely to be true about *units of analysis you didn't study*, then your work has **external validity**. This depends crucially on sampling.

So, to put this all together:

(1) if you test the idea that 6-year-old girls in a single classroom show greater enthusiasm for reading than boys in that same classroom do; and

(2) if your measurement of enthusiasm—qualitative or quantitative or both—is believable to colleagues who read your report; then

(3) your study has internal validity. If you repeat your study in another classroom in the same school and you get the same results, then

(4) the internal validity of your study deepens and your study starts to have external validity. If you repeat it again in another school in the same school district and get the same results, then

(5) the internal validity deepens further (i.e., your colleagues gain confidence in how you assessed enthusiasm) and the external validity widens further.

This chapter is about the sampling component of research design. We'll follow up in Chapter 4 with methods for collecting data—that is, about measurement.

TWO KINDS OF SAMPLES ♦

There are two kinds of samples in research: those based on probability theory—random sampling—and those that are not. Two rules apply, however, to *all* researchers, including those who deal with qualitative data as well as those who deal with quantitative data.

(1) Rule 1: If your objective is to estimate a characteristic of a whole population—like the average number of hours that people spend doing housework or the variation in their income, and so on—and you can only interview a sample of the population, then only a **probability sample** will do. Collect data from a sufficiently large, randomly selected, unbiased sample of the larger population. (More on this coming up next.)

(2) Rule 2: If you want to understand a process—like how the police in a squad car determine whether to stop someone on the street—then you want people who can offer expert explanations about the cultural norm and about variations on that norm (Handwerker et al. 1997). It's one thing to ask: "How many people did you stop on the street for questioning last week?" This requires an answer about individual behavior. It's another thing to ask: "How do people in your squad decide whether to stop someone for questioning on a street patrol?"

Sampling cultural experts is one kind of **nonprobability sample**. If your research requires a nonprobability sample, or if your research requires a probability sample but there is no way to get one (because of logistical or ethical problems), then use a nonprobability sampling method and apply it systematically. And, of course, let everyone know in your write-up exactly what you did.

Sample Size in Probability Sampling

In classical sampling terminology, a real characteristic of a population is called a **parameter**. In any group of, say, 1,000 people, the true average height—the height parameter—is the sum of all the measured heights of the people, divided by 1,000. This parameter can be estimated from an unbiased (i.e., probability) sample of the heights of those 1,000 people. An **unbiased sample** means that every member of the population has the same chance of being selected for the sample. **Random selection** is how we ensure that this is the case (see Box 3.2).

Box 3.2

Why Sampling Theory Is Important in Qualitative Research

Although ethnography, grounded theory, and other research strategies in the qualitative tradition rely heavily on nonprobability sampling, it is important for all social scientists to understand the basics of statistical sampling theory as well as the value of nonprobability samples. As we stress throughout this book, we see the great divide between qualitative and quantitative in social research as more than just dysfunctional. It's pernicious. It keeps good social scientists in both traditions blinded to the value of work in both traditions. We can't cover sampling theory here, but coverage is widely available in many methods books.

By eliminating bias—by taking the decision out of your hands—random selection ensures that whatever you find out about the sample can be generalized to the population from which it was taken, give or take a known amount of potential error.

For example, when you read that a political leader has an "approval rating of 41%, plus-or-minus three percentage points," and assuming the poll was done on an unbiased sample, you know that if the poll were taken 10,000 times, then 95% of the time the parameter (the true approval rating) would be estimated to lie between 38% and 44%—i.e., 41%, plus-or-minus three points.

The amount of error, given random selection, depends on sample size, not on the proportion of the population taken as a sample. A random sample of 1,000 out of a population of 10,000 has the same **error bounds** (those three points, plus or minus) as a sample of 1,000 out of a population of 10,000,000. All data represent something, but in statistics, a **representative sample** is one in which every unit of analysis (every person, or every church, or every magazine ad) has an equal chance of being selected for the study.

Telephone surveys, for example, are typically based on random digit dialing because, in theory, everyone in a calling area has the same chance of being contacted. Being contacted, though, doesn't necessarily mean being interviewed. Even in highly industrialized countries, like Holland, Spain, and the United States, response rates of 60% and lower are common (Díaz de Rada 2005:6; McCarty et al. 2006; Poortman and van Tilburg 2005:24).

Thus, the final sample in a well-conducted survey may not represent important segments of the population—like people who avoid surveys. This does not invalidate survey results, but it means that results have to be taken cautiously until they are repeated and that special surveys of nonresponders need to be done to fill in the blanks. Determining the sample size in survey research may be complicated, but it's a science that has known error bounds. (**Further Reading**: sampling theory in social science)

Sample Size in Nonprobability Sampling

The problem of sample size is not quite as well understood when it comes to ethnography, grounded theory, schema analysis, narrative analysis, and the like, but a lot of progress is being made and new research is coming out all the time (Guest 2015). Our advice—based on this emerging evidence—is that 20–60 knowledgeable people are enough to *uncover and understand* core themes. To explain our recommendation, we'll walk you through a few different areas of research.

The first has to do with how many interviews it takes to detect the simple existence of a theme in research on a fairly focused phenomenon, with a reasonably homogenous sample. Studies of this kind focus on well-defined cultural domains (like the list of things you can put in a salad or the list of ways to treat a cold) or on lived experience (like coping with a particular illness or surviving combat or being out of work). (See Chapter 18 for more on collecting and analyzing data about cultural domains. See Chapters 10 and 13 on studying lived experience.)

Morgan et al. (2002:76) did in-depth interviews with four different samples of people about various risks in the environment. The researchers did the usual coding for concepts, but they also plotted the cumulative number of new concepts identified after each interview across the four different studies. Their results are in Figure 3.1. In every case, the *shape* of the line is the same: The first few interviews produce a lot of new data, but by 20 interviews, the curves flatten out and hardly any new information is retrieved.

This finding is corroborated by Guest et al. (2006). These researchers interviewed 30 sex workers in Ghana and another 30 in Nigeria on how they talked with their peers about sex and condoms. The researchers coded the transcripts in batches of six, completing all the interviews from Ghana and then moving on to the interviews from Nigeria.

Figure 3.2 shows the plot of the number of new themes uncovered in the coding. Of the 114 themes identified in the entire corpus of text, 80 turn up in the first six interviews. Another 20 themes turn up in the second batch of six interviews. In other words, 100 of the 114 themes (88%) extracted from these interviews were discovered by the time the researchers had worked with 12 respondents. Just nine new themes were discovered in next 18 interviews in Ghana and only five new themes were added to the codebook to accommodate the 30 interviews from Nigeria.

Building on the findings of Guest et al. (2006) and others, Francis et al. (2010) developed a simple test for determining if your sample size is big enough to identify themes. First, you set an initial sample size (say, 10 interviews). Then, you continue interviewing and analyzing your data until no new themes emerge. (This technique is called **data saturation**. For more on theoretical saturation, a related technique, see Chapter 10.) Once you've done three consecutive interviews and found no new themes, they recommend, you can stop. In their own study of beliefs about genetic testing (with relatives of a patient with Paget's disease—a bone disorder), they found that 17 interviews were enough: 14 to identify the themes and three more to make sure they were done.

| Figure 3.1 | The Number of New Concepts Retrieved in Interviews Tapers Off in Just 20 Interviews |

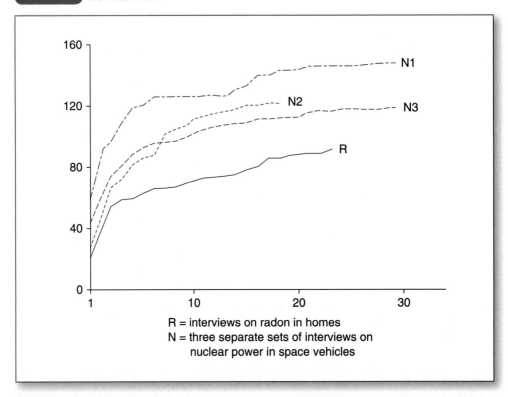

SOURCE: Morgan, M. G., B. Fischoff, A. Bostrom, and C. J. Atman. 2002. *Risk Communication: A Mental Models Approach*. New York: Cambridge University Press. Reprinted with the permission of Cambridge University Press.

NOTE: The x-axis shows the number of interviews. The y-axis shows the cumulative number of new concepts derived from all interviews. N = three separate sets of interview on nuclear power in space vehicles; R = interviews on radon in homes.

These studies give us a basic sense of how many interviews we need to do to discover themes—and how to figure out if we've done enough. From here, scholars have started to branch out, asking how many interviews we need to accomplish other research goals.

For example, Guest et al. (in press) tested the number of focus groups—rather than interviews—needed to identify themes. They ran 40 focus groups, with about eight participants in each one, focusing on African American men's views on health behaviors. Guest et al. eventually found 94 themes in their study, but 60 of them turned up in the very first focus group and 79 of them (84% of the 94) turned up by the third focus group. Their conclusion: You'd need between three and five focus groups—that is, you'd have to recruit around 24 to 40 people (if your focus groups each had 8 participants)—to find most themes.

Figure 3.2   Number of New Themes Tagged in 60 Interviews

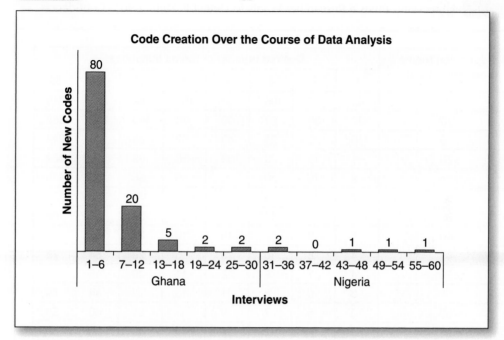

SOURCE: Guest et al. 2006:67. Used by permission.

Hagaman and Wutich (in press) tested the number of interviews needed to find **metathemes**—broad, overarching themes that cover a number of smaller themes—in a big, cross-cultural study on people's views of water and injustice in Fiji, Bolivia, New Zealand, and the United States. At the end of their study, they had identified 240 themes and nine metathemes. Like others, they concluded that about 16 interviews were enough to identify and understand locally grounded themes in each of the four sites. But they needed a lot more interviews—between 20 and 40 in each site—to identify and understand the cross-cutting metathemes, because metathemes that were common in one site were not common in others.

All of the studies we've discussed to this point are about how to determine, empirically, the number of interviews it takes to identify core themes in purposive (non-random) samples. But a new area of research focuses on estimating the number of randomly selected interview respondents you'd need to (1) identify the existence of common themes and rare themes in a population and (2) determine whether you'd found multiple occurrences of common and rare themes. (**Further Reading**: statistical estimates of sample sizes for qualitative interviews)

Fugard and Potts (2015), for example, describe a model for estimating sample size that takes into account four variables: (1) the prevalence of the theme (how often it

Figure 3.3 Sample Size Estimations, Taking Into Account How Common a Theme Is and How Many Times a Researcher Wants to Detect It, With a 90% Confidence

Population theme prevalence (%)	Desired number of theme instances							
	1	2	3	4	5	10	20	30
5	45	77	105	132	158	282	515	740
10	22	38	52	65	78	140	256	368
15	15	25	34	43	52	93	170	244
20	11	18	25	32	38	69	126	182
25	9	15	20	25	30	55	100	145
30	7	12	16	21	25	45	83	120
35	6	10	14	18	21	38	71	102
40	5	9	12	15	18	33	61	89
45	4	8	10	13	16	29	54	79
50	4	7	9	12	14	26	48	70
55	3	6	8	11	13	23	44	63
60	3	5	7	9	11	21	40	58
65	3	5	7	9	10	19	36	53
70	2	4	6	8	9	18	33	49
75	2	4	6	7	9	16	31	45
80	2	4	5	6	8	15	28	42
85	2	3	5	6	7	14	26	39
90	1	3	4	5	7	13	24	36
95	1	2	4	5	6	12	22	33

SOURCE: Fugard and Potts (2015).

appears); (2) the likelihood that people will actually talk about the theme; (3) how many times researchers want to see a unique instance of the theme; and (4) how sure you want to be that you'll detect uncommon themes.

As Figure 3.3 shows, you need to interview just one person to detect a theme held by 95% of the population with 90% confidence. But if you want to detect a theme held by only 50% of the population, with the same 90% confidence, you'd have to quadruple your sample size and interview four people. That's still not daunting, but to detect an uncommon theme, theme held by, say, 5% of the population, you'd have to interview 45 people and to identify 30 occurrences of that uncommon theme you'd have to interview 740 people.

When is detecting the existence of a theme enough? And when do you need multiple instances of a theme? If you are trying to develop a survey instrument, finding a theme just once might be what you need to move to the next stage of data collection. (See Chapter 16 on Ethnographic Decision Models and Chapter 18 on Cultural Domain Analysis for examples of studies that use theme identification to develop closed-ended surveys.) But if you want to describe a theme thoroughly or compare it across groups, you need to see more examples of it—as it's used by different people or in different contexts—to really understand it. And for that, of course, you'd need a larger sample.

What we're learning about sample size estimation for qualitative data is starting to converge with what've long known about cultural data more broadly. In 1988, Weller and Romney published Table 3.1, on the number of people you need to interview to

| Table 3.1 | Minimal Number of Informants Needed to Classify a Desired Proportion of Questions With a Specified Confidence Level for Different Levels of Cultural Competence |

Proportion of Questions	Average Level of Cultural Competence				
	.5	.6	.7	.8	.9
.95 confidence level					
0.80	9	7	4	4	4
0.85	11	7	4	4	4
0.90	13	9	6	4	4
0.95	17	11	6	6	4
0.99	**29**	**19**	**10**	**8**	**4**
.99 confidence level					
0.80	15	10	5	4	4
0.85	15	10	7	5	4
0.90	21	12	7	5	4
0.95	23	14	9	7	4
0.99	>30	20	13	8	6

SOURCE: S. C. Weller and A. K. Romney, *Systematic Data Collection*, p. 77, 1988, Sage Publications.

understand the contents of a cultural domain. This table assumes that everyone is getting the same questions and that their responses conform to set categories. In that way, it's a bit different from what you'd get from open-ended text elicitation. But even so, their answers are strikingly similar to the ones we're getting when we ask how many interviews it takes to detect themes.

Take a close look at Table 3.1. The big take-away message is in bold: Just 10 people are needed when the average knowledge (cultural competence) of the informants is only .70 (i.e., informants who would get a C on a test of knowledge about the domain). The number of informants needed rises to a lofty 29 if the average knowledge slips from .7 to .5. This confirms what we are finding in the theme identification studies—relatively small samples are large enough to find most common themes. And this is very good news for researchers of experience and cultural knowledge—the kind retrieved with in-depth interviews.

Morse (1994) recommended a minimum of six interviews for phenomenological studies and 30–50 interviews for ethnographic studies and grounded theory studies. Now, data from empirical research and statistical estimations are increasingly supporting Morse's experience-based guess. Aiming for Morse's upper limit of around 50 (or even, as we do, a bit more conservatively at 60) interviews is wise because, in many cases, this allows you to identify a theme more than once and get a fuller sense of the way it is expressed across respondents or contexts. (**Further Reading**: problems of sampling qualitative research)

Remember, every sample represents something. An unbiased (randomly selected) sample represents a population with a known probability of error. A nonprobability sample lacks this one feature. For a very, very large number of research questions, this is simply not a problem. (**Further Reading**: sample size in qualitative research)

♦ KINDS OF NONPROBABILITY SAMPLES

The most widely used nonprobability sampling methods are quota sampling, purposive sampling (also called judgment sampling), convenience sampling, network sampling (also called chain referral sampling), theoretical sampling, and key informants.

Quota Sampling

In **quota sampling**, you decide on the subpopulations of interest and on the proportions of those subpopulations in the final sample. If you are going to take a sample of adults in a small town, you might decide that, because gender is of interest to you as an independent variable, and because women make up about half the population, then half your sample should be women and half should be men. Moreover, you

Table 3.2 Quota Sampling Grid With Three Binary Independent Variables

Variables							
Salaried				Self-Employed			
≤ 39		≥ 40		≤ 39		≥ 40	
Men	Women	Men	Women	Men	Women	Men	Women
5	5	5	5	5	5	5	5

decide that half of each gender quota should be at least 40 years old and half should be younger than 40 and that half of each of those quotas should be self-employed and half should be salaried.

The result is a **sampling grid**, shown in Table 3.2.

Once you have a sampling grid, you go out and look for, say, five self-employed women who are over 40 years of age; five salaried men who are under 40; And so on. This will give you a sample of 40 people—quite typical for studies that are based on intensive study of narratives or life histories.

Silverman et al.'s Study of Breast Cancer

Silverman et al. (2001) did in-depth, hour-long interviews to learn "how women view breast cancer, their personal risk of breast cancer, and how screening mammography affects that risk" (p. 231). The researchers began by calling women across the United States at random. The first question they asked was whether the women had ever had

Table 3.3 Sampling Grid for the Quota Sample in Silverman et al.'s Study

Income							
Up to $25,000 per year				Above $25,000 per year			
Race							
White		Black		Other	White		Black		Other
Age							
≤39	40–49	50–69	≥70	≤39	40–49	50–69	≥70

SOURCE: Assembled from data in Silverman, E., S. Woolshin, L. M. Schwartz, S. J. Byram, H. G. Welch, and B. Fischoff. 2001. Women's views on breast cancer risk and screening mammography: A qualitative interview study. *Medical Decision Making*, 21:231–240. Copyright © Society for Medical Decision Making.

breast cancer. If the answer was no, the woman was eligible for the study. Silverman et al. used a quota system to select women for in-depth interviewing:

> To fill our quota sampling, we approached 191 women randomly selected within strata defined by census tract income and age provided by NDS. Ninety-eight women were disqualified because they did not meet racial, age, or socioeconomic criteria, 52 refused, and 41 agreed to participate. Of note, 35 of these women requested the personalized breast cancer risk report and all 41 accepted the $20 payment. (Silverman et al. 2001:233)

Table 3.4 shows the diverse demographics of Silverman et al.'s final sample of 41 informants.

Table 3.4 Participant Characteristics for 41 Women in the Silverman et al. Study

Demographics	Percentage
Age	
Younger than 40	15
40–49	37
50–69	34
70 or older	15
Race	
White	51
Black	24
Asian	12
Hispanic	7
Native American	5
Annual Income	
Less than $25,000	51
Education	
Did not finish high school	20
High school graduate	41
College degree	39
Ever had a mammogram	80
Breast cancer risk factors	
Family history of breast cancer	12
Personal history of breast biopsy	23

SOURCE: Silverman, E., S. Woolshin, L. M. Schwartz, S. J. Byram, H. G. Welch, and B. Fischoff. 2001. Women's views on breast cancer risk and screening mammography: A qualitative interview study. *Medical Decision Making*, 21:231–240.

Commercial polling companies use quota samples that are fine tuned on the basis of decades of research. Organizations like Gallup, Roper, Harris, and others have learned how to train interviewers not to choose respondents who are pretty much like themselves; not to select only people whom they would enjoy interviewing; not to avoid people whom they would find obnoxious or hostile; not to avoid people who are hard to contact (busy people who are hardly ever home, or people who work nights and sleep days); and not to favor people who are eager to be interviewed.

The result is quota samples that are not unbiased but that often do a good job of reflecting the population parameters of interest. In other words, quota sampling is an art that often approximates the results of probability sampling at less cost and less hassle than strict probability sampling (see Box 3.3).

Box 3.3

Quota Sampling Often Approximates Probability Sampling—But Not Always

In 1948, some pollsters predicted, on the basis of quota sampling, that Thomas Dewey would beat Harry Truman in the U.S. presidential election. The *Chicago Tribune* was so confident in those predictions that they printed an edition announcing Dewey's victory—while the votes were being counted that would make Truman president. Since then, we've known that quota sampling cannot be used for estimating accurately the percentage of people who vote for a particular candidate in a really close election, but it's excellent for many other kinds of studies.

The bottom line: Quota sampling is not an acceptable substitute for strict probability sampling when the goal is to estimate the true value of a variable in a population. If you want to know the true average age of people in a population, only a probability sample will do. On the other hand, quota samples are excellent for understanding variation in people's experience. If you want to know, for example, how children's sports— Little League Baseball, Pop Warner football, Youth Soccer, high school football—function in small communities across the United States, you'd ask people who have children playing those sports. To get at the intracultural variation, open-ended interviews with four or five really knowledgeable people in each sub-group (like Blacks, Whites, and Hispanics, for example, or young parents and grandparents) will produce the relevant data about the range of ideas that people have about these institutions. (**Further Reading**: quota sampling)

(Continued)

- Look for agreement and disagreement. Try to hunt out the areas where opinions converge, and probe for areas where views diverge.
- Once three people tell you the same thing, find some other people who can tell you something new.

Patton (1990, 2002) describes more techniques for choosing respondents in purposive samples. One set of techniques is helpful for recruiting respondents who share core traits, views, or experiences. These include recruiting respondents who (1) are homogeneous, (2) are typical or average cases, or (3) provide intense or information-rich examples. Another set of techniques is helpful for recruiting respondents who can add to your understanding of heterogeneity in the phenomenon under investigation. These include recruiting respondents who (1) vary maximally; (2) are extreme, deviant, or unusual cases; or (3) confirm and disconfirm your emerging ideas.

Having a purposive sample that contains people recruited in multiple ways can enrich your understanding of the problem you are studying.

Convenience Sampling

Convenience sampling is a glorified term for grabbing whoever will stand still long enough to answer your questions. Sometimes, convenience samples are all that's available, and you just have to make do. Studies of the homeless, for example, are usually done with convenience samples. Convenience does not mean haphazard. Good convenience samples are done with a purpose in mind. For example, you can maximize your ability to find homeless people by going to shelters and food banks.

Remember: All samples represent *something*. The trick is to make them representative of what *you* want them to be. That's what turns a convenience sample into a purposive one.

For example, Al-Krenawi and Wiesel-Lev (1999) wanted to understand the emotions of Israeli Bedouin women who had experienced genital mutilation. They interviewed a convenience sample of 12 women who had been through the ritual and 12 women who had not but had either seen it first-hand or had heard about women in their own extended families going through it. We wouldn't put much stock in the fact that a specific *percentage* of the women reported sexual problems or relationship problems with various members of their family, but the *list* of problems is very instructive because it is the basis for more in-depth research.

Network Sampling: Snowball and Respondent-Driven Sampling

Snowball sampling and **respondent-driven sampling (RDS)** are two **network sampling** methods (also known, generically, as **chain referral** methods) for studying hard-to-find or hard-to-study populations. Populations can be hard to find and study for three reasons: (1) they contain very few members who are scattered over a large area (think vegans in Wyoming); and/or (2) they are stigmatized and reclusive (like HIV-positive people who never show up at clinics until they are sick with AIDS) or even actively hiding (like intravenous drug users); and/or (3) they are members of an elite group, like criminal defense lawyers, and don't care about your need for data.

Snowball Sampling

In snowball sampling, you start with one or two "seeds"—people you want to interview and who can introduce you to others like them. The method was developed by Charles Kadushin (1968) in a classic study of elites. Using key informants and documents, you build a preliminary list of elites. These might be "people in this town whose opinions really count" or "living artists whose work everyone wants to buy" or "fellow physicians whose opinions you trust when it comes to adopting a new drug." The elite group can range from very local (a single high school) to international (opinion makers).

Once you have a preliminary list, you show it to a couple of people who are *on* the list—the seeds—and ask them to name others whom they think *should be on* the list. The process continues until the list becomes "saturated"—that is, until no new names are offered.

This is the formal version of snowball sampling. A less formal snowball sampling approach is to start with one or two seeds, interview them, and, then, at the end of those interviews, ask the person to suggest additional people with whom you might speak.

Ostrander (1980) used snowball sampling in her study of class consciousness among upper-class women in a midwestern U.S. city. She selected her first informant by looking for someone who had graduated from an elite women's college, was listed in the social register, was active in upper-class clubs—and who would talk to her. At the end of the interview, she asked the informant to "suggest another woman of your social group, with a background like yours, who might be willing to talk to me."

Elites are easy to find, but hard to interview. Doors open when one member of an elite group passes you on to another. David Griffith and his colleagues used *two* snowball samples in their study of food preferences in Moberly, Missouri. They chose an initial seed household in a middle-income neighborhood and asked a man in the house to name three people in town with whom he interacted on a regular basis. The first person cited by the informant lived in a lower-income neighborhood across town. That person, in turn, named other people who were in the lower-income bracket.

After a while, the researchers realized that, although they'd started with a middle-income informant who had children at home, they were getting mostly lower-income, elderly people in the snowball sample. So they started again, this time with a seed from an elite, upper-middle-income neighborhood. By the time they got through, Griffith et al. had a well-balanced sample of 30 informants with whom they did in-depth interviews (reported in J. C. Johnson 1990:78).

If you are dealing with a relatively small population of people who are likely to be in contact with one another, like practitioners of alternative medicine in a small town, then the formal method of snowball sampling is an effective way to build an exhaustive sampling frame quickly. Once you have an exhaustive sampling frame, you can select people to interview, either at random or purposively.

In large populations, however, people who are well known have a better chance of being named in a snowball procedure than are people who are less well known. And in large populations, people who have large networks name more people than do people who have small networks. This means that, in large populations, snowball sampling isn't likely to produce a complete sampling frame. On the other hand, snowball sampling will always produce a sample. So, if your objective is just to find hard-to-find people to interview, snowball sampling can be useful. (**Further Reading**: snowball sampling)

Respondent-Driven Sampling

Respondent-driven sampling was developed by Douglas Heckathorn (1997) and Matthew Salganik (Salganik and Heckathorn 2004) in studies of hidden populations, like injecting drug users. Like snowball sampling, RDS begins with a few informants who act as seeds. The informants are paid for being interviewed and are then asked to recruit up to three members of their networks into the study.

To move this process along, Heckathorn paid each of the seed informants in his study $10 and gave them three coupons (Heckathorn 1997). Anyone who came to Heckathorn to be interviewed and who had one of those coupons was paid the same $10. (He upped the bounty to $15 for referring a female drug injector, since they were harder to find.) Those informants, in turn, got several coupons and recruited others into the study.

There are several important improvements to snowball sampling here. First, this method avoids the ethical problem that snowball sampling presents. The people who an informant names may not want you even to know about their existence, much less be anxious to grant you an interview. Second, having members of a hard-to-find or hard-to-study population do your recruiting deals with the reluctance of some people to be interviewed. And finally, Heckathorn (1997, 2002) shows that, when it's done right, the RDS method produces samples that are less biased than are traditional snowball samples. However, they do have a tendency to recruit people who are most attracted to the reward the researcher is willing to offer. (**Further Reading**: respondent-driven and other kinds of chain referral sampling)

Theoretical Sampling

Theoretical sampling refers to the selection of cases as they are needed in the course of research. The method was formalized by Glaser and Strauss (1967) in their landmark book, *The Discovery of Grounded Theory*. Right from the title, Glaser and Strauss made clear that the method they were advancing was about discovery through systematic induction rather than about testing of hypotheses. The method involved interviewing a single person and then coding and analyzing the transcript (details about how to do all this in Chapter 10). The idea was that coding and theory building would develop together and that researchers would select cases for study as concepts, and links among concepts, emerged (Glaser and Strauss 1967:45–77; Strauss and Corbin 1998:205–12).

Building an inventory of concepts and links among concepts—i.e., understanding pattern in the data—is the discovery of grounded theory. With each advance in a theory, you can decide on what you need to learn next (to fill in holes and to advance the theory) and, therefore, *who* to interview. That's theoretical sampling. The approach is similar to what an investigative journalist or a detective would do as she moved from lead to lead, circling back when appropriate to make sure she had the story or case correct.

This method of sampling as you go and filling in an emerging theory is associated most with grounded theory, but is a hallmark of ethnography as well. Bernard, for example, used theoretical sampling in his ethnographic study of Greek sponge divers (1987). When Bernard went to Kalymnos in 1964, one of the things he wanted to understand was how people on that island were reacting to what was then a relatively recent threat to the sponge industry on which Kalymnians depended for a living: the mass marketing of the synthetic sponge.

Bernard knew he had to interview sponge merchants, boat owners, and divers—the three main actors in the Greek sponge industry—but his first interviews taught him that the industry went into decline partly because many young divers had recognized the threat of the synthetic sponge by the mid-1950s and had gone to Australia as labor migrants. This drove up the price of diving labor on the island, making natural sponges less competitive against the synthetics. By 1964, some of these labor migrants had accumulated money and had returned to the island. These men were no longer employed in the sponge industry, but their stories were important for understanding how and why the industry was changing.

It was very easy to find those returned migrants: Everyone on the island either had one in their family or knew people who did. In other words, Bernard changed his sampling procedure as he began to understand the theoretical importance of labor migration in his research.

Theoretical Sampling and Grounded Theory

Theoretical sampling is a key part of classical grounded theory. Caron and Bowers (2003), for example, used theoretical sampling in their study of people who were caring for elderly family members. Their final sample comprised 16 participants: six men (who were taking care of their wives) and 10 women (who were taking care of either their husband or a parent or, in one case, a brother-in-law). Caron and Bowers knew they wanted to compare male and female caregivers, but after a few interviews, they began selecting participants based on the presence or absence of Alzheimer's or other cognitive impairment; whether the caregiver and care recipient lived in the same house; and whether the caregiver was getting help from various services with housecleaning, cooking, and transportation (2003:1255).

Wilson et al. (2002) used a form of theoretical sampling in their grounded-theory study of HIV-positive men and women in the San Francisco Bay area. At the start, the objective was to understand how people manage the symptoms associated with various stages of HIV infection. By coding and analyzing on the fly, however, the researchers quickly found that when they asked about symptoms, the "study participants talked about their stories of medication regimens and side effects" (p. 1310). Wilson et al. began asking people explicitly about adherence to anti-retroviral drug regimes, and this became a major focus of the study. (**Further Reading**: theoretical sampling)

Key Informants

Across the social sciences, you'll see references to research participants as **respondents** or **subjects** or **informants**. Respondents (the preferred term among quantitative sociologists) respond to survey questions; subjects (the preferred term among psychologists) are the subject of some experiment or observation; and informants (the preferred term among anthropologists and some qualitative sociologists) tell you what *they think you need to know* about their culture.

Key informants are people who know a lot about their culture and are, for reasons of their own, willing to share their knowledge with you. When you do long-term ethnography, you develop close relationships with a few key informants—relationships that can last a lifetime. You don't choose these people. They and you choose each other, over time (see Box 3.6).

Box 3.6

Specialized Informants

Specialized informants have particular competence in some cultural domain. If you want to know when to genuflect in a Roman Catholic Mass, or what herb tea to give children for diarrhea, or how to avoid being busted for streetwalking, you need to talk to people who can speak knowledgeably about those things.

Good key informants are people whom you can talk to easily, who understand the information you need, and who are glad to give it to you or get it for you. Pelto and Pelto (1978:72) advocate training informants "to conceptualize cultural data in the frame of reference" that you, the researcher, use.

In some cases, you may want to just listen. But when you run into a really great informant, there is no reason to hold back. Teach the informant about the analytic categories you're developing and ask whether the categories are correct. In other words, encourage the informant to become the ethnographer.

Bernard and Jesús Salinas Pedraza have been working together since 1962. Bernard tells the following story about his work with this key informant:

In 1971, I was about to write an ethnography of his culture, the Ñähñu of central Mexico, when he mentioned that he'd be interested in writing an ethnography himself. I dropped my project and taught him to read and write Ñähñu. Over the next 15 years, Salinas produced four volumes about the Ñähñu people—volumes that I translated and from which I learned many things that I'd never have learned had I written the ethnography myself. For example, Ñähñu men engage in rhyming duels, much like "playing the dozens" among African Americans and other traditions of ritualized insults found around the world. I wouldn't have thought to ask about those duels because I had never witnessed one. (Bernard and Salinas Pedraza 1989:11–38)

Doc

One of the most famous key informants in the ethnographic literature is Doc in William Foote Whyte's *Street Corner Society* (1981 [1943]). Whyte studied "Cornerville," an Italian American neighborhood in a place he called "Eastern City." (Cornerville was the North End of Boston.) Whyte asked some social workers if they knew anyone who could help Whyte with his study. One social worker told Whyte to come to her office and meet a man whom she thought could do the job. When Whyte showed up, the social worker introduced him to Doc and then left the room. Whyte nervously explained his predicament, and Doc asked him "Do you want to see the high life or the low life?" (Whyte 1984:68).

Whyte couldn't believe his luck. He told Doc he wanted to see all he could, learn as much as possible about life in the neighborhood. Doc told him:

Well, any nights you want to see anything, I'll take you around. I can take you to the joints—the gambling joints—I can take you around to the street corners. Just remember that you're my friend. That's all they need to know. I know these places and if I tell them you're my friend, nobody will bother you. You just tell me what you want to see, and we'll arrange it. (Whyte 1984:68)

Doc was straight up; he told Whyte to rely on him and to ask him anything, and Doc was good to his word all through Whyte's three years of fieldwork. Doc introduced Whyte to the boys on the corner; Doc hung out with Whyte and spoke up for Whyte when people questioned Whyte's presence. Doc was just spectacular (see Box 3.7).

Box 3.7

Informants Sometimes Lie

Boelen (1992) visited Cornerville 25 times between 1970 and 1989, sometimes for a few days, other times for several months. She tracked down and interviewed everyone she could find from Street Corner Society. Doc had died in 1967, but she interviewed his two sons in 1970 (then in their late teens and early 20s). She asked them what Doc's opinion of Whyte's book had been and reports the elder son saying: "My father considered the book untrue from the very beginning to the end, a total fantasy" (Boelen 1992:29).

Of course, Whyte (1996a, 1996b) refuted Boelen's report, but we'll never know the whole truth.

Doc may be famous, but he's not unique. He's not even rare. All successful ethnographers will tell you that they eventually came to rely on one or two key people in their fieldwork. What was rare about Doc is how quickly and easily Whyte teamed up with him—and the fact that Whyte wrote clearly about all this.

Solid Insiders and Marginal Natives

In fact, the first informants with whom you develop a working relationship in the field may be somewhat deviant members of their culture. Michael Agar (1980:86) reports that during his fieldwork in India, he was taken on by the *naik*, or headman of the village. The naik, it turned out, had *inherited* the role, but he was not respected in the village and did not preside over village meetings.

This did not mean that the naik knew nothing about village affairs and customs; he was what Agar called a "solid insider" and yet somewhat of an outcast—a "marginal native," just like the ethnographer was trying to be (Freilich 1977). If you think about it, Agar said, you should wonder about the kind of person who would befriend an ethnographer.

In all our fieldwork—at sea, in Mexican villages, on Greek islands, in rural Cameroon, in rural communities in the United States, and in modern American bureaucracies—we have consistently found the best informants to be people who are a bit cynical about their own culture. They may not be outcasts—in fact, they are always solid insiders—but they say they *feel* somewhat marginal to their culture, by virtue of their intellectualizing of and disenchantment with their culture. They are always observant, reflective, and articulate. In other words, they invariably have all the qualities that any ethnographer would like to have.

So, Take Your Time

If you're doing long-term, participant observation ethnography, don't choose key ethnographic informants too quickly. Allow yourself to go awash in data for a while and play the field. When you have several prospects, check on their roles and statuses in the community. Be sure that the key informants you select don't prevent you from gaining access to other important informants (i.e., people who won't talk to you when they find out you're so-and-so's friend).

When Jeffrey Johnson began fieldwork in a North Carolina fishing community, he went to the local marine extension agent (the equivalent of an agricultural extension agent) and asked for help. The agent, happy to oblige, told Johnson about a fisherman whom he thought could help Johnson get off on the right foot.

It turned out that the fisherman was a transplanted northerner; he had a pension from the Navy; he was an activist Republican in a thoroughly Democratic community; and he kept his fishing boat in an isolated moorage, far from the village harbor. He was, in fact, maximally different from the typical local fisherman. The agent had meant well, of course (J. C. Johnson 1990:56).

And since good ethnography is, at its best, a good story, find trustworthy informants who are observant, reflective, and articulate—who know how to tell good stories—and stay with them. In the end, ethnographic fieldwork stands or falls on building mutually supportive relations with a very small sample of informants. (**Further Reading**: key informant interviewing)

Key Concepts in This Chapter

research design	parameter	purposive sampling
sampling	unbiased sample	(judgment sampling)
measurement	random selection	experience sampling
units of analysis	error bounds	pilot studies
validity	representative	intensive case studies
internal validity	sample	critical case studies
external validity	data saturation	hard-to-find populations
probability sample	metathemes	ethnographic sampling
nonprobability	quota sampling	convenience sampling
sample	sampling grid	snowball sampling

respondent-driven   referral sampling)   subjects
  sampling   theoretical sampling   informants
network sampling (chain respondents   key informants

Summary

- There are two kinds of data of interest to social scientists: individual data and cultural data. These two kinds of data require different approaches to sampling.

  o Individual data are about attributes of individuals in a population. To estimate the parameters of these attributes in a population requires probability sampling.
  o Cultural data require experts, which means relying on nonprobability sampling.
  o If the objective in a research project is to estimate a characteristic of a population—like the average number of hours that people spend doing housework or the variation in their income, and so on—then a probability sample is required.

- It is often impossible to do strict probability sampling under real research conditions. In these cases, use a nonprobability sample. Also, when you are collecting cultural data, rather than individual attribute data, random sampling is inappropriate.

- Regarding sample size for nonprobability samples, there is growing evidence that 20–60 knowledgeable people are enough to uncover and understand the core categories in just about any cultural domain (like the list of things you can put in a salad or the list of ways to treat a cold) or the study of lived experience (like coping with a particular illness or surviving combat or being out of work).

- Some types of nonprobability sampling are quota sampling, purposive (judgment) sampling, convenience sampling, network sampling, theoretical sampling, and key-informant sampling.

  o In quota sampling, you decide on the subpopulations of interest and on the proportions of those subpopulations in the final sample. Quota sampling resembles stratified probability sampling, but respondents are not chosen randomly. Many commercial polling companies use quota samples that are fine tuned on the basis of decades of research.
  o In purposive, or judgment, sampling, you decide the purpose you want the units of analysis (people, communities, countries) to serve. This is somewhat like quota sampling, except that there is no overall sampling design that tells you how many of each type of informant you need for a study. Purposive samples are used widely in (1) pilot studies, (2) intensive case studies, (3) critical case studies, and (4) studies of special populations and hard-to-find populations.
  o Convenience or haphazard sampling means grabbing whoever will stand still long enough to answer your questions. It is useful for exploratory research, to get a feel for "what's going on out there" and for pretesting questionnaires to

make sure that the items are unambiguous and not too threatening. Pilot studies are often done with convenience samples.

o There are two kinds of network sampling, or chain-referral sampling: snowball sampling and respondent-driven sampling. In snowball sampling, you locate one or more key individuals and ask them to name others who would be likely candidates for your research. Snowball sampling is used in studies of social networks, where the object is to find out who people know and how they know each other. Respondent-driven sampling is a form of snowball sampling and is particularly suited to studies of hard-to-find populations.

o Theoretical sampling is widely used by ethnographers and in grounded theory studies, and refers to the selection of cases as they are needed in the course of research. This method of sampling as you go and filling in an emerging theory is associated most with grounded theory, but is a hallmark of ethnography as well.

o Ethnographers also often rely on key informants—people who know a lot about their culture and are willing to share their knowledge with a researcher. Specialized informants have particular competence in some cultural domain. If you want to know what to do when a child gets sick, you need to talk to people who can speak knowledgeably about those things.

Exercises

1. What are the advantages and disadvantages of probability sampling, purposive sampling, quota sampling, and convenience sampling? When is a convenience sample called for in research?

2. Does the distinction between qualitative and quantitative data have any bearing on whether a probability or nonprobability sample is appropriate?

3. You are called on to study the reaction by students at your school to a program about binge drinking. You determine that the only way to get immediate reaction is to ask people coming out of the auditorium if they will answer your survey and, if they agree, to hand them a survey form to fill out on the spot. Develop a quota sampling grid for gender (male, female), freshman versus senior class, and ethnicity (white, African American, Hispanic, and other).

Further Reading

Sampling theory in social science. Agresti and Franklin (2007), Handwerker (2003).

Problems of sampling in qualitative research. Barroso and Sandelowski (2003), Curtis et al. (2000), Fielding and Lee (1996:253), Luborsky and Rubinstein (1995), Miles and Huberman (1994:27–34), Morse (2003, 2007), Onwuegbuzie and Leech (2007), Patton (2002:230–46).

Sample size in qualitative research. Crouch and McKenzie (2006), Green (2001), Kuzel (1999), Sandelowski (1995a), Sobal (2001).

Statistical estimates of sample size for qualitative and cultural research. Galvin (2015), Bernard and Killworth (1993); for opposing views, see Byrne (2015), Emmel (2015), Hammersley (2015).

Quota sampling. Carlson et al. (1994), Morrow et al. (2007), Moser and Stuart (1953), T. M. F. Smith (1983), Sudman (1976).

Snowball sampling. Biernacki and Waldorf (1981), Browne (2005), Cohen and Arieli (2011), Kendall et al. (2008).

Respondent-driven and other kinds of chain referral sampling. Heckathorn and Jeffri (2001), Martin and Dean (1993), Penrod et al. (2003), Salganik and Heckathorn (2004), Sudman and Kalton (1986).

Targeted sampling. Carlson et al. (1994), Martsolf et al. (2006), Kral et al. (2010), Peterson et al. (2008).

Theoretical sampling. Boeije (2002), Coyne (1997), Curtis et al. (2000), Draucker et al. (2007), C. Thompson (1999).

Key informant interviewing. Houston and Sudman (1975), Magnarella (1986), McKenna and Main (2013), Paerregaard (2002), Poggie (1972), Tremblay (1957), Wolcott (2008).

Visit the online resource site at study.sagepub.com/bernardaqd to access engaging and helpful digital content, like video tutorials on working with MAXQDA, presentation slides, MAXQDA keyboard shortcuts, datasets, stop list, and recommended readings.

CHAPTER 4

RESEARCH DESIGN II

Collecting Data

◆ INTRODUCTION

After sampling, the other big problem in research is measurement. Don't be put off by the word "measurement." It's just another way of saying "collecting data," and it's just as important for qualitative data as it is for quantitative data.

For example: Deciding whether to do metaphor analysis or grounded theory is a measurement decision. So is whether to do structured or semistructured interviewing. And so is deciding whether to code a particular theme as present or absent in a text. Each decision helps determine the data you wind up with for your analysis and the conclusions you eventually reach in your research.

We begin with a taxonomy of data collection techniques, both qualitative and quantitative.

◆ DATA COLLECTION METHODS

There are four broad categories of methods for collecting data about human thought and human behavior: (1) **experiments**; (2) **indirect observation**; (3) **direct observation**; and (4) **elicitation**, or talking to people. The difference between experiments and all other methods of collecting data is that (with the exception of natural experiments) the researcher influences the subjects *on purpose* and then observes the results. Figure 4.1 lays out the three non-experimental methods for collecting data, plus a fourth set——mixed methods (see Box 4.1).

> ### Box 4.1
>
> #### Reducing Observer and Response Effects
>
> All methods of collecting data involve some kind of observation. There is an enormous social science literature on **observer effects**–how people change their behavior in response to being watched–and **response effects**–how people change their behavior in response to being asked questions. Changing the order of questions in a survey, for example, or changing the race or gender of the person asking survey questions can influence people's responses. The object of this literature is to minimize the error produced by these effects. (**Further Reading:** response effects)

The methods in Figure 4.1 have two things in common: (1) they can be used equally for collecting qualitative or quantitative data; and (2) they are very, very labor intensive. Anyone who thinks that *qualitative* is a synonym for *easy* has a rude shock coming.

Figure 4.1 Taxonomy of Qualitative Data Collection Techniques

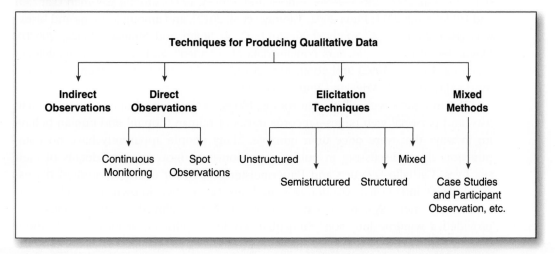

INDIRECT OBSERVATION ♦

Indirect observation involves (1) studying the traces of human behavior and thought; (2) analyzing archival data; and (3) secondary analysis, or reanalyzing data that were collected for other projects.

Behavior Traces

1. The traces of human behavior and thought are everywhere: material objects (pots, statues, buildings, steel mills), texts (diaries, speeches, interviews, lyrics), still images (paintings, graffiti, magazine ads, photographs), moving images (recordings of old radio shows, home videos of family events, newsreels, television ads, commercial movies), and recordings of sound. Some of these physical remains—like advertisements and political speeches—are created for public consumption; others—like diaries and love letters—are created for private use. But all of these, and much more, have been sources of qualitative data for social research.

There is a long tradition in political science, for example, of analyzing speeches and platforms to understand the policy positions of different candidates and parties (Benoit 2011; Laver and Garry 2000). Researchers in media studies and marketing examine printed and television advertisements to track attitudes across time and in different countries about the role of women in the household and on the job. Neto and Furnham (2005), for example, analyzed children's ads on Portuguese, English, and American television to look for how gender roles in these three countries were being portrayed (also see Furnham and Paltzer 2010; Huhman and Argo 2011).

Personal ads inform us about preferences in mate selection among heterosexuals (Glasser et al. 2009; Lance 1998; Yancey and Yancey 1997), among gay men (Lanzieri and Hildebrandt 2011; Phua 2002; Varangis et al. 2012), and among lesbians and bisexuals (Farr 2011; C. A. Smith et al. 2011; C. A. Smith and Stillman 2002a, 2002b). Obituaries of business leaders contain data about men's and women's management practices (Kirchler 1992) and about how people in different cultures memorialize the dead (Alali 1993; de Vries and Rutherford 2004).

The Internet—with all its chat rooms, blogs, newsgroups, bulletin boards, email lists, and personal web pages—records traces of human thought and human behavior in ways that were once unimaginable. Many people apparently have no compunction about discussing in public chat rooms the most intimate details of their sex lives. Carballo-Diéguez and Bauermeister (2004), for example, studied discussions about intentional, condomless anal sex (a practice known as barebacking) among gay men. Systematic examination of these archived electronic messages provided a window into something that would be difficult, at best, to ask about directly (see Box 4.2).

Archival Data

2. Research with archival data, like trace data, is inexpensive and nonreactive. Whether you're studying records of court proceedings, migrations, hospital visits, or credit card purchases, people can't change their behavior after the fact. The original data may have been collected reactively, but that's one reason why historians demand such critical examination of sources.

In assessing the value of documents, Guba and Lincoln (1981:238–39), citing G. K. Clark (1967), suggest asking the following questions: What is its history? How did it come into my hands? What guarantee is there that it is what it pretends to be? Is the document complete, as originally constructed? Who is the author? What is the author trying to accomplish? What was the document intended for? What were the maker's sources of information? What was the maker's bias? To what extent was the writer likely to want to tell the truth? Do other documents exist that might shed additional light on the same story, event, project, program, context? (see also Altheide and Schneider 2012).

Archives of qualitative data can be examined again and again to answer different research questions. The ads in the *Ladies Home Journal*, for example, have been analyzed for what they say about gender stereotypes in the products advertised to women (Mastin et al. 2004), for what they say about how women's roles have changed over time (Demarest and Garner 1992; Margolis 1984), and for what they say about women's body image (Fangman et al. 2004), among other topics.

Box 4.2

Ethical Issues in Collecting Data From the Internet

The fact that we can so easily study sensitive topics—like sexual practices, alcoholism, suicide, obesity, and response to serious illnesses—via the Internet raises ethical problems and problems of authenticity and validity. For example, if you get the personal OK from a member of a chat room to use his or her posts, verbatim, in your publications, does that violate the privacy of everyone else in the room? If you join a self-help list of recovering alcoholics to recruit respondents for a study, you might disrupt the group therapy. Institutional Review Boards across the world are wrestling with ethical problems like these to this day, as are researchers who rely on the Internet for their data (see Ess and AoIR 2002; Marham and Buchanan 2012).

The problem of authenticity was immortalized in a cartoon by Peter Steiner, published in the *New Yorker* in 1993, just as the Internet was getting started.

Figure 4.2 Anonymity on the Internet

"On the Internet, nobody knows you're a dog."

SOURCE: © Peter Steiner/The New Yorker Collection/The Cartoon Bank.

By 1999, a report by the American Association for the Advancement of Science noted: "The Internet appeals to researchers because of its access to a potentially wide geographical and diverse population. However, this may also be one of the pitfalls in such research, since it is quite easy to mislead others about one's geographical location, gender, or race" (Frankel and Siang 1999:3–4).

The Internet is a rapidly expanding source of archival data. The U.S. Library of Congress has an online collection of all known recordings of former slaves (http://memory.loc.gov/ammem/collections/voices/—the recordings were mostly made in the 1930s and 1940s) and a collection of 8,000 images documenting Chinese immigration to California between 1850 and 1925 (http://memory.loc.gov/ammem/award99/cubhtml/). It also has a collection of 2,100 baseball cards from 1887 to 1914 (http://memory.loc.gov/ammem/bbhtml/)—in case you'd like to study what baseball players wore in those days. Libraries across the world are putting collections of primary documents like these online.

Secondary Analysis

3. Secondary analysis is analysis done on data that were collected for other research projects. All major surveys—the ones that track the buying habits of high school students, political preferences of people in various ethnic groups, the health of age cohorts, and so on—provide data for secondary analysis, and there are hundreds of published studies based on these analyses.

Less well known, but of enormous value, are the corpora of qualitative data that are available for secondary analysis (Fielding 2004; Hammersley 2010a; Seale 2011). The U.K. Data Service (http://discover.ukdataservice.ac.uk/) houses the **QUALIDATA collection**, comprising original text from hundreds of studies done by social scientists in the United Kingdom.

Historical analysis is largely done on sets of documents about events, communities, organizations, and people, but if you look carefully, you'll find this kind of reanalysis across the social sciences. Khaw and Hardesty (2007) reanalyzed 19 transcripts of long interviews (between one and two hours) with women who had left relationships in which they had experienced physical violence from their partners. The original study, by Hardesty and Ganong (2006), was done to document the parenting histories of the women, but in the reanalysis, Khaw and Hardesty focused on the process by which the women came to the point where they were able to leave the relationship.

The largest archive of ethnographic data in the world is the **Human Relations Area Files** (HRAF). Started in the 1940s by George Peter Murdock, Clellan Ford, and other behavioral scientists at Yale University, the archive has grown to more than a million pages of text, extracted from nearly 7,000 books and articles, on nearly 400 societies. The archive is growing at about 40,000 pages a year, and about two-thirds of the material is available via the Internet through libraries that subscribe (http://www.yale.edu/hraf/).This archive has been the source of hundreds of published articles. (More about the HRAF in Chapters 6 and 11.)

Disadvantages of Archival and Secondary Data

There are at least three problems associated with archival and secondary data: (1) lack of authenticity; (2) lack of representativeness; and (3) measurement error.

(1) **Lack of authenticity** refers to the fact that, in secondary analysis, the data you're examining probably weren't collected with the purpose you have in mind now. If you interview 50 middle-aged women who are caring for frail, elderly parents, *you* decide what issues are important and *you* make sure that you ask each woman about each of those issues. Researchers who code archival data often find that only a few codes that interest them can be consistently applied (Hodson 1999:13). Missing data are a common problem in all research,

but at least with data you're collecting yourself, you can go back and fill in the gaps as you find them (see Box 4.3).

Box 4.3

The Missing Data Trap

All researchers deal with missing data, but the problem is especially acute in the collection of qualitative data. We miss some data because of people's unwillingness to answer a question, but in our experience most missing data come from failure to ask a question in the first place and from failure to probe for detailed answers or to record answers faithfully.

A lot of qualitative research is based on indirect observation and unstructured interviewing, in which the researcher has little or no control. Archival records are often incomplete. Corpora of text, like news articles, may simply not contain information on all events of interest in a study. Focus groups are notorious for producing missing data because not everyone participates fully throughout the discussion. What people think but do not say is missing.

In unstructured and semistructured interviews, everyone may be asked about the same topics but not be asked the exact same questions. Some people are probed on certain questions; others are not. Data are lost when they are not recorded properly. Transcriptions of video and audio eliminate certain kinds of data from the record.

We recommend recording all interviews, even if you can't transcribe them, so you'll have a record of what was actually said that you (and others) can go back to. If you are taking notes during an interview, LiveScribe® pens let you record the conversation as you write. Then, you can go back to hear what was actually being said by touching where you scribbled your note.

Field notes are the worst offenders when it comes to missing data. Researchers simply cannot write down all they see and hear, and when field notes are written up hours after an event, there is further loss. Human memory is a very poor recorder of events and conversations. In the end, we fill in the gaps with inferences, but missing data make systematic comparisons across cases difficult and make systematic testing of hypotheses questionable. This is one reason we advocate using both systematic and nonsystematic data collection methods in qualitative research.

---

(2) Lack of representativeness is a sampling problem. Sampling is a problem for all research, but it's particularly apparent in the use of archival and secondary data. The solution is to focus on internal validity and to use best practices in measurement. For example, if you have multiple coders reading a set of texts, be sure to check interrater reliability. (Go back to Chapter 3, on sampling, for more on this and see Chapter 11, on content analysis.)

Measurement error of all kinds, including missing data, plagues all data collection, qualitative and quantitative alike. It should be a simple matter to compare the number of crimes in different parts of the United States in which guns are used, but it isn't. The basic data—the Uniform Crime Reports, issued by the FBI for each of the 3,142 counties in the United States—are flawed. People in some U.S. counties tend to report when they're robbed at gunpoint. In other counties, the events go unreported and unrecorded. This doesn't stop research on the use of guns in crime. It creates opportunities to assess error and to make analyses better. All data are reductions of experience. You work with what you have and you try to eliminate bias as best you can. (**Further Reading**: secondary analysis of qualitative data)

◆ DIRECT OBSERVATION

In the immortal words of Yogi Berra, "You can observe a lot by watching" (Berra and Garagiola 1998).When you want to know what people do, rather than what they say they do, nothing beats watching them (see Bernard et al. [1984] for a review of the informant accuracy problem). Just sitting and watching the activities of a clinic or hanging out at a truck stop can produce a lot of useful information if you pay attention and take careful notes. The hard part is not taking careful notes—it's paying attention and capturing detail.

Building Explicit Awareness

Paying careful attention to detail is a skill, not a talent. It comes naturally to small children (think of a three-year-old asking in a loud voice in a supermarket: "Mommy, why doesn't that woman have any hair?"), but it doesn't come naturally to most adults. We learn early to tune out most detail—that's how cultural schemas get imprinted. Those schemas serve us well in everyday life (see Chapter 12), but they are deadly on research. **Explicit awareness** is a skill that every social researcher needs to develop.

Try this exercise: Holding a notepad, walk by a store window at a normal pace. As soon as the window is out of your vision, write down everything you can remember that was in the window. Go back and check. Do it again with another window. After repeating this exercise a few times, your ability to remember little things will start to improve. You'll find yourself making up mnemonic devices for remembering what you see. After you've done five or six windows, go back to them and try to capture more detail. Keep up this exercise (new windows, old windows) until you are satisfied that you can't get any better at it.

Here's another one. Walk through a city neighborhood, noting the languages or dialects that people speak, the music they play, the foods they eat, the number of singles (people who are alone), and pairs and groups of three or more. Repeat the exercise, going over the exact same route. You'll find yourself listening and watching for more detail and you'll see again how much you can learn from sharpening your skills at on-the-fly observation. Repeat with a new route. Keep this up (new routes, old routes) until you're satisfied that you can't get any better at it.

Here's a more demanding challenge. With two colleagues, attend a religious service that none of you have attended before. Don't take any notes, but after you leave, write up what you saw, in as much detail as you can and compare what you've written. Repeat this exercise—keep attending the service and watching carefully—until the three of you are satisfied that you have reached the limits of your ability to recall complex behavioral scenes and your notes of those scenes are substantially the same. Now repeat the exercise, but at a service with which you are familiar and your colleagues are not. See if your notes are substantially like theirs—i.e., if you've been able to develop the ability to see familiar things as if you were seeing them for the first time.

It doesn't have to be a religious service. Any really familiar scene—a bowling alley, a laundromat—will help you improve your reliability as an observer. This doesn't guarantee accuracy, but because reliability is a necessary and insufficient condition for accuracy, you have to become a reliable data-gathering instrument if you want to become an accurate one (see Box 4.4).

Box 4.4

Other Devices for Observation

If you can't take notes during an interview or at an event, then get your thoughts down on paper immediately. Avoid talking to people in the interim. Talking to others before getting your notes down will reinforce some things you heard and saw at the expense of other things (Bogdan 1972:41).

Draw a map—even a rough sketch will do—of the physical space where you spent time observing and talking to people. As you move around the map, details of events and conversations will come to you. In essence, let yourself walk through your experience.

Or get a colleague to do the observations with you. Each of you should take notes independently, then immediate afterward have a "debrief" session where you each discuss what you saw. What you are looking for is where (1) both of you saw and noted the same thing; (2) both of you saw the same thing, but only one of you noted it; (3) where the two of you disagree what you saw. We find that tape recording and transcribing such debriefs to be even better than relying on just one person's notes.

Two formal methods for direct observation of behavior are continuous monitoring and spot observation.

Continuous Monitoring

In **continuous monitoring**, or CM, you watch a person, or group of people, and record the behavior as accurately as possible. It is hard to do, but it produces uniquely valuable qualitative and quantitative data. The technique was developed in the 19th century to improve manufacturing. In a classic study, F. B. Gilbreth (1972 [1911]) measured the behavior of bricklayers—things like where they set up their pile of bricks and how far they had to reach to retrieve each brick—and made recommendations on how to lessen worker fatigue and raise productivity through conservation of motion. Before Gilbreth, the standard in the trade was 120 bricks per hour. After Gilbreth published, the standard reached 350 bricks per hour (Niebel 1982:24).

People who hired bricklayers loved the method. Bricklayers were not as happy, but the method of continuous monitoring of behavior is still used in assessing work situations (Pershing 2006), especially in tracking the work of people who engage in routinized and repetitive tasks—like doctors, nurses, and other medical personnel (Tang et al. 2007; Westbrook et al. 2010).

Rosalyn Negrón (2011) used CM to find out how much time Spanish–English bilinguals in New York City spent speaking one language or the other and exactly when they code-switched—that is, changed languages (it can happen in the middle of a sentence among bilinguals). There had been dozens of studies on this topic, based on interviews and self-reports of behavior by respondents, but CM helped fill in lots of holes in our knowledge of code switching (see Box 4.5). (Details of Negrón's study are in Chapter 14 on discourse analysis.)

Box 4.5

An Exercise in Continuous Monitoring

To get a feel for the challenge of continuous monitoring, go to an upscale department store on a school day and record the interaction behavior of 60 mother–child pairs for one minute each. (Yes, one minute. It's a long time in the continuous monitoring business.) The children will mostly be under six years of age on a school day (ignore mothers with children who are clearly older than that). Select 30 mothers with one child in tow and 30 with more than one child. Record in detail the mother's interaction with each child, including content, tone of voice, and gestures of mothers and children.

Try to guess the ages of the children and the ethnicity and socioeconomic status of the family. It's a real challenge to code for SES and ethnicity when you can't talk to the people you observe. Try using dress for SES and language or dialect for ethnicity. Do this with at least one colleague so you can both check the reliability of your observations. Repeat the exercise at an upscale and at a downscale department store. Then see if you can set up a table of the interactions and find patterns in the behaviors you've recorded. (**Further Reading**: continuous monitoring)

Spot Observation and Time Allocation Studies

If you are trying to find out *what* people do, the data will be textual, like this:

There are three people home; the grandmother is playing with the toddler, who is about two and is banging a spoon on the kitchen table; the mother is putting a load of laundry into the washing machine; the grandfather and the father are said to be out playing golf together because it's the father's day off and the grandfather is retired.

If, on the other hand, you are trying to find out *how much* people engage in a particular behavior, you need a quantitative technique. In **spot sampling**, an observer appears at randomly selected places, at randomly selected times, and records what people are doing (Gross 1984). The logic of this method for studying **time allocation** is clear: If you sample a sufficiently large number of representative acts, then the percentage of *times* people are seen doing things (working, playing, resting, eating) is a proxy for the percentage of *time* they spend in those activities. So, if women and men are observed doing some kind of work 38% and 52% of the *times* you observe them, then women work 38% of the *time* and men work 52% of the *time*—plus or minus some amount that's determined by the sample size. Your favorite statistics program will calculate this plus-or-minus amount for you and will tell you if 52% is really a bigger number than 38% or might be the result of chance, given the sample size.

Spot observation has been done across the world to track how people actually spend their days and to answer questions like: Do men or women have more leisure time? What fraction of the time are babies left alone or held in someone's arms? (A. Johnson 1975; Ricci et al. 1995; Umezaki et al. 2002).

Obviously, spot observation does not capture the *stream* of behavior the way CM does. Nor does it capture whole events in context as ethnography does. But spot observation captures many of the elements that make up the larger context and can be quite revealing when complemented with ethnography and interview data. (**Further Reading**: spot sampling and time allocation studies)

Converting Observations Into Data

Like any other phenomenon, the stream of behavior has to be converted to data. This can be done by taking extensive notes or by reducing activities to a set of fixed codes on the fly. Many researchers record their observations on audio or video recorders. It's less tedious than writing; it lets you focus your eyes on what's going on; it lets you record details later that might be left out of an on-the-spot written description; it avoids the limitations of a check list; and it lets you get information about context as well as about the behavior you're studying.

But there are tradeoffs. If you want measurements from qualitative data (like running commentaries on tape or disk), you have to code them. That is, you have to listen to and watch the audio and video recordings over and over again and decide what behaviors to code for each of the people you observe. Coding on the spot (by using a behavioral checklist or by inputting codes into a handheld computer) produces immediate quantitative data, but you lose context.

You can't code and talk into a recorder at the same time, so you need to decide what kind of data you need—exploratory or confirmatory—and why you need them before you choose a method. If you are trying to understand a behavioral process, then focus on qualitative data. If you need measurements of how much or how often people engage in this or that behavior, then focus on quantitative data.

◆ ELICITATION METHODS

Elicitation, or interviewing, is a social process—you ask people questions and they provide answers—so it's the most reactive of the data collection methods. Interviews can be unstructured, semistructured, or structured. And, of course, you can mix the types in any given study. Figure 4.3 (an expansion of one section of Figure 4.1) lays this out.

Unstructured Interviews: Informal and Ethnographic

Informal interviews look and sound like casual conversations, but they aren't. They occur everywhere—in homes, in bars, on street corners, in factory lunch rooms—and they're hard to do. Informal interviewing requires self-discipline and a trained memory to recall in detail, from brief notes taken on the fly, what happened to you throughout the day, and what people said to you.

Informal interviewing provides a wealth of information, and in some cases it's the only realistic tool available for gathering information. How else could you talk to commercial sex workers who are out hustling on the street (assuming that you don't have

Figure 4.3   Taxonomy of Elicitation Methods

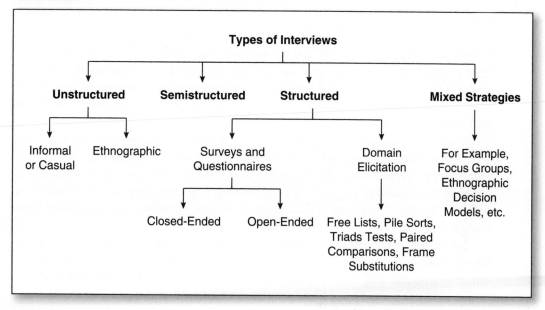

the funds to buy their time for a formal interview)? Or to long-distance truck drivers who are grabbing a quick dinner on the road while their rig is being fueled (assuming that you don't have the time to ride with them all day or all night so you can conduct a formal interview)?

Ethnographic interviews can also look and feel like casual conversations, but they are not. And they are not informal, either. Informal interviews feel like casual conversations. Ethnographic interviews have a lot of give and take, but they feel like . . . well, interviews.

Here are three questions that might turn up in an ethnographic interview: (1) "Can you tell me, from your own experience, how you decided to have an abortion?" (2) "Can you tell me about how your friend decided to have an abortion?" (3) "Can you tell me how women you know decide to have an abortion?" The first question gets directly at lived experience. The second asks for a report on the experiences of others. It's often less threatening and can produce an enormous of amount of data from which cultural norms can be extracted.

The third question goes right for the cultural norms by asking the informant to generalize from experience. The goal in ethnographic interviewing is to understand the cultural norms, but there are many ways to get there. Detailed stories about lived experience are a great way to go, but there are clearly situations in which you have to tread lightly and in which question 2 or even 3 is the best way to start and to build trust.

Typically, ethnographic interviews start with broad, general questions—what Spradley (1979) called **grand tour questions**—and are then followed up with questions about specifics. This is known as a **funnel interview**. A study of the dating practices of adolescents might begin with a question like: "What does it mean to date around here?" Later, you would ask for specifics, like: "Who do you and your friends tend to date?" "When people your age are dating, what kinds of things do they do?" And still later, you might probe for information about sexual practices: "When people your age are dating, what kinds of sexual activities do they engage in?" and then "Which of these tends to come first?"

In ethnographic interviews, the idea is to get people on a topic and get out of the way, letting them provide the information that they think is important. This makes ethnographic interviewing a fluid process, and it means that you may not be able to cover all the issues on a topic in a single sitting. Use ethnographic interviews when you have plenty of time—as in participant observation studies—and can return again and again to the same trusted informants.

Informal and ethnographic interviews help you understand the flow of everyday life, the kind of information that people are willing to divulge, and the topics that are sensitive. Informal and ethnographic interviews help build rapport and generate a lot of data—data that can be analyzed on their own or used in designing questionnaires.

Semistructured Interviews

In **semistructured interviews**, each informant is asked a set of *similar* questions. In structured interviews, each informant is asked a set of *identical* questions.

If you want to make comparisons across people or groups of people, then you really need to get at least similar information from all of them. Semistructured interviews are based on an **interview guide or protocol**—a list of questions and topics that have to be covered. The interviewer covers each topic by asking one or more questions and using a variety of probes (like "Tell me more about that") and decides when the conversation on a topic has satisfied the research objectives (Cannell and Kahn 1968:527). The interview guide, and its instructions on where and how to probe, are essential when there's more than one interviewer on a project so that people are asked roughly the same questions.

Semistructured interviews occupy an interesting position along the structured–unstructured continuum. Semistructured interviews are flexible in that the interviewer can modify the order and details of how topics are covered. This cedes some control to the respondent over how the interview goes but because respondents are asked more or less the same questions, this makes possible comparisons across interviews.

Semistructured interviews produce a *lot* of qualitative data quickly. Hardré and Sullivan (2008), for example, studied how rural high school teachers got their students motivated. In addition to applying formal questionnaires, the researchers asked 66 teachers these nine, open-ended questions:

1. What subject areas and classes do you teach?

2. What is your students' general level of achievement in your class?

3. What is your students' general level of motivation for your class?

4. How do you tell when students in your class are unmotivated or disengaged?

5. When you see that students are unmotivated, what do you do or try to do?

6. What do you believe are the features of your classroom environment that facilitate or inhibit students' academic motivation?

7. What do you believe are the features of the larger school environment, outside your classroom, that facilitate or inhibit students' academic motivation?

8. What do you believe are the features of the larger community context, outside the school, that facilitate or inhibit students' academic motivation?

9. Is there anything else that you believe is important for us to know, to understand your students' motivation? (Patricia Hardré, personal communication, December 22, 2008)

Questions that start with who, what, where, when, why, and how all generate qualitative descriptions—sometimes very long descriptions. The result in Hardré's study was 30 hours of transcripts—over 300 pages of single-spaced text in Times 12-point type, or about 135,000 words (Patricia Hardré, personal communication, December 22, 2008).

Semistructured interviews are particularly useful for interviewing people who you really can't interview formally—like children. J. B. Whiting and Lee (2003) interviewed 23 foster children, using a semistructured guide. Each part of the interview—things like "how I came to foster care" or "my family"—was printed on a separate page. The interviewer showed a child each page as a way to stimulate the interview.

Probing

Probing is the key to successful in-depth interviewing; it definitely does not mean prompting. Here's a common question in interviews: "Have you ever lived anywhere except in this city?" If the respondent says, "Yes," then a probe is in order: "Like where?" If the respondent says: "Oh, all over the country," your next response should *not* be "Chicago? New York? Denver?" That's prompting. The correct response is a probe that doesn't put words into your respondent's mouth, like "Could you name some of the places where you've lived before?"

Interview technique, including the use of probes, has been the focus of research since the 1920s. In what follows, we draw on the work by Gorden (1987), Hyman and Cobb et al. (1975), Kahn and Cannell (1957), Merton et al. (1956), Reed and Stimson (1985), Richardson et al. (1965), Warwick and Lininger (1975), Whyte (1960), Whyte and Whyte (1984), and on our own experience. (**Further Reading**: interviewing technique)

The Silent Probe

The **silent probe** involves nothing more than waiting for someone to continue their thought. Especially when you start an interview, people will ask for guidance on whether they're "giving you what you want." The silent probe is hard to learn because you have to recognize when people have more to say—and are just thinking—and not take silence as a void that absolutely has to be filled. Doing that can really kill an interview. On the other hand, if someone has really completed a response, don't sit silently waiting for them to continue. If you don't move on, you can lose credibility as an interviewer and wind up with a respondent just going through the motions to complete the task.

Silence is sometimes the way people avoid answering threatening questions. If you sense that a respondent is holding back because a question is threatening, you can fill in the void or you can let the silence continue until the respondent starts to talk. The silent probe takes practice to use effectively, but it's worth the effort.

The Echo Probe

The **echo probe** involves simply repeating the last thing someone has said and asking them to continue. It's particularly useful when an informant is describing a process or an event. "I see. So, when you arrest someone, you take them to the station house. Then what happens?" This neutral probe doesn't redirect the interview. It shows that you understand what's been said so far and encourages the informant to continue with the narrative. Don't use the echo probe too often, though, or you'll hear an exasperated informant asking: "Why do you keep repeating what I just said?"

The Uh-Huh Probe and Head Nodding

With the **uh-huh probe**, you encourage a respondent to continue with a narrative by just making affirmative comments, like "Uh-huh," or "Yes, I see," or "Right, uh-huh," and so on. In a classic experiment, Matarazzo et al. (1964a) showed how powerful this neutral probe can be. They did a series of identical, semistructured, 45-minute interviews with a group of informants. They broke each interview into three 15-minute chunks. During the second chunk, the interviewer was told to make affirmative noises, like "Uh-huh," whenever the respondent was speaking. Interviewee responses during those chunks were 31% longer than during the first and third periods. The same team (Matarazzo et al. 1964b) also found that continual head nodding by the interviewer increased the average length of respondent utterance by 48%.

The Long-Question Probe

Instead of asking, "Why did you give up drinking?" say: "People have many reasons for giving up alcohol. Can you tell me about why you chose to give up alcohol?" The trick is to use the first longer sentence—what we call the **preamble**—to create a safe and neutral context for the respondent to answer the shorter question of interest. Instead of asking "Why did you join a gang?" say: "Everyone has a story about how they got into this. How did *you* come to join this gang?"

Terse questions tend to produce terse answers and longish questions tend to provoke longer answers. In another classic experiment, Matarazzo et al. (1963) found that doubling the length of an interviewer's question from five seconds to 10 seconds doubled the length of the response from 25 seconds to 50 seconds.

Longer is not always better, but when you're conducting an in-depth interview, the key is to keep people talking and let them develop their thoughts. The more people open up, the more you can express your support and develop rapport. This is especially important in the first interview you do with someone whose trust you want to build (see Spradley 1979:80).

Long questions are also recommended for questions about sensitive topics. Instead of asking straight out, "Did you ever steal anything when you were in high school?" you might say: "We're interested in the kinds of things that kids do in high school that can get them in trouble, like shoplifting. Do you know people who shoplifted things?" After the respondent answers, *then* you can ask, "How about you? Did you ever steal anything from a store?" (**Further Reading**: improving response to sensitive and threatening questions)

The Tell-Me-More Probe

This probe involves saying: "Could you tell me more about that?" or "Why exactly do you say that?" or "Why exactly do you feel that way?" These stock probes can get tiresome for respondents, though, so use them sparingly. Otherwise, you'll hear someone finishing up a nice long discourse by saying, "Yeah, yeah, and why *exactly* do I feel like that?" (Converse and Schuman 1974:50).

We consider each of the probes above to be *nonspecific*—that is they don't direct the respondent toward or away from anything in particular. We use them to get people to talk more. The reason they work so well, is because they are based on some ingrained linguistic patterns. In normal conversations, people naturally take turns speaking. For example, in interviews, the interviewer typically asks a question that is then followed by the respondent's answer. After giving an answer, the respondent expects the interviewer to take the next turn and ask another question. The silent probe, the uh-huh probe, the echo probe, and the tell-me-more probe are just ways for you as an interviewer to take your turn without really adding any direction to the conversation. If done well, the result is an interview where the respondent does almost all of the talking.

Phased-Assertion and Baiting Probes

A particularly effective probing technique is called **phased assertion** (Agar 1996:142; Collings 2009; Kirk and Miller 1986:48. Unlike nonspecific probing, this is when you act like you already know something to get people to open up. Every journalist (and gossip monger) knows this technique well. As you learn a piece of a puzzle from one person, you use it with the next informant to get more information, and so on. The more you seem to know, the more comfortable people feel about talking to you and the less people feel they are actually divulging anything. They are not the ones who are giving away the "secrets" of the group.

Baiting probes are a type of phased-assertion that prompts some people to jump in and correct you if they think you know a little, but that you've "got it all wrong." Here you intentionally make a statement that you think your respondent will disagree with. You have to be careful, however, not to alienate the person you are interviewing. The best way to do this is to attribute the controversial statement to unnamed others such as: "Someone told me that . . . ," or "I've heard people say that. . . ." No matter how you phrase the statement, be prepared to hear what may be a very emotional response or strongly held beliefs.

Structured Interviews:
Questionnaires, Surveys, and Response Effects

In fully **structured interviews**, like a **questionnaire** or a survey, each respondent sees or hears the same set of cues, usually in the same order. Having a fixed set of questions ensures that everyone we interview responds to the same set of cues. Well, that's the idea. Actually, we know that interviews are social events and that many things can make a difference in how people respond to our questions. Researchers have been studying these response effects since surveys began. A lot of what they've learned is as valuable for producing qualitative data as it is for producing quantitative data.

The Deference Effect

Differences in race, gender, ethnicity, and age between an interviewer and an informant can produce lots of **deference** responses—people telling you what they think you want to know, in order not to offend you. Kane and Macaulay (1993:11) asked a sample of Americans how couples divide child care. Men were more likely than women to say that men and women share this responsibility—if the interviewer was a man. Huddy et al. (1997:205) asked Americans about various issues affecting women. The answers to those questions were more likely to reflect a feminist perspective—if the interviewer was a woman. Flores-Macias and Lawson (2008) found similar results in Mexico.

The Third-Party-Present Effect

Interviews are usually conducted one-on-one, but in many cases, the spouse or partner of the person being interviewed may be in the room. Does this affect responses? Zipp and Toth (2002) found that, in Britain, when spouses are interviewed together, they are more likely to agree about many things—like who does what around the house—than when they are interviewed separately. Apparently, people listen to each other's answers and modify their own answers accordingly, which puts on a nice, unified face about their relationship.

Aquilino (1993) found that when their spouse is in the room, people report more marital conflict than when they are interviewed alone. They are also more likely to report that they and their spouse lived together before marriage if their spouse is in the room. Perhaps, as Mitchell (1965) suggested long ago, people own up more to things like this when they know it will be obvious to their spouse that they are lying. (**Further Reading**: third-party-present effects)

Open- and Closed-Ended Questions

Open-ended questions allow people to respond in their own words and capture people's own ideas about how things work while **closed-ended questions** force people to respond using a predefined set of categories.

Typically, open-ended questions produce more data and are less boring for people than are their closed-ended equivalents. On the other hand (there's always a trade-off), coding and analyzing open-ended questions are labor-intensive tasks that require lots of inferences and judgment calls. The cost, in time and money, for coding and analyzing the answers to open-ended questions can mount up fast—one reason that research in the qualitative tradition involves a lot fewer respondents than does research in the quantitative tradition.

Open-ended questions also have more missing data than do closed-ended questions about the same topic. Suppose you interview 10 people about the rules of driving. Five people mention driving on the right-hand side of the road; five don't. How to interpret this? You could conclude that half the sample drives on the left (as they do in 50 countries, including England, Japan, Bangladesh, and Cyprus), but instead you go to reinterview the five people who failed to mention the right-hand rule and find that: One is from England; another simply forgot to mention the right-hand rule; a third thought that driving on the right was so obvious as not to need mentioning; a fourth is from rural Vermont and drives almost entirely on single-lane roads; and the fifth refuses to be interviewed again.

If you want to know which side of the road people drive on, then a close-ended question—"Do you drive on the right-hand of the road? (Yes or No)"—is the way to go.

In their classic work on interview techniques, Cannell and Kahn (1968) recommended using open-ended questions when the objective is to discover people's attitudes and beliefs and the basis on which someone has formed an opinion. Use open-ended questions, they suggested, when the topic is likely to be outside the experience of many respondents, if you want to assess how much people know about a topic, or if you, yourself, know little about a topic and are in the exploratory phase of research.

But if you already know, from prior research, the range of responses to a question, then, Cannell and Kahn said, use closed-ended questions. This is good advice. Well-formulated, closed-ended questions put a lot less burden on respondents. As they also pointed out 50 years ago—and as thousands of seasoned researchers have learned on the job ever since—"There is no rule against mixing types of questions" (Cannell and Kahn 1968:567).

Short and Long Responses

Answers to open-ended questions can be long, narrative accounts (like an entire life history). They can also be short descriptions of events and experiences (like a one- or two-paragraph account of a recent illness), or even one-liners in response to a specific question. In one of own studies (Ryan and Bernard 2006), we asked people across the United States what they did with the last aluminum can they had in their hands. Most of the answers were one-liners, like "I threw it in the trash," or "I recycled it," or "I was driving and just tossed it out the window."

In general, the longer the texts, the more opportunities there are for discovering new themes and relationships. (More about this in Chapter 5.) Suppose you're studying conflict in married couples. To elicit actual cases of conflict, you might tell each partner separately: "Please describe, in as much detail as you can, the conflicts between you and your partner over the last year." Some responses—the ones from really good informants—will be quite long and will cover many episodes, some serious, others not so serious.

If you want to code the narratives for the presence of anger, frustration, and retaliation, you'll need to break them into episodes of conflict. That's because most people will mention anger, frustration, and retaliation at some point in a narrative about a year's worth of marital conflict. If you leave the narratives whole, you'll wind up with no variation across them, when, in fact, some conflicts are characterized by anger, some by frustration, some retaliation, some by all three of those things, and some by all three possible pairs of those things.

Lists and Relational Responses

Open-ended questions yield two types of answers: **lists** and **relations**. When we start to study something, we are typically interested in lists, and lists are generated by the W questions: who, what, why, where, and when. Asking "What did you do last night?" gets you a list of activities. Asking "Why did you do that?" gets you a list of rationales justifying the behavior. Asking a new mother about her birthing experiences, we might ask: "Who was present?" "What medications did they give you?" "Where did the birth take place?" "When did the nurse take your pulse?"

Across many cases, lists tell us about the range, frequency, and distribution of things under study. (See Chapter 18 for techniques to analyze list data.)

Lists from the W questions are very valuable, but, as Becker (1998) argues convincingly, asking *how* questions elicits stories and narratives that tell us about relations among things.

Ask new military recruits, "Why did you decide to join up?" and you'll get answers like: "Well, my father and uncle were in the military and my grades weren't that good, so I figured I would have a hard time getting into college" and "I didn't really want to go to college, but I was getting tired of working at the mall so I figured this would be a good experience and I could use the GI bill to get a college education later." Notice the lists.

Ask them instead, "How did you decide to join the military?" and you'll get stories like this one:

> Well, my grades weren't very good in high school and my folks didn't have much money, so I started working at my uncles' garage. I'd been working for about a year when my best friend came back from boot camp before being transferred to his first station. We talked quite a bit and he said the Army was a great deal. He took me down and we talked to the local recruiter. The recruiter explained what some of the benefits were and told me about all the testing I needed to complete. I started the process the next week. My mother wasn't really sure this was a good idea, but my father and uncle thought it would give me a lot of experience. Eventually my mom said it was my choice. I passed the tests and had good enough scores to get into a mechanic position.

How questions elicit process and relationships. (By the way, this story is from some applied research we did. The story has been edited to take out all the "umms" and such. Real speech is very messy. Sometimes, as in this case, a full transcription is more than you need. Sometimes, though, as in conversation analysis, you need a true verbatim transcription. We'll cover conversation analysis in Chapter 14.)

Compare-and-contrast questions also elicit how things are related to each other. Try the following experiment the next time you have to make small talk at a party. Instead of asking the standard question, "What do you do?" and waiting for the one- or two-word reply, ask: "So, what is your job like?" If your conversation partner is at all talkative, this should elicit a fairly long descriptive list of his or her day-to-day routine.

Follow up by asking the compare-and-contrast question: "So, how does this job compare to your last job?" This will not only get you a description of a second job, it will give you information about how the two jobs are related or not related.

Compare list and relational questions to questions that produce yes-or-no answers. These types of questions often start with *is, did, does, do, has,* or *have*. For example: Did you talk to family members about joining the military? Has anyone in your family served before? These questions can also bias respondents by pointing them in a particular direction, such as when we ask, "Did you consider the GI Bill when thinking about volunteering?" Or even worse, "Do you think that joining the military was the best choice of a career?"

In our experience, novice interviewers tend to ask more of these **dichotomous questions**. If you want full, rich data from your interviews, it is best to emphasize relational and list questions and avoid dichotomous and leading questions.

◆ ACCURACY

When people say that they *prefer* a particular brand of car, or that they *love* their new job, they're talking about internal states. You pretty much have to take their word for such things. But a lot of interviewing involves asking people about their behavior—How often do they go to church? Do they eat out in restaurants? Do they use bleach when they clean their needles?—and about facts in their lives—Where did they spend Thanksgiving last year? How many brothers and sisters do they have? Do they make regular deposits to their 401k? In all these cases, **accuracy** is a real issue.

People are inaccurate reporters of their own behavior for many reasons. Here are four:

1. Once people agree to be interviewed, they have a personal stake in the process and usually try to answer all your questions—whether or not they know the answers to your questions.

2. Human memory is fragile, although it's clearly easier to remember some things (like recent surgery) than others.

3. Interviews are social encounters, and people manipulate those encounters to whatever they think is their advantage. Expect people to overreport socially desirable behavior (like giving to charity) and to underreport socially undesirable behavior (like cheating on exams).

4. People can't count a lot of behaviors, so they use general rules of inference and report what they think they usually do. If you ask people how many times they ate eggs last month, don't expect the answers to accurately reflect the behavior of your respondents.

Reducing Errors: Jogging People's Memories

Sudman and Bradburn (1974) suggest several things that can increase the accuracy of self-reported behavior:

1. ***Cued recall***. In this technique, people might consult their records to jog their memories or you might ask them questions about specific behaviors. With life histories, for example, college transcripts help people remember events and people from their time at school. Credit card statements and long-distance phone bills help people retrace their steps and remember people and events.

2. ***Aided recall***. This technique involves giving people a list of possible answers to a question and asking them to choose among them. Aided recall is particularly effective in interviewing the elderly (Jobe et al. 1996). In situations where you do multiple interviews with the same person, you can remind people what they said last time in their answer to a question and then ask them about their behavior since their last report.

3. ***Landmarks***. The title of Loftus and Marburger's (1983) article on this says it all: "Since the eruption of Mt. St. Helens, has anyone beaten you up? Improving the accuracy of retrospective reports with landmark events." Means et al. (1989) asked people to recall landmark events in their lives going back 18 months from the time of the interview. Once the list of personal landmark events was established, people were better able to recall hospitalizations and other health-related events. (**Further Reading**: improving accuracy of recall in interviews)

◆ ELICITING CULTURAL DOMAINS

Cultural domains comprise a list of words in a language that somehow "belong together." Some domains, like names for racial and ethnic groups, names of fish, and things to eat for breakfast, are easy to list. Other domains, like things that mothers do or ways to preserve the environment, are harder to list.

Cultural domains are typically hierarchical. For most native speakers of English, lemons are a kind of citrus, which are a kind of fruit, which are a kind of food. But not for everyone. Some people skip the citrus level entirely. And people vary in what they think is the content of any cultural domain. For some native speakers of English, sharks and dolphins are kinds of fish; for others, they are not. For many native speakers of English, chimpanzees are kinds of monkeys; for others, they are kinds of apes and are definitely not kinds of monkeys.

Some cultural domains comprise fixed lists. The list of terms for members of a family (mother, father, etc.) is more or less a fixed list and is agreed on by most members of a culture. But not all. For some native speakers of English, a man's wife's sister's husband is the man's brother-in-law; for others, he's his wife's brother-in-law, and for others, he's no relative at all.

Many cultural domains—like the list of carpenters' tools or the list of muscles, bones, and tendons in the human leg—are the province of specialists. The list of names of major league baseball teams in the United States is agreed on by everyone who knows about this domain, but the list of greatest left-handed baseball pitchers of all time is a matter of heated debate among experts.

The object of cultural domain analysis is to discover the content and the structure of domains—what goes with what, and how they go together.

Data for the content of domains are collected with listing tasks; data on the structure of domains are collected with relational tasks like compare-and-contrast questions or paired comparisons, pile sorts and triad tests. These tasks generate qualitative data, but because the data are collected systematically, they can be treated quantitatively. We cover the methods for collecting and analyzing data about the content and structure of cultural domains in Chapter 18.

◆ MIXED METHODS

There was a time when combining qualitative and quantitative approaches was a topic of conversation in social research. Today, the practice is so widespread, there are several excellent texts and a scholarly journal devoted to it.

In fact, many social researchers now routinely begin with informal or ethnographic interviews to get a feel for what is going on and then move to semistructured or structured interviews to test hunches or hypotheses—as Laubach (2005) did in his study of informal workplace stratification at a family-owned lending institution. Or they may start with a questionnaire and move on to open-ended interviewing in an effort to better understand the quantitative results—as Weine et al. (2005) did in their study of Bosnian refugees in Chicago.

Focus groups, participant observation, case studies (including life histories), and decision modeling—all of these may (but don't have to) involve a mix of qualitative and quantitative data. (**Further Reading**: mixed methods)

Focus Groups

Focus groups are recruited to discuss how people feel about products (like brands of beer or new electronic gadgets) and for assessing social programs (is the new day care center providing enough support for working mothers?). They are used in getting stakeholder reaction to proposed programs (how do parents, teachers, administrators, and school board members feel about the proposal to move the start of the school year up by a month?). And they are often used in the development of surveys (to explore whether questions seem arrogant or naive to respondents) or to help interpret the results of a survey.

In the hands of a skilled moderator, the group setting stimulates discussions that would not occur in simple two-person interactions and encourages people to explore similarities and differences of opinion (Patton 1987). The objective is to get a group of people talking about a particular topic and then get out of the way.

Focus groups, however, are not good tools for understanding the distribution of responses in a group. First, the responses that people give to questions are not independent. In fact, the whole idea of a focus group is to get a group dynamic going so that people will feed off one another. This means that some people may dominate while others lurk.

To make sure that we get the whole range of opinions or feelings about a topic, we always ask participants in focus groups to complete a short questionnaire about the topic we plan to discuss *before* we begin the discussion. This gets people thinking about the topic and provides data on the variation in people's beliefs and attitudes about the topic we're studying.

It's tempting to use focus groups in the exploratory phase of research, but, as Agar and MacDonald remind us (1995), you really need to be well along in your research to understand and benefit from the free-flowing rhetoric generated by a group on a roll. When people who talk the same language get together, they abbreviate in almost everything they say.

Listen to ordinary people talking about their last business or vacation trip and you'll hear things like "I got the random big screening and almost missed my flight." Think of how much you have to know to fill in around that one: You have to know about screening of passengers at airports and that some passengers are selected at random for increased inspection that may include opening of their luggage and a physical pat-down. If you convene a group of teenagers to talk about suicide or dating, you'd better have done plenty of ethnography first or you won't be able to fill in around the cultural abbreviations.

Group interviews are not all focus group interviews. Robert Thornberg (2008) studied what children in Swedish primary schools think about how school rules—don't run in the halls; raise your hand if you want to speak—are made and enforced. During his two years of ethnography, Thornberg did 49 interviews with groups of two to four students each. If you're doing field research in a tightly knit community, expect people to just come up and insert themselves into what you think are private interviews.

This happened to Rachel Baker (1996a, 1996b) when she interviewed homeless boys in temples and junkyards in Kathmandu (Nepal) and to Stanley Yoder (1995) when he interviewed mothers in Lubumbashi (Democratic Republic of Congo) about childhood diarrhea. If you insist on privacy in these situations, you might find yourself with no interview at all. Better to take advantage of the situation and just let the information flow. Be sure to take notes, of course—on who's there, who's dominant, who's just listening, and so on—in any group interview. (**Further Reading**: recruiting and running focus groups)

Participant Observation

Participant observation is the ultimate mixed method strategy. It has been used for generations by scholars across the social sciences, positivists and interpretivists alike. It puts you where the action is, lets you observe behavior in a natural context (behavior that might be otherwise impossible to witness), and lets you collect any kind of data you want.

A lot of the data collected during participant observation are qualitative: field notes taken about things you see and hear in natural settings; photographs of the content of people's houses; audio recordings of people telling stories; video recordings of people making dinner, getting married, and having an argument; transcriptions of recorded, open-ended interviews; free lists and pile sorts of items in cultural domains. But many participant observers also collect quantitative data about behavior—like counting the number of drinks people consume in a bar—and even closed-ended questionnaires.

Participant observation involves going out and staying out, learning a new language (or a new dialect of a language you already know), and experiencing the lives of the people you are studying as much as you can. Unlike passive observation where there is minimum interaction between the researcher and the object of study, participant observation means establishing rapport and learning to act so that people go about their business as usual when you show up (see Box 4.6).

Box 4.6

The Ethical Dilemma of Rapport

Participant observation, for all its virtues, is also the most ethically challenging method for collecting data. Participant observers have taken notes at breast cancer support groups (Markovic et al. 2004), listened while teen-age gangs plotted illegal acts (Fleisher 1998), hidden out with illegal refugees on the run (Bourgois 1990). ... All of this requires lots of rapport, but the phrase "gaining rapport" is a euphemism for impression management, one of the "darker arts" of fieldwork, in Harry Wolcott's memorable phrase (2005: chap. 6).

Participant observation involves immersing yourself in a culture and learning to remove yourself every day from that immersion so you can intellectualize what you've seen and heard, put it into perspective, and write about it convincingly. When it's done right, participant observation turns fieldworkers into instruments of data collection and data analysis (see Box 4.7). (**Further Reading**: participant observation ethnography)

Box 4.7

Fieldwork Without Participation

Participant observation implies fieldwork, but not all fieldwork involves participant observation. Gomes do Espirito Santo and Etheredge (2002) interviewed 1,083 male clients of female sex workers and collected saliva specimens (to test for HIV) during 38 nights of fieldwork in Dakar, Senegal. The data collection involved a team of six fieldworkers, and the lead researcher was with the team throughout the three and a half months that it took to collect the data. This was serious fieldwork, but not participant observation.

Case Studies, Life Histories, and Case Histories

Case studies are the "end-product of field-oriented research" (Wolcott 1992:36); a research strategy for developing "a comprehensive understanding" of groups under study (Miles and Huberman 1994:25); and a way to develop "general theoretical statements about regularities in social structure and process" (Becker 1970:76).

In general, the goal of doing a case study is to get in-depth understanding of something—a program, an event, a place, a person, an organization. Often the interest is in process—how things work and why—rather than variations in outcomes, in contexts rather than specific variables, in discovery rather than theory testing (Yin 2008). Like participant observation ethnography, case studies can involve many data collection methods, including direct and indirect observation along with structured and unstructured interviewing.

Case studies are often used in evaluation research (see Patton 2002). They provide lots of descriptive data, are lifelike, and simplify the data that a reader has to assess. Above all, Guba and Lincoln argue, cases studies yield "information to produce judgment. Judging is the final and ultimate act of evaluation" (1981:375).

Merriam (1998) distinguishes among ethnographic case studies (which focus on the culture of a group, like a classroom or a factory), sociological case studies (which focus on social interactions, like those between couples, between student peers, between doctors and patients, etc.), historical case studies (which examine how institutions or organizations change over time), and psychological case studies (which examine the inner workings of people's thoughts and emotions). Freud used case studies in developing his theory of psychosexual development, and Piaget studied his own children to develop his theory of cognitive development.

Life histories are case studies of people—what happened to them and how they felt as they went through various experiences and stages. Life histories produce data from which deductions are made about changes in the culture and social structure of communities. Some life histories are wide-ranging autobiographical accounts, but many are focused on particular topics, like a person's work history, migration history, reproductive history, or sexual history.

When you ask people for their life history, they will try to recount things chronologically but, as in all open-ended interviews, they'll go off on tangents. These tangents provide context and background for the events we're studying, but to keep them from becoming the focus, life histories should be elicited with an interview guide that forces you to cover everything you need to know in a particular project. Life history interviews can take several days or longer to complete.

Case histories (also known as **event histories** or **case narratives**) are in-depth narratives about specific events. For example, investigators may want to know what happened and how people felt the last time they were sick, the last time they had sex, the last time they fought with their spouse, or the last time they snuck across the border looking for work.

When you analyze a case study, be careful not to overgeneralize. Don't let case studies "masquerade as a whole," warn Guba and Lincoln, "when in fact they are but a part, a slice of life" (1981:377). (**Further Reading**: case studies and life histories)

Ethnographic Decision Modeling

Ethnographic decision modeling (EDM) is a mixed method that involves ethnographic interviewing, systematic coding, and structured questionnaires. In one of our projects (Ryan and Bernard 2006), we asked 21 people to tell us stories about why they recycled or didn't recycle the last aluminum can they had in their hand. Coding of those stories produced 30 reasons, like "There was a recycling bin handy, so why not?" and "Hey, I was in my car and I didn't want to stain the carpet, so I threw the can out the window" and "I was home and we recycle everything at home, so naturally. . . ."

Then we asked 70 different people what they did with the last aluminum can they had in their hand and, no matter what they said in response, we asked them all 30 of those reasons we had extracted from the story-telling phase: Were you in your car at the time? Do you usually recycle other things at home? Was recycling bin handy? And so on. Finally, using all the responses, we built a model to account for recycling behavior and tested that model on another, independent sample of people. We'll cover this example in depth and EDM in general in Chapter 16.

CHOOSING A DATA COLLECTION STRATEGY ◆

The methods we've outlined here are strategies for collecting data. Each method—participant observation, semistructured interviewing, indirect observation, life histories, and so on—comprises many techniques. And each of these strategic methods has advantages and disadvantages. In deciding which method to use, consider two things: **data complexity** and **data distance**.

Data Complexity

Focus groups are more complex than are one-on-one interviews. Open-ended questions produce more complex data than do closed-ended ones. Long interviews produce more complex data than do short ones.

Complex data are likely to be a rich source of information—and quotes that you can use in your write-up—and they are wonderful for

1. Exploratory questions, like: How do licensed massage therapists feel about having to share their fees with physicians and chiropractors who refer patients?

2. Understanding processes, like: How do people in this community make wine at home?

3. Generating potential explanatory models, like: What causes people to abandon home-based remedies for an illness and consult a nurse or physician?

However, data from broadly focused interviews and from multiple speakers are difficult to compare across individuals. When you want to know the average of anything—whether it's people's age or their weight or how strongly they feel about that new labor contract they're negotiating—you simply have to have data that you can compare across people.

We recommend starting exploratory projects with hypothetical or normative/cultural questions and then moving on to individual/personal questions and finally to episodic questions. For example, if we wanted to talk to cops about violence against them, we might begin by asking a hypothetical question, like: "What would you do if a suspect drew a knife?" Or a normative/cultural question, like: "What's the accepted practice when you happen to come upon an act of domestic violence?"

As the interview progressed, and the respondent felt more comfortable, we might probe about the actual experiences with violence of some colleagues. And if the interview progressed sufficiently, we might ask about their actual experiences with violence and, finally, about the specifics of a real encounter.

Unstructured and semistructured interviews are typically conducted as face-to-face encounters, though it is possible to conduct them over the phone or via chat rooms on the web. Structured interviews can be conducted face to face or can be self-administered questionnaires, telephone interviews, or done over the web. Use face-to-face interviews with people who do not usually provide information (like elites), with illiterate people, or with people who have no phone or live in hard-to-reach places.

Face-to-face interviews have several advantages. You can clarify questions as you go, and such interviews can be much longer than either telephone or self-administered questionnaires. In face-to-face encounters, people can't flip ahead to anticipate questions or change answers they have already given. And in a face-to-face interview, you can be sure that the responses have been provided by the person for whom the questions were intended.

Data Distance

Data distance is about the amount of information lost in the process of recording it. Thinking about data distance is a kind of validity check. It tells us how good a proxy the data are for the phenomenon we're trying to study. A focus group is a complex interaction of individuals discussing a variety of issues. An audio recording of a focus group has no data on hand gestures and facial expressions. Voice tones that indicate emotional, cynical, or enthusiastic responses are lost when the recording is transcribed.

A video camera can record a lot more of the activity, but it can only capture what falls within the range of its lens. You can usually place a video camera so that it captures all movement in a classroom, but the camera can't locate the classroom in its larger school context and cannot assess environmental data like temperature, moisture, or smells.

Figure 4.4 Data Distance by Data Complexity

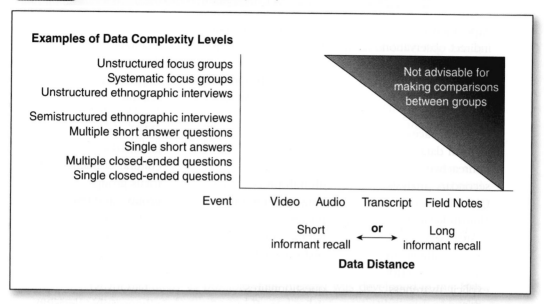

Human observers can see around moving bodies, can locate a situation in larger contexts, and can record information on environmental conditions. But human observers get overloaded with information very quickly; unless an observer is trained in taking verbatim notes (with shorthand), much of the conversation will go unrecorded, especially when two or more people talk at once.

Field notes are an essential part of all qualitative data collection, even when you have audio or video recordings. But clearly, the notes are a massive reduction of data—which is another way of saying data loss. In writing field notes, we filter what to record, choosing some things and ignoring others, and we lump different observations and events into thematic categories. In this sense, producing field notes is a process of identifying themes, but it can also introduce systematic bias.

The longer you wait to write up your notes, the more errors you're likely to make. There will be errors of omission (we forget events, even whole conversations) and errors of commission (we infer the existence of events and conversations that did not happen). We recommend that all unstructured and semistructured interviews be recorded, unless people explicitly ask not to be recorded. If you must rely entirely on notes, then write them up immediately after each interview. Above all, never sleep on data. They vanish into the night.

As either data complexity or data distance increases, it becomes more difficult to make systematic comparisons. As Figure 4.4 shows, we do not recommend making comparisons using field notes as the only source of data, nor do we recommend making comparisons across complex cases like unstructured focus groups.

After collecting qualitative data, the next steps are identifying and coding themes—the subjects of Chapters 5 and 6.

- o Semistructured interviews are flexible, in that the interviewer can modify the order and details of how topics are covered. This cedes some control to the respondent over how the interview goes, but because respondents are asked more or less the same questions, this makes possible comparisons across interviews.

- Probing is the key to semistructured interviewing.

  - o There are several kinds of probes, including: the silent probe (just waiting for a response); the echo probe (repeating what the respondent said and asking for more); the uh-huh probe (nodding and making affirmative sounds to encourage the respondent to go on); the tell-me-more probe (asking the respondent to say more about what she or he just said); the long-question probe (a long run-up to the actual question sometimes makes it easier for people to answer sensitive questions); and phased assertion (acting like you already know something to get people to open up).

- In structured interviews, each respondent sees or hears the same set of cues.

  - o Questionnaires are subject to many response effects, including the deference effect (people telling you what they think you want to know, in order not to offend you); the third-party-present effect (spouses who are interviewed together are more likely to agree about things like who does what around the house).
  - o Open-ended questions allow people to respond in their own words and capture people's own ideas about how things work. If you already know, from prior research, the range of responses to a question, then use closed-ended questions.

- Open-ended questions yield two types of answers: lists and relations.

  - o When we start to study something, we are typically interested in lists, and lists are generated by the W questions: who, what, why, where, and when. Asking "What did you do last night?" gets you a list of activities. Across many cases, lists tell us about the range, frequency, and distribution of things under study. (See Chapter 18 for techniques to analyze list data.) Lists from the W questions are very valuable, but as Becker (1998) argues convincingly, asking *how* questions elicits stories and narratives that tell us about relations among things.

- A lot of interviewing involves asking people about their behavior—How often do they go to church? Do they eat out in restaurants? Do they use bleach when they clean their needles?—and about facts in their lives—Where did they spend Thanksgiving last year? How many brothers and sisters do they have? Do they make regular deposits to their 401k? In all these cases, accuracy is an issue.

  - o Sudman and Bradburn (1974) suggest the following to increase the accuracy of self-reported behavior: cued recall (looking over credit card statements or their college transcript can help people remember some events); aided recall (giving people a list of possible answers to a question and asking them to choose among them); landmarks (asking people to recall landmark events in their lives and then using those landmarks to cue recall of other events that occurred around the same time).

- Cultural domains comprise a list of words in a language that somehow "belong together." Some domains, like names for racial and ethnic groups, names of fish, and things to eat for breakfast, are easy to list. Other domains, like things that mothers do or ways to preserve the environment, are harder to list.

  o The object of cultural domain analysis is to discover the content and the structure of domains—what goes with what and how they go together. Data for the content of domains are collected with listing tasks; data on the structure of domains are collected with techniques like pile sorts and triad tests.

- Some methods combine both qualitative and quantitative approaches.

  o Some mixed methods covered in other chapters are focus groups, group interviews, participant observation, case studies, life histories, case histories, and ethnographic decision modeling.

- Consider data complexity and data distance in choosing a data collection method.

  o Focus groups are more complex than are one-on-one interviews. Open-ended questions produce more complex data than do closed-ended ones. Long interviews produce more complex data than do short ones. We recommend starting exploratory projects with hypothetical or normative/cultural questions and then moving on to individual/personal questions and finally to episodic questions.

  o Data distance is about the amount of information lost in the process of recording it. A video camera can record a lot more of the activity, but it can only capture what falls within the range of its lens. Human observers can see around moving bodies, can locate a situation in larger contexts, and can record information on environmental conditions. But human observers get overloaded with information very quickly.

Exercises

1. How do researchers who work with qualitative data deal with the problem of validity? Find two or more research articles that (1) are based on the collection and analysis of qualitative data and (2) deal explicitly with the problem of interval versus external validity. Explain how the authors dealt with the problem of validity in their research.

2. To get familiar with the various methods of data collection, find research articles that (1) are based on the collection and analysis of qualitative data and (2) are based on each of the three non-experimental methods, including indirect observation, direct observation, and elicitation.

3. Take careful notes on any three-hour bloc of your day. That night, enter the notes on your computer and try to expand on the notes as you type. The first time you do this, you should become acutely aware of how hard it is to take careful notes and how much harder it is to expand on the notes. Do this for five days and keep track of how much you can recall about events of the day. Watch for two things: (1) the level of detail should get greater as you get more practice, and (2) you should start to see patterns in your data.

4. A good way to learn the craft of interviewing is with life histories. Begin with a favorite aunt or uncle, or a family friend who is much older than you. As you set up your recorder, tell the person that you'd like them to start at the beginning and give you as much detail as possible about each event they describe in their life.

   Don't be surprised if the first thing your respondent says is something like: "I was born in Canton, Ohio, in 1940. I went to Manning High School and when I graduated I joined the army." The object here is to learn how to get details. Ask people to tell you about their earliest memories and follow the threads you get from that. Ask them to name their friends in grade school and high school and ask if they know what those friends are doing now. Ask about movies and music they remember from when they were kids. Did they dance? If so, what were the names of the dances they did back then? Life histories should take five or 10 hours of interviewing if you're doing them right. By the time you repeat this exercise with your second respondent, you'll be asking questions you'd never thought of before and moving the interview along with some of the techniques discussed in this chapter.

5. Get a team of five or six people together to learn about running a focus group. Have the team read up on how to run focus groups. Decide on a topic together. Focus groups about consumer products seem to work well, assuming that everyone in the group has experience with the products. Take turns being the moderator of the group. Try to keep the conversation going for an hour. Have one member of the group video each session so that you can all learn from the experience, no matter who is the moderator.

6. Do a computer bibliographic search for the term "response effect." What are gender-of-interviewer and race-of-interviewer effects? Are there differences in these effects for telephone interviews versus face-to-face interviews?

Further Reading

Response effects. Aquilino (1994), Barnes et al. (1995), Borgers et al. (2004), Bradburn, Sudman et al. (1979), Davis et al. (2010), Dijkstra and van der Zouwen (1982), Finkel et al. (1991), Javeline (1999), Malhotra (2008), Millar and Dillman (2011), Narayan and Krosnick (1996), Schuman (2008, 2009), Schwarz (1999), Singer and Presser (1989), Sudman and Bradburn (1974, 1982), Tanur (1992), Tourangeau and Bradburn (2010), van der Vaart et al. (2006), Wentland and Smith (1993).

Secondary analysis of qualitative data. Hammersley (2004, 2010a), Haynes and Jones (2012), Heaton (2008), N. Moore (2007), Murray (2012), Seale (2011), Silva (2007), and other articles in a special issue of Sociological Research Online (http://www.socresonline.org.uk/12/3/contents.html). See Corti and Backhouse (2005) and other articles in a special issue of Forum: Qualitative Social Research (http://www.qualitative-research.net/index.php/fqs/issue/view/12).

Continuous monitoring. Beck (2007), Brewis and Lee (2010), Devine et al. (2010), Weigl et al. (2009).

Spot sampling and time allocation studies. Baksh et al. (1994), Messer and Bloch (1985), Scelza (2009), Tirella et al. (2007).

Interviewing technique. Behr et al. (2012), Conrad and Schober (2010), Converse and Schuman (1974), Gubrium and Holstein (2002), Holstein and Gubrium (1995), Kvale and Brinkmann (2009), Levy and Hollan (2014), Mishler (1986), Rubin and Rubin (2005), Schaeffer et al. (2010).

Improving response to sensitive and threatening questions. Bradburn (1983), Bradburn, Sudman et al. (1979), Johnston and Walton (1995), Joinson et al. (2008), Tourangeau and Yan (2007), Wutich et al. (2009). See Catania et al. (1996), Gribble et al. (1999), Hewitt (2002), Wiederman et al. (1994).

The third-party-present effect. Aquilino et al. (2000), Blair (1979), Boeije (2004), Bradburn (1979), Edwards et al. (1998), Hartmann (1994), Pollner and Adams (1997), Seale et al. (2008), T. W. Smith (1997), Taietz (1962).

Improving accuracy of recall in interviews. Beegle et al. (2012), Reimer and Mathes (2007), van der Vaart and Glasner (2007), Wansink et al. (2006).

Mixed methods. Axinn and Pearce (2006), Creswell (2003), Creswell and Plano Clark (2011), Greene (2008), R. B. Johnson (2006), R. B. Johnson and Onwuegbuzie (2004), LeCompte and Schensul (2013), Mertens (2005), Saks and Allsop (2007), Tashakkori and Teddlie (1998, 2010). For empirical studies using mixed methods, see the *Journal of Mixed Methods Research*.

Recruiting and running focus groups. Barbour (2007), Carey (2012), Krueger and Casey (2009), Morgan (1997), Morgan and Krueger (1998), Puchta and Potter (2004), Stewart and Shamdasani (1990), Vaughn et al. (1996).

Participant observation. For detailed discussions of participant observation in various disciplines see Agar (1996), Becker (1998), Bernard (2011), Crabtree and Miller (1999), DeWalt and DeWalt (2011), Fenno (1990), Gummesson (2000), C. D. Smith and Kornblum (1996), Spradley (1980), Winchatz (2010), and Wolcott (2005).

Case studies and life histories. Adriansen (2012), De Chesnay (2015), Gerring (2007), van der Vaart and Glasner (2011), Yin (2014).

Visit the online resource site at study.sagepub.com/bernardaqd to access engaging and helpful digital content, like video tutorials on working with MAXQDA, presentation slides, MAXQDA keyboard shortcuts, datasets, stop list, and recommended readings.

CHAPTER 5

FINDING THEMES

Authors' note: We rely heavily in this chapter on our article Ryan and Bernard, *Field Methods* 15(1): 85–109. Copyright © 2003 Sage Publications.

♦ INTRODUCTION

Analyzing text involves five complex tasks: (1) discovering themes and subthemes; (2) describing the core and peripheral elements of themes; (3) building hierarchies of themes or codebooks; (4) applying themes—that is, attaching them to chunks of actual text; and (5) linking themes into theoretical models.

In this chapter, we focus on the first task: discovering themes and subthemes. Then, in Chapter 6, we discuss methods for describing themes, building codebooks, and applying themes to text. In Chapter 7, we move on to building models.

In Chapter 19, we'll show you how to use some computer methods (cluster analysis and multidimensional scaling) to find themes in text. In this chapter, we'll focus on techniques, like line-by-line analyses, that (so far) only people can do, and on simple word counts that can be done by a computer and that support human coders in their search for themes in texts. Each technique has advantages and disadvantages. As you'll see, some methods are better for analyzing long, complex narratives, while others are better for short responses to open-ended questions. Some require more labor and skill, others less (see Box 5.1).

But first . . .

Box 5.1

Automated Text Analysis . . . Not Quite Around the Corner, But on Its Way

Computer analysis of text has been going on since the 1960s (see Ogilvie et al. 1966), but things really got rolling in the 1990s (Salton et al. 1996) and this now is a fast-moving area of artificial intelligence in engineering and informatics. These new systems can read free text created by physicians and offer support for clinical decisions for specific illnesses, like pneumonia and cervical cancer (Aronsky et al. 2001; Wagholikar et al. 2012).

They can do this because the guidelines for diagnosis of these illnesses are so clearly established. There are, after all, only so many words in the vocabulary of diagnosis that a physician can choose from to diagnose any particular illness. There is a long way to go before machines replace human coders in parsing texts about human experiences (see Noll et al. 2013), but work on this problem is advancing quickly, with obvious applications in the social sciences. Many programs are available today that plow through mountains of text—all of Shakespeare's work, for example, or tens of thousands of blog pages—and isolate potential themes. (See Box 11.5 for more on automated content analysis.) (**Further Reading**: automated text analysis)

WHAT'S A THEME? ♦

This question has a long history. Thompson (1932–36) created an index of folktale motifs, or themes, that filled six volumes. In 1945, Morris Opler, an anthropologist, made the identification of themes a key step in analyzing cultures. He said:

> In every culture are found a limited number of dynamic affirmations, called *themes*, which control behavior or stimulate activity. The activities, prohibitions of activities, or references which result from the acceptance of a theme are its *expressions*. . . . The expressions of a theme, of course, aid us in discovering it. (Opler 1945:198–99)

Opler established three principles for analyzing themes. First, he observed that themes are only visible (and thus discoverable) through the manifestation of expressions in data. And conversely, expressions are meaningless without some reference to themes. Second, Opler noted that some expressions of a theme are obvious and culturally agreed on, while others are subtler, symbolic, and even idiosyncratic.

And third, Opler observed that cultural systems comprise sets of interrelated themes. The importance of any theme, he said, is related to (1) how often it appears; (2) how pervasive it is across different types of cultural ideas and practices; (3) how people react when the theme is violated; and (4) the degree to which the number, force, and variety of a theme's expression is controlled by specific contexts (see Box 5.2).

Box 5.2

Terms for Themes

Today, social scientists still talk about the linkage between themes and their expressions, but use different terms to do so. Grounded theorists talk about "categories" (Glaser and Strauss 1967), "codes" (Miles and Huberman 1994), or "labels" (Dey 1993:96). Opler's "expressions" are called "incidents" (Glaser and Strauss 1967), "segments" (Tesch 1990), "thematic units" (Krippendorf 1980), "data-bits" (Dey 1993), and "chunks" (Miles and Huberman 1994). Lincoln and Guba refer to expressions as "units" (1985:345). Corbin and Strauss (2008:51) call them "concepts" that are grouped together in a higher order of classification to form categories.

Here, we follow Agar's lead (1979, 1980) and remain faithful to Opler's terminology. To us, the terms "theme" and "expression" more naturally connote the fundamental concepts we are trying to describe. In everyday language, we talk about themes that appear in texts, paintings, and movies and refer to particular instances as expressions of goodness or anger or evil. In selecting one set of terms over others we surely ignore subtle differences, but the basic ideas are just as useful under many glosses.

♦ WHERE DO THEMES COME FROM?

Induced themes come from data, while **a priori themes** (also called **deduced themes**) come from prior understanding of whatever phenomenon we are studying. A priori themes come from characteristics of the phenomena being studied—what Aristotle identified as essences and what dozens of generations of scholars since have relied on as a first cut at understanding any phenomenon. If you are studying the night sky, for example, it won't take long to decide that there is a unique, large body (the moon), a few small bodies that don't twinkle (planets), and millions of small bodies that do twinkle (stars).

A priori themes can come from the literature about a topic; from local, commonsense constructs; and from researchers' values, theoretical orientations, and personal experiences (Bulmer 1979; Maxwell 1996; Strauss 1987).

The decisions about what topics to cover and how best to query people about those topics are a rich source of a priori themes (Dey 1993:98). In fact, the first pass at generating themes often comes from the questions in an interview protocol (Coffey and Atkinson 1996:34). Even with a fixed set of open-ended questions, there's no way to anticipate all the themes that will come up before you analyze a set of texts (Dey 1993:97–8).

Andriotis (2010), for example, explored the way newspapers reported the activities of British spring-breakers at Greek resorts. A review of the literature on spring-break-type behavior across the world turned up four major themes: alcohol consumption (and especially binge drinking), drug use, sexual behavior, and other risk taking (like unprotected sex, ledge walking, stunt driving, etc.). After preliminary coding, however, Andriotis dropped drug use (it was reported rarely in the 186 newspaper articles he was studying) and added a new theme: host community reaction to the behavior of the tourists.

The act of discovering themes is what grounded theorists call **open coding**, and what classic content analysts call qualitative analysis (Berelson 1952) or **latent coding** (Shapiro and Markoff 1997). There are many recipes for arriving at a preliminary set of themes (Tesch 1990:91). We'll describe eight observational techniques—things to look for in texts—and four manipulative techniques—ways of processing texts. These 12 techniques are neither exhaustive nor exclusive. They are often combined in practice. (**Further Reading**: finding themes)

♦ EIGHT OBSERVATIONAL TECHNIQUES: THINGS TO LOOK FOR

Looking for themes in written material typically involves pawing through texts and marking them up, either with different colored pens or by swiping words and phrases in different colors on the computer screen. Sandelowski (1995b:373) says that text analysis begins with proofreading the material and simply underlining key phrases "because they make some as yet inchoate sense." For recorded interviews, the process of identifying themes begins with the act of transcription. Whether the data come in the format of video, audio, or written documents, handling them physically is always helpful for finding themes.

Here's what to look for:

1. Repetitions

"Anyone who has listened to long stretches of talk," says D'Andrade, "knows how frequently people circle through the same network of ideas" (1991:287). Repetition is easy to recognize in text. Claudia Strauss (1992) did several in-depth interviews with Tony, a retired blue-collar worker in Connecticut. Tony referred again and again to ideas associated with greed, money, businessmen, siblings, and "being different." Strauss concluded that these ideas were important themes in Tony's life. To get an idea of how these ideas were related, Strauss wrote them on a piece of paper and connected them with lines to snippets of Tony's verbatim expressions—much as researchers today do with text analysis software.

Owen (1984) used repetition and forcefulness as indicators of a theme in his study of narratives about family relationships. If a concept occurred at different places in a narrative and was emphasized by the informant (in vocal inflection, or dramatic pauses or volume), then he took that as evidence of a theme. Owen distinguished between what he called recurrences and repetitions—where recurrences are different uses of a concept or theme in a narrative, using different words—and repetitions involve the use of the *same* words for a concept—but the idea is the same: The more the same concept occurs in a text, the more likely it is a theme. How many repetitions makes an important theme, however, is a question only you can decide.

2. Indigenous Typologies or Categories

Another way to find themes is to look for unfamiliar, local words, and for familiar words that are used in unfamiliar ways—what Patton calls **indigenous categories** (2002:454–56; and see Linnekin 1987). Grounded theorists refer to the process of identifying local terms as **in vivo coding** (Corbin and Strauss 2008:65; Strauss 1987:28). Ethnographers call this the search for typologies or classification schemes (Bogdan and Taylor 1975:83) or **cultural domains** (Spradley 1979:107–19).

In a classic ethnographic study, Spradley (1972) recorded conversations among tramps at informal gatherings, meals, and card games. As the men talked to each other about their experiences, they kept mentioning the idea of "making a flop," which turned out to be the local term for finding a place to sleep for the night. Spradley searched through his recorded material and his field notes for statements about making a flop and found that he could categorize them into subthemes such as kinds of flops, ways to make flops, ways to make your own flop, kinds of people who bother you when you flop, ways to make a bed, and kinds of beds. Spradley returned to his informants and asked for more information about each of the subthemes.

For other classic examples of coding for indigenous, categories, see Becker's (1993) description of medical students' use of the word "crock" and Agar's (1973) description of drug addicts' understandings of what it means to "shoot up."

3. Metaphors and Analogies

In pioneering work, Lakoff and Johnson (2003 [1980]) observed that people often represent their thoughts, behaviors, and experiences with **metaphors and analogies**. Analysis, then, becomes the search for metaphors in rhetoric and deducing the schemas, or broad, underlying themes that might produce those metaphors (D'Andrade 1995; Strauss and Quinn 1997).

Naomi Quinn (1996) analyzed over 300 hours of interviews from 11 couples to discover themes in the way Americans talk about marriage. She found that when people were surprised that some couple had broken up, they said they thought the couple's marriage was "like the Rock of Gibraltar" or that the marriage had been "nailed in cement." People use these metaphors, says Quinn, because they know that their listeners (people from the same culture) understand that cement and the Rock of Gibraltar are things that last forever.

Agar (1983) examined transcripts of arguments presented by independent truckers at public hearings of the Interstate Commerce Commission on whether to discontinue a fuel surcharge. One trucker explained that all costs had risen dramatically in the preceding couple of years and likened the surcharge to putting a bandage on a patient who had internal bleeding. With no other remedy available, he said, the fuel surcharge was "the life raft" that truckers clung to for survival (Agar 1983:603).

Natural human speech is full of metaphors. More on this in Chapter 12, on schema analysis.

4. Transitions

Naturally occurring shifts in content may be markers of themes. In written texts, new paragraphs may indicate shifts in topics. In speech, pauses, changes in tone of voice, or the presence of particular phrases may indicate transitions and themes.

In semistructured interviews, investigators steer the conversation from one topic to another, creating transitions, while in two-party and multiparty natural speech, transitions occur continually. Analysts of conversation examine features such as turn-taking and speaker interruptions to identify these transitions. More about this in Chapter 14.

5. Similarities and Differences

What Glaser and Strauss (1967:101–16) labeled the "**constant comparison method**" involves searching for similarities and differences by making systematic comparisons across units of data. Typically, grounded theorists begin with a line-by-line analysis, asking: "What is this sentence about?" and "How is it similar or different from the preceding or following statements?" This keeps the researcher focused on the data rather than on theoretical flights of fancy (Charmaz 1990, 2000; Glaser 1978:56–72; Strauss and Corbin 1990:84–95).

Here's an exchange from our study of what people say about helping the environment (Bernard et al. 2009):

Interviewer: So, what can people do to help the environment?

Informant: (long pause) Ya' know the thing that's interesting to me is I don't understand toxic waste roundup, but if there could be more of that . . . it seems that only once a year they round up toxic waste and I know I poured stuff down the sink I shouldn't (laughing) and poured it like on the (pointing to the ground) (pause). Also reporting violations. (pause) I had a friend who reported these damn asbestos tiles (which were on her apartment building roof).

The reference to asbestos is different from the reference to the toxic waste roundup. On the other hand, asbestos is a toxic substance. At this point, we might tentatively record "getting rid of toxic substances" as a theme.

Another comparative method involves taking pairs of expressions—from the same informant or from different informants—and asking: "How is one expression different or similar to the other?" Here's another informant in our study of what Americans think they can do to help the environment:

Interviewer: Any pressing issues that you can think of right now?

Informant: well I don't know what you can do to solve it but the places for hazardous waste are few and far between from what I understand—that some people are dumping where they shouldn't (pause) and I don't know what you can do because nobody wants any of the hazardous wastes near them.

In comparing the two responses, we asked: "Is there a common theme here, in hazardous waste and toxic waste?" If some theme is present in two expressions, then the next question to ask is: "Is there any difference in degree or kind in which the theme is articulated in both of the expressions?"

Degrees of strength in themes may lead to the naming of subthemes. Suppose you compare two video clips and find that both express the theme of anxiety. Looking carefully, you notice that anxiety is expressed more verbally in one clip and more through subtle hand gestures in the other. Depending on the goals of your research, you might code the clips as expressing the theme of anxiety or as expressing anxiety in two different ways.

You can find some themes by comparing pairs of whole texts. As you read a text, ask: "How is this one different from the last one I read?" and "What kinds of things are mentioned in both?" Ask hypothetical questions like: "What if the informant who produced this text had been a woman instead of a man?" and "How similar is this text to my own experiences?" These hypothetical questions will force you to make comparisons, which often produce moments of insight about themes.

Bogdan and Biklen (1982:153) recommend reading through passages of text and asking: "What does this remind me of?" Below, we'll introduce more formal techniques for identifying similarities and differences among segments of text, but we always start with the informal methods, underlining, highlight, and comparing.

6. Linguistic Connectors

Look carefully for words and phrases that indicate attributes and various kinds of causal or conditional relations (Casagrande and Hale 1967).

Causal relations: "because" and its variants 'cause, 'cuz, as a result, since, and so on. For example: "Y'know, we always take 197 there 'cuz it avoids all that traffic at the mall." But notice the use of the word "since" in the following: "Since he got married, it's like he forgot his friends." Text analysis that involves the search for linguistic connectors like these requires very strong skills in the language of the text because you have to be able to pick out very subtle differences in usage.

Conditional relations: In conditional relations, the occurrence of one thing, A, is conditional on another thing, B. This shows up as "if" or "then" (and if–then pairs), "rather than," and "instead of." For example: "If you pass the bar exam on the first try, you'll get lots of job offers." "You can drink a lot more [alcohol] if you coat your stomach with milk first."

Taxonomic categories: The phrase "is a" (as in "a moose is a kind of mammal") is often associated with taxonomic categories: "Vitamin C is a great way to avoid colds." Again, watch for variants. Notice how the "is a" relation is embedded in the following: "When you come right down to it, lions are just big pussy cats."

Time-oriented relations: Look for words like "before," "after," "then," and "next." "There's a trick to that door. Turn the key all the way to the left, twice, and then push hard." The concept of time-ordered events and relations can be very subtle: "By the time I bike home, I'm sweating like a pig." "It's so damn hot, your glasses fog when you go out."

X-is-Y relations: Casagrande and Hale (1967) suggested looking for attributes of the form X is Y: "Lemons are sour," "The Greek islands are still a bargain," "This is just bullshit," "He's lucky he's alive."

Contingent relations: Look for phrases of the form if X, then Y follows, or X causes Y or Y is caused by X: "If mortgage rates go above 7%, people will rent instead of buying houses." "For a strong harvest, plant with the full moon." This relation can be expressed in the negative, too: "They won't wear a condom, no matter what you do."

Spatial relations: Look for phrases of the form X is close to Y: "I found my way around pretty good in the new place [supermarket] because stuff is together. Milk and cheese and eggs and stuff are always together and all that stuff is near the meat" (see Box 5.3).

Box 5.3

More Linguistic Connectors

Operational definitions: X is a tool for doing Y: "You can use Excel to do basic stuff, but if you really wanna work on text you gotta get a real program for that."

Example definitions: X is an instance of Y: "So now [referring to undergraduates] they're using the Internet to find papers they can use; new technology, same old plagiarism."

Comparison definitions: X resembles Y: "Iraq is like Vietnam in some ways, but we need to remember the differences."

Class inclusions: X is a member of class Y: "Geeks and nerds are both dorky, but a geek is a nerd who can get hired."

Synonyms: X is equivalent to Y: "Telling me you can't afford to go is just a wimpy way of saying kiss off."

Antonyms: X is the negation of Y: "Not picking up after your dog is the definition of a bad neighbor" [the implication is that the act is the negation of "good neighbor"].

Provenience: X is the source of Y: "A foolish consistency is the hobgoblin of little minds" (Emerson's famous dictum [see Emerson 1907:89]).

Circularity: X is defined as X: "Yellow means like when something is lemon colored."

SOURCE: Casagrande and Hale (1967).

7. Missing Data

This method works in reverse from typical theme-identification techniques. Instead of asking "What is here?" we can ask "What is missing?" Women who have strong religious convictions may fail to mention abortion during discussions of birth control. In power-laden interviews, silence may be tied to implicit or explicit domination (Gal 1991). In a study of birth planning in China, Greenhalgh reports that she could not ask direct questions about resistance to government policy. People made "strategic use of silence," she says, "to protest aspects of the policy they did not like" (1994:9). Obviously, themes discovered like this need to be looked at critically to make sure that we are not finding only what we are looking for (see Box 5.4).

Box 5.4

Data Can Be Missing on Themes We Think Are Important

In Lyn Richards's pioneering study of a new suburb outside Melbourne, Australia, one of the driving research questions was "How do residents in a new outer suburb cope with isolation and loneliness?" This was to be a five-year study, but by the end of the first year "none of those talking to the researchers were reporting that they were lonely" (Singh and Richards 2003:10–11). Perhaps a year was just not enough for loneliness to set in. Perhaps informants were hiding something. Or was the theory wrong? Maybe nobody was lonely in the new suburb? This challenge to the theory guided Richards in the subsequent years of the study.

Gaps in texts may not indicate avoidance at all, but simply what Spradley (1979:57–58) called **abbreviating**—leaving out information that everyone knows. As you read through a text, look for things that remain unsaid and try to fill in the gaps (Price 1987). This can be tough to do. Distinguishing between when people are unwilling to discuss a topic from their simply assuming that you already know about it requires a lot of familiarity with the subject matter. If someone says, "John was broke because it was the end of the month," they're assuming that you already know that many people get paid once a month and that people sometimes spend all their money before getting their next pay check.

When you first read a text, some themes will simply pop out at you. Highlight them—with highlighters, if you prefer to work with paper, or in your text management program. Then read the text again. And again. Look for themes in the data that remain unmarked. This tactic—marking obvious themes early and quickly—forces the search for new and less obvious themes in the second pass (Ryan 1999).

8. Theory-Related Material

By definition, rich narratives contain information on themes that characterize the experience of informants, but we also want to understand how qualitative data illuminate questions of theoretical importance. Spradley (1979:199–201) suggested searching interviews for evidence of social conflict, cultural contradictions, informal methods of social control, things that people do in managing impersonal social relationships, methods by which people acquire and maintain achieved and ascribed status, and information about how people solve problems.

Bogdan and Biklen (1982:156–162) suggested examining the setting and context, the perspectives of the informants, and informants' ways of thinking about people, objects, processes, activities, events, and relationships. Strauss and Corbin (1990:158–75) urge us to be more sensitive to conditions, actions/interactions, and consequences of a phenomenon and to order these conditions and consequences into theories. "Moving across substantive areas," says Charmaz, "fosters developing conceptual power, depth, and comprehensiveness" (1990:1163).

There is a trade-off, of course, between bringing a lot of prior theorizing to the theme-identification effort and going at it fresh. Prior theorizing, as Charmaz says (1990), can inhibit the forming of fresh ideas and the making of surprising connections. And by examining the data from a more theoretical perspective, researchers must be careful not to find only what they are looking for. Assiduous theory avoidance, on the other hand, brings the risk of not making the connection between data and important research questions.

The eight techniques just described require only pencil and paper. Next, we describe four techniques that require more physical or computer-based manipulation of the text itself.

FOUR MANIPULATIVE TECHNIQUES: ♦
WAYS TO PROCESS TEXTS

Some techniques are informal—spreading texts out on the floor, tacking bunches of them to a bulletin board, and sorting them into different file folders—while others require software to count words or display word-by-word co-occurrences. And, as we'll see, some techniques require a fair amount of skill in computer analysis. But more of that later . . .

9. Cutting and Sorting

After the initial pawing and marking of text, cutting and sorting involves identifying quotes or expressions that seem somehow important—these are called **exemplars**—and then arranging the quotes/expressions into piles of things that go together (Lincoln and Guba 1985:347–51). By the way, this kind of work can be done with cards or with computer software. There is no right way to do it. What matters is that the process feels comfortable and productive.

There are many variations on this technique. We cut out each quote (making sure to maintain some of the context in which it occurred) and paste the material on a small index card. On the back of each card, we write down the quote's reference—who said it and where it appeared in the text. Then we lay out the quotes randomly on a big table and sort them into piles of similar quotes. Then we name each pile. These are the themes.

When it comes to pile sorting, there are two kinds of people: **splitters and lumpers**. Splitters maximize the differences between items and generate more fine-grained themes, while lumpers minimize the differences and identify more over-arching themes. The objective is to identify the widest possible range of themes at the end of the process. To accomplish this, some researchers find it best to split first and lump later, while others find it best to lump first and split later.

In a project with two or three researchers, each member of the research team should sort the exemplar quotes into named piles independently. This usually generates a longer list of themes than you get in a group discussion. After sorting the piles independently, the researchers can decide together which piles can be merged, which should be split, and which are good candidates for further analysis.

Barkin et al. (1999) interviewed clinicians, community leaders, and parents about what physicians could say to adolescents, during routine well-child exams, to prevent violence among youth. There were three questions at the center of the project: (1) What could pediatricians potentially do to deal with youth violence? (2) What barriers did they face? (3) What resources were available to help them?

Two coders read through the transcripts and pulled out all segments of text associated with these questions. The two coders identified 84 statements related to potential, 74 related to barriers, and 41 related to resources. All the statements were pulled out and put onto cards.

Next, four other coders independently sorted all the quotes from each major theme into piles of things that they thought were somehow similar. Talking about what the quotes in each pile had in common and naming those piles helped Barkin et al. identify subthemes. In really large projects, have pairs of researchers sort the quotes and decide on the names for the piles. Record and study the conversations that researchers have while they're sorting quotes and naming themes in order to understand the underlying criteria they are using (see Box 5.5). (**Further Reading**: pile sorting [card sorting] for themes)

Box 5.5

Formal Analysis of Pile Sorts

Pile sorts produce **similarity data**—that is, a matrix of what goes with what—and similarity data can be analyzed with some formidable visualization methods, like **multidimensional scaling** and **cluster analysis**. These methods let you see patterns in your data.

Barkin et al. (1999) converted the pile-sort data 199 statements (84 potential + 74 barriers + 41 resources) into a quote-by-quote similarity matrix, where the numbers in the cells indicated the number of coders (0, 1, 2, 3, or 4) who had placed the quotes in the same pile. They used multidimensional scaling and cluster analysis to identify groups of quotes that the coders thought were similar.

More about **matrix analysis**, including multidimensional scaling and cluster analysis, in Chapters 7 and 18.

---

10. Word Lists and Key-Words-in-Context (KWIC)

Word lists and the **key-word-in-context (KWIC)** technique draw on a simple observation: If you want to understand what people are talking about, look closely at the words they use. To generate word lists, you identify all the unique words in a text and then count the number of times each occurs.

As part of a 12-year longitudinal study, Thomas Weisner and Helen Gamier (1992) told parents of adolescents: "Describe your children. In your own words, just tell us about them." From the transcripts, Ryan and Weisner (1996) produced a list of all the unique words. Then they counted the number of times each unique word was used by mothers and by fathers. The idea was to get some clues about themes that could be used for coding the full texts.

Overall, the words that mothers and fathers used to describe their children suggested that they were concerned with their children's independence and with their children's moral, artistic, social, athletic, and academic characteristics, but mothers were more likely to use "friends," "creative," "time," and "honest" to describe their children while fathers were more likely to use "school," "good," "lack," "student," "enjoys," and "independent." Ryan and Weisner used this information as clues for themes that they would use later in actually coding the texts. (Details about this study are in Chapter 9.)

Word-counting techniques produce what Tesch (1990:139) called **data condensation** or **data distillation**. By telling us which words occur most frequently, these methods can help us identify core ideas in researchers a welter of data. But condensed data like word lists and counts take words out of their original context, so if you do word counts, you'll also want to use a KWIC program.

The classic KWIC method is essentially a modern version of a **concordance.** A concordance is a list of every substantive word in a text, shown with the words surrounding it. Concordances have been done on sacred texts from many religions and on famous works of literature from Euripides (Allen and Italie 1954), to Beowulf (Bessinger and Smith 1969), to Dylan Thomas (Farringdon et al. 1980).

Before computers, concordances were arranged in alphabetical order so you could see how each word was used in various contexts. These days, KWIC lists are generated by asking a computer to find all the places in a text where a particular word or phrase appears and printing it out in the context of some number of words (say, 30) or sentences (say, two) before and after it. You (and others) can sort these instances into piles of similar meaning to assemble a set of themes. More about the KWIC method and word lists in Chapter 17.

11. Word Co-Occurrence

Word co-occurrence, also known as **collocation**, comes from linguistics and **semantic network analysis**. It's based on an observation, by J. R. Firth (1935, 1957), that many words commonly occur with other words to form an idea that would not be obvious from the individual words—collocations like "green with envy," "shrouded in mystery," "maiden voyage," and "vaguely remember."

In 1959, Charles Osgood created word co-occurrence matrices—i.e., matrices that show how often every pair of words co-occurs in a text—and analyzed those matrices to describe the relation of major themes to one another. It was rather heroic work back then, but computers have made the construction and analysis of co-occurrence and collocation matrices easy today and have stimulated the development of semantic network analysis (Barnett and Danowski 1992; Danowski 1982, 1993). More about this, too, in Chapter 19.

12. Metacoding

Metacoding examines the relationship among a priori themes to discover potentially new themes and overarching metathemes. The technique requires a fixed set of data units (paragraphs, whole texts, pictures, etc.) and a fixed set of a priori themes, so it's less exploratory than many of the techniques we've described.

For each data unit, you ask which themes are present and, where appropriate, the direction and strength of each theme. The data are recorded in a unit-by-theme matrix. This matrix can then be analyzed statistically.

Factor analysis, for example, indicates the degree to which themes coalesce along a limited number of dimensions. Visualization methods—like multidimensional scaling and correspondence analysis—show graphically how units and themes are distributed along dimensions and into groups or clusters. (More on multidimensional scaling in Chapters 7 and 18.)

Jehn and Doucet (1996, 1997) asked 76 U.S. managers who worked in Sino–American joint ventures to describe recent interpersonal conflicts with their business partners. Each person described two conflicts: one with a same-culture manager and another with a different-culture manager.

Two coders read the 76 intracultural and 76 intercultural conflict scenarios and evaluated them on a 5-point scale for 27 themes that Jehn and Doucet had identified from the literature on conflict. This produced two 76x27 scenario-by-theme matrices—one for the intracultural conflicts and one for the intercultural conflicts. Jehn and Doucet analyzed these matrices with factor analysis. This method reduced the 27 themes to just a handful. Jehn and Doucet then pulled out quotes from their original data to illustrate the most important themes.

Quotes that characterized the first factor for intercultural relations were: "There is a lot of hate involved in this situation," and "The dislike is overwhelming," and "I was very angry." Quotes that characterized the second factor were: "I was very frustrated with my co-worker" and "Their inconsistencies really aggravated me." And quotes that characterized the third factor were: "She's a bitch" and "We are constantly shouting and screaming." Jehn and Docuet labeled these factors personal animosity, aggravation, and volatility in intercultural business relations (1997:2).

Numerical methods like these work best when applied to short, descriptive texts of one or two paragraphs. They tend to produce a limited number of large, meta-themes, but these are just the kind of themes that may not be apparent, even after a careful and exhaustive reading of a text. Metacoding is a nice addition to our theme-finding tool kit.

SELECTING AMONG TECHNIQUES ♦

Figure 5.1 and Table 5.1 lay out the characteristics of the techniques to help you decide which method is best in any particular project, given your own time and skill constraints. Looking for repetitions and similarities and differences and cutting and sorting can be applied to any kind of qualitative data and don't require special computer skills. It is not surprising that these techniques are the ones used most frequently in qualitative research.

There are five things to consider in selecting one or more of these 12 techniques: (1) the kind of data you have; (2) how much skill is required; (3) how much labor is required; (4) the number and types of themes to be generated; and (5) whether you are going to test the reliability and validity of the themes you produce.

Figure 5.1 Selecting Among Theme Identification Techniques

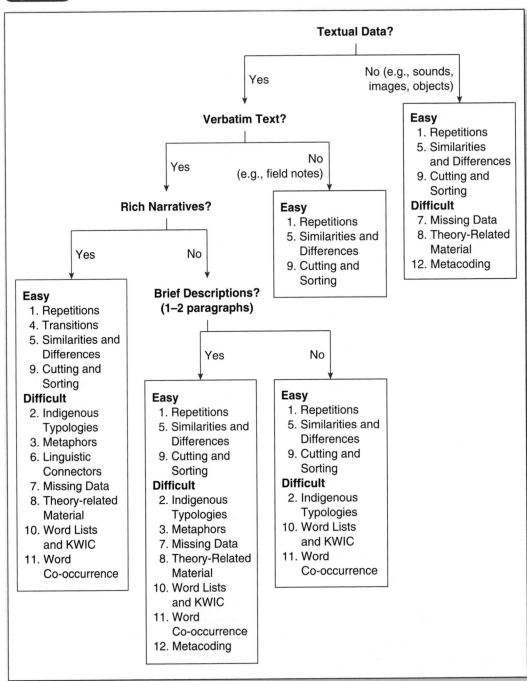

Table 5.1   Practical Characteristics of Theme Discovery Techniques

	Technique	Labor Intensity	Expertise			Stage in Analysis	Number of Themes Produced	Type of Theme Produced
			Language	Substantive	Methodological			
1	Repetitions	Low	Low	Low	Low	Early	High	Theme
2	Indigenous Typologies	Low	High	Low	Low	Early	Medium	Theme, Subtheme
3	Metaphors	Low	High	Low	Low	Early	Medium	Theme
4	Transitions	Low	Low	Low	Low	Early	High	Theme
5	Similarities and Differences	Low-High	Low	Low	Low	Early	High	Theme
6	Linguistic Connectors	Low	High	Low	Low	Late	High	Theme
7	Missing Data	High	High	High	High	Late	Low	Theme
8	Theory-Related Material	Low	Low	High	High	Late	Low	Theme
9	Cutting and Sorting	Low-High	Low	Low	Low	Early or late	Medium	Theme, Subtheme, Metatheme
10	Word Lists and KWIC	Low	Medium	Low	Low	Early	Medium	Theme, Subtheme
11	Word Co-Occurrence	Medium	Medium	Low	High	Late	Low	Theme, Metatheme
12	Metacoding	Medium	Medium	High	High	Late	Low	Theme, Metatheme

1. Kind of Data

With the exception of metacoding, all 12 of the techniques we've described here can be applied to lengthy narratives. However, as texts become shorter and less complex, looking for transitions, metaphors, and linguistic connectors is harder to do. Discovering themes by looking for what is missing is inappropriate for very short responses to open-ended questions because it is hard to say whether missing data represents a new theme or is just the result of the way the data were elicited. And short texts are inefficient for finding theory-related material.

For audio and video data, we find that the best methods involve looking and listening for repetitions, similarities and differences, missing data, and theory-related material—and doing metacoding.

One more reminder about field notes as texts: In writing field notes, we choose what data are important to record and what data are not. Any patterns (themes) that we discover in field notes may come from our informants—but may also come from biases that we brought to the recording process.

2. Skill

Not all techniques are available to everyone. You need to be truly fluent in the language of the text to look for metaphors, linguistic connectors, and indigenous typologies or to spot missing data. If you are working in a language other than your own, it's best to stick to the search for repetitions, transitions, similarities and differences, and etic categories (theory-related material) and to have native speakers do any sorting of exemplars. Word lists and co-occurrences, as well as metacoding, also require less language competence and so are easier to apply.

Using word co-occurrence or metacoding requires know-how about producing and managing matrices, as well as skill in using methods for exploring and visualizing data. If you don't have training in the use of multidimensional scaling, cluster analysis, factor analysis, and correspondence analysis, then use techniques like cutting and sorting, word lists, and KWIC.

Word lists and KWIC are easily done on a computer with many of the popular **CAQDAS** packages. CAQDAS (pronounced "cactus") stands for "computer assisted qualitative data analysis software." Consult the CAQDAS Networking Project website (http://www.surrey.ac.uk/sociology/research/researchcentres/caqdas/) for information on these resources. (**Further Reading**: computer-assisted qualitative data analysis software)

3. Labor

A generation ago, observation-based techniques required less effort than did process techniques. Today, computers and software have made counting words and co-occurrences of words, as well as analysis of matrices very easy, though the cost, in time and effort, to learn these computer methods can be daunting.

Some of the observation-based techniques (searching for repetitions, indigenous typologies, metaphors, transitions, and linguistic connectors) are best done by eyeballing, but this can be really time consuming. In team-based applications research, the premium on getting answers quickly often means a preference for methods that rely on computers and less on human labor.

In our own work, we find that a careful look at a word frequency list and some quick pile sorts are goods ways to start. Studying word co-occurrences and metacoding require more work and produce fewer themes, but they are excellent for discovering big themes that can hide in mountains of texts.

4. Number and Kinds of Themes

In theme discovery, more is better. It's not that all themes are equally important. You still have to decide which themes are most salient and how themes are related to each other. But unless themes are discovered in the first place, none of this additional analysis can take place.

We know of no research comparing the number of themes that each technique generates, but in our experience, looking for repetitions, similarities and differences, transitions, and linguistic connectors that occur frequently in text produces more themes, while looking for **indigenous metaphors** and indigenous categories (which occur less frequently) produces fewer themes. Of all the observation techniques, searching for theory-related material or for missing data produces the smallest number of new themes.

Of the process techniques, the cutting-and-sorting method, along with word lists and KWIC analysis, yield many themes and subthemes, while word co-occurrence and metacoding produce a few, larger, more inclusive metathemes. But at the start of any project, the primary goal is to discover as many themes as possible. And this means applying several techniques until you reach saturation—that is, until you stop finding new themes.

Cutting and sorting expressions into piles is the most versatile technique. You can identify major themes, subthemes, and even metathemes with this method and although the analysis of this kind of data is enhanced by computational methods, much of it can be done without a computer. In contrast, techniques that apply to aggregated data such as word co-occurrences and metacoding are particularly good at identifying more abstract themes but really can't be done without the help of good software.

5. Reliability and Validity

"There is," says Ian Dey (1993:110–11) "no single set of categories [themes] waiting to be discovered. There are as many ways of 'seeing' the data as one can invent." In their study of Chinese and American managers (above), Jehn and Doucet (1996, 1997) used three different discovery techniques on the same set of data and each produced a different set of themes. All three of their theme sets have some intuitive appeal, and all three yield analytic results that are useful. But Jehn and Doucet might have used any of the other techniques we've described here to discover even more themes.

How can we tell if the themes we've identified are valid? That is, are the concepts we've identified really in the text? The answer is that there is no ultimate demonstration of validity. The **validity of a concept** depends on the utility of the device that measures it and on the collective judgment of the scientific community that a concept and its measure are valid (Bernard 2012:51; Denzin 1970:106).

Reliability, on the other hand, is about agreement among coders and across methods and across studies. Do coders agree on what theme to assign a segment of text? Strong interrater reliability—about which more in Chapter 11—suggests that a theme is not just a figment of your imagination and adds to the likelihood that the theme is also valid (Sandelowski 1995b).

Lincoln and Guba's (1985) team approach to sorting and naming piles of expressions is so appealing because agreement need not be limited to members of the core research team. Jehn and Doucet (1996, 1997) asked local experts to sort word lists into themes, and Barkin et al. (1999) had both experts and novices sort quotes into piles. The more agreement among team members, the more confidence we have that emerging themes are internally valid.

Some researchers recommend that respondents be given the opportunity to examine and comment on themes (Lincoln and Guba 1985:351; Patton 1990:468–69). This is certainly appropriate when one of the goals of research is to identify and apply themes that are recognized or used by the people whom one studies, but this is not always possible. The discovery of new ideas derived from a more theoretical approach may involve the application of etic rather than emic themes—that is, understandings held by outsiders rather than those held by insiders. In these cases, researchers should not expect their findings necessarily to correspond with the ideas and beliefs of study participants. (**Further Reading**: reliability and validity in qualitative research)

◆ AND FINALLY . . .

We have much to learn about the process of finding themes in qualitative data. Since the early 1960s, researchers have been working on fully automated, computer-based methods for identifying themes in text. These computer-based content dictionaries, as they're known, may not sit well with some. After all, if the "qualitative" in qualitative methods means analysis by humans, then how can we give over such an important piece of qualitative analysis—theme identification—to machines?

The answer, of course, is that ultimately, we are responsible for all analysis. We are comfortable using text management software to help us recognize connections in a set of themes, and we are comfortable letting machines count words and create matrices for us from texts. Text analysts of every epistemological persuasion can hardly wait for voice recognition software to become sufficiently effective that it will relieve us of all transcription chores. Computer-based content dictionaries that can parse a text and identify its underlying thematic components will, we believe, be just another tool that will (1) make the analysis of qualitative data easier and (2) lead to much wider use and appreciation of qualitative data in all the social sciences.

Key Concepts in This Chapter

induced themes	contingent relations	cluster analysis
a priori (deduced themes)	spatial relations	matrix analysis
open coding	operational definitions	word lists
latent coding	example definitions	key-word-in-context
indigenous categories	comparison definitions	(KWIC)
in vivo coding	class inclusions	data condensation
cultural domains	synonyms	(data distillation)
metaphors and	antonyms	concordance
analogies	provenience	collocation
constant comparison	circularity	semantic network
method	abbreviating	analysis
causal relations	exemplars	metacoding
conditional relations	splitters and lumpers	CAQDAS
taxonomic categories	pile sorts	indigenous metaphors
time-oriented relations	similarity data	validity of a concept
x-is-y relations	multidimensional scaling	reliability

Summary

- Analyzing text involves five tasks: (1) discovering themes and subthemes; (2) describing the core and peripheral elements of themes; (3) building hierarchies of themes or codebooks; (4) applying themes—i.e., attaching them to chunks of actual text; and (5) linking themes into theoretical models. This chapter focuses on the first task: discovering themes and subthemes.

- There are two kinds of themes: Induced themes come from data, while a priori themes (also called deduced themes) come from prior research, from commonsense constructs and from researchers' experiences. Research projects may involve both kinds of themes.

- In looking for themes, there are at least eight things to look for in texts. These include (1) repetitions; (2) indigenous categories (local words for topics of importance); (3) the use of metaphors and analogies; (4) naturally occurring shifts in content; (5) similarities and differences in pairs of statements about a topic; (6) use of linguistic connectors, like "because," "rather than," and "instead of," is a kind of, time statement (like "before" and "after that,"), if–then statements, spatial statements (like "close to"), comparisons, synonyms, and antonyms; (7) missing data; and (8) theory-related material (like evidence of social conflict, cultural contradictions, informal methods of social control, things that people do in managing impersonal social relationships, methods by which people acquire and maintain achieved and ascribed status, and information about how people solve problems).

    o Other techniques in looking for themes require more physical or computer-based manipulation of the text itself. These include (1) creating cards with quotes from a text, sorting them into piles of similar quotes, and naming each pile; (2) creating word lists and concordances with a key-words-in-context program; (3) looking for co-occurrences and collocations; and (4) metacoding (examining the relationship among themes to discover potentially new themes and overarching metathemes).

- Consider five things in selecting techniques for finding themes: (1) the kind of data you have; (2) how much skill is required; (3) how much labor is required; (4) the number and types of themes to be generated; and (5) whether you are going to test the reliability and validity of the themes you produce. For example, looking for transitions, metaphors, and linguistic connectors is hard to do in short responses to open-ended questions because it is hard to say whether missing data represent a new theme or is just the result of the way the data were elicited. And short texts are inefficient for finding theory-related material.
- Cutting and sorting expressions into piles is the most versatile technique for finding major themes, subthemes, and even metathemes. Cutting-and-sorting, along with word lists and KWIC analysis, yields many themes and subthemes, while word co-occurrence and metacoding produce a few, larger, more inclusive metathemes. At the start of any project, use several techniques until you reach saturation—that is, until you stop finding new themes.

Exercises

1. This is an exercise in coding induced themes. Download 10 stories from newspapers in any country about some current event that is making national or international news. With another student, read the stories line by line and highlight words and phrases that seem to you to indicate various themes. Name the themes as you go.

    Start by doing just one story together with your colleague. After you finish highlighting one story, compare your notes and discuss each theme. Whenever there's a discrepancy between coders, discuss the issues and come to an agreement. Then go on to the next story and repeat the process. Some new themes may come up in the second story. Be sure that you and your colleague resolve any disagreements before moving on to the next story.

The idea here is simply to reduce a set of texts to a set of themes and to do so in a way that is agreed upon by two people. Don't be surprised if you wind up with a few themes that you can't agree on.

2. This is an exercise in understanding the concept of deduced themes. With a colleague, read 10 studies based on classic content analysis and isolate the codes that were used in those studies. There are thousands of studies based on classic content analysis of print media, films, blogs, and social media. You can find examples by going to scholar.google.com and searching for "content analysis." Limiting the entries to the most recent year will get you several hundred possibilities.

3. This is another exercise in understanding the concept of deduced themes. Download 20 stories from nationally known newspapers in any country about some current event that is making national or international news. Ten of those stories should come from a newspaper with a conservative (right-wing) editorial policy, and 10 should come from a left-wing paper.

   In the United States, for example, the *Wall Street Journal* and the *New York Times* would fit this description. In Canada, the *National Post* and the *Toronto Star* would fill the bill. In the United Kingdom, you might use the *Daily Mail* and the *Daily Mirror*. With a colleague, discuss the content of the story and develop a small set of a priori themes.

Further Reading

Finding themes Bradley et al. (2007), Yeh and Inman (2007). Finding themes in group research: Carey and Gelaude (2008), MacQueen et al. (2008), Necheles et al. 2007.

Automated text processing Colley and Neal (2012), Grimmer and Stewart (2013), Van Holt et al. (2013).

Pile sorting Eastman et al. (2005), Hsiao et al. (2006), Nolle et al. (2012), Patterson et al. 1993, Sayles et al. (2007).

Computer-assisted qualitative data analysis software Text analysis info (http://www.textanalysis.info/), CAQDAS Networking Project (http://www.surrey.ac.uk/sociology/research/researchcentres/caqdas/).

Reliability and validity in qualitative research Kirk and Miller (1986), Long and Johnson (2000), Moret et al. (2007), Ryan (1999).

Visit the online resource site at study.sagepub.com/bernardaqd to access engaging and helpful digital content, like video tutorials on working with MAXQDA, presentation slides, MAXQDA keyboard shortcuts, datasets, stop list, and recommended readings.

CHAPTER 6

CODEBOOKS AND CODING

INTRODUCTION ◆

In Chapter 5, we discussed how to discover themes. In this chapter, we discuss the actual process of coding—that is, organizing lists of themes into codebooks and applying codes to chunks of text. Finally, we lay out some methods for finding chunks of text that are

125

typical of each theme. This helps us understand the core and peripheral elements of each theme and is an important part of analysis—which begins in Chapter 7.

◆ THREE KINDS OF CODES

Codebooks contain three kinds of codes: (1) **structural codes** (2) **thematic codes** and (3) **memos** Structural codes describe things like features of the environment in which data are collected, features of the respondent, features of the interviewer, and so on (L. Richards and T. Richards 1995; T. Richards 2002). Theme codes show where the themes we've identified actually occur in a text. Memos are field notes about codes and contain our running commentary as we read through texts (Corbin and Strauss 2008:117–40, 200–26, 230–44, 249–60, 264–70).

Table 6.1 is a piece of a coded focus group transcript showing all three kinds of codes. The transcript is from a study by Mark Schuster and his colleagues (Eastman et al. 2005; Schuster et al. 2000) in Los Angeles about the feasibility of running classes at corporate work sites to help parents better communicate with their adolescent children about relationships and sex.

One structural code (on the far left column in Table 6.1) tells us that the focus group took place in Corporation 1; a second code indicates where different topics in the interview protocol begin and end (in this example, there are two topics represented); a third indicates the gender of the speakers; and a fourth tells us which moderator was running the group at the time of each snippet.

Schuster et al. could have assigned codes for other features of the focus group, like the time of day the group was conducted or whether the focus group met onsite or offsite. And they could have coded for characteristics of the speakers, like age or ethnicity if they'd wanted to.

Theme codes are the most common kinds of codes. These are the codes we use for marking instances of themes in a set of data. You may see thematic codes called **referential codes** (L. Richards and T. Richards 1995) because these codes refer to where a theme is located in a text. We might also call them **index codes** because, like the index in the back of a book, they tell us where to look in a text if we want to find material about a particular theme. There are two thematic codes in Table 6.1. Italicized text marks Theme #1, called "Communication," and underlined text references Theme #2, called "Potential Barriers."

The segment in small caps between the square brackets is a memo. These features are identified in the legend in the lower right corner of Table 6.1 (see Box 6.1).

Blocking off theme areas makes analysis easier later on: We can search the transcript and find where particular themes occur. This can be done with a word processor, but it's even easier with a text analysis program. And with a text analysis program, you can search for places in the transcript where two or more themes occur.

Table 6.1 Examples of Structural Codes, Theme Codes, and Memos

Structural Codes				Thematic Codes and Memos	
Work Site	Interview Topic	Speaker's Gender	Speaker	Transcript	
Corporation #1			Moderator	If we were going to offer a parenting program, what would you like to hear that would catch your interest or make you want to attend this type of program? How could we market it?	
	Topic #1	M	1	I don't know. . . . I know my wife would like it a lot. She would lead me into it, but. . . .	
		M	2	*Probably stressing the communication, somehow portraying that and the problems communicating because that's a universal. We were talking yesterday, that that's the biggest challenge, or one of the biggest challenges, so somehow portraying that well and grabbing attention that way.* [THIS IS PART II OF A 2-DAY SESSION. PREVIOUS DAY, PARTICIPANTS DISCUSSED HOW THEY COMMUNICATED WITH THEIR ADOLESCENTS ABOUT SEX AND RELATIONSHIPS.]	
		F	3	I think you'd have to sell the success. What is it that you plan on accomplishing with this? If you can tell me that at the end of this thing, our relationship will be better, my daughter will be a better achiever, you know, I won't lose my temper as often; that would do it.	
		F	4	Money-back guarantee.	
	Topic #2		Moderator	If we said, "OK, tonight we want you to have a conversation with your child about sex." What would be hard or easy about that?	
		F	4	I've taken a couple of classes through the years, and my kids get a kick out watching me sit and do homework. And so if I let them know, this is my homework, and gosh mom gets homework too, ya, and that could be kinda fun for them to know that you've gotta sit and read a book and do a report or have a discussion. You know, you're my homework tonight.	

SOURCE: Adapted from Eastman et al. (2005) and Schuster et al. (2000).

Legend: Italics = Theme #1, communication; underline = Theme #2, potential barriers; small caps = memo.

Box 6.1

Kinds of Memos

The transcript in Table 6.1 contains some memos embedded right into the running text. Corbin and Strauss distinguish three kinds of memos (2008:117–42): (1) code memos; (2) theory memos; and (3) operational memos.

(1) Code memos describe the researcher's observations and thoughts about the concepts that are being discovered.

(2) Theory memos summarize our ideas about the existence of themes, about how themes are linked, and about what causes themes to exist in the first place. For example, if you are analyzing a set of texts about the experience of giving birth, you may notice that some women mention the pain; others don't, or even play it down. Noticing and memoing how the theme of pain is linked to other themes is an act of theory making, as is noticing and memoing the circumstances in a woman's life that make the mention of pain predictable.

(3) Operational memos are about practical matters. For example, the memo in the middle of the transcript in Table 6.1 indicates that the same participants had met the day before to talk about how they communicated with their adolescent children about sex and relationships.

The concept of memoing comes from grounded theory and is an integral part of that method. We'll discuss memos in more detail in Chapter 10, on grounded theory.

♦ BUILDING CODEBOOKS

Like themes, codebooks can be built up from data—the inductive approach—or from theory—the deductive or a priori approach. Boyatzis (1998) laid out two different pathways for building codes, as shown in Figure 6.1.

The inductive (or data-driven) path has five steps. First, you reduce the raw data into manageable pieces. Second, you identify themes. In this second step, you use the techniques we covered in Chapter 5. Some theme identification techniques, though, can generate a lot of themes, and not all of them are good candidates for coding and write-up. In the third stage, you compare these themes across respondents, groups, or contexts to find the ones that have interesting patterning—this is a powerful way to find promising themes for your analysis.

Once you select a subset of themes to focus on, you are ready to create codes. As a final step, after you've had a chance to work with the codes a bit, you'll want to assess interrater reliability (more on that in a minute).

Figure 6.1   Boyatzis's Steps for Developing Themes Inductively and Deductively

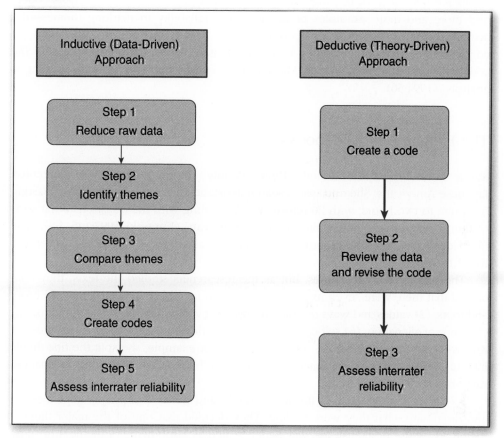

SOURCE: Adapted from Boyatzis (1998), p. 44.

The deductive (or theory-driven) path has just three steps. The first step is to identify concepts in the literature that will be the focus of your analysis (we covered how
to do this in Chapter 2). These concepts form the basis of your codes.

It may seem like the deductive approach is easier or quicker because, after the
literature review, you can skip straight to code creation. In our experience, deductive
approaches to codebook creation can be just as time consuming as inductive ones.
That's because the second step, when you revise the code again and again to narrow
the gap between concept and data, can take a lot of work. At the end of this second
phase, you'll have a code that reflects both a theoretical concept (as it appears in the
literature) and the textual data (the way people really talk about it). In the final step,
too, you'll check interrater reliability.

It can be helpful to think about inductive and deductive approaches to code
development as separate pathways, but in reality many researchers use a combination

of the two approaches (Dey 1993:104). We're in that camp, too. We find that code-books are often a work in progress right up until a project is almost over. As coders find more and more examples of themes, their reliability in marking themes—the actual process of coding—goes up (Carey et al. 1996; Krippendorff 1980:71–84). As coders refine their understanding of the content of a code, the description in the codebook gets more detailed. As Miles and Huberman said so elegantly: "Coding is analysis" (1994:56).

The Evolution of Codebooks I

Karen Kurasaki (2000) studied ethnic identity among *sansei*, third-generation Japanese Americans. She and two research assistants did in-depth interviews, lasting from one to two hours, with 20 informants, beginning with the question "What sorts of things remind you that you're Japanese-American" (Kurasaki 1997:145–149). The interviews were transcribed and then studied by all three researchers to develop a list of themes.

The first list had 29 themes, but as the researchers studied the texts, they concluded that there were seven major themes, shown in Table 6.2: (1) a sense of history and roots; (2) values and ways of doing things; (3) biculturality; (4) sense of belonging; (5) sense of alienation; (6) self-concept; and (7) worldview. As the analysis progressed, Kurasaki split the major themes into subthemes. For example, she split the first theme into (a) sense of having a Japanese heritage and (b) sense of having a Japanese American social history.

As the coding progressed further, Kurasaki and her two assistants kept meeting and discussing what they were finding. They decided that one of the major themes, theme 5 (a sense of alienation), was better treated as a subtheme of theme 4 (a sense of belonging). Then they decided that one of the subthemes, 4.4 (searching for a sense of community), was redundant with codes 4.1, 4.2, 4.3, and 4.5, and that code 7.1, social consciousness (shown crossed out in Table 6.2), should instead be labeled an orientation toward promoting racial tolerance (Kurasaki 1997:50–56).

The Evolution of Codebooks II

Here's another example. Across the world, the vast majority of illness episodes are treated at home. Ryan (1995) studied how ordinary people in Cameroon react at home when they get sick. Every week for five months, Ryan and several assistants visited 88 extended family households in rural Cameroon. They asked if anyone had been sick and, for each of 429 illness episodes, they asked the primary caregiver to describe what happened and what had been done about it.

Table 6.2 Kurasaki's Inductive Codebook

First-Order Category	Second-Order Category	First Numeric Codes	Second Numeric Codes
Sense of history and roots	Sense of having a Japanese heritage	1.1	1.1
	Sense of having a Japanese American social history	1.2	1.2
Values and ways	Japanese American values and attitudes of doing things	2.1	2.1
	Practice of Japanese customs	2.2	2.2
	Japanese way of doing things	2.3	2.3
	Japanese American interpersonal or communication styles	2.4	2.4
	Japanese language proficiency	2.5	2.5
Biculturality	Integration or bicultural competence	3.1	3.1
	Bicultural conflict or confusion	3.2	3.2
Sense of belonging	Sense of a global ethnic or racial community	4.1	4.1
	Sense of interpersonal connectedness with same ethnicity or race of others	4.2	4.2
	Sense of intellectual connectedness with other ethnic or racial minorities	4.3	4.3
	Searching for a sense of community	4.4	deleted
Sense of alienation	Sense of alienation from ascribed ethnic or racial group	5.1	4.5
Self-concept	Sense of comfort with one's ethnic or racial self	6.1	5.1
	Searching for a sense of comfort with one's ethnic or racial self	6.2	5.2
Worldview	~~Social consciousness~~ Orientation toward promoting racial tolerance	7.1	6.1
	Sense of oppression	7.2	6.2

SOURCE: Kurasaki (1997, 2000:186).

Ryan knew from earlier work in the village the kinds of treatments that were available to people there, so that part of his codebook was set. He planned to code each illness for the caregiver's ideas about its cause, its severity, and its outcome as well as for its signs, symptoms, and duration. Because he planned to compare people's

Table 6.7 Portion of Code Book for Workplace Ethnographies

CAS
EID:

DATE: q1(Mo=)   q1a(Da=)   q1b(Yr=)

CODER: q2(2 col):

BOOK CODE: q3 (3 col):

T1   BOOK TITLE AND AUTHOR'S LAST NAME: Page #s: (Include in Text)

T2   MODAL OCCUPATION: Page #s: (Include in Text)

T3   INDUSTRY: Page #s: (Include in Text)

T4   COUNTRY/REGION: Page #s: (Include in Text)

T5   OBSERVER'S ROLE: Page #s:

of1   YEAR STUDY BEGAN: 9999 - No Info   Page #s:

of1a   YEAR STUDY ENDED: 9999 - No Info   Page #s:

ORGANIZATIONAL FACTORS

Technology/organization

Code	Factor	Values					Page #s
of2a	Occupation:	00 - Professional	01 - Management/Supervisor	02 - Clerical	03 - Sales	04 - Skilled	Page #s:
		05 - Assembly	06 - Unskilled	07 - Service	08 - Farm	09 - No Info	
of2b	Craft:	1 - Yes	2 - No			9 - No Info	Page #s:
of2c	Direct Supervision:	1 - Yes	2 - No			9 - No Info	Page #s:
of2d	Bench:	1 - Straight Piece	2 - Quota/Bonus	3 - Hourly	4 - No Bench Guaranteed	9 - No Info	Page #s:
of2e	Assembly Line:	1 - Yes	2 - No			9 - No Info	Page #s:

140

Code	Variable	1	2	3	4	7	9	
of2f	Automated:	1 - Yes	2 - No				9 - No Info	Page #s:
of2g	Microchip:	1 - Yes	2 - No				9 - No Info	Page #s:
of2h	Bureaucratic:	1 - Yes	2 - No				9 - No Info	Page #s:
of2i	Corporatist:	1 - Yes	2 - No				9 - No Info	Page #s:
of2j	Worker Ownership:	1 - Co-op	2 - ESOP	3 - None			9 - No Info	Page #s:
of3	Employment Size:	(6 col): _____					999999 - No Info	Page #s:
of4	Employment Growth:	1 - Decline	2 - Stable	3 - Growing			9 - No Info	Page #s:
of5	Level of Competition:	1 - Low	2 - Medium	3 - High			9 - No Info	Page #s:
of6	Product Market Stability:	1 - Stable	2 - Unstable				9 - No Info	Page #s:
of7	Productivity:	1 - Declining	2 - Stable	3 - Increasing			9 - No Info	Page #s:
of8	Locally Owned:	1 - Yes	2 - No				9 - No Info	Page #s:
of9	Subcontractor:	1 - Yes	2 - No				9 - No Info	Page #s:
of10	Divisional Status:	1 - Yes	2 - No				9 - No Info	Page #s:
of11	Owned by a Conglomerate:	1 - Yes	2 - No				9 - No Info	Page #s:
of12	Corporate Headquarters:	1 - Yes	2 - No				9 - No Info	Page #s:
of13	Corporate Sector:	1 - Core	2 - Periphery				9 - No Info	Page #s:
of14	Unions (type):	1 - None	2 - Craft	3 - Industrial	4 - Combined		9 - No Info	Page #s:
of15	Unions (strength):	1 - Weak	2 - Average	3 - Strong		7 - NA	9 - No Info	Page #s:
of16	Turnover:	1 - Low	2 - Medium	3 - High			9 - No Info	Page #s:
of17	Layoff Frequency:	1 - Never	2 - Seldom	3 - Sometimes	4 - Frequent		9 - No Info	Page #s:

SOURCE: Hodson, R. (1999). Analyzing documentary accounts (pp. 74–80). Copyright © 1999 Sage Publications.

Table 6.8 Example of Tagging and Value Coding

ID	Sex	Narratives	Diagnosis	Signs and Symptoms						Treatments				Duration
				Cough	Sore Throat	Vomiting	Fever	Chills	Fatigue	Home Remedy	OTC	Western Medical	CAM	
108	M	**Sinus/upper respiratory infection/asthma.** *Drainage into lungs, down back of throat, lower breathing capacity, used peak flow meter, shortness of breath, cough, fatigue, wanted to sleep more. Annually occurring. Wheezing, used inhaler three times a day, about every four hours. Had symptoms for three days before going to health center. Coughing up phlegm, sinus headache, ears popped, runny nose. Amoxicillin for two weeks. Dizzy, lightheaded. Lungs felt tight, harder to breathe.*	Sinus/ upper respiratory infection/ asthma	Y	N	N	N	N	Y	N	Y	Y	N	3 days or 14 days?
116	F	*The last time I had a **cold** my throat was sore. It felt like I had needles in my tonsils. Every time I would swallow it felt like needles were digging in farther and farther. It also felt as though my throat was closing up making it hard to breathe. My nose was stuffed up but it was running like a faucet. There was a lot of pressure in my head like my head was in a vice. I had a horrible headache like someone was smashing my head with a hammer. Every muscle in my body ached. It felt like I couldn't move. I had a 102 degree fever. Sometimes I was so hot I felt like I was on fire. Then the next minute it was like I was in an ice-cube bath! I had difficulty breathing not only because my throat felt like it was closing but also because I felt like someone was sitting on my chest.*	Cold	?	Y	N	Y	Y	N	N	N	N	N	?

ID	Sex	Narratives	Diagnosis	Signs and Symptoms						Treatments				Duration
				Cough	Sore Throat	Vomiting	Fever	Chills	Fatigue	Home Remedy	OTC	Western Medical	CAM	
118	F	The last time I had a **cold** was back in November, I think. *I was tired, crabby, had a sore throat, runny nose, and a bit of a cough.* I remember going to Wal Mart to look for the new Cold-Eeze throat lozenges that my mother swears by. They have zinc in them and are supposed to reduce the length of your cold. I couldn't find them at Walt Mart because they are a pretty hot item. So I think I just suffered this way throughout the cold with no medication because I'm not a big believer in their benefits (unless, of course, my mother swears by it). I did have some peppermint tea that the midwife at work gave me. I work as an office assistant at a birth center). I tried to get more sleep than usual, but I didn't take any time off of work or school. I remember trying not to kiss my boyfriend (that's pretty tough, you know!) so that he wouldn't get sick, too. My cold lasted probably five days. It was about the fourth time I had been sick that semester which is quite unusual for me. I usually only get sick only once or twice a year.	Cold	Y	Y	N	N	N	N	Y	N	N	N	5 days

Signs and symptoms are tagged with *italics*; treatments and behavioral modifications are tagged with <u>underlining</u>; and diagnosis is tagged with **bold**.

Note that the chunks that are tagged vary in size from a single word (like cold) to several lines. Symptoms and treatment categories take dichotomous values (yes or no). Duration is coded in days, a numerical variable. And gender of informant, a structural variable, is coded as M and F.

Once you have chunks of text marked with underlining or italics or small caps, and so on, you can search for those attributes using your word processor's FIND command. And once you're familiar with the tagging and retrieval process using a word processor, it's easy to automate the procedure so you can find segments very quickly (see Box 6.3).

Box 6.3

Coding and Inference

Assigning values to a unit of text can be a high- or low-inference act. When someone says they "had a cough, runny nose and headache," it doesn't take much inference to code the variable coughing as Yes. But consider narrative 116 in Table 6.8. The respondent says: "Then the next minute it was like I was in an ice-cube bath!" Coding this as having chills requires more interpretation. If you think this is a high-inference problem, think of all the subtle and not so subtle ways in which people can report that they threw up.

And consider Narrative 108. Here, the respondent says that he waited three days before going to the health center, but then reports he took Amoxicillin for two weeks. So, how long did the episode last? It's common for people to take antibiotics for two weeks, but the signs and symptoms probably disappeared long before the pills were gone. If you don't ask "So, how long did that cold last?" you have to decide whether to assign a three-day value to the episode (the time it took the informant to get to a clinic) or a five–seven-day value (the time it takes for most colds to come and go) or a two-week value (the time the informant was on those antibiotics).

For more complex projects—and to make coding easier even for small projects—use a full-featured text analysis program, like Atlas/ti® or NVivo® or MaxQDA® or Dedoose®. Figure 6.2 shows the schema for doing this, using narrative 118 in Table 6.8.

The mechanics vary from program to program, but the idea is pretty much the same in full-featured text analysis software these days. Basically, the codes are linked to chunks of text or to points in the text, and the codes and memos are all linked. You

Figure 6.2 Linkages Between Texts, Codes, and Memos

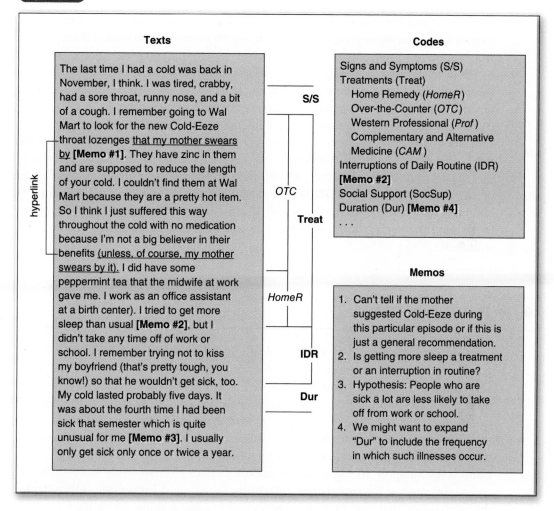

build a codebook as you go, highlighting a chunk of text and assigning it a code by opening up a codebook window. If the code exists already (if you've used it before for some other chunk of text), you just click on the code and the highlighted chunk of text (or the point in the text) is then associated with that code. If you need a new code, you name it and add it to the codebook.

As you code, you think of things to say about the text—memos. Wherever you like, you indicate the presence of a memo. A window opens and you start typing your observations. Memos are linked to the text so that later, as you read through your marked-up text, you can click on any memo indicator (like the bolded word memo in Figure 6.2) and the memo will pop up in a window. You can add, delete, or edit memos as your analysis progresses. Memos are the essence of grounded theory, about which more in Chapter 10.

With many text analysis programs, you can treat still photos, video, and sound recordings just as if they were written texts. In other words, you can mark segments of video with codes and then retrieve those segments later. For example, in a 37-minute video of teacher–pupil interaction in a kindergarten class, you might use OBED as a code for the theme "instruction on obedience." That code can be tucked into the video anywhere you think it belongs—say, in a 22-second chunk between 14 minutes, 21 seconds and 14 minutes, 43 seconds. Later, you can retrieve all the chunks of video that were tagged OBED. For digital photos (of people, of billboards, of buildings, or whatever), mark the actual chunks—the physical spaces— of the image by swiping the surface and tucking in the codes. (**Further Reading**: text analysis software)

◆ MULTIPLE CODERS

Even on small projects, like those typically associated with MA and PhD. theses, you should try to have more than one coder. Constructs typically start out fuzzy and become concrete as you become more experienced with a set of texts. And even if you are working on your own, it pays to have at least one other person to talk to about the themes you see in your corpus of text. For example, some researchers use member checks to discuss their emerging understandings of themes with key informants or other members of the study population (Charmaz 2006). (See Chapter 10 for more on member checks.) Also, with more than one coder, you can test for **intercoder reliability** (also called **interrater reliability)**— the probability that two or more coders see the same thing when they evaluate and code a text.

Intercoder reliability is vital if you're going to do statistical analysis on your data, but it's also important for retrieving examples of text that illustrate themes. If one coder marks themes, you have to rely on that coder—and usually, that means you— not to miss examples of themes. Having multiple coders increases the likelihood of finding all the examples in a text that pertain to a given theme. The best-known measure of intercoder reliability is **Cohen's kappa**. More on kappa in Chapter 11, on content analysis.

Training Coders

We can't stress sufficiently the importance of training coders to recognize themes consistently. There are six principles for this.

1. Give all coders a written codebook to which they can refer during the actual marking of data.

2. After reviewing the codebook as a group, have coders independently code a set of real examples.

3. Review their responses and bring the group together to discuss and resolve discrepancies.

4. Update the codebook as coders come to agreements about the content of themes.

5. Once coders start coding the bulk of the data, do random spot checks to keep coders alert and to find out if they are running into situations that you had not anticipated in designing the codebook.

6. If there are continued problems, repeat steps 3 and 4 and, if you make any changes, go back over previously coded material to make sure it is all coded consistently. (**Further Reading**: training coders)

How Many Coders Are Enough?

This is a perennial question in text analysis, and the answer depends on five things:

1. The experience of coders (some coders are better than others). Depending on the project, you might need coders who have special knowledge—of the language, of the research setting, or even of theoretical concepts. Lampert and Ervin-Trip (1993:199–200) advocate recruiting a diverse team of coders to help develop codes that are valid across a wider range of social contexts.

2. The core/periphery dispersion of the theme. Themes that have a clear core are easy to pick out in text.

3. The level of inference required to see a theme. The more inference it takes, the harder it is for two or more coders to agree that they see it in a text.

4. The number of times that any given theme appears in the text. The rarer a theme's occurrence and the more important it is to find all occurrences, the more coders you want to look for it.

5. The consensus among coders about the presence of a theme.

In large projects, having multiple coders can run into real money. A single 90-minute interview can easily generate 30–50 pages of transcribed text. With 150 interviews, that's at least 4,500 pages—about 12–16 average size books. Coding all that text, at five pages per hour and $20 per hour, would cost $18,000 for one coder, not counting the time to get the coder up to speed on recognizing the themes in the text.

Trimming Codes and Coders

We can reduce the workload and the cost by: (1) lowering the number of codes; (2) reducing the amount of text to be coded; and (3) using fewer coders. Most codebooks are hierarchical, with a small set of superordinate categories and a larger set of subordinate categories. The maximum number of themes that can be dealt with in a journal article is closer to a dozen than it is to a hundred. For some projects, focusing on the major categories is appropriate.

We nearly always wind up with more data than are required in a particular project. We design interviews to capture the broadest range of data and when we build codebooks we tack on every theme that seems useful at the time. As analysis gets underway, however, some of the themes that we thought were so important earlier may not continue to be important. This is a common experience among analysts of text. The three coders on Miles's project to evaluate six public schools developed 202 codes and wound up with just 26 big themes by the time they had done all the trimming (Miles 1979:593ff).

If your analysis interest narrows, focus on the portions of text that are most likely to contain the themes you're really interested in. This is easy to do when you have semistructured interviews because you know where in each text you're likely to find information on each major theme.

For themes that are found throughout a set of texts, it is sometimes enough to analyze a sample of texts, rather than the whole set. Even the workload in a smaller sample of texts can be reduced by rapidly scanning for particular themes. Once coders are really familiar with the constructs being studied in a project, they can read very quickly through the material and—especially if they are free to use loose definitions of constructs—identify paragraphs that contain the constructs.

Whenever a theme of interest is found, the paragraph is cut from the corpus and stored in a separate document of theme hits. To ensure against bias, a second coder should scan the text and look for theme occurrences that the first scanner might have missed. These paragraphs are also pulled and stored in the document of theme hits.

Finally, the higher the consensus you get among coders, the fewer coders you need for any particular project (Romney et al. 1986:325–27). We can reduce the number of coders by training them very well, though this creates the possibility of another kind of bias—finding themes that we want to find and not others. Giving coders free rein to find lots of new codes or having them look only for codes that we've already determined are of interest in a particular project is a choice. And every choice in research comes with its own problems.

THE CONTENT OF CODEBOOKS ◆

The key to good coding is a good codebook. In a good codebook, each theme needs to be described in sufficient detail so that coders can identify and mark the theme when they see it in the data. Table 6.9 shows part of the codebook from Ryan's (1995) study of illness narratives in Cameroon.

Start by giving each theme a **mnemonic** Then, as MacQueen et al. (1998) recommend, provide a short description, a detailed description, a list of inclusion and exclusion criteria for each theme, and some typical and atypical examples from the text as well as examples that seem close to but do not represent the theme. This aids in consistency of coding.

Mnemonics

Table 6.9 details three themes: signs and symptoms, over-the-counter (OTC) drugs, and home remedies. Ryan used S/S, OTC, and HomeR as mnemonics for these themes (see Box 6.4).

No matter how obvious some codes are (like DIV for divorce), you'll never remember the full set of codes for any project a year after you've completed it, so be sure to write up a detailed codebook in case you forget what NAITRAV (has the informant ever traveled to Nairobi?) or whatever-abbreviations-you-dreamed-up-at-the-time-you-did-the-coding mean.

You can use numbers or words as theme codes (whatever you're most comfortable with), but make sure that your codebook is explicit and in plain English (or plain Spanish, or French, or Russian . . .).

INTRODUCTION TO DATA ANALYSIS

INTRODUCTION: WHAT IS ANALYSIS ◆

Analysis is the search for patterns in data and for ideas that help explain why those patterns are there in the first place. Analysis starts before you collect data—you have to have some ideas about what you're going to study—and it continues throughout the research effort. As you develop ideas, you test them against your observations; your observations may then modify your ideas, which then need to be tested again, and so on.

As we pointed out on the first page of this book, analysis is the essential qualitative act. Many methods for quantitative analysis—things like regression analysis, cluster analysis, factor analysis, and so on—are really methods for **data processing** They are tools for finding patterns in data. Interpreting those patterns—deciding what they mean and linking your findings to those of other research—that's real **data analysis**.

Where do we get ideas from about patterns? Human beings are really good at this. In fact, they make patterns up all the time. Children look at clouds and make up stories about the shapes. For eons, people have labeled sets of stars and made up stories about them. Psychologists ask people to make up a story about ink blots. Once you have data in your hands, you won't have any trouble seeing patterns. In fact, you'll have to take real care not to read patterns into data. If you work on it, your natural penchant to see patterns everywhere will diminish as you do more and more research, but it's always a struggle. And the problem can get worse if you accept uncritically the folk analyses of articulate or prestigious people.

From a humanistic standpoint, it's important to seek the **emic**—that is, insider—perspective and to document folk analyses (Lofland et al. 2006). Those analyses may sometimes be correct. But it is equally important to remain skeptical, to retain an **etic**—that is, outsider—perspective, and not to "go native" (Miles and Huberman 1994:216).

The Constant Validity Check

As research progresses—as your interviews pile up—work on switching back and forth between the emic and the etic perspectives. Ask yourself whether you are buying into local folk explanations or perhaps rejecting them out of hand without considering their possible validity. It isn't hard to check yourself once in a while during research, but it's very hard to do it systematically.

Here are five guidelines.

1. Watch for disagreements among knowledgeable informants. When knowledgeable informants disagree about anything, find out why.

2. Check informant accuracy whenever possible. For example, check people's reports of behavior or of environmental conditions against more objective evidence. If you were a journalist and submitted a story based on informants' reports without checking the facts, you'd never get it past your editor's desk. We see no reason not to hold social scientists to the standard that good journalists face every day.

3. Welcome negative evidence. If a case turns up that doesn't fit with what you know—a middle-class suburban teenager who doesn't like hanging out at malls, for example—ask yourself if it's the result of: (a) normal intracultural variation; (b) your lack of knowledge about the range of appropriate behavior; or (c) a genuinely unusual case.

4. Continue to look for alternative explanations for phenomena, even as your understanding deepens. American folk culture holds that women left the home for the workforce because of something called women's liberation. An alternative explanation is that the oil shock of the 1970s produced double-digit inflation, cut the purchasing power of men's incomes, and drove women into a workforce where they faced discrimination and unequal pay—and were radicalized (Margolis 1984). Both explanations, one emic and one etic, are interesting for different reasons.

5. Try to fit negative cases into your theory. When you run into a case that doesn't fit your theory, then examine your theory. It's easier to ignore inconvenient data than to reexamine your pet ideas, but the easy way is hardly ever the right way in research.

DATABASE MANAGEMENT ♦

Analysis may be the search for patterns, and human beings may be good at seeing patterns, but we can apply some methods systematically to help the process along. This means getting narratives and other forms of qualitative data digitized and into a computer or organized and tagged so that we can apply methods of **database management**

If you do 30 open-ended interviews that average an hour and a half each, you could easily wind up with a thousand double-spaced pages of text to deal with. That's where database management comes in.

When you use your library's online catalogs to find books and articles, you're using database management systems. To find books and articles on bilingual education and achievement, you would use the Boolean expression "bilingual education AND achiev*." The * is a commonly used **wildcard** In this case, it would mean "find all the books that are about bilingual education and about anything that starts with achiev, like achieve, achieving, achiever, or achievement."

You can apply this same logic to any set of records (things) and fields (the characteristics of those things). If you've got a thousand tunes on your phone or media player and you want to organize them into play lists, then each tune is a record in a database and the fields are things like artist, title, publisher, date of release, and genre. If you have a thousand photographs from a research project, then each one is a record in a database. You can ask the database "Which photos are about children?" or "Which photos are about old men?" or "Which are about children AND about eating?" If you've *coded* each photo for those themes (children, old men, eating), then the software shows you which records satisfy your query.

If your photos are from old family albums, you can number the records (the photos) on the back from 1 to *n* and use the numbers as the record names in a database.

And if your photos are digital (or scanned in from paper or slides), you can code them directly with a database management program. Microsoft Excel®, for example, is advertised as a spreadsheet for numbers, but you can use it to manage any list of things.

Using a Text Analysis Program

Text analysis programs, like Atlas/ti®, NVivo®, Dedoose®, MaxQDA®, and so on, are special purpose database management programs with tools for handling and asking questions of text.

Suppose you have a hundred transcribed life histories. You could ask questions like: "Which chunks of these texts are about migration and about women who are under 30 years of age?" A good text analysis program will (1) find the segments of text that you've coded for the theme of migration; (2) produce a provisional list of those segments; (3) examine each segment in the provisional list and find the respondent's name or ID code; and (4) look up the respondent in the respondent information file.

If the respondent is a man or is a woman over 30, the program drops the segment of text from the provisional list. Finally, the program reports which, if any, segments of text conform to all the criteria you listed in your question. With the right software, asking questions like this takes a couple of seconds, even with 10,000 pages of text. But deciding which questions to ask—which is analysis, after all—is your job, not the program's.

Many text analysis programs also let you build networks of codes and produce reports and diagrams of how codes are related to one another in a set of texts. (**Further Reading**: text analysis software)

◆ DATA MATRICES

One of the most important concepts in all data analysis—whether we're working with quantitative or qualitative data—is the **data matrix**. There are two kinds of data matrices: **profile matrices** and **proximity matrices**. Profile matrices are also simply called data matrices. These are the familiar case-by-attribute matrices that are used across the sciences to record data. If you've ever entered data into a spreadsheet, like Excel, you've had experience with profile matrices.

Proximity matrices are a different species altogether. They contain data about how similar or dissimilar a set of things are. Those mileage charts that you see on road maps are proximity matrices. They tell you, for every pair of cities on a map, how far apart they are. We'll have more to say about proximity matrices later. First, profile matrices. . . .

Profile Matrices

The vast majority of analysis in the social sciences, whether it's qualitative or quantitative, is about how properties of things are related to one another. We ask, for example, "Does how much money a family has affect the SAT scores of its children?" "Does having been abused as a child influence whether a woman will remain in a physically abusive marriage?" "Is the per capita gross national product of a nation associated with the average level of education?" "Are remittances from labor migrants related to the achievement in school of children left behind?"

This kind of analysis is done on a profile matrix. You start with a series of things—**units of analysis**—and you measure a series of **variables**, or **attributes**, for each of those things. Each unit of analysis is *profiled* by a particular set of measurements on some variables. Table 7.1 is an example of a typical profile matrix.

In this table, an interviewer has stopped a hundred people who were coming out of a supermarket and recorded seven pieces of information: How much the person spent; the person's gender, age, and education (in years); whether the person lived in a house or an apartment and whether they owned or rented; and how many people lived with them.

These data produce a 100 × 7 (read this as: "100-by-7") profile matrix. Two profiles—two data cases—are shown in Table 7.1.

Person #1 reported spending $67.00, is male, is 34 years old, graduated from high school, and lives in a house, which he rents, with four other people. Person #2 reported spending $19.00, is female, is 60 years old, completed college, and lives in an apartment, which she owns, by herself.

Table 7.1   Profile Matrix of Two Cases by Seven Variables

Case	Spent	Gender	Age	Education	Home or Apartment	Own (Y/N)	Number in House
1	67	M	34	12	H	N	5
2	19	F	60	16	A	Y	1

Profile Matrices With Qualitative Data I—Van Maanen's Study

The profile matrix shown in Table 7.1 was constructed from survey data (asking people the same questions about their grocery shopping experience), but the form of a profile matrix is the same, whether the data are quantitative or qualitative. Van Maanen et al. (1982) compared a traditional commercial fishing operation with a modern operation. Table 7.2 shows what they found in the analysis of their field notes. Simple inspection of Table 7.2 gives you an immediate feel for the results of Van Maanen et al.'s descriptive analysis.

Table 7.2 Van Maanen et al.'s Findings About Kinds of Commercial Fishing

	Traditional fishing (e.g., Gloucester, MA)	Modern fishing (e.g., Bristol Bay, AK)
Social organization		
Backgrounds of fishermen	Homogeneous	Heterogeneous
Ties among fishermen	Multiple	Single
Boundaries to entry	Social	Economic
Number of participants	Stable	Variable
Social uncertainty	Low	High
Relations with competitors	Collegial and individualistic	Antagonistic and categorical
Relations with port	Permanent, with ties to community	Temporary, with no local ties
Mobility	Low	High
Relations to fishing	Expressive (fishing as lifestyle)	Instrumental (fishing as job)
Orientation to work	Long-term, optimizing (survival)	Short-term, maximizing (seasonal)
Tolerance for diversity	Low	High
Nature of disputes	Intra-occupational	Trans-occupational
Economic organization		
Relations of boats to buyers	Personalized (long-term, informal)	Contractual (short-term, formal)
Information exchange	Restrictive and private	Open and public
Economic uncertainty	Low (long-term)	High (long-term)
Capital investment range	Small	Large
Profit margins	Low	High
Rate of innovation	Low	High
Specialization	Low	High
Regulatory mechanisms	Informal and few	Formal and many
Stance toward authority	Combative	Compliant

SOURCE: Van Maanen, J., Miller, M., and Johnson, J. C. (1982). An occupation in transition: Traditional and modern forms of commercial fishing. *Work and Occupations, 9,* 193–216. Copyright © 1982 Sage Publications.

There are two units of analysis in Table 7.2: the two communities where Van Maanen et al. did their ethnographic fieldwork. One community, Gloucester, Massachusetts, represented the traditional American fishing occupation; the other, Bristol Bay, Alaska, represented a more factory-like fishing operation.

Notice that in Table 7.2, the two units of analysis—the cases—are in the columns and the attributes of the cases are in the rows. This is the opposite of how the data were set up in Table 7.1. It is common in exploratory research to have many units of analysis (like respondents to a questionnaire) and relatively few variables. By contrast, in confirmatory research it is common to have a few units of analysis (like informants who provide narratives) and a great many variables, or attributes (like themes). For formatting purposes, it is easier to put whatever you have fewer of in the columns and whatever you have more of in the rows (see Box 7.1).

Box 7.1

Qualitative and Quantitative Data Matrices

Another way of saying this is that in studies based primarily on quantitative data, we typically know a little about many things, and in studies based primarily on qualitative data, we typically know a lot about a few things. In a telephone survey, for example, we can ask hundreds or even thousands of people a few questions. In a study based on in-depth interviews, we might spend an hour or more with respondents and get information about many different topics. With just a few units of analysis in this kind of study, it is easier to look for patterns when we have the cases in the columns and the attributes of the cases in the rows.

Table 7.2 tells us that the social organization of the traditional fishing operation in Gloucester is more homogeneous, more expressive, and more collegial than that of the modern operation, but profits are lower. Based on the qualitative analysis, Van Maanen et al. were able to state some general, theoretical hypotheses regarding the weakening of personal relations in technology-based fishing operations. This is the kind of general proposition that can be tested by using fishing operations as units of analysis and their technologies as the explanatory variable.

Profile Matrices With Qualitative Data II—Fjellman and Gladwin's Study

Fjellman and Gladwin (1985) studied the family histories of Haitian migrants to the United States. Table 7.3 shows a matrix of information about one family. Table 7.3 is a profile matrix with the cases (the people) in the columns and the variables (the years in which people joined or left the family) in the rows.

Table 7.3 Fjellman and Gladwin's Table for One Haitian Family in the United States

Year	Jeanne	Anna (mother)	Lucie (sister)	Charles (brother)	Marc (adopted son)	Helen (aunt)	Hughes and Valerie (cousins)	Number in Household
1968	+							1
1971	+	+	+	+				4
1975	+	+	+	+	+			5
1976	+	+	−	−	+			3
1978	+	+	−	+	+		*	4
1979	+	+	−	+	+	+	*	5
1982	+	+	−	−	+	+	*	4

SOURCE: S. M. Fjellman and H. Gladwin, Haitian family patterns of migration to South Florida, *Human Organization* 44:307. Copyright © 1985, Society for Applied Anthropology. Reprinted with permission.

The family began in 1968 when Jeanne's father sent her to Brooklyn, New York, to go to high school. The single plus sign for 1968 shows the founding of the family by Jeanne. Jeanne's father died in 1971, and her mother (Anna), sister (Lucie), and brother (Charles) joined her in New York. Thus, there are four plus signs for 1971. Jeanne adopted Marc in 1975. She moved to Miami in 1976, with her mother and Marc, and Lucie and Charles stayed on in New York. The two minus signs in the row for 1976 indicate that Jeanne's sister and brother were no longer part of the household founded by Jeanne.

Lucie married in 1978 (husband not shown), and Charles went to Miami to join Jeanne's household. That same year, Jeanne began applying for visas to bring her cousins Hughes and Valerie to Miami. The asterisks show that these two people were in the process of joining the household in 1982 when the family history data were collected. Aunt Helen (Anna's sister) joined the family in 1979. Finally, Charles returned to New York in 1982 to live again with his sister, Lucie.

Fjellman and Gladwin present seven of these family history charts in their article, and they provide the historical detail—like why Jeanne went to the United States in the first place and why Charles left Jeanne's household in 1976—in vignettes below each chart. We need the historical detail to understand how the family developed over the years, but reducing everything to a matrix of pluses and minuses lets us see the patterns of family growth, development, and decay. (**Further Reading**: matrices of qualitative data)

PROXIMITY MATRICES ◆

If profile analysis is about how *properties of things* are related to one another, then **proximity analysis** is about how *things* (not their properties or attributes) are related to one another. Profile matrices contain measurements of variables for a set of items. Proximity matrices contain measurements of relations, or proximities, between items.

There are two types of proximity matrices: similarity matrices and dissimilarity matrices. In a **similarity matrix**, bigger numbers mean that things are more alike, or, conceptually, closer together. In a **dissimilarity matrix**, bigger numbers mean that things are less alike, or farther apart. Table 7.4 is a dissimilarity matrix. It shows the driving distances between all pairs of nine cities in the United States. The bigger the number in the cells, the more "dissimilar" or further apart two cities are on the map.

Visualization Methods—Seeing Patterns in Proximity Matrices

It's much easier to see patterns in graphs of relations than in matrices of them, like Table 7.4. In fact, you could stare at the 9 × 9 (read: nine-by-nine) matrix of relations in Table 7.4 all day and never see the big picture. Figure 7.1 is a multidimensional scaling (MDS) map of the data in Table 7.4, and it shows the big picture.

Table 7.4   A Dissimilarity Matrix for Distances Among Nine U.S. Cities

City	Boston	New York	District of Columbia	Miami	Chicago	Seattle	San Francisco	Los Angeles	Denver
Boston	0	206	429	1504	963	2976	3095	2979	1949
New York	206	0	233	1308	802	2815	2934	2786	1771
District of Columbia	429	233	0	1075	671	2684	2799	2631	1616
Miami	1504	1308	1075	0	1329	3273	3053	2687	2037
Chicago	963	802	671	1329	0	2013	2142	2054	996
Seattle	2976	2815	2684	3273	2013	0	808	1131	1307
San Francisco	3095	2934	2799	3053	2142	808	0	379	1235
Los Angeles	2979	2786	2631	2687	2054	1131	379	0	1059
Denver	1949	1771	1616	2037	996	1307	1235	1059	0

SOURCE: ANTHROPAC 4.0 Methods Guide, by S. P. Borgatti (1996:28). Reprinted with permission of the author.

Figure 7.1 Multidimensional Scaling of Distances Among Nine Cities

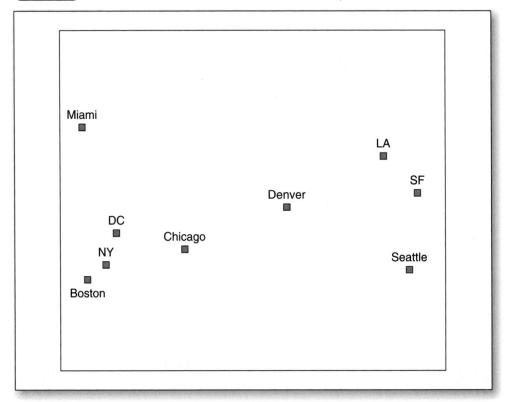

MDS is one part of a family of data **visualization methods**—a way to see all the relations in a matrix of relations. So, in Figure 7.1, we expect New York to be about equally close to Washington, DC, and to Boston. We expect San Francisco to lie between Los Angeles and Seattle and for all three of those cities to be far from Boston, New York, and DC. And so on. Sure enough, the relations in Figure 7.1 conform to all our expectations.

Well, most of them. Because of our early training in school, we expect Miami to be in the lower right of the map and for Seattle to be in the upper left. The MDS program doesn't care about our culturally derived expectations. It just graphs all the numerical relations in a matrix, and all of those relations (in this case, how many miles apart various cities are from one another) are, in fact, perfectly represented in Figure 7.1. More about MDS in Chapters 18 and 19.

If you've had a course in statistics and seen a **correlation matrix**, then you've had experience with a similarity matrix. The bigger the number in each cell—the higher the correlation—the more alike two things are. Table 7.5 is a similarity matrix of 15 emotions. This matrix comes from a qualitative data collection exercise called a **triad test**.

Table 7.5 A Similarity Matrix for 15 Emotions

		1 LOVE	2 ANGE	3 DISG	4 SHAM	5 FEAR	6 ANGU	7 ENVY	8 ANXI	9 TIRE	10 HAPP	11 SAD	12 LONE	13 BORE	14 HATE	15 EXCI
1	LOVE	0.00	0.09	0.08	0.21	0.10	0.08	0.35	0.16	0.10	0.82	0.20	0.14	0.08	0.41	0.74
2	ANGER	0.09	0.00	0.85	0.19	0.59	0.64	0.46	0.32	0.00	0.17	0.40	0.09	0.04	0.95	0.11
3	DISGUST	0.08	0.85	0.00	0.76	0.76	0.66	0.55	0.63	0.08	0.08	0.38	0.08	0.14	0.70	0.13
4	SHAME	0.21	0.19	0.76	0.00	0.22	0.75	0.51	0.38	0.57	0.10	0.57	0.39	0.09	0.47	0.06
5	FEAR	0.10	0.59	0.76	0.22	0.00	0.57	0.40	0.71	0.05	0.11	0.55	0.59	0.08	0.86	0.21
6	ANGUISH	0.08	0.64	0.66	0.75	0.57	0.00	0.85	0.47	0.20	0.10	0.70	0.31	0.08	0.69	0.09
7	ENVY	0.35	0.46	0.55	0.51	0.40	0.85	0.00	0.44	0.06	0.08	0.08	0.30	0.28	0.47	0.11
8	ANXIOUS	0.16	0.32	0.63	0.38	0.71	0.47	0.44	0.00	0.16	0.29	0.30	0.17	0.20	0.39	0.40
9	TIRED	0.10	0.00	0.08	0.57	0.05	0.20	0.06	0.16	0.00	0.14	0.63	0.44	0.73	0.04	0.13
10	HAPPY	0.82	0.17	0.08	0.10	0.11	0.10	0.08	0.29	0.14	0.00	0.34	0.09	0.04	0.08	0.85
11	SAD	0.20	0.40	0.38	0.57	0.55	0.70	0.08	0.30	0.63	0.34	0.00	0.71	0.31	0.24	0.19
12	LONELY	0.14	0.09	0.08	0.39	0.59	0.31	0.30	0.17	0.44	0.09	0.71	0.00	0.59	0.06	0.06
13	BORED	0.08	0.04	0.14	0.09	0.08	0.08	0.28	0.20	0.73	0.04	0.31	0.59	0.00	0.14	0.19
14	HATE	0.41	0.95	0.70	0.47	0.86	0.69	0.47	0.39	0.04	0.08	0.24	0.06	0.14	0.00	0.28
15	EXCITEMENT	0.74	0.11	0.13	0.06	0.21	0.09	0.11	0.40	0.13	0.85	0.19	0.06	0.19	0.28	0.00

In this case, 40 people looked at 70 triads of emotions—Anger/Love/Fear, Sad/ Bored/Hate, Anger/Bored/Love, and so on—and told us which emotion was least like the other two. (This is a replication of pioneering work by A. Kimball Romney [Romney et al. 1997] and colleagues [C. C. Moore et al. 1999]). The similarity measurements in Table 7.5 are percentages. Looking across the first row of Table 7.5, we see that love and anger are 0.09 alike, which means that 9% of the time our informants said that love and anger were similar. By contrast, 82% of the time our informants said that love and happy were similar.

If the 9 × 9 matrix of intercity distances in Table 7.4 looked complicated, the 15 × 15 matrix in Table 7.5 is hopeless—far too complex to analyze with the naked eye. Figure 7.2 shows the MDS plot for these data. It's a two-dimensional plot, and it looks like the two dimensions are nice versus not-so-nice emotions (with nice emotions on the bottom of the picture and not-so-nice emotions on the top) and active versus passive emotions (with the most active emotions on the right and the more passive emotions over on the left).

And how is all this qualitative? Well, the triad tests are all qualitative—the informant sees sets of names and chooses one. The data (people's choices) are converted into numbers (Table 7.5), but the numbers are just a way to record the choices that people made in doing the triad task. And the words become numbers only long enough

Figure 7.2 Multidimensional Scaling of Similarities Among 15 Emotions

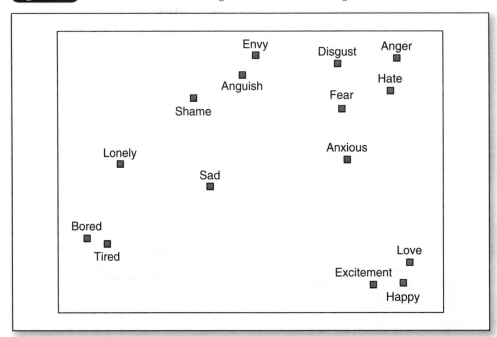

to process them and turn them into a picture—a purely qualitative outcome—that we can interpret.

With or without numbers, though, causal models are best expressed as some kind of model, or flow chart, the subject of the next chapter.

Key Concepts in This Chapter

data processing	data matrix	similarity matrix
data analysis	profile matrix	dissimilarity matrix
emic	proximity matrix	visualization methods
etic	units of analysis	correlation matrix
database management	variables or attributes	triad test
wildcard	proximity analysis	

Summary

- Analysis is the search for patterns in data and for ideas that help explain why those patterns are there in the first place.

  o We distinguish between things like regression analysis, cluster analysis, factor analysis, and so on, which are methods for data processing and for finding patterns in data, and interpreting those patterns—deciding what they mean and linking your findings to those of other research—which is real data analysis.

  o From a humanistic standpoint, it's important to seek the emic—that is, insider—perspective and to document folk analyses (Lofland et al. 2006). Those analyses may sometimes be correct. But it is equally important to remain skeptical, to retain an etic—i.e., outsider—perspective.

- Text analysis programs don't actually analyze your data, but analyzing text can be assisted with these special-purpose database management programs.
- An important concept in data analysis is the data matrix.

  o In a profile matrix, the rows are the units of analysis (like people or texts) and the columns are characteristics or features of those units. In a proximity matrix, the rows and the columns are the same things and the cells of the matrix show how similar or dissimilar the things are to one another. A proximity matrix that contains the distances between pairs of cities on a map is a dissimilarity matrix. A proximity matrix that contains correlations is a similarity matrix.

  o The data in a profile matrix can be quantitative or qualitative.

- Visualization methods, like multidimensional scaling, are used to make sense of complicated, proximity data.

Exercises

1. Discuss the difference between data processing and data analysis. Include a discussion of some quantitative methods for analyzing quantitative data. Go back to Figure 1.1 and discuss the four components in that figure in light of what you've learned so far.

Further Reading

Text analysis software. See http://caqdas.soc.surrey.ac.uk/ and Lewins and Silver (2014).

Matrices of qualitative data. Miles and Huberman (1994).

Visit the online resource site at study.sagepub.com/bernardaqd to access engaging and helpful digital content, like video tutorials on working with MAXQDA, presentation slides, MAXQDA keyboard shortcuts, datasets, stop list, and recommended readings.

CHAPTER **8**

CONCEPTUAL MODELS

INTRODUCTION ◆

A major part of data analysis involves building, testing, displaying, and validating **models**. Models are simplifications of complicated, real things. If you ever played with toy cars or dolls when you were a child, you've had first-hand experience with **physical models**. If you've wasted as much time as we have playing computer games, where you pretend to be a magician or a warrior or a criminal or a crime fighter, you've worked with **virtual models**.

If you've watched the news during a hurricane and seen predictions of where the hurricane will go and how strong it will be when it gets there, you've seen **numerical models** that were turned into **visual models** (to make them easier to understand).

◆ STATISTICAL MODELS AND TEXT ANALYSIS

In fact, understanding numerical models is a very good way to understand modeling in general. Here's a typical **statistical model**:

STARTING WAGE = .87 +.10EDUC + .08VT + .13PW + .17MARSTAT + .11FO (Graves and Lave 1972:53)

This little model describes the starting wages of 259 Navajo men who migrated during the 1960s from the Navajo reservation to Denver. It took Theodore Graves and Charles Lave (1972) about three years of tough work to get this model. Here's what it says:

1. Start with 87 cents an hour (remember, this was the 1960s).

2. Add 10 cents for every year of education beyond the first 10 years (it turned out that each year of education, up to 10 years, produced the same wage benefit).

3. Then add 8 cents an hour for having strong vocational training (in things like carpentry or plumbing).

4. Add another 13 cents an hour for each dollar the man earned in his best job before migrating to Denver (the PW stands for previous wage).

5. Add 17 cents if the man is married.

6. And finally, because most Navajo men on the reservation in the 1960s were sheep herders, add 11 cents if the migrant's father had worked for wages (FO is father's occupation) (Graves and Lave 1972:53–54) (see Box 8.1).

Box 8.1

What's Qualitative About This Model?

It may seem strange for us to present a statistical model in a book on qualitative research methods, but the fact is, although statistical models are built on quantitative data, models are models, no matter what kind of data you have. All researchers, qualitative and quantitative alike, build models of abstract concepts connected by propositions or hypotheses—like this:

A → B

This simple, qualitative model says "Something called A leads to, or causes, something called B." The statistical model by Graves and Lave is a series of abstract concepts (education, marital status, etc.) connected by plus signs, which are propositions to the effect that "all these things added together account for the difference in starting wages when Navajo men get to Denver from the reservation."

If you take the numbers out of the statistical model, you get a picture—an entirely qualitative model—like the one in Figure 8.1, which says:

Five things—education, vocational training, wage on last job on the reservation, father's job on the reservation, and marital status, in no particular order—contribute materially to how much a Navajo man would earn when he migrates to Denver from the reservation.

Figure 8.1 Graves's Initial Conceptual Model of Variation in the Hourly Wage Rate for Navajo Men in Denver

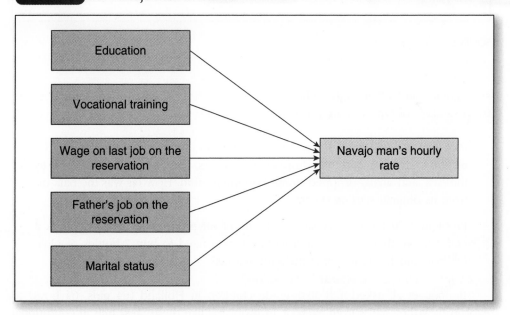

SOURCE: Graves and Lave (1972).

Adding Weights to Directions

Statistical models can get very complex, with arrows going in both directions and between pairs of concepts. Figure 8.2 shows Boonen et al.'s (2013) model for how 125

Figure 8.2 Path Analysis of How Children in Holland Solve Math Story Problems

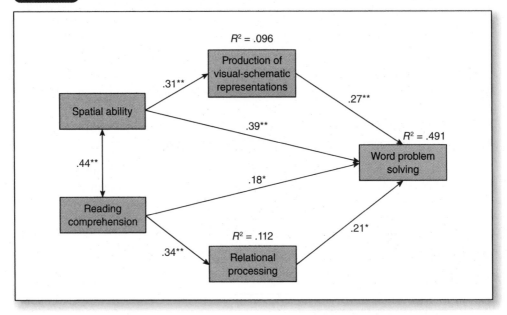

SOURCE: Boonen et al. (2013).

sixth graders in Holland solve what educators call "story problems" in math. Here are two examples of typical story problems:

Problem 1: A balloon first rose 200 meters from the ground, then moved 100 meters to the east, and then dropped 100 meters. It then traveled 50 meters to the east, and finally dropped straight on the ground. How far was the balloon from its original starting point?'

Problem 2. At the grocery store, a bottle of olive oil costs 7 euros. That is 2 euros "more than" at the supermarket. If you need to buy 7 bottles of olive oil, how much will it cost at the supermarket?

Boonen et al. asked 128 sixth-grade children in Holland (64 girls, 64 boys) to explain how they had solved each of 14 problems like these. Research in educational psychology has shown that children's ability to solve story problems involve a set of skills, including spatial reasoning, the ability to visualize problems, reading comprehension, and what's called "relational processing." (Understanding metaphors, for example, involves relational processing.)

Some of the children in Boonen et al.'s study drew diagrams (e.g., a balloon rising) in addition to offering a narrative or used gestures to show how elements of the problem were related to one another. In coding the narratives, Boonen et al. coded these diagrams and gestures as visual representations.

The number of problems (out of 14) that the children got right was the dependent variable—i.e., what Boonen et al. hoped to explain. Read Figure 8.2 as follows: Almost half (0.491=49.1%) of the variance in the ability of these sixth graders' ability to solve math story problems is accounted for by the two skills the researchers hypothesized would be involved (the production of visual-schematic representations and relational processing) plus the two underlying abilities for those skills (spatial ability and reading comprehension).

The path analysis in Figure 8.2 is a nice example of quantitative analysis from qualitative data.

Conceptual Models in Qualitative Research

Conceptual models like these are as useful in qualitative research as they are in quantitative research. Figure 8.3 is a conceptual model, built from an entirely qualitative study, of the stages of women's weight loss and weight regain. Wysoker (2002:170) wanted to account for the fact that "Women will continue to try to lose weight, despite the long history of losing weight and gaining the lost weight back."

Read Figure 8.3 as follows: In Phase I, women become desperate about losing weight. The desperation comes from two main sources: a concern for health and a desire to conform to social pressures (e.g., about being thin). Desperation leads to dieting (Phase II). Dieting has emotional and physical costs, but those are offset by the satisfaction of weight loss and a sense of control. Phase III involves maintaining the weight loss. This is easier said than done, which leads to weight regain (Phase IV), and this triggers the feelings of desperation that eventually produce Phase I again.

All models, whether built on qualitative or quantitative data, are reductions of complex realities. We build models to better understand these complexities and to help others understand them as well.

The rest of this chapter takes you through the steps in building models and introduces some of the models that researchers use to simplify complex cases or to show how complex processes unfold over time. Variations of these models appear in many different kinds of analyses of qualitative data, including grounded theory, discourse analysis, schema analysis, analytic induction, content analysis, and ethnographic decision modeling. (**Further Reading**: building conceptual models)

Figure 8.3 Wysoker's Model of Women's Weight Gain and Weight Loss

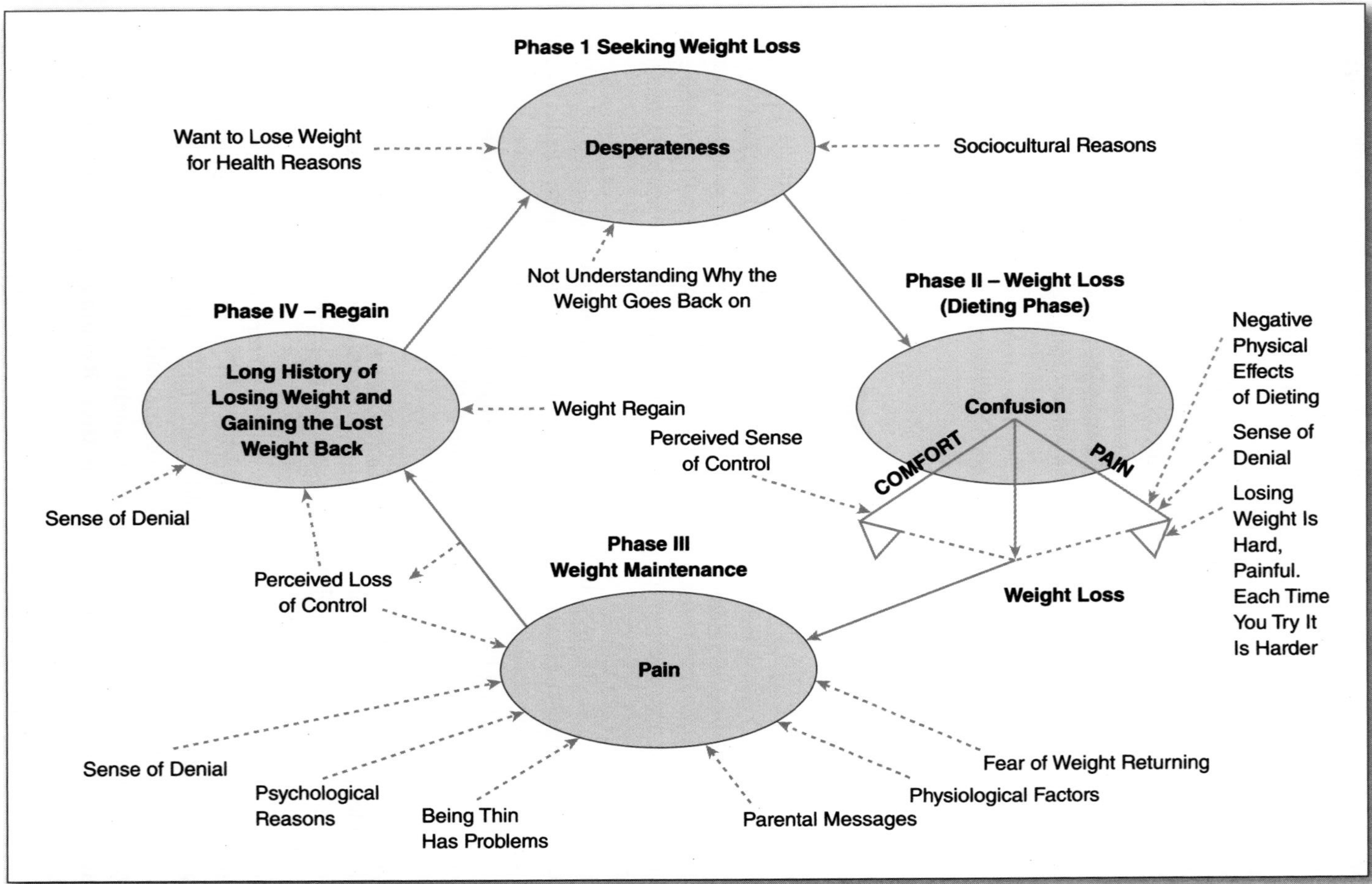

SOURCE: Wysoker, A. 2002. A conceptual model of weight loss and weight regain: An intervention for change. *Journal of the American Psychiatric Nurses Association* 8:168–173. © 1991 by Amy Wysoker. Reprinted with permission from the author.

BUILDING MODELS ♦

There are three steps in building models: (1) Identify the key constructs to be included; (2) show linkages among the constructs—that is, identify how the constructs are related and represent the relationships visually; and (3) test that the relationships hold for at least the majority of the cases being modeled. These steps are not always in sequence. You'll find yourself going back and forth among them as you develop models.

STEP 1: IDENTIFYING KEY CONCEPTS ♦

This is about choosing among the many themes you've identified in your data and prioritizing those themes in terms of their impact on whatever you're studying. In any project, you'll wind up with dozens, even hundreds, of themes in your codebook. Analysis is about whittling the number down and figuring out how the whittled-down set works.

The first step is to separate core from periphery themes, or what grounded theorists call **selective coding** for salience and centrality. **Salience** is about how important a concept is. How often a concept appears in the data is one sign of how important it is. Another sign is how **ubiquitous** a concept is—i.e., how often it appears in lots of different contexts. Concepts that appear across many respondents and in many situations are likely to be salient. Other signs of salience include how strongly people express their feelings about something or how severe the results of a concept or activity might be (i.e., children with blood in their stools might be a rare event, but when it occurs, mothers think of it as being highly salient).

Centrality is about the degree to which a concept is linked to other concepts. Concepts that are linked to many others are likely to be at the core of—that is, central to—any model.

Identifying key concepts means making choices about what you can cover in your analysis. No model can cover everything. Some concepts will just have to be excluded, or at least deferred until the next paper. At some point in the process, every researcher has to ask: "Is this something I really need to explain here? Or is it tangential to my main concern right now?"

Getting a Handle on Things

With hundreds of pages of transcripts and notes, how do you actually make those choices?

Richard Addison (1992) followed nine newly minted physicians in their first year of residency in family medicine. He spent hours and hours interviewing them, their spouses, and others involved with their training, and he observed them as they went about practicing medicine. He began to analyze his notes and interviews while he was still collecting data. He started with **in vivo coding**, highlighting words and phrases that residents used—words like "punting," "pimping," "dumping," and "surviving"—in describing their experiences.

Addison started writing notes about those words and put the notes on index cards. He cut up segments of text from the transcripts and put those on cards, too. He sorted the hundreds of cards into piles that seemed to have some common thread. By the time he was done, he says, "every horizontal surface above floor level was filled with cards and cut-up transcripts." He goes on:

> I began to see progressions and flows. I started making lists of groups of practices, people, reactions, and events and connecting these lists on big sheets of white paper. Since no horizontal surfaces were left, I removed pictures and prints and tacked these lists and categories onto walls. Suddenly, 3 or 4 months after beginning, out of this wealth of seeming chaos, I had a flash of clarity: The central organizing theme for the residents as they began the residency was "surviving." It seemed to both describe and unify their practices in a way that made sense. (1992:117–18)

In big projects, with hundreds or thousands of people and themes, you can use a computer for analyzing pile-sorting data like these (see Chapter 18). For relatively small projects, like those in most thesis and dissertation research, touching and moving your data around physically, like Addison did, is a great way to shop for ideas. (For details of this technique, see the section on cutting and sorting themes in Chapter 5.)

◆ STEP 2: LINKING KEY CONSTRUCTS

Once key coding categories start to emerge, it's time to link them together in theoretical models. Grounded theorists call this **axial coding**. It almost inevitably involves returning to the data for further analysis. For example, after Addison recognized that "surviving" was a central concept in young physicians' experience of their residency, he reanalyzed his transcripts, interviews, notes, and index cards with reference to surviving:

> I began seeing a different, more cohesive organization that seemed to incorporate previously scattered experiences and practices. I constructed a diagram that encompassed most of the lists and categories from my wall charts. This beginning diagram or attempted pictorial whole of what happened to these individuals as they began their residency looked something like a child's drawing of an extraterrestrial's digestive system. It was the first of many attempts to make diagrammatic sense of their existence. (1992:118)

Addison doesn't tell us how he identified (and named) the links between each of his key constructs. We suspect that he did a compare-and-contrast exercise across his transcripts, writing memos and looking for particular types of relationships.

But once he had the links in mind, the next step is to lay them out. And this means choosing a model type. Figures 8.4–8.14 show some common types of models in social research.

Conditional Matrices

Figure 8.4 is an adaptation of what Strauss and Corbin (1990:158–75) call a **conditional matrix**. The small circle at the bottom of the figure represents some action or interaction: a discussion between a doctor and a patient; crossing the U.S.–Mexican border illegally in search of work; moving a dying person to a hospice; buying a $300 pair of running shoes; sharing (or not sharing) a drug needle with a stranger.

Figure 8.4   Conditional Matrix

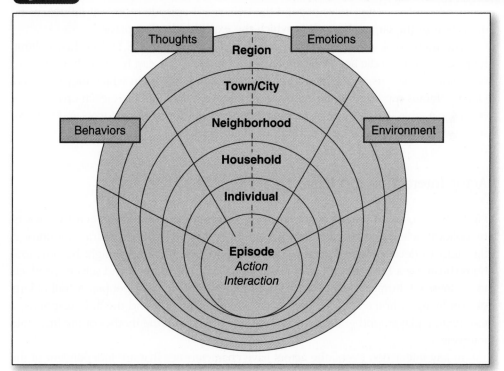

SOURCE: Adapted from Corbin and Strauss, 2008:94. *Basics of Qualitative Research: Techniques and Procedures for Developing Grounded Theory*. 3rd. ed. Thousand Oaks, CA: Sage Publications.

Table 8.1 A General Framework for Key Aspects of Experience and Levels of Influence

	Episode	Individual	Household	Neighborhood	Town/City	Region
Behaviors						
Thoughts						
Emotions						
Environment Social Physical						

SOURCE: Strauss, A., and Corbin, J. (1990). *Basics of Qualitative Research: Grounded Theory Procedures and Techniques.* Newbury Park, CA: Sage. © 1990 Sage Publications.

In trying to understand human experience we focus on behavior, thoughts, and emotions and on the social and physical circumstances in which thinking, feeling, and acting takes place. The circles beyond the behavioral episode represent influences on the action or the larger contexts in which the experience takes place.

The framework can also be presented as a matrix (Table 8.1). The first column represents the episodic action or interaction of interest and can be described in terms of people's behaviors, thoughts, and emotions and the context in which they occurred. Other columns represent larger and larger forces that may influence each episode. We often use a table like this one to help us organize questionnaire protocols and to make sense of complex textual data during our analysis phase.

Actor Interaction Models

Figure 8.5 shows a framework for studying **interaction events** between two actors. In political science, the actors in interaction events are often countries (country A threatens to declare war on country B). In economics, the actors might be organizations (business A buys its supply of raw material from business B and sells its products to business C). In most qualitative research, interactions involve people: A frail elderly person living at home asks for help from a home-care aide and the aide responds; a toddler in a playground grabs a toy from another child and the mother of the first child intervenes.

In any interaction event, the actors have characteristics that are independent of the interaction itself—things like beliefs and experiences—but that influence the interaction. Each person acts and behaves as an individual before and during an event, but some

Figure 8.5 Framework for Studying Interaction Events

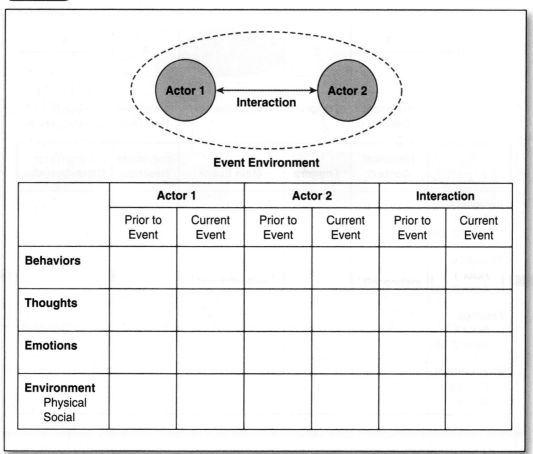

	Actor 1		Actor 2		Interaction	
	Prior to Event	Current Event	Prior to Event	Current Event	Prior to Event	Current Event
Behaviors						
Thoughts						
Emotions						
Environment Physical Social						

interactions—ordinary conversations, for example—are the product of joint action. These features of interaction can be represented in a table, also shown in Figure 8.5.

Process Models

Figure 8.6 is a **process model** that represents how events unfold over time. This framework divides any event into five stages: (1) the event itself; (2) the immediate triggers (environmental, social) that led to the event; (3) the larger historical context in which the event was based; (4) the immediate response or reaction to the event; and (5) the event's long-term consequences.

Decision models can be represented in a **branching tree diagram**—also called a **dendrogram**—as in Figure 8.8 or in an **IF–THEN chart**, as in Figure 8.9. The dendrogram in Figure 8.8 shows James Young's model for how people in Pichátaro, Mexico, make their initial decision on how to react to an illness. The IF–THEN chart in Figure 8.9 shows Ryan and Martínez's (1996) model for how mothers in San José, Mexico, decided on how to respond to their infants' and toddlers' diarrhea. More about decision models in Chapter 16.

Transition Models

Figures 8.10 and 8.11 are **transition models**. When people make decisions—about buying a car or about choosing a college—they move from one emotional state to another. When people make medical decisions, for example, their first reaction (or state) may be to just wait and see. They may take some pills they have lying around that they got from a doctor in a previous illness. The models in Figures 8.10 and 8.11 show how these kinds of health care decisions unfolded in a village in Cameroon where Ryan worked.

Note that there are more lines in Figure 8.10 than in Figure 8.11. Ryan had 429 cases of illness in the set of families he studied for a year. If just one transition occurred in a case, it got a connecting line in the model shown in Figure 8.10. Figure 8.11 shows what happened when Ryan set the cut-off at 5%—at least 5% of the cases at one point moved to the next transition point. Notice that in both Figures 8.10 and 8.11, there are **recursive transitions**: People might try one home remedy after another before the illness either stopped or they broke out of the loop and did something else.

Activity Models

Figure 8.12 is an example of an **activity record**. This one comes from Werner's (1992) discussion of changing a tire. The model shows that the phrase "change a tire" can have more than one interpretation. At the macro level, the phrase means to get ready, jack up the car, remove the nuts, remove the wheel, put on the wheel, replace nuts, remove the jack, and finish up. At the micro level, it assumes the car is already jacked up and refers only to removing the nuts, removing the wheel, putting on the wheel, and replacing the nuts.

Taxonomies

Taxonomies are models of how we think a set of things are related. Taxonomies are used in all sciences as models of complex reality (e.g., think of the Linnaean tradition

Figure 8.8 Young's Decision Model for the Initial Choice of Treatment

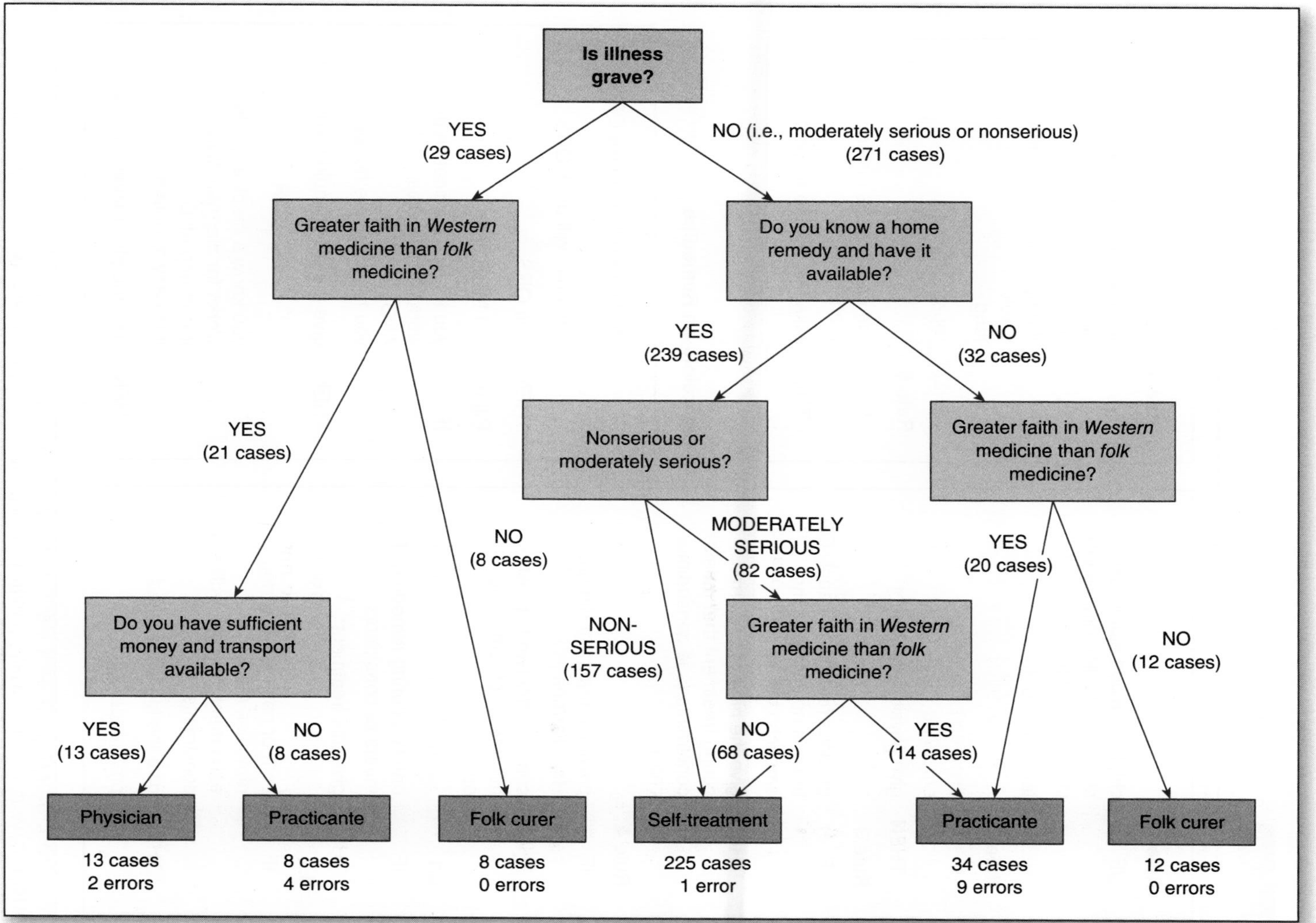

SOURCE: This article was published in *Social Science and Medicine*, 15, Young, J. C. "Non-use of physicians: Methodological approaches, policy implications, and the utility of decision models," pp. 499–507. Copyright Elsevier (1981). doi:10.1016/0160-7987(81)90024-7

Figure 8.9 Ryan and Martínez's If–Then Model for the Initial Choice of Treatment

Rule 1

IF child has blood stools OR child has swollen glands OR child is vomiting

THEN take child to doctor

Rule 2

IF diarrhea is caused by *empacho*

THEN give physical treatment

Rule 3

IF previous rules do not apply OR there is no cure with the empacho treatment

THEN give the highest preferred curing treatment that meets constraints (see constraint chart)

Rule 4

IF previous treatment did not stop diarrhea

THEN compare the two highest treatments of remaining options

4.1

IF one is a curing remedy AND meets its constraints

THEN give this treatment

4.2

IF both or neither are curing remedies AND each meet their respective constraints

THEN give the highest ranked preference

Rule 5

IF the previous treatment did not stop the diarrhea
AND
the episode is less than 1 week long

THEN repeat Rule 4

Rule 6

IF the episode has lasted more than 1 week

THEN take the child to a doctor

Constraints on Remedies

IF you know how to make ORS
AND
your child will drink ORS

THEN give ORS

Pill or Liquid Medication

IF you know a medication that works for diarrhea
AND
you have it in the house

THEN give the pill or liquid medication

OR

IF you know a medication that works for diarrhea AND it is cheap AND it is easy to obtain

THEN give the pill or liquid medication

SOURCE: G. W. Ryan and H. Martínez, 1996. Can we predict what mothers do? Modeling childhood diarrhea in rural Mexico. *Human Organization* 55:47–57. http://dx.doi.org/10.17730/humo.55.1.p0n23832j8q34743

Figure 8.10 Transition Between Types of Treatment

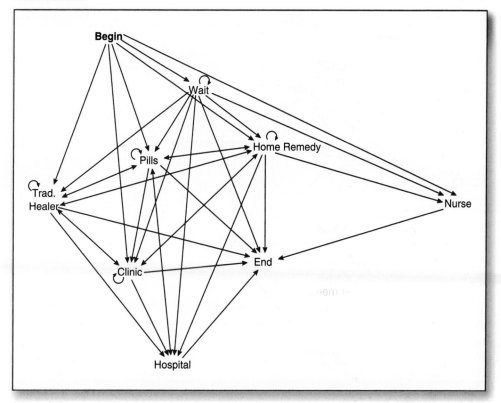

SOURCE: Reprinted from Ryan, G. 1998. Modeling home case management of acute illness in a rural Cameroonian village. *Social Science and Medicine* 4 (2): 209–225. DOI: http://dx.doi.org/10.1016/S0277-9536(97)00151-2 with permission of Elsevier.

NOTE: Arrows indicate that at least one transition occurred.

of taxonomies of living things in biology). Figure 8.13 is an example of a folk, or cultural, taxonomy. Bernard (2011) elicited this taxonomy of "kinds of cars and trucks" from an informant named Jack in West Virginia in the 1970s. More about building folk taxonomies in Chapter 18 on cultural domain analysis.

Mental Maps

Figure 8.14 comes from a study by James Boster and Jeffrey Johnson (1989) of two groups of fishermen in North Carolina. One group, the experts, were commercial fishermen. The other, the novices, were weekend anglers. Both groups did a pile sorting task with cards that had pictures of 42 different kinds of fish. The two graphics in

Figure 8.11 Transition Between Treatment Modalities

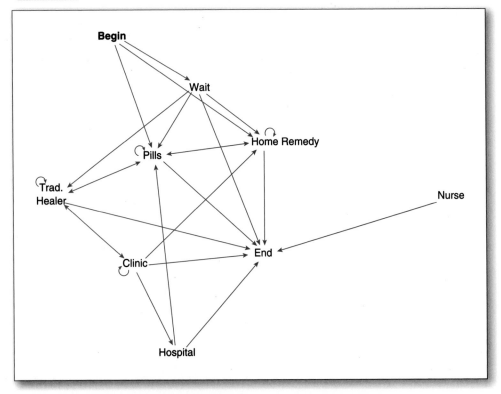

SOURCE: Reprinted from Ryan, G. 1998. Modeling home case management of acute illness in a rural Cameroonian village. *Social Science and Medicine* 4 (2): 209–225. doi: http://dx.doi.org/10.1016/S0277-9536(97)00151-2 with permission of Elsevier.

NOTE: *N* = 429. Arrows indicate transitions that took place more than 5% of the time.

Figures 8.14 shows models of what the two groups of fishermen thought about how the fish were related. Boster and Johnson found that experts judged the fish on function and shape, while novices judged fish primarily on their shape. These kinds of models are known as **mental maps**. They are produced from qualitative data like pile sorts and other systematic data collection methods. More about these methods, too, in Chapter 18.

◆ STEP 3: TESTING THE MODEL

Model building is an iterative process. We start with a case and state a theory. Then we look at another case and see if it fits our theory. If it does, we move on. If it doesn't, then we modify the theory to accommodate the new case. This constant comparison

Figure 8.12 An Example of an Activity Record

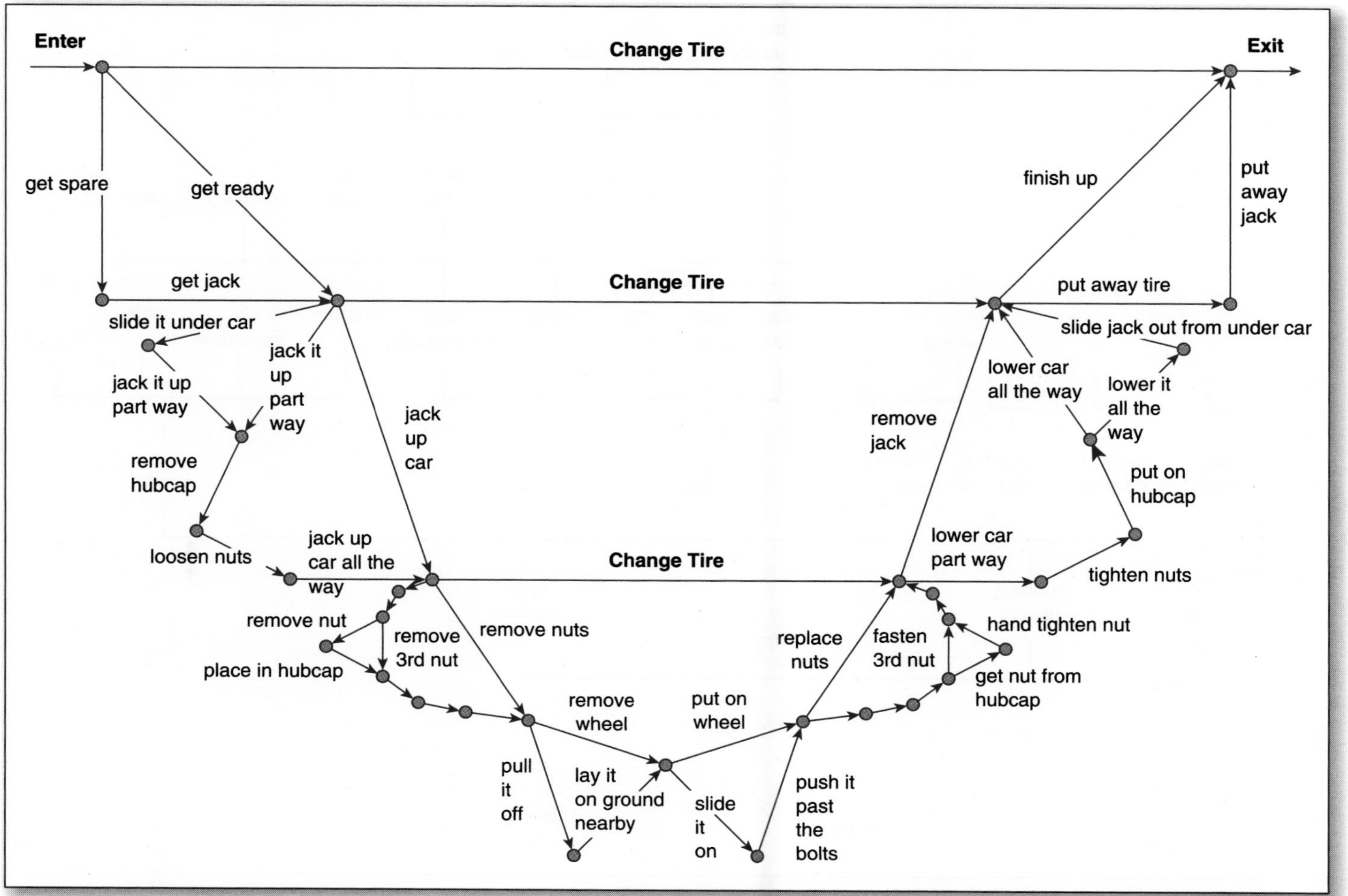

Enter

Change Tire

Change Tire

Change Tire

Exit

get spare

get ready

get jack

slide it under car

jack it up part way

jack it up part way

remove hubcap

jack it up part way

loosen nuts

jack up car all the way

remove nut

place in hubcap

remove 3rd nut

pull it off

lay it on ground nearby

slide it on

push it past the bolts

get nut from hubcap

hand tighten nut

fasten 3rd nut

replace nuts

put on wheel

remove wheel

remove nuts

jack up car

lower car part way

lower car all the way

remove jack

tighten nuts

put on hubcap

lower it all the way

slide jack out from under car

finish up

put away tire

put away jack

SOURCE: Werner, O. (1992). How to record activities. *Cultural Anthropology Methods Journal, 4*(2), 1–3. Copyright © 1992 Sage Publications.

Figure 8.13 Part of Jack's Taxonomy of Cars and Trucks

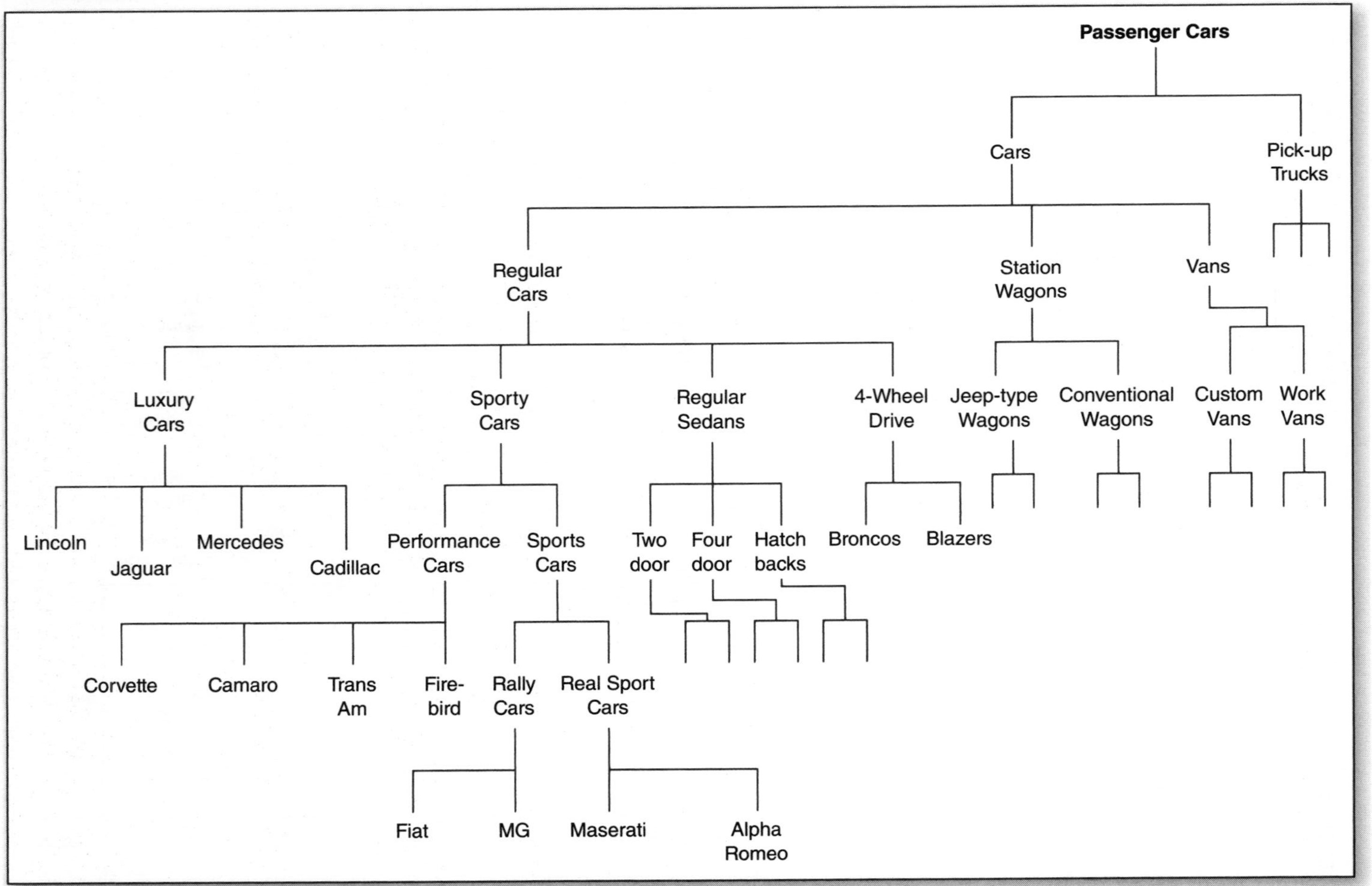

SOURCE: H. R. Bernard. (2011). *Research Methods in Anthropology: Qualitative and Quantitative Approaches.* 5th Edition. AltaMira Press.

Figure 8.14 Two Mental Models of Fish

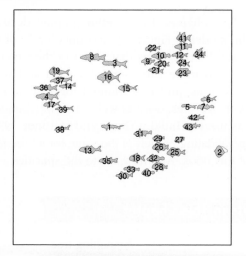 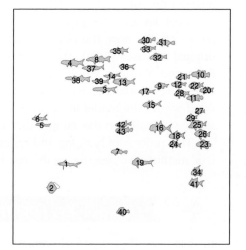

A multidimensional scaling of the similarities among the fish according to the North Carolina experts (Kruskal stress = .18).

A multidimensional scaling of the similarities among the fish according to the North Carolina novices (Kruskal stress = .10).

SOURCE: Reproduced by permission of the American Anthropological Association from American Anthropologist, Volume 91, Issue 4, Pages 866–889, December 1989. Not for sale or further reproduction.

of theory and cases, called **negative case analysis**, forces us to defend our theories and to look for new explanations.

The danger in negative case analysis is that every new case is seen as unique. In fact, in some sense, every case of anything is unique, but in building and testing models, the idea is to look for the commonalities and to simplify things. If every case is seen as unique, then theories become so complicated and so overspecified that they are useless. (**Further Reading**: negative case analysis)

Eventually, we reach some sort of closure—when new cases add little new information. When the incremental improvement in a model becomes minimal with each new case, grounded theorists say they have reached model saturation.

The real worth of a model, though, is not in its building, but in its testing—that is, whether it stands up against a new set of cases that weren't used in building the model in the first place.

Go back and look at Figure 8.9, the IF–THEN model that Ryan and Martínez built to account for what mothers in Mexico did in response to episodes of their children's diarrhea. Ryan and Martínez asked 17 mothers in San José, Mexico, who had children under five years old, what they did the last time their children had diarrhea. Then they went systematically through the treatments, asking each mother why she had used X instead of A, X instead of B, X instead of C, and so on down through the list.

We'll lay out the process in detail in Chapter 16, on ethnographic decision modeling. For now, the point is that the model in Figure 8.9 accounts for 15 of the original 17 cases (89%). To accommodate the two cases that didn't fit their model, Ryan and Martínez would have had to add more rules—one for each additional case. They tested the model on 20 new cases, and it accounted for 17 (84%). In other words, the model in Figure 8.9, with six rules, does as well on an independent sample as it did on the sample that was used to build it (Ryan and Martínez 1996).

This process of building and testing/validating models is the same for all the analytic methods we describe in the rest of this book. And now, on to the specifics.

Key Concepts in This Chapter

models	centrality	branching-tree
physical models	in vivo coding	diagram
virtual models	axial coding	dendrogram
numerical models	conditional matrix	IF–THEN chart
visual models	interaction events	transition models
statistical models	process model	recursive transitions
conceptual models	decisions under	activity record
selective coding	conditions of	taxonomies
salience	uncertainty	mental maps
ubiquitous	decision models	negative case analysis

Summary

- A major part of data analysis involves building, testing, displaying, and validating models. Models are simplifications of complicated, real things.
  - o Different kinds of models include physical models, virtual models, numerical models, and visual models.
- A good way to understand how models work is to start with a statistical model— that is, seeing how much you can predict some outcome of interest (like starting wage of a person new to the workforce) from background variables (like her or his education).

  - o Although statistical models are built on quantitative data, models are models, no matter what kind of data you have. All researchers, qualitative and quantitative alike, build models of abstract concepts connected by propositions or hypotheses.

- For example, **A → B** is a qualitative model that says "Something called A leads to, or causes, something called B."

- All models, whether built on qualitative or quantitative data, are reductions of complex realities. We build models to better understand these complexities and to help others understand them as well.
- There are three steps in building models: (1) Identify the key constructs, or themes to be included; (2) show linkages among the constructs—i.e., identify how the constructs are related and represent the relationships visually; and (3) test that the relationships hold for at least the majority of the cases being modeled. These steps can be repeated and repeated as models develop.

  - The first step is to separate core themes from periphery themes. The more often a concept appears—particularly if it appears across many respondents and in many situations—the more important it is likely to be. Centrality is about the degree to which a concept is linked to other concepts. Concepts that are linked to many others are likely to be at the core of—i.e., central to—any model.
  - Identifying key concepts means making choices about what you can cover in your analysis. No model can cover everything. Some concepts will just have to be excluded, or at least deferred until the next paper. Some researchers use pile sorting to find central concepts. But at some point in the process, every researcher has to ask: "Is this something I really need to explain here? Or is it tangential to my main concern right now?"

- Some common visual display models used in the social sciences include the conditional matrix, actor-interaction models, process models, decision models, transition models, activity models, taxonomies, and mental maps.
- The real value of a model is not in its building, but in its testing—that is, whether it stands up against a new set of cases that weren't used in building the model in the first place.

Exercises

1. Here are some processes that are of interest to many social researchers. For one of these, draw a model of how you think the process works.

   deciding to buy a car

   recovering from open-heart surgery

   adjusting to life after the death of a spouse

   choosing a college

losing weight and keeping it off

adjusting to life after being released from prison

treating a cold

Your model should have a starting point and an outcome. When you produce the model, write up how you might test the links you propose.

Further Reading

Building conceptual models. Miles and Huberman (1994). See literature on grounded theory (Chapter 10).

Negative case analysis. Boeije (2002), Bowen (2008), Dey (1993), Draucker et al. (2007), Emigh (1997), Lincoln and Guba (1985), McCreaddie (2010), Miles and Huberman (1994), Spiggle (1994).

Visit the online resource site at study.sagepub.com/bernardaqd to access engaging and helpful digital content, like video tutorials on working with MAXQDA, presentation slides, MAXQDA keyboard shortcuts, datasets, stop list, and recommended readings.

CHAPTER 9

COMPARING ATTRIBUTES
OF VARIABLES

INTRODUCTION

Many techniques have been developed over the years for systematic analysis of qualitative data. Two of them—semantic network analysis and cultural domain analysis—require the use of computers. Others (comparing attributes of variables, word counts and concordances, content analysis, analytic induction, ethnographic decision modeling, grounded theory, conversation analysis, and schema analysis) don't require the use of computers,

Units of Analysis

One of the first things to do in any research project is decide on the **units of analysis**. In Table 9.1, the units are texts and, of course, the people who provided the texts. In fact, in most social research, and especially in qualitative research, the units of analysis are people: female Mexican immigrants, male nurses, bureaucrats in the Department of Justice, women in German trade unions, runaway adolescents who are living on the street, people who go to chiropractors, Hispanic patrol officers in the Los Angeles Police Department.

But other things can be units of analysis, too. Depending on the research you're doing, you can compare newspapers, folktales, countries, or cities. If it can fit into a row in a matrix—and irrespective of whether the descriptors are words or numbers—then it's a unit of analysis.

The rule about units of analysis is: Always collect data on the lowest level unit of analysis possible. For example, if you want to know a household's income, collect data on the income contribution of each member. Then you can aggregate to the household level. But if you ask people to tell you about their household's income to start with, you can never disaggregate the data to find out how much each person contributed.

If you're studying the relationship between child-rearing practices and religion, collect data on the child-rearing practices of each person in the household—the mother, the grandmother, elder siblings, and so on. You can aggregate those data later and code each household as having, say, strict versus permissive child-rearing practices.

Attributes

We can appreciate qualitative data just by observing them as wholes—looking, listening, feeling—but a different kind of analysis can be done by focusing on features, or attributes of variables. A variable is something that can take more than one value, and the values of variables can be words or numbers. Income per year from tips is a variable; number of pregnancies is a variable; gender, religion, political party affiliation—all are variables.

Listen to experts as they discuss different renditions of the same piece of music—say, a piano sonata by Chopin. You'll hear talk about things like harmonic pungency, the force of the attack, the muddiness of the lower registers, and so on. These are all qualitative variables, and, like all variables, they vary from unit of analysis to unit of analysis (in this case, from rendition to rendition of the same piece).

In Table 9.1, the verbatim illness descriptions are in column 3. Then, following that, the descriptions are reduced to a set of variables in columns 4 through 8. Column 4 shows the data for the variable called "Diagnosis." In this project, this variable can take one of two attributes: cold or flu. If we compare informants on this variable, we see that informants 32, 47, and 18 reported having had a cold and informants 17, 15, and 24 reported that they had the flu.

Univariate Analysis

In column 8, we see that for informants 17, 15, and 18 the illness episodes lasted a week or less, but for informants 32, 47, and 24 the illness episodes lasted more than a week. The previous sentence is an example of **univariate analysis**, or comparing results within one column at a time. All systematic data analysis should begin with univariate analysis.

Univariate analyses are really, really focused and tell us a lot about a little. Mark Schuster and his colleagues (1998) asked 419 African American mothers who had recently given birth in Los Angeles, "What is your biggest fear for [child's name] growing up?" Mothers were prompted to give more than one answer—"Anything else you're afraid of for your child?"

After classifying the responses into 16 categories, Schuster et al. (1998) found that more than half the fears were in the medical and public health categories, but that the number-one concern was fear of gangs, violence, or both (39%). These findings have important policy implications—something the American Academy of Pediatrics has taken up in recommending counseling to families about preventing violence, in general, and firearm injuries, in particular.

Bivariate Analysis

Bivariate analysis involves comparing data across two columns. For example, if we sort Table 9.1 first by diagnosis and then by the variable concern (was the informant ever frightened or overly concerned about the illness), we would find four diagnostic/concern categories: cold/yes, cold/no, flu/yes, and flu/no. In this four-way categorization, cases 18 and 47 are similar as each belongs to the same cold/no category and cases 15 and 24 are similar as each belongs to the same flu/no category.

Multivariate Analysis

Multivariate analysis involves comparing three or more columns simultaneously. For example, informants 18 and 15 seem quite similar to each other on several variables. Informant 18 rated the overall severity of the illness as a 4, its worst point as a 4, and its duration as about 3.5 days; informant 15 rated the overall severity as a 5, its worst point as a 4, and its duration as about 3 days. Informants 17 and 24 are identical on the first two of these three variables (7 and 9), but informant 24 reported that the illness lasted for two weeks—twice as long as the one week reported by informant 17.

These two cases seem very different from that of informant 47, who said that she had a very mild cold (rating it just 1 out of a possible 7) that never got very bad (rating its worst point just 2 out of 10), but that lasted a long time (10 days).

There are some numbers in these descriptive statements, but the analyses are qualitative. The principle is the same, however, no matter how many cases or how many variables we compare at once: *Our knowledge of relations is the result of actively and systematically making comparisons.*

But as soon as we get more than a handful of cases, we need more formal techniques than inspection to keep things straight and to calculate similarities and differences. Fortunately, there are many computer programs to help you find patterns in both qualitative and quantitative multivariate data (see Box 9.1).

Box 9.1

Multivariate Statistics and Weak Relations

There is a limit to the relations that can be detected in the kind of data we're talking about here—that is, text. With enough cases, we can use statistical methods to tease out weak relations among multiple variables.

Weak relations can be very important in our lives. Some people have an increased risk of certain kinds of cancer because of environmental or genetic factors. Typically, though, it takes population-level studies—studies based on many thousands of cases—to detect those increased risks. African Americans are more likely than Whites in the United States to experience prison, hunger, and violent death. We can tell this because we have population-level studies on which to base the measurement of differences.

◆ LEVELS OF MEASUREMENT

Notice that column entries in Table 9.1 vary in what's known as **level of measurement**. That is, some columns are filled with qualitative data (words, like cold or flu, or even whole texts, as in column 3), and some contain numbers. The values of variables come in three major levels of measurement: nominal, ordinal, and interval.

Nominal Variables

The values of a **nominal variable** comprise a list of names. Religions have names, like Baptist, Hindu, and Shinto, so religion is a nominal variable. Occupations have names, like chauffeur, ornithologist, and zookeeper, so occupation is a nominal variable. Ethnic groups, body parts, rock stars . . . all are nominal variables. The themes in a codebook are nominal variables if they are coded as present or absent.

In statistics, nominal variables are called "qualitative" because they don't involve any quantities. Coding men as "1" and women as "2" does not make gender a quantitative variable. You can't add up all the 1s and 2s and calculate the average gender. Assigning the number 1 to men and the number 2 to women is just substituting one name (the name of a number) for another (nominal comes from Latin, *nomen*, or name).

Here's an example of a typical nominal, or qualitative, variable from a survey:

Do you identify with any religion? (check one)

☐ Yes   ☐ No.

If you checked "yes," then what is your religion? (check one)

☐ Protestant   ☐ Catholic   ☐ Jewish   ☐ Muslim   ☐ Other religion

---

Notice the use of the "other" category. The defining feature of nominal measurement is that it is **exhaustive** and **mutually exclusive**. Inserting the other category makes the measurement exhaustive.

Mutually exclusive means that things can't belong to more than one category of a nominal variable at a time. The instruction to "check one" makes the list mutually exclusive.

Note, though, that life is complicated. People whose parents are of different races may think of themselves as biracial or multiracial. In 2000, the U.S. Census began offering people the opportunity to check off more than one race—and about seven million Americans did just that. By 2010, about nine million people claimed multiracial status (Jones and Bullock 2012). Occupation is a nominal variable, but people can be homeopaths and jewelers at the same time; they can be pediatric oncology nurses and eBay entrepreneurs.

In Table 9.1, whether the informant reported a cold or a flu is a nominal variable. Depending on the analysis, we could add subcategories: simple colds, cold/flu combo, sinus infection, and so on.

Ordinal Variables

Ordinal variables also have the properties of mutual exclusivity and exhaustiveness, but they have an additional property: Their values can be rank ordered. Anything measured as high, medium, or low (like socioeconomic class) is an ordinal variable.

Anyone labeled "middle class" is lower in the social class hierarchy than someone labeled "upper class" and higher in the same hierarchy than someone labeled "lower class." Ordinal variables, though, do not contain information about how much something is more than or less than something else.

The familiar "on a scale of 1 to 5" preamble to survey questions tells you that an ordinal variable is coming. Consider the variable: "like a lot," "like somewhat," "neutral," "dislike somewhat," "dislike strongly." A person who likes something a lot may like it twice as much as someone who says they like it somewhat, or five times as much, or half again as much. There is no way to tell.

In Table 9.1, Informant 47 said that, overall, her cold was about a 1 on a 7-point scale, and Informant 18 said that his cold was about a 4. We don't know if 4 is four times as bad as a 1 or twice as bad. All we know is that 4 is more serious than 1, at least in the mind of Informant 18.

Thomas Weisner and his colleagues (1991) studied families that had children with developmental delays. Working from interviews and questionnaires, raters assessed each family on: (1) its involvement with and attendance at a church or temple; (2) its shared sense of spirituality; (3) the support it received from a church or temple; and (4) how much religion influenced everyday actions and decisions. Readers of qualitative research reports need context to understand scale values. Weisner and his colleagues provided exemplars in the form of vignettes, shown in Table 9.2, for each of the ordinal categories.

Table 9.2 Qualitative Exemplars of Ordinal Scales

Ordinal Rating	Exemplary Description
Nonreligious family	The Ehrlich family was headed by a grandmother, who was raising her granddaughter who had developmental delays. This family had no religious affiliation and attended no church or temple. They received no support from any religious groups and did not engage in any religious activities in the home. The grandmother was not taking her granddaughter to church at the time. When asked whether religion had provided any kind of support for her, or what else had been helpful, the grandmother replied: "No. Nothing, really. I just, really nothing, (I) just take care of her." As with many other nonreligious families in our sample, the Ehrlich family did have some history of formal religious training or experience in their past, but was not currently involved in religious activity.
Moderately nonreligious family	The Stein family was Jewish and attended temple occasionally, but they were not formal or active members. However, the Steins did indicate that they prayed regularly in their home. When asked whether religion was helpful, this mother replied: "It does play a part, more for me than my husband. But, I am very religious, I guess, in a vague way. My husband is not particularly religious at all."

Ordinal Rating	Exemplary Description
Moderate to high religious family	The Crandalls had a young son with developmental delays who had several problems at birth and continued to have speech and coordination problems. The family held membership in and regularly attended a nearby Congregational Church. This mother, who taught Vacation Bible School one summer, said of the church, "It's a nice experience for our entire family. Jason loves Sunday School."
Highly religious family	Religion was an integral part of the Robinson's everyday life. Their daughter Cathy was born prematurely and had major medical problems, necessitating four hospitalizations in her first year; her development was delayed in all areas. The Robinsons were active members of a 7th Day Adventist church, where they were involved in many activities. Prayer was a part of the Robinsons' daily lives. "We started doing things like praying together as a family, and having that faith foundation has strengthened our commitment to one another and our relationship with one another, and I think it's brought us closer together."

SOURCE: Weisner, T. S., L. Beizer, and L. Stolze 1991. Religion and families of children with developmental delays. *American Journal of Mental Retardation* 95:647–62.

Interval Variables

Interval variables have all the characteristics of nominal and ordinal variables—an exhaustive and mutually exclusive list of attributes that have a rank-order structure—and one additional property: The distances between the attributes are meaningful. Nominal variables are qualitative; ordinal variables are semi-quantitative; and interval variables are fully quantitative (see Box 9.2).

Box 9.2

About Interval/Ratio Variables

Technically, most of what we commonly call interval variables are really **ratio variables**. Ratio variables have all the properties of interval variables, plus one: They have a true zero point. Income, for example, is a common ratio variable: $50 is exactly twice $25 and exactly half of $100.

True interval variables—with real intervals and no zero point—are rare. In SAT scores, for example, the difference between a 600 and 700 is 100 points and the difference between 300 and 400 is 100 points. The intervals (SAT points) are the same, but a score of 600 is way more than twice as good as a score of 300. (A score of 600 is actually one standard deviation above the mean and a score of 300 is two standard deviations below the mean.) Common measurements for temperature are at the interval level. Whether you measure temperature in Fahrenheit or Celsius, a zero on those scales doesn't mean the absence of temperature.

Some examples of interval/ratio variables we've seen recently in the social science literature include: number of times married and number of years married; years in current job and months since last job; distance (in miles or minutes) to the nearest public school; number of pounds of fish caught last week; and number of hours last week spent in preparing food.

"Number of years of education" looks like an interval variable, but a year of grade school is not the same as a year of graduate school, so this variable usually gets chunked into an ordinal one: up to sixth grade, high school, some college, college degree, some postgraduate work, postgraduate degree. Sometimes, you just have to be sensible. And notice that, although a person who is 20 is twice the age of someone who is 10, this says nothing about the difference in social or emotional maturity. Conceptual variables, like social maturity, tend to be measured at the ordinal level.

◆ CONVERTING TEXT TO VARIABLE DATA

There are trade-offs between the complexity and richness of **nonvariable data**— whole texts, whole pieces of music, whole films, whole television ads—and the simplicity of variable data. On the one hand, nonvariable data, like the verbatim descriptions in Table 9.1, are a rich account of what people thought was most salient to report about their last experience with having a cold or flu. On the other hand, the complexity of nonvariable data makes them difficult to use for making comparisons in their raw form.

Consider cases 32 and 47 in Table 9.1. The two cases are similar in that both report coughing and having a sore throat, but they are quite distinct on many other dimensions. One describes having a runny and stuffed-up nose with sneezing; the other reports having body aches and loss of appetite. One had trouble sleeping; the other felt like sleeping all the time. One reports when the illness started and how long it lasted; the other doesn't cover either of these topics.

How similar are these cases? This question gets even more complex if we want to know whether case 18 (the other case of a cold) is more similar to case 32 than to 47. One way to tackle this problem is to use the value coding processes we covered in Chapter 6. In Table 9.3, we have coded each of the verbatim descriptions in Table 9.1 for eight signs and symptoms of a cold and/or flu: cough, runny/stuffed nose, nausea/ vomit, fever, fatigue, sore throat, body ache, and loss of appetite.

Each of the eight themes (variables) in Table 9.3 could take one of three values: 1 if the sign or symptom was mentioned; 0 if it was explicitly mentioned as not being present; and a dot • if it was not mentioned at all. Then (over in the right-hand column of Table 9.3) we summed up all the signs and/or symptoms that were mentioned. Finally, we sorted the table so that examples of cold were at the top and flu at the bottom.

Table 9.3   Signs and Symptom Codes Derived From Verbatim Illness Descriptions

ID	Sex	Verbatim Illness Description[1]	Diagnosis	Signs and Symptoms								
				Cough	Runny, Stuffed Nose	Nausea, Vomiting	Fever	Fatigue	Sore Throat	Body Ache	Loss Appt.	Sum
32	F	Tired, aching, running nose, stuffed nose, sneezing, coughing, difficulty sleeping, uncomfortableness, sore throat—lots of Kleenex.	Cold	1	1	•	•	1	1	1	•	5
47	F	It was February and I came down with a cold. Just a sore throat, achy body, and a cough. Felt like sleeping all the time and didn't feel like eating anything unless it was salty. It took a week or a week and a half to get over.	Cold	1	•	•	•	1	1	1	1	5
18	M	Headache—throbbing in temples—moved around head. Cough—hacking—sometimes—phlegm. Congestion—in sinuses and rib cage. Labored breathing—reduction of 20-10 airflow, tight chest. Fatigue—strong desire to sleep and nap.—did not do activities running and going to gym for day to day and a half—felt weak and did not have desire to do much—could not concentrate—bad headache and a little stressed.	Cold	1	1	•	•	1	•	•	•	3
		The last time I had the flu I was VERY ill. It began at my head and arms and swept down my body in a big ache. All my muscles were sore, I felt like I was dying. I think I had fever blisters in my mouth, I had a sore throat, but did not lose my appetite nor was I sick to my stomach.	Flu	•	•	0	•	1	1	1	0	3

(Continued)

Table 9.3 (Continued)

ID	Sex	Verbatim Illness Description[1]	Diagnosis	Signs and Symptoms								
				Cough	Runny, Stuffed Nose	Nausea, Vomiting	Fever	Fatigue	Sore Throat	Body Ache	Loss Appt.	Sum
17	F	I just remember being laid out on our sofa for 3 days, every muscle in my body aching like I'd been beat up or through severe athletic training. The whole episode lasted around 7 days.										
15	M	The last time I had a cold/flu was in Feb 98. I laid in bed for 2 days with a headache, a stomach ache, fever, body pain. I had spells of dizziness and nausea. I pretty much slept for most of 48 hrs. I was still tired and worn out for a couple of days beyond the initial illness.	Flu	•	•	1	1	1	•	1	•	4
24	M	I had the flu 5 months ago. I was always tired and it was hard to think straight. At some points though I actually kind of enjoyed it. No one expected much out of you. I don't know if it was the medicine or the fever, but at times I felt like I had a buzz. Of course I had all the common symptoms. I would wake up at night either sweating my ass off or shaking horribly from being so incredibly cold. I remember one night I was so cold and shaking so bad it woke my roommate up because I was shaking the bunk beds. He was not cold at all.	Flu	•	•	•	1	1	•	•	•	2

NOTES: 1. Please recall the last time that you had a cold or the flu and describe it in as much detail as possible. 2. What kind of illness did you have? 3. Where you ever frightened or overly concerned about your condition? 4. Please place a mark on the scale to indicate the severity of your illness (visual scale resembled a thermometer marked 1–10), with 10 considered to be the worst health state. 5. Please rate the severity of your illness by circling the one number that best describes the severity at its *worst* during the episode. 6. How many days did it last?

LEVELS OF AGGREGATION ♦

After you make decisions about the units of analysis (rows), features of comparisons (columns) and level of measurement (cells), the next step is to decide at what **level of aggregation** you want to make comparisons. There are three levels of aggregation for comparisons: (1) pairwise; (2) within-group; and (3) cross-group.

Pairwise Comparison

Pairwise comparisons describe the similarity between any two rows of a table. We can compare informants 32 and 47, 32 and 18, 17 and 15, 17 and 24, and so on. There are six informants in Tables 9.1 and 9.3. The formula for comparing things two at a time from any list is

$$n(n-1)/2$$

so, in this case, with six informants, we can do 6(5)/2=15 comparisons. Going systematically through all possible pairwise comparisons is the central idea in the **constant comparative method** used by grounded theorists and other qualitative researchers everywhere for finding themes. (See Chapters 5, 9, and 10.)

Within-Group Comparison

If we want to compare more than two things at a time, we use **within-group comparisons** (also called **intragroup comparisons**). This involves scanning multiple rows simultaneously to search for things like **range**, **central tendency** (like the mean, or average), and **distributions** of variables.

For example, the top portion of Table 9.1 contains descriptions of illness by women. We see that two out of three women reported colds and were the same people who reported being somewhat concerned about their condition. Their overall assessment of severity was from 1 to 7 (range) and averaged 3.67 days (1+3+7/3=3.67). These events lasted anywhere from seven to 14 days (again, range), with an average of 10.33 days.

Cross-Group Comparison

Cross-group comparisons (also called **intergroup comparisons**) takes the process one more step. From Table 9.1, we see that none of the men expressed concern for his health, but two out of three women did. On the other hand, the three men reported colds/flus lasting from three to 14 days (average 6.83), with severity ranging from 4 to 7 (average 5.33)—more severe than the colds/flus reported by women but lasting less time than those reported by women.

These are self-report data, so we're dealing here with what people perceive, not with measures of physical reality, as would be the case if we had the results of a physician's examination on all these cases. Also, with so few cases, we can't generalize the results to the whole population. Still, you can see how cross-group comparison can be a very powerful tool for identifying patterns in populations. Even with just a few cases, we can see patterns emerging and can start formulating hypotheses, like "On average, men will report having a harder time with colds and flu than will women but will be reluctant to express concern."

This may not work out when we get more cases, but that's fine. The idea here is to use the data we have in hand and get some ideas about what's going on. These few cases give us something to look for when we collect more cases. In fact, they help us focus interviews as we move through a project. Most qualitative research projects are based on fewer than a hundred interviews. You want to make those interviews count, so start doing the analysis on the first few and keep expanding the analysis as you get more data.

◆ MANY TYPES OF COMPARISONS

Table 9.4 summarizes the comparisons that can be made with combinations of levels of comparisons, levels of measurement, and levels of aggregation.

Table 9.4 Types of Comparisons

Levels of Aggregation	Dimensions of Comparison		
	Univariate	Bivariate	Multivariate
Pairwise	I	IV	VII
	(nv, n, o, ir)	(nv, n, o, ir)	(nv, n, o, ir)
Within-Group	II	V	VIII
	(nv, n, o, ir)	(nv, n, o, ir)	(nv, n, o, ir)
Cross-Group	III	VI	IX
	(nv, n, o, ir)	(nv, n, o, ir)	(nv, n, o, ir)

LEVELS OF MEASUREMENT: nv = nonvariable, n = nominal, o = ordinal, ir = interval/ratio.

There are two important points here. First, all the comparisons described in Table 9.4 can be made using qualitative data. In the case of variable-based comparisons, you may need to add an extra step to convert nonvariable data, like text, into nominal-, ordinal-, or interval-level variables.

Second, different methodological traditions emphasize certain types of comparisons over others. For example, classic content analysis of texts (Chapter 11) involves within-group and cross-group comparisons and always requires the conversion of text or images to at least nominal-level variables. Grounded theory and schema analysis (Chapters 11 and 12), by contrast, rely on whole texts—i.e., nonvariable data—and rarely involve conversions of texts to variables.

During the discovery phase of both grounded theory and schema analysis, the method of constant pairwise comparison plays an important role in the identification of themes. As the process of building models moves on, within-group and cross-group comparisons become more important.

Analytic induction (Chapter 15), particularly the method known as qualitative comparative analysis (QCA), produces aggregate, within-group models and uses text that has been converted to nominal variables. The analysis of nominal, free list data (Chapter 18) is a type of univariate comparative analysis (usually at the within- and cross-group comparative levels).

If this all seems a bit opaque right now, come back and read this section again after you've gone through the later chapters on all these methods for analyzing texts.

Comparing the Columns

Up to this point, we have been making comparisons across pairs of rows or groups of rows (units of analysis). Much of social science research, however, is about identifying general associations between variables and how they are co-distributed in a population. These associations are found by making comparisons across columns.

Table 9.5a shows the bivariate relationship between illness diagnosis (cold, flu) and concern (yes, no) in Table 9.1. The rows in Table 9.5a represent the values associated with one dimension (Diagnosis), and the columns represent the values of the other (Concern). The numbers in each cell represent the number (and percentage) of cases that meet the conditions indicated by the intersection of two variables.

From the data in Table 9.1, we see that informant 32 reported a cold and was concerned, but informants 47 and 18, who also reported colds, were not concerned. From Table 9.5b, we see that only six (14%) of the 43 people who reported a cold also reported being concerned, but nine (about 53%) of the 17 students who reported a case of the flu also reported being concerned. The students in our research see flu as the more serious of the two illnesses.

Table 9.5 Bivariate Comparison of Illness Narratives in Table 9.1

Table 9.5a					Table 9.5b					
Data from Table 9.1 ($n = 6$)					Data from Entire Sample ($N = 60$)					
	Concern						Concern			
	Yes		No		Total		Yes		No		Total
Diagnosis	Freq.	%	Freq.	%	Freq	Diagnosis	Freq	%	Freq	%	Freq
Cold	1	33.3	2	66.6	3	Cold	6	14.0	37	86.0	43
Flu	1	33.3	2	66.6	3	Flu	8	47.1	9	52.9	17
	2	33.3	4	66.6	6		14	23.3	46	76.7	60

1. Data taken from Table 9.1 ($n = 6$).

2. Data taken from entire sample on which Table 9.1 was based ($n = 60$).

◆ AND FINALLY . . .

Many projects that are based on texts involve the kinds of analyses we've outlined in this chapter—that is, comparisons of themes or variables. Some studies may involve only qualitative data and qualitative comparisons. Increasingly, however, we find studies that combine both qualitative and quantitative data and analyses.

It is fashionable to call these **mixed-methods** studies. A sensible mix of qualitative and quantitative data, however, has always been the natural order of science. Particular studies in any science may be mostly based on qualitative data or mostly based on quantitative data. But all fields of science, from sociology to ornithology, advance as a result of studies based on both kinds of data.

In the chapters that follow, we take up the various methods for analyzing qualitative data.

Key Concepts in This Chapter

attributes of variables
units of analysis
univariate analysis
bivariate analysis
multivariate analysis
level of
  measurement
nominal variable
exhaustive

mutually exclusive
ordinal variable
interval variable
ratio variable
nonvariable data
level of aggregation
pairwise comparison
constant comparative
  method

within-group (intragroup)
  comparison
range
central tendency
distributions
cross-group (intergroup)
  comparison
mixed methods

Summary

- Data analysis begins by comparing attributes of variables. "All knowing is comparative," said Donald Campbell (1988:372), and he was right. Astronomers, historians, and social scientists alike achieve knowledge by making comparisons. This star is brighter than that one; this war was more costly in blood and treasure than that one; women, on average, live longer than men do, in the industrialized societies of the world, but men live longer than women do in the non-industrialized societies of the world. Whether we use qualitative or quantitative data, we know things because we compare new experiences with the ones we already have.

- In making comparisons, we ask three questions:

  1. What things are we comparing? What are the units of analysis?
  2. What attributes of these units are we using to make the comparison?
  3. How will we measure similarities and differences on each of the attributes?

     o The rows in a data matrix represent the units of analysis and define what we're comparing (the answer to question 1). The columns represent the attributes of variables (the answer to question 2). And each cell represents one person's response to each question (the answer to question 3).

- In most social research, the units of analysis are people: female Mexican immigrants, male nurses, bureaucrats in the Department of Justice, women in German trade unions, runaway adolescents who are living on the street.

  o Other things can be units of analysis: We can compare newspapers, folktales, countries, or cities. If it can fit into a row in a matrix—and irrespective of whether the descriptors are words or numbers—then it's a unit of analysis.
  o Collect data on the lowest level unit of analysis possible. If you want to know a household's income, collect data on the income contribution of each member. Then you can aggregate to the household level. But if you ask people to tell you about their household's income to start with, you can never disaggregate the data to find out how much each person contributed.

- Each unit of analysis can be characterized by a series of variables and attributes of variables. A variable is something that can take more than one value, and the values of variables can be words or numbers. Income per year from tips is a variable; number of pregnancies is a variable; gender, religion, political party affiliation—all are variables.

- Some relations are weak, but weak relations can be very important in our lives. Some people have an increased risk of certain kinds of cancer because of environmental or genetic factors. Typically, though, it takes population-level studies—studies based on many thousands of cases—to detect those increased risks.

- The values of variables come in three major levels of measurement: nominal, ordinal, and interval. The values of a nominal variable comprise a list of names. Religions have names, like Baptist, Hindu, and Shinto, so religion is a nominal variable.

  o The defining feature of nominal measurement is that it is exhaustive and mutually exclusive.

  o Ordinal variables also have the properties of mutual exclusivity and exhaustiveness, but their values can be rank ordered. Anything measured as high, medium, or low (like socioeconomic class) is an ordinal variable.

  o Interval variables have all the characteristics of nominal and ordinal variables—an exhaustive and mutually exclusive list of attributes that have a rank-order structure—plus, the distances between the attributes are meaningful.

  o Nominal variables are qualitative; ordinal variables are semi-quantitative; and interval variables are fully quantitative.

  o Most of what we commonly call interval variables are really ratio variables. Ratio variables have all the properties of interval variables, plus one: They have a true zero point. Income for example, is a common ratio variable: $50 is exactly twice $25 and exactly half of $100.

  o True interval variables—with real intervals and no zero point—are rare. In SAT scores, for example, the difference between a 600 and 700 is 100 points and the difference between 300 and 400 is 100 points. The intervals (SAT points) are the same, but a score of 600 is more than twice as good as a score of 300.

- There are trade-offs between the complexity and richness of nonvariable data—whole texts, whole pieces of music, whole films, whole television ads—and the simplicity of variable data.

  o Texts can contain rich accounts of what people think and do. The complexity of nonvariable data, like whole texts, makes them difficult to use for making comparisons in their raw form.

- After you make decisions about the units of analysis (rows), features of comparisons (columns), and level of measurement (cells), the next step is to decide at what level of aggregation you want to make comparisons. There are three levels of aggregation for comparisons: (1) pairwise; (2) within-group; and (3) cross-group.

  o Pairwise comparisons describe the similarity between any two rows of a table.

  o Within-group comparisons (also called intragroup comparisons) involves scanning multiple rows simultaneously to search for things like range, central tendency (like the mean, or average), and distributions of variables.

  o Cross-group comparisons (also called intergroup comparisons) takes the process one more step, like comparing the answers of men and women to the same question.

- Many projects that are based on texts combine both qualitative and quantitative data and analyses—on mixed methods.

  o A sensible mix of qualitative and quantitative data has always been the natural order of science. Particular studies in any science may be mostly based on qualitative data or mostly based on quantitative data. But all fields of science, from sociology to ornithology, advance as a result of studies based on both kinds of data.

Exercises

1. In 300 words or less, describe the last time you had a cold or flu. Be sure to cover how you felt with it coming on and what you did about it. How did it interfere with your regular routine? On a scale of 1 to 5, how severe was your illness (with 5 being very severe and 1 being mild). How many days did it last? Did you go to a doctor or clinic? Set up a matrix, like the one in Table 9.1, and insert the data from your description.

2. Code your description for the presence or absence of the eight symptoms in Table 9.3: cough, runny nose, vomiting, fever, fatigue, sore throat, body ache, and loss of appetite. Also code for whether the episode you described was a cold or flu.

3. Once you've done exercises 1 and 2 for your own description of a cold or flu episode, ask three friends or acquaintances the questions in exercise 1, above, and repeat exercises 1 and 2 for the three new descriptions.

4. Distinguish among univariate, bivariate analysis, and multivariate analyses.

5. What are the properties of nominal, ordinal, and ratio variables? Name three of each kind of variable.

Further Reading

Analyzing qualitative data. Auerbach and Silverstein (2003), Bryman and Burgess (1994), Dey (1993), Flick (2002), Gibbs (2007), LeCompte (2000), Miles (1979), Miles et al. (2013), L. Richards (2005), Silverman (2011).

Visit the online resource site at study.sagepub.com/bernardaqd to access engaging and helpful digital content, like video tutorials on working with MAXQDA, presentation slides, MAXQDA keyboard shortcuts, datasets, stop list, and recommended readings.

CHAPTER **10**

GROUNDED THEORY

INTRODUCTION: ON INDUCTION AND DEDUCTION ◆

This chapter and the next are about two very different kinds of text analysis: grounded theory and content analysis. The two methods reflect the two great epistemological approaches for all research: **induction** and **deduction**.

In its idealized form, inductive research involves the search for pattern from observation and the development of explanations—theories—for those patterns through a series of hypotheses. The hypotheses are tested against new cases, modified, retested against yet more cases, and so on, until something called **theoretical saturation** happens—new cases stop requiring more testing.

In its idealized form, deductive research starts with theories (which come from common sense, from observation, or from the literature), derives hypotheses from them, and moves on to observations—which either confirm or disconfirm the hypotheses.

Real research is never purely inductive or purely deductive, but for some kinds of research problems, a mostly inductive or a mostly deductive approach is called for. Inductive research is required in the **exploratory phase** of *any* research project, whether the data are words or numbers. Deductive research is required in the **confirmatory stage** of any research project—again, irrespective of whether the data are qualitative or quantitative.

In general, the less we know about a research problem, the more important it is to take an inductive approach—to suspend our preconceived ideas as much as we can and let observation be our guide. As we learn more and more about a research problem, the more important it becomes to take a deductive approach.

Suppose we want to understand why preadolescent boys and girls join urban gangs. We would begin by observing some boys and girls who are in gangs and some who aren't. We would look for patterns in their behavior. As we learn about those patterns we would form hypotheses.

Here's one: Holding neighborhood constant, kids who have two biological parents are less likely to join gangs than are kids who have one biological parent or are in single parent families or are in foster homes. Eventually, we would want to test our ideas about patterns (our hypotheses, in other words) against new observations.

This paradigm for building knowledge—the continual combination of inductive and deductive research—is used by scholars across the humanities and the sciences alike and has proved itself over thousands of years. If we know anything about how and why stars explode or about how HIV is transmitted or about why women lower their fertility when they enter the labor market, it's because of this combination of effort.

Human experience—the way real people actually experience real events—is endlessly interesting because it is endlessly unique. In a way, the study of human experience is always exploratory and is best done inductively. On the other hand, we also know that human experience is patterned. A migrant from Mexico who crosses the U.S. border one step ahead of the authorities lives through a unique experience and has a unique story to tell, but 20 such stories will surely reveal similarities. (**Further Reading**: induction and deduction in social science)

◆ OVERVIEW OF GROUNDED THEORY

The same goes for men in Montreal who have lived through hand-to-hand combat, women in Sydney who are fighting breast cancer, and men in Beijing who are trying to give up smoking. Each has a unique experience; each has a unique story to tell; and similarities, if there are any, are revealed in the aggregate of those unique stories.

Discovering patterns in human experience requires close, inductive examination of unique cases plus the application of deductive reasoning.

And the same goes for **social processes**, not just for **lived experiences**. People who are in jail for committing violent crimes; people who are living with AIDS; people who are studying abroad for a year—all of them have been through a long, long process, with many stages and many choices made along the way. And in each case, the process is unique for each person. But there are patterns, too, with one stage leading to the next and the next. Discovering patterns in social processes also requires close, inductive examination of unique cases plus the application of deductive reasoning.

That's where **grounded theory** (GT) comes in. This inductive method was developed by two sociologists, Barney Glaser and Anslem Strauss, in a seminal book titled *The Discovery of Grounded Theory: Strategies for Qualitative Research* (1967). As the title implies, the aim is to *discover* theories—causal explanations—grounded in empirical data, about how things work.

Glaser and Strauss were not the first to recognize the value of qualitative data for developing theory about social processes and human experience. The genius of their book—as important and fresh today, in our view, as it was in 1967—was their systematic, yet flexible methods for doing the job. Glaser and Strauss did more than just claim the usefulness of qualitative data. They showed us how to treat qualitative data as a serious source of scientifically derived knowledge about social and psychological processes.

Where Do Grounded Theory Data Come From?

Data for a GT study come from in-depth interviews about people's lived experiences and about the social processes that shape those experiences. All the lessons about interviewing from Chapter 4 apply here. You need to be aware of things like the **deference effect**—people telling you what they think you want to hear. You need to learn how to probe effectively—to get people talking and then letting them talk. You need to learn to ask questions that may be threatening—about drug use, suicide, sexual behavior—and appear comfortable doing so.

GT interviews can be ethnographic—focused on the culture—but many grounded theorists prefer what Levy and Hollan (1998) call person-centered interviews. In an ethnographic interview, one might ask: "Tell me how *people in biochemistry* get trained to do science." In a person-centered interview, the question would be: "Tell me how *you* were trained to do science?"

Kathy Charmaz uses in-depth interviewing "to explore, not to interrogate" (2002:679). Figure 10.1 shows the kinds of questions that Charmaz uses in a GT interview. These are the same kinds of questions that characterize a **life story interview** (Atkinson 1998, 2002), or what Kvale and Brinkman call a **life world interview** (2009:124).

Figure 10.1   Examples of Questions in a Grounded Theory Interview

Initial Open-Ended Questions

1. Tell me about what happened [or how you came to _____]?

2. When, if at all, did you first experience _____ [or notice _____]?

3. [If so,] What was it like? What did you think then? How did you happen to _____? Who, if anyone, influenced your actions? Tell me about how he/she influenced you.

4. Could you describe the events that let up to _____ [or preceded _____]?

5. What contributed to _____?

6. What was going on in your life then? How would you describe how you viewed _____ before _____ happened? How, if at all, has your view of _____ changed?

7. How would you describe the person you were then?

Intermediate Questions

1. What, if anything, did you know about _____?

2. Tell me about your thoughts and feelings when you learned about _____?

3. What happened next?

4. Who, if anyone, was involved? When was that? How were they involved?

5. Tell me about how you learned to handle _____.

6. How, if at all, have your thoughts and feelings about _____ changed since _____?

7. What positive changes have occurred in your life [or _____] since _____?

8. What negative changes, if any, have occurred in your life [or _____] since _____?

9. Tell me how you go about _____. What do you do?

10. Could you describe a typical day for you when you are _____? [Probe for different times.] Now tell me about a typical day when you are _____.

11. Tell me how you would describe the person you are now. What most contributed to this change [or continuity]?

12. As you look back on _____, are there any other events that stand out in your mind? Could you describe it [each one]? How did this event affect what happened? How did you respond to _____ [the event; the resulting situations]?

13. Could you describe the most important lessons you learned about _____ through experiencing _____?

14. Where do you see yourself in two years [five years, ten years, as appropriate]? Describe the person you hope to be then. How would you compare the person you hope to be and the person you see yourself as now?

15. What helps you to manage _____? What problems might you encounter? Tell me the sources of these problems.

16. Who has been the most helpful to you during this time? How has he/she been helpful?

Ending Questions

1. What do you think are the most important ways to _____? How did you discover [or create] them? How has your experience before _____ affected how you handled _____?

2. Tell me about how your views [and/or actions depending on topic and preceding responses] may have changed since you have _____?

3. How have you grown as a person since _____? Tell me about your strengths that you discovered or developed through _____. [If appropriate] What do you most value about yourself now? What do others most value in you?

4. After having these experiences, what advice would you give to someone who has just discovered that he or she _____?

5. Is there anything that you might not have thought about before that occurred to you during this interview?

6. Is there anything you would like to ask me?

SOURCE: Charmaz, K. (2002: 677–78). Qualitative interviewing and grounded theory analysis. In J. F. Gubrium and J. A. Holstein (Eds.), *Handbook of Interview Research* (pp. 675–94). Thousand Oaks, CA: Sage. Copyright © 2002 Sage Publications.

GT has grown and changed over the years, but in one form or another, it is the most widely used method across the social sciences for collecting and analyzing interview data about how people experience the mundane and the exotic, the boring and the enchanting moments of life.

Some recent examples: how economic and cultural constraints delay marriage for professional women, in Shanghai, China (To 2013); how journalists report on weather extremes and climate change in the American Southwest (Gustafson 2012); how women in a small town act out class differences while having coffee (Yodanis 2006); how the wives of Japanese students and businessmen in the United States cope during their temporary separation from Japanese culture (Toyokawa 2006). (**Further Reading**: grounded theory)

Changes in Grounded Theory Since 1967

Today, there are several competing schools of grounded theory. Glaser and A. Strauss took different paths, developing competing schools of GT. Glaser has remained more committed to the mostly inductivist approach (1992, 2002); Strauss (first in 1987 on his own and then with Julie Corbin in 1990, 1998, and 2008 [Corbin and Strauss 2008]) allowed for more use of deduction. Strauss and Corbin (1998:48–52) advocate reading the literature on a topic as part of GT; Glaser (1998) warns against it. Strauss and Corbin are for more use of deduction; Glaser is for less.

For Glaser (1992), the original two layers of coding in the GT method—fragmenting the text into concepts and then putting it back together in larger theoretical categories—is enough. Strauss and Corbin (1998) have added a third layer they call axial coding, in which the researcher looks to discover the relationships among concepts.

For Glaser (and for us, by the way), the traditional GT method is applicable to any kind of social research and any kind of data (Glaser 1978, 2001, 2002). For others, the traditional GT method is too objectivist. In an influential series of books and articles, Kathy Charmaz has developed an alternative GT method, called constructivist grounded theory (Charmaz 1995a, 2000, 2002, 2006). Traditional objectivist GT, says Charmaz, "accepts the positivistic assumption of an external world that can be described, analyzed, explained, and predicted: truth, but with a small t. That is, objectivist GT is modifiable as conditions change" (2000:524). For constructivists, by contrast, informants and researchers create data together, interactively, during an interview. Charmaz's version of GT is firmly in the tradition of interpretive social science, with an emphasis on meaning.

In the original formulation of GT, one of its key elements was **theoretical sampling**—deciding on what cases to study based on the content of the developing theory (Glaser 1978:36; Glaser and Strauss 1967:45–77; Strauss and Corbin 1998:143–61), so that sampling, coding, and theory building all develop together.

Theoretical sampling remains central to the method, even for interpretivists like Charmaz (2000:519). A review of hundreds of studies, however, in which researchers claim to be doing GT, shows that this key component of the method is not widely followed. Rather, many studies today that fly under the banner of grounded theory are based on the analysis of already collected interview texts. In these studies, scholars may develop a theory on half their data and then check it on the other half. This adds an element of verification to the method as well.

Should all these variations be called grounded theory? That depends on who you ask, but we don't see any harm in doing so. For us, what's important is that useful theories are generated and tested. (For a review of this issue, see Cutliffe 2005 and Greckhamer and Koro-Ljungberg 2005.)

Whichever epistemological position you favor, objectivist or constructivist, once you have data, all GT analysis involves the same basic steps: (1) coding text and theorizing as you go; (2) memoing and theorizing as you go; and (3) integrating, refining, and writing up theories. Notice that theorizing is in all three steps. The discovery of grounded theory is a supremely iterative process. You keep building and testing theory all the way through to the end of a project. We treat the three key steps in turn.

1. Coding and Theorizing

In GT research, the search for theory begins with the very first line of the very first interview you code. How to get started? Begin with a small chunk of text and code *line by line*. Identify potentially useful concepts. Sandelowski's (1995a:373) advice on this is on the money for us: Mark key phrases, she says, "because they make some as yet inchoate sense."

Name the concepts. Move on to another chunk and do this again. And again. And again. This is what Strauss and Corbin (1998:101–21) call **open coding** and Charmaz (2002) calls **initial coding**. Whatever you decide to call it, this is a process of **fragmenting data** into conceptual components. (See Chapter 5 for more on the mechanics of finding and coding themes.)

The next step involves a lot more theorizing, but now it's in service to **defragmenting the text**. As you code, pull examples of all concepts together and think about how each concept might be related to larger, more inclusive concepts—called **categories** in the language of GT—that you can look for in texts. This involves the **constant comparative method** (Glaser and Strauss 1967:101–115; Strauss and Corbin 1998:78–85, 93–99), and it goes on throughout the GT process, right up through the development of complete theories.

Coding for categories is variously called **focused coding** (Charmaz 2002:686) or **theoretical coding** or **axial coding** (Strauss and Corbin 1998:123–42).

Milica Markovic (2006) used this method in her study of 30 Australian women—17 immigrants and 13 native born—who had been diagnosed with some form of gynecological cancer (ovarian, cervical, endometrial, uterine). Markovic's goal was to understand why many women in Australia delay getting medical help for obvious symptoms of these cancers. Table 10.1 shows part of her first interview, with Tipani, a 59-year-old immigrant.

Notice the italics in Markovic's transcript (the right-hand column of Table 10.1). Markovic read the text a line at a time, tagging pieces with italics and creating codes—that is, names—for the italicized pieces whenever she could. You can do this with a word processor (italics, underlining, highlighting, various type fonts), or even by hand, using different colored highlighter pens, though most researchers today would use a text management program.

The important thing is to get your impressions about concepts down and to give the concepts descriptive names. This gives you a map of what to look for in subsequent interviews. For example, Tipani had at first seen her symptoms as something positive—as "bad blood coming out." Markovic interpreted this as Tipani's applying familiar ideas (menstruation and menopause) to an unfamiliar situation and, more generally, as an example of "women's lay understanding of health problems" (see Box 10.1).

Figure 10.2 Charmaz's Memo About the Concept of Suffering as a Moral Status

Suffering is a profoundly moral status as well as a physical experience. Stories of suffering reflect and redefine that moral status. With suffering comes moral rights and entitlements as well as moral definitions—when suffering is deemed legitimate. Thus the person can make certain moral claims *and* have certain moral judgments conferred upon him or her.

Deserving

Dependent

In Need

Suffering can bring a person an elevated moral status. Here, suffering takes on a sacred status. This is a person who has been in sacred places, who has seen known what ordinary people have not. Their stories are greeted with awe and wonder. The self also has elevated status. . . .

Although suffering may first confer an elevated moral status, views change. The moral claims from suffering typically narrow in scope and power. The circles of significance shrink. Stories of self within these moral claims may entrance and entertain for a time—unless someone has considerable influence and power. The circles narrow to most significant others.

The moral claims of suffering may only supersede those of the healthy and whole in crisis and its immediate aftermath. Otherwise, the person is less. WORTH LESS. Two words—now separate—may change as illness and aging take their toll. They may end up as "worthless." Christine's statement reflects her struggles at work to maintain her value and voice.

And so I went back to work on March 1st, even though I wasn't supposed to. And then when I got there, they had a long meeting and they said could no longer rest during the day. The only time I rested was at lunchtime, which was my time, we were closed. And she said, my supervisor, said I couldn't do that any more and I said, "It's my time, you can't tell me I can't lay down." And they said, "Well you're not laying down on the couch that's in there, it bothers the rest of the staff." So I went around and I talked to the rest of the staff, and they all said, "No, we didn't say that, it was never brought up." So I went back and I said, "You know, I was just was talking to the rest of the staff, and it seems that nobody has a problem with it but you," and I said, "You aren't even here at lunchtime." And they still put it down that I couldn't do that any longer. And then a couple of the other staff started laying down at lunchtime, and I said, you know, "This isn't fair. She doesn't even have a disability and she's laying down," so I just started doing it.

Christine makes moral claims, not only befitting those of suffering, but of PERSONHOOD. She is a person who has a right to be heard, a right to just and fair treatment in both the medical arena and the workplace.

SOURCE: Charmaz, K. (2011). Qualitative interviewing and grounded theory analysis. In J. F. Gubrium and J. A. Holstein (Eds.), *Handbook of Interview Research* (pp. 675–94). Thousand Oaks, CA: Sage. Copyright © 2011 Sage Publications.

3. Building and Refining Theories

As coding categories emerge, the next step is to link them together in theoretical models around a central category that holds everything together (Glaser and Strauss 1967:40; Strauss and Corbin 1998:146–48).

Here again, the constant comparative method comes into play, along with **negative case analysis**—looking for cases that do not confirm your model (Lincoln and Guba 1985:309–13). The procedure is simple and clear: You generate a model about how whatever you're studying works, right from the first interview, and you see if the model holds up as you analyze more interviews.

This is how Markovic proceeded, as she analyzed those 30 interviews with women in Australia who had been diagnosed with some form of gynecological cancer. Here is her model, based entirely on the interview with Tipani (shown in Table 10.1):

> In the presence of an unusual symptom, women (more specifically, immigrant women) seek advice from their peers. If they (or those whom they ask for advice) interpret their symptoms in light of their previous life experiences and normalize the severity of the symptoms, women wait until their next regular appointment for an ongoing health problem before reporting their cancer symptoms to a health professional. On the other hand, if women experience disruptions to their everyday life (that is, symptoms that cannot be normalized easily), this influences their decision to report the symptoms to a health professional earlier. (Markovic 2006:418)

Markovic's second informant, Betty, produced some new themes, but overall, Betty's story confirmed the preliminary hypothesis. Betty's symptoms were not the same as Tipani's, but like Tipani, Betty found reasons to normalize her symptoms and the result was the same: a delay in diagnosis despite the fact that the symptoms were disruptive of daily life.

Markovic's third informant, Tulip, reported that she went to see a physician at the first signs that something was wrong. According to Tulip, her first physician referred her to another, the second one referred her to a third, and the third referred her to a hospital for tests. The tests confirmed that Tulip had ovarian cancer. Markovic modified her hypothesis to accommodate this otherwise negative case.

> Unusual symptoms that cannot be interpreted as normal, given the woman's individual life circumstances, influence her prompt seeking of advice from a health professional. A health professional, however, may provide referral for diagnostic tests and to a specialist other than a gynecologist, which can lead to diagnostic delays. (Markovic 2006:420)

Markovic's next informant, Barbara, reported being sent for several ultrasounds that came back negative. The doctor told her she had an enlarged liver from "all that alcohol you drink." Barbara shot back:

> Listen here, if the pubs had to depend on me buying alcohol, they'd go broke. . . . I said to him, *Aren't you getting sick and tired of sending me for all these ultrasounds* and everything?" So he said, "Look, I'll refer you to [a woman's hospital] to see what they say." (Markovic 2006:420)

With each new interview she coded, Markovic compared all reported events to one another—the constant comparative method again—and found that many women had experienced incorrect diagnoses and having their concerns dismissed by clinicians. She modified her hypothesis again, "to accommodate the reported lack of responsiveness of health providers to women's distress and women's perception that the onus was being placed on them to be persistent in seeking professional health advice" (Markovic 2006:421).

In the end, 19 of the 30 women whom Markovic interviewed said they had experienced delays in diagnosis. This became the **core category** for analysis. Among the 19 who experienced delays, 14 *had not* normalized their symptoms and *had* told their doctors that the symptoms were disruptive. Seven of those 14 reported having had their symptoms initially dismissed by physicians, and six of the seven were immigrants.

Figure 10.3 shows Markovic's final grounded theory, or model, to account for all 30 of her cases.

♦ A GT PROJECT: SCHLAU'S STUDY OF ADJUSTMENT TO BECOMING DEAF AS AN ADULT

Let's go through one more GT project to illustrate the pieces. Jane Schlau (2004) used GT in her doctoral research on the adjustment to acquired deafness—that is, adjustment to deafness among people who, like her, lost their hearing after learning to communicate with full hearing. She interviewed 24 people by email (the perfect medium for interviewing the deaf) about their experiences and generated 216 pages of material. Schlau did not use theoretical sampling. This was her complete corpus.

Schlau coded line by line and, as is typical at the initial stage of GT, she generated a lot of codes—128 of them—shown in Table 10.3.

Next, Schlau compared and contrasted all these initial codes across all her respondents, looking for similarities and differences and reducing the number of codes. She combined codes like ambivalence, denial, and depression into a category

Figure 10.3 Markovic's Grounded Theory of Delays in Diagnosing Women's Cancer in Australia

1. If women can normalize their symptoms by placing the symptoms in the context of their life cycle or as normal signs of female physiology, they are likely to delay seeking advice from a professional, causing a delay in proper diagnosis. The likelihood of this happening in these cases is low: five out of thirty women (17%) fall in this category.

2. These women eventually visit a health professional when the symptoms become more severe. This suggests that public education about the signs of gynecological cancer is an appropriate intervention for this part of the problem.

3. Among the twenty-five women who visited doctors soon after symptoms appeared, fourteen reported that their physicians either dismissed their concerns (i.e., normalized the symptoms) or referred them to inappropriate diagnostic tests and specialists. These tests, which did not suggest any underlying pathology, caused further delays in proper diagnosis by the clinicians, according to these women.

4. Most women reported that they experienced some delay in accessing the public health care system (they were put on waiting lists), but most women would not have been on the list for longer than a couple of weeks or so.

5. The report of a prompt diagnosis (eleven of thirty cases) was accompanied by any or some combination of the following: reports of regular screening and a Pap test (which detected cervical cancer); symptoms incongruent with women's life cycle (lump on the vulva, vaginal bleeding among younger women); accidental finding of gynecological cancer during regular health exams; and diagnostic acumen on the part of clinicians.

SOURCE: Markovic, M. (2006). Analyzing qualitative data: Health care experiences of women with gynecological cancer. *Field Methods, 18,* 413–29.

Table 10.3 Listing of 128 Open Codes From Schlau's Study of the Deaf

Acceptance	Death	Groups	Meeting others	Self
Accommodations	Denial	Guilt	Mental health	Self-acceptance
ADA	Dependence	"Hearies"	Mental illness	Self-concept
Adaptation/change	Depression	Hearing again	Money	Sign
Adjustment	Disability	Hearing aids	Music	Sleep
Advocacy	Disclosure	Hearing dogs	Notice	Social
Ambivalence	Discovery	Helping others	Other disabilities	Speechreading

(Continued)

Table 10.3 (Continued)

Asking for help	Doing for others	Holidays	Others	Stigma
Attitude	Dreams	Humor	Phone	Stress
Avoidance	Driving	Identity	Pity	Substitutes
Awareness	Drugs	Impact on life	Positives	Suicide
Before hearing loss	Educating others	Inclusion	Preconceived attitudes	Support
Bias/choice	Education	Interventions	Pretending	Surrender
Bluffing	Effects on others	Intimacy	Process	Talk to others
Can't do	Emotions	Isolation	Psychology	Talking about it
Career	Employment	Knowing others	Reading/research	Technology
Changes	Escape	Knowledge	Reality	Time
Choice	Exclusion	Kübler-Ross	Realization	Tolerance
CI	Existentialism	Learning	Reflection	Travel
Communication	Expectations	Life	Regrets	Treatment
Communication needs/assertiveness	Family	Limits	Religion	Trust
Confirmation	Fatigue	Lip-reading	Replacements	Vocational rehabilitation
Control	Final comments	Loss	Resentment	Voice
Conversations	Friends	Lost words	Responsibility	Wanting to hear again
Courage	Gave-up	Marriage	Risk	
Deaf	Grief	Medical	Safety	

SOURCE: Schlau (2004:71).

she called emotional reactions. She combined bluffing, lip reading, and several other open codes into one she called communication. She reduced the 128 codes to 44, shown in Table 10.4, and then reduced all of those codes to just seven major codes: In the Beginning, Reactions/Stigma, Symptoms, Talking about it, Defining Moments, Coming to terms/New reality, and Learning (Schlau 2004:73–74).

Table 10.4 Forty-Four Open Codes in the Second Stage of Schalu's Coding

Acceptance	Driving	Intimacy	Self/identity
Adjustment	Education	Isolation	Sign Language
Advocacy	Effect on/from others stigma	K-R/death	Social
Avoidance/escape	Emotions	Medical	Stress
Can't do/limits	Family	Music	Substitutes
Career/employment	Fatigue	Phone	Psychiatric
Changes/ adjustment/dealing	Final Comments	Positives	Talks about deafness to family/others/disclosure
CI	Finances	Reading/research	Technology
Communication	Hearing aids	Reality	Travel
Control vs. uncontrollable	Impact on life/loss	Reflection	Vocational rehab
Dependence	Interventions/ support/LDAs	Religion	Voice

SOURCE: Schlau (2004:161–162).

Schlau saw these seven codes as parts of a core theme, adjusting to acquired deafness. When she reached this point in her analysis, Schlau went back over the texts and did **selective coding** to learn in depth as much as her data could tell her about how each of the 24 participants in her research had adjusted to acquired deafness.

Everyone adjusted, but not everyone adjusted in the same way. All 24 of Schlau's informants reported similar experiences at the onset of hearing loss. That's the in-the-beginning code, and all of them reported defining moments (like the first time they realized that they couldn't talk on the phone).

Shlau's grounded theory of adjustment to acquired deafness is shown in Figure 10.4.

VISUALIZING GROUNDED THEORIES ♦

Many grounded theorists find that visualizing the emerging theory with one or more of the modeling formats described in Chapter 8 helps them integrate their models of how things work.

Figure 10.4 Schlau's Grounded Theory of Adjustment to Acquired Deafness

The discovered grounded theory illustrates how the process of becoming deafened begins the same way for everyone. All participants, once aware of hearing loss, sought medical attention. When hearing loss was confirmed, they had strong emotional reactions. These emotional reactions were also noted in my pilot study and in Zieziula and Meadows (1992). As participants went through medical procedures and experienced countless emotions, they also obtained hearing aids, in an effort to mitigate the effects of hearing loss.

Following these reactions, the process participants went through varied based upon the individual. Factors such as personality, the influences of parents and upbringing, are just a couple of the variables that effected individual adjustment. However, all participants experienced the physicality of deafness—the symptoms of being deaf. All participants discussed changes in their lives, based upon the effects of deafness on communication. The reciprocity of communication, as stated by Goffman (1959, 1967) structures our everyday interactions. When this basic tenet of communication breaks down, due to deafness and the resultant inability to receive communication, reality is changed. As reality changed for the participants, as they experienced the effects and symptoms of deafness, they all had some defining moment, where the realization of the need for change "hit." The loss of the ability to use or participate in an activity that once took no thought—such as watching television or using the phone—was a reality check for all participants. This brought the participants to the point of coming to terms with being deafened and forming a new reality.

Here is where differences among participants were clearly noticeable. Those who were "Accepted" all had deaf friends. They all had some family support; all signed to some degree; all found positives in deafness; all were willing to disclose their deafness and all reflected and learned to be deaf. Those who were "Struggling" all collected SSDI. They all had little or no family support; they did not sign; they did not have deaf friends; they either told selected people they were deaf or they tried to hide their deafness. Ultimately, they did not experience double-loop learning and avoided internalizing a change in their reality.

Those who were "Resigned" to deafness also generally had little family support. They were not interested in sign language; generally found nothing positive about their deafness; told only select people they were deaf and had only hearing friends or were isolated. They also did not experience double-loop learning through reflection, but most did experience some reflection and were often aware of changes they could make but had not internalized these changes.

SOURCE: Schlau (2004:161–162).

Margaret Kearney and her colleagues (1995) interviewed 60 women who reported using crack cocaine an average of at least once weekly during pregnancy. The semi-structured interviews lasted from one to three hours and covered childhood, relationships, life context, previous pregnancies, and actions taken in the current pregnancy related to drug use, prenatal care, and self-care.

Kearney et al. coded and analyzed the transcripts as they went. As new topics emerged, investigators asked about the topics in subsequent interviews. In this way, they linked data collection and data analysis in one continuous effort. As they identified categories, they looked to see how categories were related to other things and to one another. They recorded their ideas and impressions about these interactions in the forms of memos, and they used the relationships they discovered to form a preliminary model.

With each subsequent transcript, they looked for negative cases and pieces of data that challenged their emerging model and adjusted it to include the full range of variation that they found in the transcripts.

By the end of their analysis, Kearney et al. (1995) identified five major categories that they called value, hope, risk, harm reduction, and stigma management. Women valued their pregnancy and their baby-to-be in relation to their own life priorities (value); women expressed varying degrees of hope that their pregnancies would end well and that they could be good mothers (hope); and they were aware that cocaine use posed risks to their fetus but they perceived that risk differently (risk). Women tried in various ways to minimize the risk to the fetus (harm reduction) and they used various stratagems to reduce social rejection and derision (stigma management).

By the time they had coded 20 interviews, Kearney et al. realized that the categories harm reduction and stigma management were components of a more fundamental category that they labeled "evading harm" and that the categories value, hope, and risk were components of a more fundamental category that they labeled "facing the situation."

After about 30 interviews had been coded, they identified and labeled an overarching psychological process they called "salvaging self" that incorporated all five of the major categories. This was the core category in their theory. By the time they'd done 40 interviews, Kearney et al. (1995) felt they had reached theoretical saturation—they were not discovering new categories or relations among categories. Just to make sure, they conducted another 20 interviews and confirmed the theoretical saturation.

Figure 10.5 shows the graphic model that Kearney et al. produced to represent their understanding of how the process worked. Notice how each of the substantive themes in their model is succinctly defined by a quote from a respondent. (**Further Reading**: visualizing models and theories)

Verifying the Model

Once the theory was built, Kearney et al. took the next step and verified it in two ways—emically and etically. (See Box 6.4 for the definition of emic and etic themes.) First, Kearney et al. did what Lincoln and Guba (1985:314–16) call **member checks**. They took their model back to stakeholders in their study—members of the project staff, health and social service professionals who were familiar with the population, and a group of 10 pregnant drug users who were not among those interviewed for the study—and asked if the model rang true.

Figure 10.5 The Development of Kearney's Core Category in a Grounded Theory of Cocaine Use Among Pregnant Women

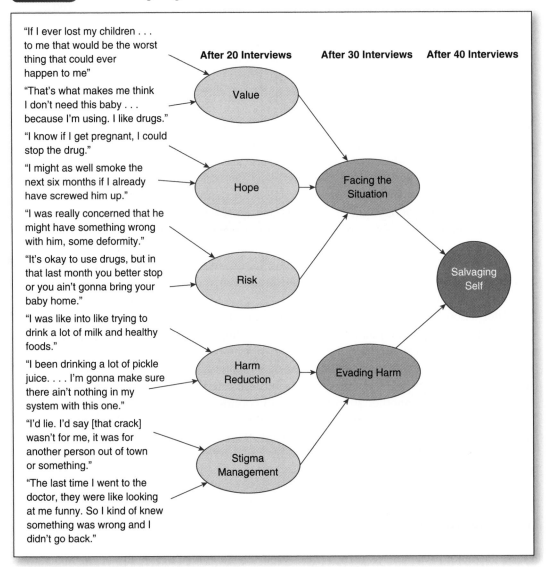

SOURCE: Adapted from Kearney, M. et al. 1995:210. Salvaging self: A grounded theory of pregnancy on crack cocaine. *Nursing Research* 44(4) July/August:208–13.

It did. Later, Kearney did an etic verification—checking her model against another set of data—by studying women who were trying to recover from drug and alcohol addiction but weren't pregnant. Those women reported that they, too, were trying everything they could to salvage some sense of self (Kearney, personal communication; see also Kearney 1996, 1998).

Key Concepts in This Chapter

induction
deduction
theoretical saturation
exploratory phase
confirmatory stage
social processes
lived experiences
grounded theory
deference effect
life story interview

life world interview
theoretical sampling
open coding
initial coding
fragmenting data
defragmenting the text
categories
constant comparative
   method
focused coding

theoretical coding
   or axial coding
constant
   comparisons
intercoder reliability
memoing
negative case analysis
core category
selective coding
member checks

Summary

- The two great epistemological approaches for all research are induction and deduction. Inductive research involves the search for pattern from observation and the development of explanations—theories—for those patterns through a series of hypotheses. Deductive research starts with theories (which are derived from common sense, from observation, or from the literature), derives hypotheses from them, and moves on to observations—which either confirm or disconfirm the hypotheses.

  o Real research is never purely inductive or purely deductive, but for some kinds of research problems, a mostly inductive or a mostly deductive approach is called for. Inductive research is required in the exploratory phase of *any* research project, whether the data are words or numbers. Deductive research is required in the confirmatory stage of any research project—again, irrespective of whether the data are qualitative or quantitative.

  o In general, the less we know about a research problem, the more important it is to take an inductive approach—to suspend our preconceived ideas as much as we can and let observation be our guide. As we learn more and more about a research problem, the more important it becomes to take a deductive approach.

- Grounded theory was an inductive approach developed by two sociologists, Barney Glaser and Anselm Strauss, in a seminal book titled *The Discovery of Grounded Theory: Strategies for Qualitative Research* (1967).

  o As the title implies, the aim is to discover theories—causal explanations—grounded in empirical data, about how people experience life. Some recent examples: how professional women in Shanghai, China, choose marriage partners (To 2013); how journalists report on weather extremes and climate change in the

American Southwest (Gustafson 2012); how women in a small town act out class differences while having coffee (Yodanis 2006).

- Today, there are several competing schools of grounded theory. Glaser and A. Strauss took different paths, developing competing schools of GT. Glaser has remained more committed to the mostly inductivist approach (1992, 2002); Strauss (first in 1987 on his own and then with Julie Corbin in 1990, 1998, and 2008) allowed for more use of deduction. Kathy Charmaz developed an alternative GT method, called constructivist grounded theory (Charmaz 1995a, 2000, 2002, 2006). For constructivists, informants and researchers create data together, interactively, during an interview.

  o The grounded theory of Glaser, Strauss, and Corbin is more in the tradition of positivist social science. Charmaz's version of GT is in the tradition of interpretive social science with an emphasis on meaning.

- Whichever epistemological position you favor, objectivist or constructivist, once you have data, all GT analysis involves the same basic steps: (1) coding text and theorizing as you go; (2) memoing and theorizing as you go; and (3) integrating, refining, and writing up theories. Theorizing is in all three steps.

  o GT begins by coding a small chunk of text line by line, identifying and naming useful concepts, and then moving on to another chunk. The idea behind this first level of coding is to fragment the text into conceptual components. The next step involves defragmenting the text, pulling examples of all concepts together and thinking about how each concept might be related to larger, more inclusive concepts, called categories in the language of GT.

  o Coding for categories (variously called focused coding or theoretical coding or axial coding) is based on the method of constant comparison—thinking about how you might have a used a concept earlier in the text, considering whether you need a new theme or concept, and recoding earlier segments to reflect your developing understanding (also see Chapter 5).

  o Memos are field notes about codes and contain our running commentary as we read through texts. They are the foundation for theory. As coding categories they can be linked together in theoretical models around a central category that holds everything together (Glaser and Strauss 1967:40; Strauss and Corbin 1998:146–48).

  o Here again, the constant comparative method comes into play, along with negative case analysis—looking for cases that do not confirm your model (Lincoln and Guba 1985:309–13). The procedure is simple and clear: You generate a model about how whatever you're studying works—right from the first interview—and you see if the model holds up as you analyze more interviews.

- Many grounded theorists find that visualizing their theory with one or more of the modeling formats described in Chapter 8 helps them integrate their models of how things work. They may also conduct member checks—taking their model back to stakeholders in their study and asking if the model rings true.

Exercises

1. Life history interviews and person-centered interviews are harder to do than they might seem. Most people respond to a request for a life history interview by listing some key dates and events—when they were born, where they went to school (high school, college), when they got married, and perhaps a few jobs they'd held over the years. Getting people to open up and really talk, in depth, with real detail, about episodes in their lives takes practice and patience. Do a life history interview with someone you *don't know well.*

2. Do an interview to collect data on someone's lived experience. Don't use the same informant you interviewed for the life history exercise. Some candidates for interesting interviews: becoming a [fill in anything here—nurse, university administrator, Little League coach, migrating from a different country, adjusting to life in the country they live in now]; coping with [fill in anything here—widowhood, a serious illness, losing a job]; learning how to [fill in anything here—repair a motorcycle engine, draw faces accurately, do some martial art at the level of a black belt, play a musical instrument at a professional level, become fluent in a new language as an adult].

3. After doing one lived-experience interview, code it for themes. Teach the codes you developed to a friend and ask the friend to code your interview. Did you code the same pieces of the interview with the same codes? Discuss and resolve the discrepancies in your coding.

4. Write a memo for each theme you identify in Exercise 3. The memos should make explicit any patterns you think you see emerging in the data. Those patterns will also make you aware of the kind of information you would need to get in the next interview, if you were doing theoretical sampling for a grounded theory project.

Further Reading

Induction and deduction in social science. Dewey (1910), Hobhouse (1891), Kaplan (1964), Gordon (1991).

Grounded theory. In addition to the key volumes on GT already mentioned in the text, see Birks and Mills (2011), Bryant and Charmaz (2007), Charmaz (2014), Dey (1999),

But the big difference between grounded theory and content analysis is their epistemological pedigree: In grounded theory, the idea is to let understanding emerge from the close study of texts. This comes from the great tradition of inductive science. Content analysis involves the tagging of a set of texts or other artifacts (photos, magazine ads, TV commercials, buildings) with codes that are derived from theory or from prior knowledge and then analyzing the distribution of the codes—again, usually statistically. This comes from the great tradition of deductive science.

There is no point in talking about which of these traditions is better. They're both terrific if you use them to answer appropriate questions. (For more on induction and deduction, see the beginning of Chapter 10 and Further Reading in Chapter 10.)

♦ HISTORY OF CONTENT ANALYSIS

Content analysis has very deep roots. Wilcox (1900) studied the content for June and September 1898, and September 1899, of 147 newspapers in the 21 most populous cities of the United States. He came up with 18 categories of content—including war news (the Spanish American War was big news in 1898), foreign news, business news, sporting news, society news, news of crime and vice, editorials, want ads, retail ads, and so on—and estimated the number of column inches devoted to each category in each paper.

At the time, newspapers were being criticized for focusing too much on sensational stories, particularly about crime and vice (the cliché in journalism that "If it bleeds, it leads" was as true then as it is now). Wilcox found that the worst offender devoted 19% of its space to crime and vice, while, on average, just 3% of the total space in American newspapers in 1898 was devoted to crime and vice (1900:67, 70). Still, as Krippendorff notes (2004a:5), Wilcox criticized the greed that drove some publishers to focus on sensational news.

Wilcox's methods were crude. He doesn't tell us how he came up with the 18 categories, and he made all the decisions about coding the papers himself. But for the time, Wilcox's study was front-edge work. Since then, of course, there have been great advances in sampling and measurement and content analysis has become an important method of investigation across the social sciences.

The systematic application of scientific methods for analyzing text got a real boost with the study of political propaganda, particularly in the period before and during World War II. (See Krippendorff [2013:14–19] and Neuendorf [2002:23–45] for excellent reviews.) (See Box 11.1.)

By 1955, content analysis had become an established method in political science, communications, and other fields. That year, the Social Science Research Council's Committee on Linguistics and Psychology sponsored a conference on content analysis, bringing together experts from across the social sciences. Their contributions appear in a landmark volume edited by de Sola Pool (1959). Since then, extensive reviews have appeared every decade or so. (**Further Reading**: reviews of content analysis)

Box 11.1

How Evidence From Content Analysis Became Admissible in Court

When the Nazis came to power in the 1930s, the U.S. Federal Communications Commission began monitoring short-wave radio broadcasts from Germany. Analysts established 14 major propaganda themes in the Nazi media. In 1942, the U.S. Department of Justice sued William Dudley Pelley for sedition, claiming that Pelley was publishing pro-Nazi propaganda in the United States while the United States was at war with Germany.

In court, the Department of Justice relied on work by independent coders who had been asked to classify 1,240 items in Pelley's publications as belonging or not belonging to one of those 14 Nazi propaganda themes. Harold Lasswell, a political scientist and expert on propaganda analysis, testified that 1,195 of the items (96.4%) "were consistent with and suggested copying from the German propaganda theme" (*United States v. Pelley* 1942). Pelley was convicted, the conviction was upheld by the U.S. Circuit Court of Appeals, and the admissibility in court of evidence based on this simple method of content analysis was established (Goldsen 1947; Lasswell 1949:49).

DOING CONTENT ANALYSIS ♦

There are seven big steps in content analysis—and a lot of little ones:

1. Formulate a research question or a hypothesis, based on existing theory or on prior research.

2. Select a set of texts to test the question or hypothesis.

3. Create a set of codes (variables, themes) in the research question or hypothesis.

4. Pretest the variables on a few of the selected texts. Fix any problems that turn up with regard to the codes and the coding so that the coders become consistent in their coding.

5. Apply the codes to the rest of the texts.

6. Create a **case-by-variable matrix** from the texts and codes.

7. Analyze the matrix using whatever level of analysis is appropriate.

We'll go over these, in turn, using two studies—one by George Cunningham and colleagues (2004) and one by Elizabeth Hirschman (1987). The one by Cunningham et al. tests research questions; the one by Hirschman tests formal hypotheses.

Cunningham's Study of Media Bias

Interest in media bias has never waned since Wilcox's day. Cunningham et al. (2004) studied whether the coverage of women athletes in the *NCAA News* reflected women's place in college athletics in general. Following the seven steps outlined above, here's how they did the research:

1. Formulate a research question or a hypothesis, based on existing theory or on prior research. In 1972, a law was passed in the United States to ensure that colleges and universities made all academic and sports programs available equally to men and women. Since then, more and more women have been participating in college sports, but coverage of women's sports in the media has not kept pace. Many studies have documented the fact that proportionately more coverage is given to men's sports in newspapers, magazines, radio, and television.

Those media are for-profit businesses and may be responding to what they think their customers want. But Schifflett and Revelle (1994) found that from 1988 to 1991, even the *NCAA News*—which is distributed to members of the National Collegiate Athletic Association—was biased against coverage of women's athletics.

Cunningham et al. (2004) set out to test whether things had changed in the *NCAA News* in the decade after Shifflett and Revell did their study. Cunningham et al. didn't have any hypotheses, but they did have two solid research questions:

Research question 1. Did the *NCAA News* provide equitable coverage for men's and women's athletics in 1999–2001?

Research question 2. Did the coverage of women's athletics in the *NCAA News* improve since Shifflett and Revelle's (1994) study? (See Box 11.2.)

Box 11.2

About Research Questions and Hypotheses

Hypotheses are predictions about the relationship between two or more variables. For example, we might predict that income and education are related. And we might go further and specify the direction of the relation: The more education, the higher the income.

Research questions are just that—questions about things a researcher wants to know. An example:

How do Mexican Americans and Anglo Americans in Dallas, Texas, react to a diagnosis of Type 2 diabetes?

Do the alcohol consumption practices of students at public and private universities differ? If so, how do they differ?

Research questions are most appropriate when we're at the exploratory stage of any research project. When we know more about a topic—like alcohol consumption practices at public and private universities or how Mexican Americans and Anglo Americans in Dallas, Texas, react to a diagnosis of Type 2 diabetes—it's time to be brave and venture some guesses about how variables are actually related.

Hypotheses are derived from prior observation—your own or that of others (in other words, the literature)—and from theory. For example, Wu-Tso et al. (1995) found that young Asian Americans consume more foods higher in fat and cholesterol and lower in fiber than do older Asians. This led Nguyen et al. (2015) to hypothesize that: "Among Asian Americans, acculturation measured as (a) years of United States residency and (b) percentage of life living in the United States is positively correlated with being obese."

Much research has shown that, for men and women professionals alike, gaps in employment are related to lower income (Reitman and Schneer 2005) and other researchers have found that parenthood has a bigger impact on professional women's careers than on men's careers (Abele and Spurk 2011). All this provided the basis for Evers and Sieverding (2014) to predict that the number of children that women physicians have negatively influences their career success.

Relative deprivation theory is based on the idea that we define our sense of being deprived in relation to the deprivation of others. From that theory, we might hypothesize that assistant professors of sociology won't feel as bad about assistant professors of finance getting double their salary as they would if assistant professors of, say, political science or anthropology were paid a lot more.

Many theories in social science generate interesting hypotheses. Here are just a few: stages of change theory, social learning theory, the self-fulfilling prophesy, cognitive dissonance theory, the fallacy of eyewitness testimony, the theory of relative deprivation, the availability heuristic, the Sapir-Whorf hypothesis, diffusion of innovations theory, priming theory, theory of reasoned action.

2. Select a set of texts to test the questions or hypotheses. After setting up a research question, the first thing to do is decide on the **units of analysis**—i.e., what segments of text or other qualitative data will be coded and analyzed. Among content analysts, this is known as **unitizing** (Krippendorff 2004a:98; Neuendorf 2002:71–74).

The NCAA News was published twice a month in 1999 and 2001, so the sampling universe was 48 issues. Rather than just selecting a random grab of issues, Cunningham et al. (2004) randomly selected one of the two issues of the *News* published each month during 1999 and 2001. The **sampling universe** here was 48 issues, of which 24 issues (one for each month of 1999 and one for each month of 2001) were selected.

This sampling procedure ensured that whatever patterns Cunningham et al. found in their sample could be generalized with confidence to the rest of the issues for 1999 and 2001. Later, during analysis, they would test whether the patterns they found in 1999 and 2001—like the proportion of space devoted to pictures of male athletes and the proportion devoted to female athletes—were statistically different from one another. If the findings were statistically indistinguishable, then they could generalize their findings with confidence to the three-year period 1999–2001, not just to 1999 *and* 2001.

Next, repeating what Schifflett and Revelle (1994) had done in their earlier study of the *NCAA News*, Cunningham et al. (2004) went through the 24 issues they had selected and marked all the articles that were about athletes, coaches, and teams, rather than about schools, facilities, administrators, and so on. The articles marked for study comprised 5,745 paragraphs and 1,086 photographs to read and code. In the Cunningham et al. study, then, the paragraph and the photo were the units of analysis.

3. Create a set of codes (variables, themes) in the research question or hypothesis. Exactly as Shifflett and Revell had done, Cunningham et al. coded the articles for gender (i.e., whether an article was primarily focused on men, primarily focused on women, focused on both sexes or on neither sex); location (where the article appeared in the issue); length (in square inches); and content. Paragraph content was coded as: (1) factual information related to athletics; (2) factual information not related to athletics; (3) personal information related to athletics; and (4) personal information not related to athletics (Cunningham et al. 2004:863).

The photos were coded for six themes: (1) competing athlete; (2) athlete in competitive context but not competing; (3) head shot of the athlete(s) or coach(es); (4) head shot of a person other than an athlete or coach (i.e., administrator); (5) a group photograph of persons other than players or coaches (e.g., committee members); and (6) other (Cunningham et al. 2004:863).

For location, Cunningham et al. coded articles and photos as appearing on: (1) the front page; (2) the back page; or—for pieces inside the issue—(3) at the top of the page; or (4) somewhere else on the page.

Of the 5,745 paragraphs, 2,342 were about men and 1,723 paragraphs were about women, for a total of 4,065 codable paragraphs. The other paragraphs were about neither sex or about both sexes and were not coded.

4. Pretest the variables on a few of the selected texts. Fix any problems that turn up with regard to the codes and the coding so that the coders become consistent in their coding. For the paragraphs, Cunningham et al. (2004) did **pretests** on three issues of the *NCAA News* that were not part of the main sample. For the photos, they found nearly perfect agreement on the content codes and the length for 50 photos selected from one issue of the *News*.

5. *Apply the codes to the rest of the texts.* Keep checking for coder reliability. Cunningham et al. used **latent coding** in marking the paragraphs. In **manifest coding**, only words and phrases in the text count as indicators of themes. In other words, the meaning is *manifest* in the language itself. Latent coding, in contrast, involves interpretation—reading for meaning, taking context into account, and identifying the presence of constructs or themes (Box 11.3).

Box 11.3

Manifest and Latent Coding

In the early days of content analysis, some researchers insisted on sticking to manifest coding to ensure reliability (see, e.g., Berelson 1952:18), but over the years, with the development of statistical tests for reliability, latent coding has become the norm.

Manifest coding is highly reliable. You only have to train coders, or a computer, to see a list of words and phrases to ensure high reliability. Latent coding, however, gives you the freedom to find themes in texts, even if certain words are not there. This is very important. It is, in fact, why we tell ethnographers to code their field notes every day. You can attend a wedding ceremony, for example, and write five single-spaced pages of notes that night about your observations—and to never use the word "marriage." When you go back to your notes six months later and do a computer search for everything about marriage, your five pages of notes about that wedding won't even pop up.

Cunningham et al. (2004) kept checking their coders' work by reading randomly selected paragraphs out of context. All of this attention paid off: Cohen's kappa, a popular measure of coder reliability (more about how to calculate kappa later), was very high for all their themes. When the coding phase was over, the investigators talked about and resolved any inconsistencies in the coding.

Cunningham et al. found 100% agreement on the coding for 100 photos from two randomly selected issues. At that level of agreement on a large sample of items in a study, it is unnecessary to run a complete interrater reliability check.

6. *Create a case-by-variable matrix from the texts and codes.* There were two data matrices in the Cunningham et al. study—one for paragraphs and one for photos. The matrix for paragraphs would have had 4,065 rows and six columns and would have looked something like Table 11.1.

Column 1 is a **unique identifier**—just a number—between 1 and 4,065. These refer to the 2,342 paragraphs about men and the 1,723 paragraphs about women. Column 2 would have the year 1999 or 2001, but might just as well have a 1 or a 2 to identify which year each paragraph came from. With just two genders to mark, column 3 will have a 1 or 2, but can just as well be coded with a 1 or a 0. There are four possible locations (front page, back page, etc.), so column 4 will have a number from 1 to 4. Length, in column 5, will contain a real number, like 3.4 or 4.1, indicating the number of square inches taken up by paragraph. Finally, because the researchers were coding for four possible content themes, column 6 will contain a number from 1 to 4.

Cunningham et al. (2004) first tested whether the amount of news coverage for women's teams, as measured by the percentage of paragraphs devoted to those teams, was different for the two years. In 1999, women's teams received 41% of all coverage compared to 44% in 2001. This meant that Cunningham et al. could combine the data from the two years for the rest of their analyses.

7. *Analyze the matrix using whatever level of analysis is appropriate.* Recall the first research question: Did the *NCAA News* provide equitable coverage for men's and women's athletics in 1999–2001? Well, it depends on what you count and how you count it. Women comprised 42% of all college athletes in those years and received 42.4% of the coverage in the *NCAA News* (and 39.7% of the photo coverage). Also, the average length of paragraphs was identical for men and women (2.25 square inches) and paragraphs about women and women's teams were equally likely to contain information

Table 11.1 Schematic for the Data Matrix of the Study by Cunningham et al. (2004)

Paragraph	Year	Gender	Location	Length	Content
1					
2					
3					
4					
5					
•					
•					
•					
•					
•					
4065					

about athletics (rather than personal information) as were paragraphs about men and men's teams. On these measures, women received coverage equal to that for men.

Paragraphs about women and women's teams, though, were more likely to appear in prominent spots (front or back page or top of a middle page) than were paragraphs about men and men's teams. On that measure, women did better than the men. On the other hand, 51% of all intercollegiate athletic teams in those years were women, so getting 42.4% of the coverage was somewhat less than that for men.

What about the second research question: Did the coverage of women's athletics in the *NCAA News* improve since the Shifflett and Revelle (1994) study? In 1990–91, women were 33% of all student athletes, and women's teams were 46% of intercollegiate competition. Shifflett and Revelle found that women got 26.5% of the coverage in the *NCAA News*. The data from the Cunningham et al. (2004) study show the *NCAA News* had erased all of the deficit in coverage of individual women athletes by 1999–2001 and had cut the deficit of women's team coverage from 19.5% (the difference between 46% and 26.5%) to 8.6% (the difference between 51% and 42.4%). (**Further Reading**: content analysis of media)

Hirschman's Study of People as Products

1. Formulate a research question or hypothesis, based on existing theory or on prior research. Drawing on social exchange theory and on studies of human mate selection, Elizabeth Hirschman (1987) analyzed the content of personal advertisements. The data in Hirschman's study are over 30 years old, but her findings are still important today (more on this later).

In **social exchange theory**, human interaction is seen as a series of exchanges of goods and services. The goods can be material, but they can also be nonmaterial—things like beauty, prestige, recognition, love, respect, and so on (see Blau 1964; Donnenworth and Foa 1974; Homans 1961a, 1961b). Researchers of human mate selection have shown that women tend to prefer men of higher social and economic status and that men tend to prefer women of greater physical beauty (see Buss 1985; Dunbar and Barrett 2007; Pawlowski and Jasienska 2008; Sefcek et al. 2007).

From the literature on exchange theory, Hirschman reasoned that men and women would offer and seek 10 kinds of resources from one another in personal ads: physical characteristics, money status, educational status, occupational status, intellectual status, love, entertainment, and information about demographic characteristics (age, marital status, residence), ethnicity, and personality. From the literature on mate selection, Hirschman expected to find a pattern, shown in Table 11.2, of resources offered and sought.

Table 11.2 is a schematic for a series of hypotheses. Two hypotheses, for example, are (1) men seek physical beauty and love more than women do in personal

Table 11.2 The Expected Pattern of Resource Exchange in Personal Ads

Women Are Expected to Offer and Men to Seek	Men Are Expected to Offer and Women to Seek
Physical attractiveness	Money
Love	Educational status
Entertainment	Intellectual status
Information about their demographic characteristics (age, marital status, residence)	Occupational status
Ethnicity	
Personality	

SOURCE: Adapted from Hirschman (1987:103).

ads; and, conversely; (2) women offer physical attractiveness and love more than men do. To test her hypotheses, Hirschman needed a corpus of personal ads . . . which brings us to step 2.

2. Select a set of texts to test the question or hypothesis. Hirschman randomly sampled 100 female-placed ads and 100 male-placed ads in *New York Magazine* and *The Washingtonian* from May 1983 to April 1984.

By sampling the ads at random, Hirschman was assured that whatever she found in the corpus she analyzed could be generalized to the content of all the ads in the two magazines. It could not, of course, be generalized to all magazines in the New York or Washington area, much less to magazines in any other city.

For example, in another New York–area magazine, *The Village Voice*, explicitly sexual traits and services were already common in personal ads in the 1980s. In *New York Magazine* and *The Washingtonian*, sexual traits and services were less than 1% of all resources sought and offered in 1983–84, so Hirschman excluded those from her analysis. If you wanted to replicate Hirschman's study today—for any magazine or Internet personal-ads site anywhere—you would sample ads that do not contain explicitly sexual services or characteristics.

3. Create a set of codes (variables, themes) in the research question or hypothesis. In this case, the variables, or themes, are the 10 resources that Hirschman had posited would be in the ads. The real work here is building a coding scheme—deciding on how to code the text in the ads.

For example, "NYU grad" or "MA in modern French lit" would count as "educational status." "Tall," "thin," "shapely," "good looking," "fit," "handsome," and so on, would count as "physical features." Information about personality might be words and phrases like "shy," "fun loving," "young at heart," "active," and so on. Information about ethnicity would be things like "Black," "White," "Hispanic," "Asian," and so on, and "small town girl" would be coded as demographic information (residence).

4. Pretest the variables on a few of the selected texts. Fix any problems that turn up with regard to the codes and the coding so that the coders become consistent in their coding. Hirschman gave 10 men and 11 women the list of 10 resource categories and a list of 100 resource items taken from 20 additional ads. She asked the 21 respondents to match the 100 resource items with the resource category that seemed most appropriate. In this case, Hirschman did not do a pretest with her actual coders. The 21 pretest respondents, however, provided strong support for the variables that Hirschman had developed. The respondents were able to categorize all 100 test items.

5. Apply the codes to the rest of the texts. Hirschman gave a male and female coder the entire set of 405 ads. (She wound up with 405 ads instead of 400 because she miscounted in the sampling and decided to keep the five extra ads. This kind of human error is easy to make in any study like this.) There were a total of 3,782 resources offered or sought in the 405 ads. The two coders worked apart and did not know the hypotheses that Hirschman was testing. They coded each of the 3,782 resources into the 10 resource categories. The coding took three weeks. This is not easy work to do.

Hirschman then checked for problems. Of 3,782 resource items coded, the coders differed on their categorization of 636 (16.8%), and in another 480 cases (12.7%) one coder neglected to categorize an item that the other coder had tagged. Hirschman resolved the 636 coding discrepancies—that is, she decided which coder was right. For the 480 coding omissions, Hirschman checked the ad and made sure that the resource item was correctly coded by the one coder who saw it. If this was the case (as it always was, apparently), then the resource was assigned to the ad by both coders.

6. Create a case-by-variable matrix from the texts and codes. In this case, the data matrix would have looked something like Table 11.3.

The first column of Table 11.3 is the number of the ad, from 1 to 405. These are the cases, or units of analysis, for this data set. Column 2 is for the name of the magazine. With just two magazines, the entries in column 2 would be 1 or 0, where 1 might mean *New York Magazine* and 0 would mean *The Washingtonian.*

The cells in column 4 would have a 1 or a 0 to indicate whether the ad had been placed by a man or a woman. Next would come 20 columns, two for each of the 10 resource categories. For each of the 405 ads, these columns would indicate how many of each of the 10 resource categories had been sought or offered.

Table 11.3 The Data Matrix for Hirschman's Study of Personal Ads

Ad #	Mag	Female placed	Physical features offered	Physical features sought	Money offered	Money sought	Educ status offered	Educ status sought	Occup status offered	Occup status offered	Etc.
1											
2											
3											
4											
•											
•											
•											
•											
•											
405											

SOURCE: Adapted from Hirschman (1987:103).

7. Analyze the matrix using whatever level of analysis is appropriate. Hirschman analyzed her data statistically. Her main concern was to test for differences in gender. Is the content of female-placed ads different from that of male-placed ads?

Before doing this, she tested whether there were differences in the content by city. If the content of the ads placed in Washington were really different from those placed in New York, then she would have had to analyze the two data sets (one for Washington and one for New York) separately for the effects of gender. Hirschman ran an analysis of variance, or ANOVA, and found that, whatever differences there were by gender in the content of the ads, those differences weren't affected by the city of origin. For the rest of the analyses, Hirschman could combine all her data, from both cities.

To set up the tests for gender effects, Hirschman counted the number of times each of the ten resources was offered and sought in each ad. Because the ads were of different length (some people included three or four of the 10 resources in their ad; some included six or seven . . . or even 10; and some repeated resources two or more times), Hirschman converted the counts of resources in each ad to percentages. If an ad listed six resources and two of them were about physical characteristics (tall, wavy hair), then physical characteristics were counted in that ad as 2/6, or 33%. Now Hirschman had a set of percentages, like those in Table 11.4.

Table 11.4 The Data From Hirschman's Study of Personal Ads

Resource	Mean Offered by Women	Mean Sought by Women	Mean Offered by Men	Mean Sought by Men
Physical status	.221	.090	.151	.223
Money	.018	.080	.059	.010
Educational status	.013	.008	.013	.009
Occupational status	.067	.032	.086	.011
Intellectual status	.048	.050	.030	.059
Love	.061	.168	.063	.158
Entertainment services	.107	.071	.080	.103
Demographic info	.217	.219	.283	.195
Ethnicity info	.091	.007	.090	.053
Personality info	.144	.200	.131	.150

SOURCE: Hirschman (1987:103).

We can tell a lot just by looking at the data in Table 11.4. For example, men mentioned money (think words and phrases like "solid income" and "well-paying job") in 5.9% of their offers, and women mentioned something to do with money in 1.8% of theirs. Women sought monetary resources more than men did (8% vs. 1%). Women offered something to do with physical status (think of words and phrases like "tall," "trim," "fit," "full figured") more than men did (22.1% vs. 15.1%), and men sought physical traits more than women did (22.3% vs. 9%). These statistics are pretty much what was expected in the 1980s from prior research on this topic. Men and women seek and offer the rest of the resources—including love—in more or less the same proportions.

We say "more or less" because that's the way the numbers look to us when we read the table. Fortunately, there is a simple test to tell if pairs of proportions, like those in Table 11.4, are statistically different—i.e., if the differences are big enough to indicate that they probably didn't occur by chance. The results are in Table 11.5. (We do not cover how to calculate the statistics in this book. The appropriate tests are covered in all standard statistics texts.)

Four of Hirschman's hypotheses were confirmed: (1) Men seek physical attractiveness more than women do. (2) Women offer physical attractiveness more than men do. (3) Women seek money more than men do. (4) Men offer money more than women do. All the other comparisons were statistically nonsignificant.

Table 11.5 Summary of Hirschman's Findings

Resource	Hypotheses		Confirmation	
	Men	Women	Men	Women
Physical status	Seek	Offer	Seek	Offer
Money status	Offer	Seek	Offer	Seek
Education status	Offer	Seek	ns	ns
Occupation status	Offer	Seek	ns	ns
Intellectual status	Offer	Seek	ns	ns
Love	Seek	Offer	ns	ns
Entertainment	Seek	Offer	ns	ns
Demographic info	Seek	Offer	ns	ns
Ethnicity info	Seek	Offer	ns	ns
Personality info	Seek	Offer	ns	ns

SOURCE: Hirschman (1987:103).

NOTE: ns = not significant statistically.

Washington, DC, and New York City are supposed to be hip places, yet the way men and women wrote their own personal ads in 1983–1984 conformed to traditional gender role expectations. Now, 30-plus years later, much has changed. The Internet has made sexually explicit ads more accessible and has made it easy for people of every color, religion, sexual orientation, and ethnicity to seek partners of a similar kind. But because of Hirschman's pioneering work, we can tell if and *how much* men and women market themselves differently to one another today.

This is a developing area of research. (**Further Reading**: content analysis of personal ads)

◆ INTERCODER RELIABILITY

The reliability of coding has long been a concern for content analysts (Woodward and Franzen 1948), and the measurement of reliability has been a major theme in all reviews of the field (Berelson 1952:171–95; Holsti 1969:127–49, Krippendorff 1980:129–68, 2013:267–329; Neuendorf 2002:211–56; Weber 1990:17–24). With two or more coders, we can test **intercoder reliability**—whether people think that the same constructs apply to the same chunks of text. The benefit of this is that we can be more certain of the counts we make when we add up the number of times any particular theme is mentioned in a text.

In turn, reliable counts mean increased confidence in measures of association between themes. Consider the following two sentences:

> Among the 12 men in our study, 10 (83%) said that they were abused by police who arrested them, and nine of those 10 (90%, or 75% of all men in our sample) described arguing with police during the event.

> Among the 16 women arrested during the demonstration, five (31%) said that they were abused and one of those 5 (20%, or 6% of all women in our sample), described arguing with police during the event.

The counts and associations in these two sentences are more credible if two or more coders marked the texts on which the analysis is based *and* agreed with one another about the presence of each theme (report of being abused, report of arguing with police).

There is an obvious and simple way to measure agreement between a pair of coders: Line up their codes and calculate the percentage of agreement. This is shown in Table 11.6 for two coders who have coded 10 texts for a single theme, using a binary code, 1 or 0—that is, they are coding the text for whether the theme is present or absent, not whether the theme is there a little bit or a lot or not at all.

Both coders have a 0 for texts 1, 4, 5, 7, and 10, and both coders have a 1 for text 2. These two coders agree a total of six times out of 10—five times that the theme, whatever it is, does not appear in the texts, and one time that the theme does appear. On four out of 10 texts, the coders disagree. On text 9, for example, coder 1 saw the theme in the text, but coder 2 didn't. Overall, these two coders agree 60% of the time.

Adjusting for Chance

The total observed agreement is a popular method for assessing reliability, but it has long been recognized that coders can agree on the presence or absence of a theme

Table 11.6 Measuring Simple Agreement Between Two Coders on a Single Theme

Units of Analysis (Documents/Observations)										
Coders	1	2	3	4	5	6	7	8	9	10
1	0	1	0	0	0	0	0	0	1	0
2	0	1	1	0	0	1	0	1	0	0

SOURCE: Adapted from Hirschman (1987:103).

The **Human Relations Area Files** (HRAF) at Yale University is the world's largest archive of ethnography. Since the 1940s, professional coders have been theme coding ethnographies of cultures from around the world. The coders at HRAF follow a codebook, called the **Outline of Cultural Materials**, developed by Murdock and others (2004 [1961]). For example, there are codes for demography, family, entertainment, social stratification, war, health and welfare, sickness, sex, religious practices, and so on. Within each major theme, there are subthemes, just like any other codebook for analyzing text. For example, under demography, there is a subcode for mortality, another for external migration, and so on. Under the code for family, there are subcodes for marriages, nuptials, termination of marriages, and so on.

Today, the archive is about a million pages of text, taken from almost 8,000 books and articles, on over 400 cultural groups. The archive is growing at about 40,000 pages a year, and about 60% of the material is available on the Internet through libraries that subscribe (hraf.yale.edu). This archive, known as the **eHRAF World Cultures Database**, is used by researchers in psychology, political science, sociology, anthropology, and other fields to test hypotheses in which whole cultures—rather than, say, personal ads—are the units of analysis.

Doing Cross-Cultural Text-Based Research

There are five steps in steps in a study based on the HRAF (Otterbein 1969). These steps are analogous to those for any content analysis study:

1. State a hypothesis that requires cross-cultural data.

2. Draw a representative sample of the world's cultures.

3. Find the appropriate OCM (Outline of Cultural Materials) codes in the sample.

4. Code the variables according to whatever conceptual scheme you've developed in forming your hypothesis.

5. Run the appropriate statistical tests and see if your hypothesis is confirmed.

Using this method, Flaxman and Sherman (2000), for example, found that in societies in which only plants (like corn) were the staples, pregnant women were significantly less likely to experience morning sickness than were women in societies where animal products were staples. Barber (1998) found that the frequency of male homosexual activity was low in hunting and gathering societies and increased with the complexity of agricultural production. Ethnographic reports of male homosexuality were also more likely for societies in which women did not control their own sexuality—a well-known correlate of increased reliance on complex agriculture. (**Further Reading**: cross-cultural studies of ethnographic text)

AUTOMATED CONTENT ♦ ANALYSIS: CONTENT DICTIONARIES

Computer-based **content dictionaries** are used in **automated content analysis**. To build these content dictionaries, words are assigned, one at a time, by human coders, to one or more categories, or themes, according to a set of rules. The rules are part of a computer program that parses new texts and assigns words to categories. Over time, researchers can assign new words to one of the categories or add new categories.

For example, one rule would tell the computer how to interpret the word "will" as a verb (he will go home"). Later, the word "will" might show up in a text as a noun ("she had a strong will to live"). And later still, the rules might have to distinguish the word "will" as yet another noun ("she left nothing to charity in her will"). As the dictionary grows, it becomes more sophisticated, making automated content analysis increasingly powerful. When you hear "This call may be monitored for quality assurance purposes," it's likely that the conversation will be turned into text that will be submitted to a computer for content analysis.

Recently, Van Holt et al. (2013) built and tested a computer-based content dictionary for coding ethnographic materials at HRAF. The test was a set of 25 paragraphs from a book about Somalian culture that had been coded by the professional human coders at HRAF. Taking the human-coded themes as the gold standard, the computer got 88% of the themes right. As with all technology, we won't be surprised to see computers doing text analysis in ways we don't currently imagine (Box 11.5).

Box 11.5

History of Automated Content Analysis

Work in this field began over 50 years ago. Computers filled whole buildings back then and were hard to use, but pioneers like Benjamin Nicholas Colby and Phillip Stone were undeterred. In his study of Navajo and Zuni responses to thematic apperception tests, Colby's (1966:379) initial impression was that the Navajo regarded their homes as havens and places of relaxation and that the Zuni depicted their homes as places of discord and tension.

To test this idea, Colby created a special-purpose dictionary that contained two-word groups that he and his colleagues had developed before looking at the data. One word group, the "relaxation" group, comprised the words assist, comfort, easy, affection, happy, and play. The other, the "tension" group, comprised the words destruction, discomfort, difficult, dislike, sad, battle, and anger.

(Continued)

(Continued)

Colby examined the 35 sentences that contained the word home and one of the words in either of the two-word groups. Navajos were more than twice as likely to use words from the relaxation group when talking about home as they were to use words from the tension group. Zuni were almost twice as likely to use tension words as they were to use relaxation words. Colby (1966:378) also found that the Navajo were more likely to use words associated with exposure such as storm, cold, freezing, hot, heat, and windy.

Colby was not surprised at the results, noting that the Navajo were sheepherders and were concerned about protecting their sheep from the elements and the Zuni were crop growers and were concerned about the water they need to grow their corn. What *was* surprising was that the texts were generated from pictures that had nothing to do with sheep or crops.

Around the same time, Stone and his colleagues began work on an ambitious system called the *General Inquirer* (Kelly and Stone 1975; Stone et al. 1962; Stone et al. 1966). They tested an early version on 66 suicide notes—33 written by men who had actually taken their own lives and 33 written by men who were asked to produce simulated suicide notes. The control group men were matched with the men who had written actual suicide notes on age, occupation, religion, and ethnicity. The *General Inquirer* program parsed the texts and picked the actual suicide notes 91% of the time (Ogilvie et al. 1966).

By 1990, computers were much more powerful than they were in the 1960s, and the General Inquirer, with what by then had become the Harvard Psycho-Sociological Dictionary, version IV, could tell whether the word "broke" meant "fractured," or "destitute," or "stopped functioning," or—when paired with "out"—"escaped" (Rosenberg et al. 1990). Work continues on the Harvard dictionary (the latest version is called Harvard-IV-4 TagNeg, or H4N), and dictionary-based markup of text is producing better and better results as time goes on.

Loughran and McDonald (2011), for example, found that many of the words counted as negative in H4N—words like tax, cost, liability, vice, and crude—are not typically negative in the finance reports (known as 10-Ks) that publicly traded companies are required by law to file each year. Loughrand and McDonald developed a list of over two thousand words that typically do have a negative meaning when someone is talking about finances. (**Further Reading**: automated content analysis and content dictionaries)

Key Concepts in This Chapter

explicit and covert meanings	case-by-variable matrix	pretests
manifest and latent content	units of analysis	latent coding
	unitizing	manifest coding
	sampling universe	unique identifier

social exchange theory
intercoder reliability
binary
nominal variables
ordinal variables
Cohen's kappa

Krippendorff's
  alpha
Human Relations Area
  Files
Outline of Cultural
  Materials

eHRAF World Cultures
  Database
content dictionaries
automated content
  analysis

Summary

- Content analysis is a set of methods for systematically coding and analyzing qualitative data.

  ○ Grounded theory is inductive: The idea is to let understanding emerge from the close study of texts. Content analysis is based on deductive reasoning and involves the tagging of a set of texts or other artifacts (photos, magazine ads, TV commercials, buildings) with codes that are derived from theory or from prior knowledge and then analyzing the distribution of the codes.

- Content analysis goes back to work done in the late 19th century to determine whether newspapers were focusing too much on sensational topics, like crime and vice. Wilcox (1900) found that the worst offending newspaper devoted 19% of its space to crime and vice, while, on average, just 3% of the total space in American newspapers in 1898 was devoted to crime and vice.

  ○ Methods improved over time and by 1955, content analysis was an established method in political science, communications, and other fields. Content analysis was instrumental in convicting William Dudley Pelley for publishing pro-Nazi propaganda in the United States while the United States was at war with Germany.

- There are seven big steps in content analysis:

  1. Formulate a research question or a hypothesis, based on existing theory or on prior research.

  2. Select a set of texts to test the question or hypothesis.

  3. Create a set of codes (variables, themes) in the research question or hypothesis.

  4. Pretest the variables on a few of the selected texts. Fix any problems that turn up with regard to the codes and the coding so that the coders become consistent in their coding.

  5. Apply the codes to the rest of the texts.

  6. Create a case-by-variable matrix from the texts and codes.

  7. Analyze the matrix using whatever level of analysis is appropriate.

need to understand that sentence, including its implications. For example, if you are in New York when you hear this sentence, you know that Alice traveled by plane. You know that "last week" is less than seven days ago. Even if you don't know that Los Angeles is 2,753 miles from New York, you know that it's much too far for Alice to have driven to LA and back or to have taken a train in the time available. You also know that, although Alice would rather she didn't have to, she thinks it's worth spending a lot of time and money on keeping this client happy.

Here's another one: "Fred lost his term paper because he forgot to save his work." This is a causal statement (A happened *because of* B). We know that Fred's forgetting to save did not actually *cause* him to lose his term paper. Several links in the causal chain are left out. These links are easily filled in by listeners who have the background to do so: Fred was going along, happily typing his term paper into a computer. He neglected to save his work periodically, as he had surely been advised to do many times over the years. Without warning, some unforeseen event occurred—like a total crash of Fred's hard disk—and Fred wound up having to type his term paper in all over again. Again, think of all the information—about computer crashes and data-loss disasters, not to mention term-paper typing—you need in order to fill in and understand this sentence.

As with many kinds of text analysis, the most important methodological skill you can have for schema analysis is to be really, really steeped in the language and culture of the people you are studying.

◆ HISTORY OF SCHEMA ANALYSIS

Schema analysis comes from Frederick Bartlett's (1964 [1932]) pioneering experiments on memory and meaning. In the early days of modern psychology, the most influential researcher on memory was Hermann Ebbinghaus. Prose, said Ebbinghaus, contained phrases that could, by turns, be funny or sad, soft or harsh. All of this variation was uncontrollable, so Ebbinghaus developed 2,300 nonsense syllables by systematically putting vowels between pairs of consonants . . . bok, gub, tiv, and so on (1913:22–23). The idea was to test people's memory without introducing the clutter of meaning.

Bartlett argued that meaning was integral to memory and sought a different experimental technique. It would be messier, but it would let him study memory and meaning together. He hit on the idea of asking subjects—Cambridge University students—to memorize and repeat back folktales (prose with meaning) that were culturally bizarre to them. Around 1916, Bartlett began asking people to read and recall a Kathlamet Indian folktale called "The War of the Ghosts." The tale had been collected in Bay Center, Washington, by Franz Boas, who translated it into English (Boas 1901:5; D. Hymes 1985:392). Here it is:

One night two young men from Egulac went down to the river to hunt seals and while they were there it became foggy and calm. Then they heard war-cries, and they thought: "Maybe this is a war-party." They escaped to the shore, and hid behind a log. Now canoes came up, and they heard the noise of paddles, and saw one canoe coming up to them. There were five men in the canoe, and they said: "What do you think? We wish to take you along. We are going up the river to make war on the people." One of the young men said, "I have no arrows." "Arrows are in the canoe," they said. "I will not go along. I might be killed. My relatives do not know where I have gone. But you," he said, turning to the other, "may go with them."

So one of the young men went, but the other returned home. And the warriors went on up the river to a town on the other side of Kalama. The people came down to the water and they began to fight, and many were killed. But presently the young man heard one of the warriors say, "Quick, let us go home: That Indian has been hit." Now he thought: "Oh, they are ghosts." He did not feel sick, but they said he had been shot. So the canoes went back to Egulac and the young man went ashore to his house and made a fire. And he told everybody and said: "Behold I accompanied the ghosts, and we went to fight. Many of our fellows were killed, and many of those who attacked us were killed. They said I was hit, and I did not feel sick." He told it all, and then he became quiet. When the sun rose he fell down. Something black came out of his mouth. His face became contorted. The people jumped up and cried. He was dead. (Bartlett, F. 1964 [1932]. *Remembering: A Study in Experimental and Social Psychology.* Cambridge: Cambridge University Press. Reprinted with the permission of Cambridge University Press.)

In some of Bartlett's experiments, people read the story twice and were asked to recall it after a few minutes or, in some cases, after several years. This was long before voice recorders, so Bartlett took detailed notes about what people recalled and didn't recall. Over time, Bartlett saw some pattern emerge in the way people recalled this story.

One key finding was what W. F. Brewer (2000:72) calls **transformations to the familiar**—recasting unfamiliar things into more familiar terms. So, for example, instead of repeating "Something black came out of his mouth," someone in pre–World War I England might have said "He foamed at the mouth" or "His soul passed from his mouth" (p. 73). People also left out things that seemed irrelevant to them—like the fact that the young man made a fire when he went to his house. This event, said Brewer (p. 72), was not crucial to the plot and so was forgotten when subjects repeated the story. But this detail would have made perfect sense to any Kathlamet man in 1899: The first thing you do when you come home, he would have said, is make a fire. (**Further Reading**: schema theory)

♦ MENTAL MODELS

Bartlett sought a theory to explain the systematic distortions and transformations over time in the retelling of stories. Even before his work, it was well known that human beings process thousands of bits of information every day about real objects and events. Bartlett reasoned that our experience of this reality is far too complex to deal with on an image-by-image basis. There must be some underlying structures—some simplifications—that help us make sense of the information to which we are exposed (Casson 1983).

These underlying simplifications, or schemas, are what Rumelhart (1980) famously called "the building blocks of cognition." They are generalizations from our prior experience and comprise "rules . . . for imposing order on experience" (Rice 1980:153). *Schema analysis, then, is the search for those rules and how they are linked together into mental models.*

Like physical models—of airplanes or DNA molecules—**mental models** are reduced, simpler versions of complex realities, but they exist in our minds, like grammars for actions rather than for words. When we run into a new situation—an object, a person, an interaction—we compare it to the schemas we have already stored in memory—not to each individual object, person, or interaction we've experienced over the years (D'Andrade 1991).

For example, when we buy a car, we expect to haggle over the price, but when we order food in a restaurant, we expect to pay the price on the menu. We know instinctively not to leave a tip at a fast-food counter, though this rule can be relaxed (as at Starbucks) if we see a big jar, labeled "Tips," on the counter where we pay for the food. And when someone we hardly know says "Hi, how's it going?" we know that they don't expect us to stop and give them a full rundown on how our life is going these days. If we did stop and launch into a peroration about our life, we'd be acting outside the prevailing schema—**breaking frame**, as Goffman (1974) put it—and making people very uncomfortable. (**Further Reading**: mental models)

Universal, Individual, and Cultural Schemas

Some mental models, or schemas, may be universal, reflecting the fact that there are some experiences that are common to all humanity. For example, every human being is born into a system in which parents are powerful and infants are helpless. This common experience by every person in the world, argues Govrin (2006:629), produces a universal "underdog schema"—the tendency to feel sympathy with the oppressed.

Lévi-Strauss (1963) observed that all human beings experience the world as a set of binary categories—like male–female, sacred–profane, and raw–cooked. Kinship systems across the world are organized around very clear distinctions, many of them binary—like lineal and collateral kin, male and female kin, consanguineal and affinal kin, and so on (D. Jones 2003, 2004:215).

If an underdog schema is universal and if reducing complex things to sets of dualities is universal, then these schemas almost certainly have some Darwinian significance—i.e., they probably result in greater likelihood of human reproductive success. The same can be said for the universal disgust that humans display at things that are likely carriers of pathogens, like feces, vomit, lice, and so on (Oaten et al. 2009).

On the other hand, because every human being grows up with a unique set of experiences, some schemas are idiosyncratic—the unique angle that each of us has on some things. The sales tax in New York City is 8.875%. A local cultural rule in New York says "Double the tax on restaurant bills to figure out the tip." But some people have a rule that says tip exactly 20% of the bill in a restaurant, no matter what. So, if the bill is $34.28, the tip (with a separate, rounding-up-to-the-nearest-penny rule applied) would be $6.86. Others may apply a 15% rule and others may have a complicated algorithm, taking into account the kind of restaurant, the perceived markup rate on the wine (yes, really; we know people who do this), and the judged quality of service.

Somewhere between universal and idiosyncratic schemas are cultural schemas: They are developed through experience but are held by a population (Rice 1980:154). For example, Blair-Loy (2003) describes the conflict that some women in executive positions feel about two widely held and competing schemas in current U.S. culture: DEVOTION TO FAMILY and DEVOTION TO WORK. (**Further Reading**: cultural schemas or models)

KINDS OF SCHEMAS ♦

Some schemas—the **what-goes-with-what schemas**—are about objects: What kinds of foods go together in a Chinese meal? What kinds of clothing and accessories are appropriate for a bride? What kinds of animals will you find in a zoo? One important schema for Americans is about how the components of a good marriage fit together (Quinn 1997). More on this later.

Some schemas—**what-happens-when schemas**—are culturally shared scripts about how regularly occurring sets of behaviors play out.

One famous script, for going out to a restaurant, was described by Schank and Abelson (1977). The script has four main components: ENTERING, ORDERING, EATING, and EXITING. (Upper case is conventionally used to represent those underlying—i.e., unspoken, perhaps even unconscious—"building blocks of cognition" that Rumelhart [1980] talked about.)

Each of the main components contains one or more additional scripts. The ORDERING script, for example, comprises scripts for: EXAMINING the menu,

CHOOSING food, SUMMONING the waiter or waitress (Casson 1983:448; Schank and Abelson 1977:42–43). The EXITING schema has scripts for PAYING THE BILL, TIPPING, and LEAVING.

These ordered schemas together tell you when to order (after entering and sitting down); when to pay (after you've eaten); and when to tip (after paying the check). Schank asked his daughter, Hanna, to tell him what it's like to go to a restaurant. Beginning at less than three years and month months of age, she was already developing a complex script for this activity. By four years and two months of age, Hanna had integrated paying at the end of the meal into the script.

There are culturally shared scripts for appropriate behaviors while waiting in a doctor's office for an appointment, scripts for how to enter and leave a classroom after the lecture has begun, and scripts for how to change a tire (see Figure 8.1).

And some schemas—the **how-things-work schemas**—are folk theories. There is a cultural schema in Mexico for how people get diabetes (Daniulaityte 2004) and another in Haiti for how people contract AIDS (Farmer 1994). There are culturally shared schemas about why you see your breath outdoors during the winter (Collins and Gentner 1987) and about how thermostats work to keep your house warm (Kempton 1987). We'll take you through the THERMOSTAT AS VALVE versus THERMOSTAT AS FEEDBACK metaphor at the end of this chapter.

◆ METHODS FOR STUDYING SCHEMAS

There are three widely used methods for studying schemas: (1) experiments, (2) interviewing, and (3) analyzing metaphors.

1. Experiments

Building on Bartlett's pioneering work, Rice (1980) conducted some experiments using Eskimo folktales. First, following Rumelhart (1975), Rice developed what she called the American cultural schema for telling a story: There is a PROTAGONIST who has a PROBLEM or series of problems; the protagonist EVALUATES THE SITUATION in each problem and TAKES ACTION; and the action has some RESOLUTION, which can be positive or negative in terms of solving the protagonist's problem.

In one experiment, Rice made two versions of some Eskimo stories. One version was the complete Eskimo version, in English—more or less replicating Bartlett's work from around 1916. The other version was adapted to make it fit the idealized American story schema, with a protagonist, a problem, an action, and a resolution. The participants in both versions of this experiment read the story and then wrote it out from recall. They also came back a week later and recalled the story again.

Rice's results provide strong support for Bartlett's earlier findings: People add the American schema structure to the stories that lack it (Rice 1980:163). For example, in one story, the protagonist is a boy who is reproached for not hunting even though he is old enough to do so. The boy doesn't respond and nothing happens to him as a result. This is a violation of the American story schema in which outcomes of one kind or another—good, bad, or indifferent—are expected for a problem in a story. "By the one-week recall," says Rice:

> 8 of the 12 subjects had modified this sequence so as to mend this hole. There are two strategies for this. Five subjects provided some sort of response on the boy's part: "but he didn't want to" or "he preferred to beg." Another three dropped the admonition altogether, an efficient solution. (1980:166)

When the passages fit the American story schema (as the passages did in the Americanized versions of the stories), people agreed about which events they remembered. And people recalled more exactly worded phrases from the Americanized versions of the stories than from the Eskimo versions. Thus, as Bartlett had found in his early work, people distort stories in recall to fit their cultural expectations (their schemas) about what stories ought to be like.

Most college students have a schema for what a graduate student's office ought to look like. Brewer and Treyens (1981) left students alone in a psychology graduate student's office for 35 seconds (the students were told that the experimenter had to go check the lab to see if the previous subjects had finished). The students were taken to another room and asked to write down everything they could remember about the office they had just left. There were no books in the office, but nine out of 30 subjects remembered seeing books.

Schemas like the one for what an office should look like or the ones for ethnic stereotypes—or how people of various ethnicities and skin color are supposed to think and behave—can be tough to shake. (**Further Reading**: experimental schema analysis)

2. Interviewing: Schemas From Text

Naomi Quinn and her students collected and transcribed interviews about marriage from 11 North American couples. Some of the couples were recently married; others had been married a long time. The couples came from different parts of the country and represented various occupations, educational levels, and ethnic and religious groups. Each of the 22 people was interviewed separately for 15–16 hours, and the interviews were transcribed.

In a series of articles, Quinn (1982, 1987, 1992, 1996, 1997, 2005b) has analyzed this body of text to discover and document the concepts underlying American marriage and to show how these concepts are tied together—how they form a cultural model, a schema, shared by people from different backgrounds about what constitutes success and failure in marriage.

Quinn's method is to "exploit clues in ordinary discourse for what they tell us about shared cognition—to glean what people must have in mind in order to say the things they do" (1997:140). She begins by looking at patterns of speech and the repetition of key words and phrases, paying particular attention to informants' use of metaphors and the commonalities in their reasoning about marriage (see Box 12.1).

Box 12.1

Linkages and Language Competence

Schema analysis requires a deep understanding of the metaphors that informants use in talking about marriage or dinner parties or energy costs or Little League. This means either native or near-native language competence for this kind of analysis. Don't even try to do schema analysis if you aren't really fluent in the language of your informants.

D'Andrade notes that "perhaps the simplest and most direct indication of schematic organization in naturalistic discourse is the repetition of associative linkages" (1991:294). "Indeed," he says, "anyone who has listened to long stretches of talk—whether generated by a friend, spouse, workmate, informant, or patient—knows how frequently people circle through the same network of ideas" (p. 287).

In a study of blue-collar workers in Rhode Island, Claudia Strauss (1992) refers to these ideas as "personal semantic networks." On reading and rereading her intensive interviews with one of the workers, Strauss found that he repeatedly referred to ideas associated with greed, money, businessmen, siblings, and "being different." Strauss displays the relationships among these ideas by writing the concepts on a sheet of paper and connecting the ideas with lines and explanations.

This is the same method used by grounded theorists. In fact, one of the key features of many late-model text management programs is the ability to build on a computer screen the networks of themes that represent underlying schemas.

For example, Nan, one of Quinn's informants, uses a popular metaphor: "Marriage is a manufactured product"—something that has properties, like strength and staying power, and that requires work to produce. Some marriages are "put together well," and others "fall apart" like so many cars or toys or washing machines (Quinn 1987:174).

Sometimes Quinn's informants would talk about their surprise at the breakup of a marriage by saying that they thought the couple's marriage was "like the Rock of Gibraltar" or that they thought the marriage had been "nailed in cement." People use these metaphors because they assume that their listeners know that cement and the Rock of Gibraltar are things that last forever (1997:145–46).

Quinn concluded that just eight themes were needed to classify the hundreds of metaphors about marriage in her corpus of text:

> (1) metaphors of *lastingness,* such as, "It was stuck together pretty good" or "It's that feeling of confidence about each other that's going to keep us going"; (2) metaphors of *sharedness,* such as, "I felt like a marriage was just a partnership" or "We're together in this"; (3) metaphors of *mutual benefit,* such as, "That was really something that we got out of marriage" or "Our marriage is a very good thing for both of us"; (4) metaphors of *compatibility,* such as, "The best thing about Bill is that he fits me so well" or "Both of our weaknesses were such that the other person could fill in"; (5) metaphors of *difficulty,* such as, "That was one of the hard barriers to get over" or "The first year we were married was really a trial"; (6) metaphors of *effort,* such as, "She works harder at our marriage than I do" or "We had to fight our way back almost to the beginning"; (7) metaphors of *success or failure,* such as, "We knew that it was working" or, conversely, "The marriage was doomed"; and (8) metaphors of *risk,* such as, "that so many odds against marriage" or "The marriage was in trouble." (Quinn 1997:142)

These eight classes of metaphors, Quinn argues, represent underlying concepts that are linked together in a schema that guides the discourse of ordinary Americans about marriage:

> Marriages are ideally lasting, shared and mutually beneficial. Marriages that are not shared will not be mutually beneficial and those not mutually beneficial will not last. Benefit is a matter of fulfillment. Spouses must be compatible in order to be able to fill each other's [emotional] needs so that their marriages will be fulfilling and hence beneficial. Fulfillment and, more specifically, the compatibility it requires, are difficult to realize but this difficulty can be overcome, and compatibility and fulfillment achieved, with effort. Lasting marriages in which difficulty has been overcome by effort are regarded as successful ones. Incompatibility, lack of benefit, and the resulting marital difficulty, if not overcome, put a marriage at risk of failure. (Quinn 1997:164)

The use by informants of similar metaphors and the repetition of similar words and phrases indicate commonalities in how people share their reasoning. In other words, just as in the search for themes in any set of texts, the search for cultural models involves being alert to patterns of speech and to the repetition of key words.

3. Analyzing Metaphors

Quinn's work owes a lot to Lakoff and Johnson's (2003 [1980]) pioneering study of metaphors. Scholars of literature have always recognized the importance of metaphors in rhetoric. Lakoff and Johnson studied metaphors in everyday discourse and distinguished between conceptual metaphors—deeply embedded similes, like LOVE IS WAR—about how the world works—and metaphors that are simply surface representations of conceptual metaphors in language. "The way we think," argued Lakoff and Johnson, "what we experience, and what we do every day is very much a matter of metaphor" (p. 3).

Listen carefully to everyday speech and the power of Lakoff and Johnson's insight becomes clear. If someone says, "He's drowning in debt," the image of a person drowning is not meant literally, but the metaphor works as a "figure of speech" (literally, an image made with words) because native speakers of English share some basic concepts. We understand, for example, when someone says "Debt can sink you," or "Debt can bury you" or "He got into a really big hole when he took on that mortgage." The underlying concept—the conceptual metaphor—is that DEBT IS STRUGGLE, but it is reflected in many linguistic metaphors.

One way to get a list of metaphors is to collect a large amount of text, as Quinn did, on a particular topic, and comb through it. For many languages today, however, there are compilations of metaphors and proverbs—short phrases or sayings that encapsulate the cultural wisdom of a people. Those archival resources offer the opportunity for schema analysis.

Lakoff and Kövecses (1987), for example, studied idiomatic expressions in American English that focus on the concept of anger. They found about 300 entries in Roget's *University Thesaurus* under "anger," including things like:

> He lost his cool.
> He channeled his anger into something constructive.
> He's wrestling with his anger.
> You're beginning to get to me.
> Watch out! He's on a short fuse.
> When I told my mother, she had a cow.

Lakoff and Kövecses argue that, not only do all these surface expressions have something to do with anger, they have something to do with each other. For example, one underlying idea is that anger is the HEAT OF A FLUID IN A CONTAINER. Lakoff and Kövecses find this in such metaphors as:

> Simmer down!
> You make my blood boil.
> Let him stew.

This proposed schema is corroborated by the extension that when anger becomes too intense, the person explodes (Lakoff and Kövecses 1987:199), as in:

She blew up at me.
We won't tolerate any more of your outbursts.
When I told him, he just exploded.
He blew a gasket.
She erupted.
She's on a short fuse.
That really set me off.

Lakoff and Kövecses argue that the underlying metaphor for anger is that ANGER IS HEAT (1987:197), but that this is further subordinated to a more general metaphor of the BODY AS A CONTAINER FOR THE EMOTIONS ("she couldn't contain her joy; he was filled with anger; she was brimming with rage"). Thus, anger is the HEAT OF A FLUID IN A CONTAINER ("You make my blood boil; Let him stew; Simmer down!") (p. 198). (**Further Reading**: metaphor analysis)

FOLK THEORIES: KEMPTON'S ♦ STUDY OF HOME THERMOSTATS

Folk theories, or **folk models**, are everyday theories about how things work or why things exist: Why do so few women go into physics? Why have American automobile manufacturers lost ground to Japanese and European manufacturers? How is obesity related to overall health? To understand these theories, we need to study "cognition in the wild" (Hutchins 1995).

Kempton (1987) interviewed 12 people in Michigan about how they controlled the heat in their homes during the winter. He inferred from the interviews that people were applying one of two possible theories about heat control: the THERMOSTAT AS FEEDBACK THEORY or the THERMOSTAT AS VALVE THEORY. People who have the feedback theory—we can call it the feedback schema—about how their heating system works believe that the furnace gets turned on when the thermostat senses that the temperature has fallen below some level. If the thermostat is set at, say, 72 degrees, then, when the temperature falls below 72, the furnace comes on and pours out heat until the house is at 72 again. Then the furnace shuts off.

There is, in other words, a "feedback" between the thermostat and the furnace. In this theory, the thermostat regulates the amount of *time* that the furnace runs, but while it's running the furnace is thought to run at a constant speed and intensity. As Kempton points out, this emic understanding of how furnaces work is thought by heating engineers to be simplified, but essentially correct (1987:228).

People who hold the THERMOSTAT AS VALVE THEORY see the thermostat as analogous to the gas pedal on a car. Just as a car goes faster the more you push on the gas pedal, so the furnace works harder and puts out more heat the higher the thermostat is set. As Kempton shows, this widely held schema translates into energy-inefficient behavior. When people who have this schema walk into their house on a cold day and the house is at 50 degrees, they may turn their thermostat up to 90 degrees, figuring that the house will heat faster than it would if they set the thermostat to 70. They figure they can turn the thermostat down to 70 when the temperature in the house reaches that mark. Much of the time, however, they miss the mark and are reminded to turn the thermostat down when the temperature in the house reaches 80 degrees and they notice that it feels too hot.

Kempton came up with the hypothesis that people have either a feedback or a valve theory about how the thermostat works early in his study of home heating control. He went back later and looked through the text of his 12 interviews for statements or metaphors that indicated which, if either, theory each of his informants held. One informant said: "You just turn the thermostat up and once she gets up there [to the desired temperature] she'll kick off automatically" (Kempton 1987:228). That informant was using a feedback theory. Another informant said that the furnace was like "electric mixers. The higher you turn them, the faster they go" (p. 230). That informant was clearly using a valve theory.

If you've ever tried to make an elevator come more quickly by repeatedly hitting the call button, you might have a valve theory of elevators. (**Further Reading**: folk theories.)

Key Concepts in This Chapter

cultural schemas	transformations to the familiar	what-happens-when schemas
cultural models	mental models	how-things-work schemas
cognitive simplifications	breaking frame	folk theories
scripts	what-goes-with-what schemas	folk models

Summary

- Schema analysis is based on the observation that everyday life is too complex for people to learn one scene at a time. Just as we don't learn a list of sentences, we don't learn a list of behaviors or scenes. There must be rules—a grammar—that help us make sense of so much information.

o Schemas let culturally skilled people fill in the details of a story. We often hear things like "Fred lost his data because he forgot to save his work." We know that Fred's forgetting to save his work didn't actually *cause* him to lose his data. A whole set of links are left out in ordinary conversations, but they are easily filled in by listeners who have the background to do so.

- Research on schemas comes from work on human memory.

  o Early researchers on memory used nonsense syllables (like bok, gub, tiv) to test people's memory without introducing the clutter of meaning.

  o Frederick Bartlett argued that meaning was integral to memory and sought a different experimental technique. Beginning in 1916, he asked people in England to memorize and repeat stories that were culturally bizarre to them, like an American Indian folktale called "The War of the Ghosts." When people repeated the stories, they transformed unfamiliar things into more familiar terms and they left out things that were not common to their own experience.

  o To explain the systematic distortions and transformations in the retelling of stories, Bartlett reasoned that our reality is far too complex to deal with on an image-by-image basis. There must be some underlying structures—some schemas—that help us make sense of the information to which we are exposed. Schemas, then, are generalizations from our prior experience.

- Schemas can be universal, idiosyncratic, and cultural.

  o Universal schemas reflect the fact that there are some experiences that are common to all humanity. For example, there may be a universal underdog schema—the tendency to feel sympathy with the oppressed—because all humans are born into a system in which parents are powerful and infants are helpless.

  o At the other extreme, because every human being grows up with a unique set of experiences, some schemas are idiosyncratic—the unique angle that each of us has on some things.

  o Somewhere between universal and idiosyncratic schemas are cultural schemas. These are, like schemas, developed through experience but are held by a population.

- There are what-goes-with-what schemas, what-happens-when schemas, and how-things-work schemas.

  o What-goes-with-what schemas are about objects: What kinds of foods go together in a Chinese meal? What kinds of clothing and accessories are appropriate for a bride?

  o What-happens-when schemas are culturally shared scripts about regularly occurring sets of behavior. Children in the United States learn very early the script for ordering and eating food in a fast-food restaurant and add new pieces to the

Finally, if women were present at their mother's death, they often described the death scene. Here are two contrasting scenes—one about a death accompanied by suffering and the other about a peaceful death—which Rubinstein nonetheless counts as similar parts of these narratives:

1. And she kept on talking. And a lot of it was about things from the past. But whatever it was, even when my brother and sister got there, we couldn't, umm, none of us got through to her. Her eyes were just moving around . . . and she even suffered to the very end, I mean, in her own way. It wasn't a peaceful death, really. (1995:270)

2. Most of the family was there, and my mother was having more difficulty breathing and I had her in my arms trying to talk to her, reassuring her that I loved her and one thing and another. And she died. . . . Yes, right in my arms, which was a beautiful way to die. It was like my mother's gift of peace to me, knowing that I could not have been any closer. (1995:271)

Notice the transcription in these narratives. The author selectively uses "kinda" instead of "kind of" to convey the conversational tone of the story. He also inserts brackets to indicate things that were implied, but not said, in the narrative. And there is only the barest attempt to include the kind of detailed information about false starts and tokens (like umm and uh).

Notice, too, how the focus of the analysis is on the themes—like the medicalization of death, the impossible dilemmas that arise in deciding on medical care for the terminally ill, the emotional pain for daughters of not being able to find the "mother-who-was" in mothers who are demented—and on how themes are combined and ordered in predictable ways. (**Further Reading**: event narratives)

Comparing Narratives: Bletzer and Koss's Study

Systematic comparison is a hallmark of analysis in the social sciences, whether the data are text or numbers. Keith Bletzer and Mary Koss (2006) analyzed 62 narratives by poor women in the southwestern United States who had survived rape, including 25 Cheyenne women, 24 Anglo women, and 13 Mexican American women. The women in all three groups were, on average, about the same age (mid-30s) and were recruited at health clinics that served their respective communities. In particular, the women recruited had mentioned on a screening survey that they had had an "'unwanted sexual experience' that involved force" (Bletzer and Koss 2006:10).

This exemplary use of quota sampling was just the right design for getting at the research question in the project: How do low-income women of different cultural backgrounds—holding region of the country and socioeconomic status constant—tell the story of being victims of sexual violence? Notice especially that the researchers had participants from the majority culture (Anglo women) so that useful comparisons could be made and that they limited their sample of Mexican American women to those who had been raised at least to adolescence in Mexico. (See Chapter 3 for more on quota sampling.)

During the interview, each woman was asked to tell her own story of rape, in her own words. The researchers looked at the stories in terms familiar to students of sexual violence: initial reaction, long-term consequences, mourning, and attempts at recovery. In addition to themes, they looked for narrative structuring devices.

For example, Anglo women used **nested stories** in their narratives; the Mexican American women made less use of this device; and the Cheyenne women didn't use it at all but typically ordered the phases of their stories more than did the Anglo or Mexican American women (Bletzer and Koss 2006:18). Anglo women also used **narrative markers** (like "so, then . . ." "so, anyways . . ." "and then . . ." etc.) more than did the women in the other two groups (p. 21).

All the women used the metaphor of feeling soiled and dirty after being raped (Bletzer and Koss 2006:22):

"Angry, scared, degraded. Felt like I was worthless." (Anglo)

"Then when I got pregnant out of it, it just made me feel dirty." (Anglo)

"I just felt dirty and degraded. I wanted to hide so nobody could see me." (Anglo)

"I felt low, I felt raunchy." (Cheyenne)

"I felt sick, dirty. I wanted to kill myself." (Cheyenne)

"It made me feel like I was dirty, nasty. . . . Made me feel real dirty." (Cheyenne)

"Anguish, very strong. Desperation, and sadness, painful sadness." (*Angustía, muy grande. Una desesperación, y tristeza, dolorosa.*) (Mexicana). (Bletzer and Koss 2006:16)

Bletzer and Koss also note what *isn't* in the narratives: Many of the Anglo and Mexican American women, they say, expressed thoughts of revenge against their assailants, but none of the Cheyenne women did (Bletzer and Koss 2006:17). In fact, the Cheyenne women almost never named men in their accounts of rape; Mexican women named people with whom they had good relations; and the Anglo women named intimates as well as people with whom they had troubled relations (p. 14).

account. They made notes about "anything within the text that appeared interesting or significant" and developed themes "which were felt to capture the essence" of Beth's account (p. 226).

Here is Beth talking about what it's like in the morning before she takes her medicine:

> And I'm in like a fog and it, and it, you can't, you can't think straight, you can't erm, it's a horrible feeling, you feel as if er you you're not connecting, you know, that's all I can explain it, your brain isn't telling your body what to do, it isn't telling you how to speak. (p. 227)

And here is Beth describing what it's like to try and walk:

> And like you have to, when you put your, get up on your feet, you say, "now go on put that foot in front of the other" and you have to physically make yourself do a step and a step at a time, you have to tell your body what to do, it doesn't just doing it by thinking. (p. 228)

Garot's Study of Screeners for Subsidized Housing

Garot (2004) studied government workers whose job it was to screen applicants for subsidized housing. He observed 43 of these screening interviews and took notes on the interactions between the workers and their clients. Right after each screening interview, he interviewed the workers about their reactions to what had happened.

There is a lot at stake in housing eligibility interviews. The resources (the subsidies) available are limited, and the intake workers have to turn people down. The workers can feel terrible guilt, especially when rejected clients get emotional or angry and plead their case—sometimes in tears. Garot describes how the workers deal with this—how they avoid using the word "no," how they develop a kind of "detached concern," and how they ease clients "from hope to rejection" (2004:744). One device is to give the exact same speech to everyone who is being denied—which means memorizing it.

Here is what the workers told clients who were ineligible for a housing subsidy:

> You don't have a preference [for a subsidy] at this time. To have a preference, you must either be paying 50% of your income towards your rent, live in substandard housing, or have been evicted for a reason other than the nonpayment of rent. If not, we'll keep you on the waiting list, so that if your situation changes we can call you back in. (Garot 2004:744)

Understandably, people plead in the hope that they can persuade the case worker. Here, Manuel lets the case worker (Anna) know that he and his family could be out on the street.

Anna:	So we'll keep you on the waiting list, and if your income decreases or your rent is higher, review it with us.
Manuel:	Right now, this apartment is not really ours. The owner doesn't wanna rent to us. Where'm I gonna go?
Anna [quietly]:	I don't know.
Manuel:	He prefers Section 8 [a program in which the government subsidizes the rent of private houses to poor people]. I'm gonna be out of a place. That's why I'm applying for this.
Anna:	I suggest you try to find a place here that's not too expensive.
	[Manuel and his family get up and leave the office.]

(Garot 2004:744)

This kind of interaction takes its toll. Here's Anna explaining to Garot how she has dealt with this stress:

Anna: I went through a period a few years ago where I was so stressed out, and I was having these horrible migraine headaches. I didn't realize at the time it was because I was having a hard time dealing with saying "no" all the time. [anguished tone] You know, seeing people come in here, and they're like, on the border, where you know, OK they can't qualify by the numbers, but you knew that they were in desperate need. So you couldn't help them. You have to sit there and look at them and say "no." [Anna pauses and looks at me, apparently burdened. Then with a sigh she shrugs off such drama and continues in a more lighthearted spirit.] It took me a while to be able to deal with that, and realize, OK, so I didn't help them, but there's someone else who did qualify who needed it more than they did, but, you know, had the numbers and stuff. It took me a while, but I did. (Garot 2004:758)

As you can see, the method here is to produce a convincing description of what other people have experienced. It may be accompanied by an explanation, but the big goal is to make readers understand the lived experience of the people you've studied. Doing that, like so much of good research, is a craft. You get better and better at it as you do more and more of it. (**Further Reading**: phenomenology)

Key Concepts in This Chapter

sociolinguistics	themes	interpretive analysis of
hermeneutics	nested stories	text
phenomenology	narrative markers	Biblical exegesis
structural regularities	heritage narratives	bracketing

Summary

- Human beings are natural storytellers. You can ask people anything about their personal experience and you'll get a narrative. Narrative analysis is the search for regularities in how people, within and across cultures, tell stories.

  - One major genre of narratives involves recounting an event: What happened? How did it happen? Why did it happen? What was the result? The object is to discover themes and recurring structures.
  - Like any empirical data, narratives can be systematically compared in the search for themes.

- There are three major traditions of narrative analysis in the social sciences: sociolinguistics, hermeneutics, and phenomenology.

  - Sociolinguistic studies of narrative focus on the structure of the story and on regularities in how people, within and across cultures, tell stories. In this tradition, the narrative itself is the object of interest.
  - Hermeneutics is the interpretive study of text and the search for the larger meaning of a narrative. Here, the narrative is a vehicle for understanding the cultural and historical context in which stories get told.
  - Phenomenology is the study of personal narratives as windows into people's lived experience. Here, the object of study is the experience of the person telling a story, not just the story itself.

- In the sociolinguistic tradition

  - Rubinstein (1995) found strong structural regularities and consistent themes in the way women told the story of their mother's death. Most women medicalized the death with stories about surgery and there is often a detailed death scene, with discussion of the dilemmas that arise in deciding on medical care for the terminally ill, and recounting of the emotional pain for daughters of not being able to find the "mother-who-was" in mothers who are demented.

o Bletzer and Koss (2006) compared the narratives of 62 poor women in the southwestern United States who had survived rape. There were clear differences in the structure of the narratives across ethnic groups. Anglo women used nested stories in their narratives; Mexican American women made less use of this device; and Cheyenne women didn't use it at all but typically ordered the phases of their stories more than did the Anglo or Mexican American women. All the women used the metaphor of feeling soiled and dirty after being raped. Many of the Anglo and Mexican American women expressed thoughts of revenge against their assailants, but none of the Cheyenne women did.

o Bridger and Maines (1998) analyzed 400 articles, letters, and editorials in Detroit's two largest newspapers in reaction to the planned closing in 1989 of 42 out of 112 Catholic churches in Detroit. One of the major themes was about how the Second Vatican Council, held from 1962 to 1965, had created a climate of openness in the Catholic Church, with more participation by priests and the laity in important local decisions. Critics said that the local Cardinal had ignored these new principles in his decision making. This **heritage narrative** reduced the closings from 42 to 31 churches showing that heritage narratives can have a real impact on political decisions.

o Folktales and myths reflect a society's values, and analysis of these narratives stresses the discovery of those values. Mathews (1992) collected 60 tellings of La Llorona, a widely told folktale in rural Mexico. The tale involves infidelity ("walking the streets") by a woman or by her husband, but in the end, the woman always kills herself. Most marriages in the rural village where Mathews worked were arranged by parents and involved an exchange of resources between families. Once resources like land are exchanged, parents can't, or won't, take back a daughter if she wants out of a marriage. The only way a woman can end her marriage, Mathews explains, is suicide (1992:150). The folktale is a cultural artifact, but its force as a morality play is that it is rooted in a political—economic feature of the speech community that tells and retells it.

• Hermeneutics in social science is an outgrowth of the Western tradition of Biblical exegesis—constantly interpreting the words of sacred texts (the Old and New Testaments) to understand their original meaning and their directives for living in the present.

o It is exegesis on the U.S. Constitution that has produced entirely different interpretations across time about the legality of slavery, abortion, women's right to vote, the government's ability to tax income, and so on.

o Herzfeld's (1977) study of the *khelidonisma*, or swallow song, sung in modern Greece as part of the welcoming of spring, showed that inconsistencies in the lyrics reflect structural principles that underlie the rite of passage for welcoming spring in rural Greece. For example, "March, my good March" appears in one song while "March, terrible March" appears in another. Herzfeld shows that the word "good" is used ironically in Greek where the referent is a source of anxiety. This kind of ever-deepening hermeneutic analysis requires intimate familiarity with the local language and culture, so that the symbolic referents emerge during the study of cultural expressions.

o Fernández (1967) analyzed the sermon of an African cult leader, using his intimate knowledge of the local language and culture to explain the societal significance of words and phrases, including the Ngombi, iron, the miracle between the thighs, the blood of the nursing mother, and the chatter of the widow. Fernández shows how these words were part of an exhortation by the preacher for his flock to protect marriage and pregnancy. The Ngombi, for example, is the voice of the goddess of fecundity, and gifts of iron were traditional for bride price. At the time, the local people had experienced a 40-year decline in fertility, the consequence of an epidemic of venereal disease, and the existence of the cult was in jeopardy.

• A phenomenological study involves six steps: (1) identifying a phenomenon whose essence you want to understand; (2) identifying your biases and bracketing them—doing as much as you can to put them aside; (3) collecting narratives about the phenomenon from people who are experiencing it; (4) using your after bracketing intuition to identify the essentials of the phenomenon; (5) laying out those essentials in writing with exemplary quotes from the narratives; and (6) repeating steps 4 and 5 until you are sure that there is no more to learn about the lived experience of the person you're studying.

• Steps 2 and 5 are the hardest.

o Zakrzewski and Hector (2004) studied the lived experience of men who were recovering from addiction to alcohol. Zakrzewski is himself a recovering addict. This gave him empathy for the men he was interviewing but it also meant that he carried a lot of his own biases into the project. To counter this, he went through a bracketing interview in which he was asked the same question that the participants would be asked.

o Selecting quotes that make clear how a person being studied actually experienced something requires that the researcher achieve empathic understanding of the phenomenon being studied.

o Garot (2004) studied government workers whose job it was to screen applicants for subsidized housing. The resources (the subsidies) available are limited, and the intake workers have to turn people down. Garot quotes his informants as they explain to him how they dealt with this stress.

Exercises

1. Collect several tellings of a well-known folktale in your native language and describe in detail the differences in the tellings. For speakers of English, for example, you might choose Cinderella, Snow White, or Little Red Riding Hood. This exercise should reveal the variation in what we may think of unvarying components of our culture.

2. Ask five seniors at your school to tell you the story of how they came to the college or university where you are studying and how they decided on their major. Analyze the stories (narratives). Are there common themes? Do the themes emerge in a common sequences? Some common questions about these narratives are: Was this college their first choice? Did they know people here before they enrolled? Did their parents or other relatives have a connection to the school? Did they try other majors before settling on the one they are in? What are their career plans? Did career plans have anything to do with their selection of the school and the major?

3. Interview a person whose race or ethnicity is different from yours. Record the interview. Ask them to describe a situation in which they felt awkward or unwelcome because of their race or ethnicity. Listen to the interview and note when you feel any biases emerging—where you find yourself agreeing strongly or disagreeing strongly with what the other person is saying. Can you bracket those biases? That is, can you ask direct questions about those things of another respondent, whose race or ethnicity is also different from yours, without leading the respondent or showing disapproval?

Further Reading

Overviews of narrative analysis. Gubrium and Holstein (2009), Herman (2007), Luc and Vervaeck (2005), Riessman (2008).

Event narratives. Baker-Ward et al. (2005), Blum-Kulka (1993), Bohenmeyer (2003), Brenneis (1988), Cornwell and Atia (2012), Koven (2002), Ledema et al. (2006), Quinn (2005a). See Reimer and Mathes (2007) on methods for improving accuracy in the collection of event histories.

Heritage and national narratives. Alkon (2004), Ashworth (2004), Brand (2010), Glover (2003), Hale (2001), Hyams (2002).

Analyzing folktales. Burke (1998), Doyle (2001), Malimabe-Ramagoshi et al. (2007), Piirainen 2011, Raby (2007).

Hermeneutics in social science. Bauman (1978), Dilthey (1989 [1883], 1996), Gadamer et al. (1988), Guignon (2006), Ricoeur (1981, 1991), H. Silverman (1991). Examples of hermeneutic analysis: King (1996), Mann (2007), Yakali-Çamoglu (2007).

Social research on folk songs and popular music. Ascher (2001), Cachia (2006), Harris (2005), Hoffman (2002), Izugbara (2005), Lomax (1968, 2003), Messner et al. (2007), Stewart and Strathern (2002).

Sermons, stories, lectures, political speeches, jokes, and life histories. Sermons: Brailey (2007), Hamlet (1994), Hopkins (2010), Moss (1994). Stories: Bareiss (2014), Blustein et al. (2013), McKelvey (2014), Wells (2011), White (2006). Lectures: Javidi and Long (1989), Nikitina (2003). Political speeches: Elahi and Cos (2005), Guthrie (2007), Murphy and Stuckey (2002), Tan (2007). Jokes: Davies (2006), Holmes (2006), Lampert and Ervin-Trip (2006), Norrick (2001), Tsang and Wong (2004). Life Histories: Angrosino (1989), Behar (1990), Blix et al. (2013), Cole and Knowles (2001), Hatch and Wisniewski (1995), Hinck (2004), Hoggett et al. (2006), Presser (2004), Rich (2005), Roy (2006). Also see the journal *Narrative Inquiry* (beginning in 1991).

Phenomenology. Bondas and Eriksson (2001), Giorgi (1986), Herrmann (1991), Howard (1994), Moran (2000), Sokolowski (2000), Staudigl and Berguno (2013), Taylor et al. (2001), van Manen (1990).

Visit the online resource site at study.sagepub.com/bernardaqd to access engaging and helpful digital content, like video tutorials on working with MAXQDA, presentation slides, MAXQDA keyboard shortcuts, datasets, stop list, and recommended readings.

CHAPTER **14**

DISCOURSE ANALYSIS II

Conversation and Performance

INTRODUCTION

Discourse analysis is the study of (1) grammar beyond the sentence; (2) language in use; and (3) the rhetoric of power (Schiffrin et al. 2001:1).

1. The first kind of study—**grammar beyond the sentence**—is about the rules that govern the construction and flow of naturally occurring speech, including narratives and conversations. We're accustomed to thinking about grammar as a set of rules for building sentences, but it's much more than that. Every native speaker of every natural language in the world also learns the grammar—the rules—for telling stories and for cooperatively building conversations.

There are many kinds of stories—folktales, jokes, life events, sermons, and speeches, for example—and there are rules in each language for telling and understanding each kind of story. And there are many kinds of conversations—conversations at a dinner table, conversations between parents and children, conversations between spouses, conversations among members of a jury, between pilots and air traffic control, conversations in a bar, and on and on.

Conversation analysis reveals how people work together in all these different circumstances, according to a set of rules, to build their interactions. Performance analysis, or **ethnopoetics**, focuses on how people set up stories and how they tell them.

2. The second kind of study—**language in use**—focuses on how people pursue their goals in naturally occurring speech. Here, the topics range from: how people extract bribes from one another (Mele and Bello 2007); to how teachers get children to behave in classrooms (De Fina 1997; Morine-Dershimer 2006); to how and when bilinguals switch between languages (Negrón 2007; Scotton and Ury 1977).

3. The third kind of study starts from the observation that people in complex societies understand and reenact in speech the power differences that pervade those societies. Studies in this tradition—called **critical discourse analysis**—focus on how the content of discourse establishes, reflects, or perpetuates power differences between actors in society.

These approaches to analyzing human discourse are not mutually exclusive. The analysis of a single interaction between a doctor and a patient, for example, can contain elements of all three approaches: a discussion of the turn taking (grammar beyond the sentence); a discussion of how the doctor tries to get the patient to comply with orders (language in use); and a discussion of how the rhetoric reinforces the doctor's position of power over the patient (critical analysis). More about this later. (**Further Reading**: reviews of discourse analysis)

♦ GRAMMAR BEYOND THE SENTENCE

This tradition of discourse analysis is grounded in linguistics. Linguists recognize five levels of grammar: phonology, morphology, syntax, semantics, and discourse.

Phonology is the study of the sounds of a language and the rules governing their use. For example, the guttural ch in the name Bach is used in many languages, but not in English. The vowel sound æ in cat is pretty common, but it doesn't exist in Spanish.

The basic sounds that are available in any particular language are the language's **phonemes**. There are 42–44 phonemes in English (depending on the dialect). Unfortunately, we only have 26 squiggles in our alphabet to represent all those sounds, but we make do by letting some letters and combinations of letters do double duty. For example, there are three pronunciations of the letter e in the word "represented." (Go ahead, count them. The first is eh as in pet. The second is ee as in street. The third is ə, called a **schwa** in phonetics. It's the same sound as the second o in doctor.)

Each level of grammar has its own set of rules. The rules of **phonology** are learned very early in life, of course. For example, there is a phonological rule in English that forbids the sound combination pt at the beginning of words but allows it in the middle and at the end (think of aptitude and inept). Speakers of Greek, though, don't have this rule, so they have no problem pronouncing the pt in pterodactyl, Ptolemy, and ptomaine poisoning, which speakers of English pronounce as if the p weren't there—as in terodactyl, tolemy, and tomaine.

Morphology comprises the rules for making meaningful units, or **lexemes**, out of phonemes. Some lexemes are always attached to others (think of un-, ig-, il- and im-, which mean "not" in unnatural, ignoble, illegal, and immoral), but most lexemes are simply words that stand on their own, like "hairy" and "eggplant."

Syntax is what we usually think of as the grammar of a language. It is the set of rules for stringing lexemes together to make phrases and sentences that native speakers recognize as well formed. Languages with long literary traditions, like English, Arabic, Hindi, Japanese, and such, have developed formal grammars of syntax—all that stuff about parsing sentences you learned in grade school—but the syntax of any language is much, much more complicated than that. It involves all the rules that you follow in decoding new sentences that come your way and in making up new ones every day that others have to decode.

Semantics is the set of rules governing the variable meaning of words and phrases in context. It's the semantic rules of grammar that make word play possible. For example, if someone says to you, "It was so nice to have you here today" (as you're leaving their home), and you reply, "It was so nice being had," you are using your knowledge of the semantic rules of American English grammar to make a joke. And you'd also better know the cultural rules for when you can get away with such things or the joke won't be funny.

Finally, there's **discourse**, the part of the grammar beyond the sentence. Linguistics-based discourse analysis is the study of the rules governing the construction of whole conversations and narrative performances.

♦ CONVERSATION ANALYSIS

Conversation analysis is the search for the grammar of ordinary discourse, or **talk-in-interaction**. It is the study of how people take turns in ordinary discourse—who talks first (and next, and next), who interrupts, who waits for a turn.

If you listen carefully to ordinary conversations between equals, you'll hear a lot of sentence fragments, false starts, interruptions, overlaps (simultaneous speech), and repeating of words and phrases. As students of conversation have learned, however, there is order in all that seeming chaos as participants respond to each other (even in strong disagreements and shouting matches) and take turns (Goodwin 1981:55ff).

The grammatical rules of turn taking are, like the rules that govern the formation of sentences, known to native speakers of any language. But unlike the other rules of grammar, the rules for taking turns are flexible and allow turn taking to be negotiated, on the fly, by participants in a conversation. At the molecular level, then, every conversation is unique, but the study of many conversational exchanges can expose the general rules, within and across cultures, that govern how conversations start, evolve, and end (see Box 14.1).

Box 14.1

Turn-Taking Rules in Institutions

In many institutional settings, turn taking in meetings is regulated by someone acting as leader. Even these rules can be subtle. At a convention of Alcoholics Anonymous in Southeast Asia, a meeting described by O'Halloran (2005:541) operated on an unspoken, but apparently well-understood rule: A member would rise and go the microphone at the speaker's table. This simple act was sufficient to claim a turn.

And pilots all over the world have a special turn-taking rule: They absolutely must learn to let each other finish each sentence before jumping in with the next one (Nevile 2007).

Unique sentences are produced all the time, by speakers of thousands of languages across the world. The sentence you are reading right now might never have been uttered or written before, but every native speaker of English reading this book knows the rules governing how the sentence was formed. We produced the sentence and you are decoding it on the fly. In natural languages, a finite number of rules, operating on a finite number of words, produce an infinite number of well-formed sentences.

This **generative principle**—that systems with a finite number of rules can produce an infinite number of unique outcomes—was first articulated in 1836 by

Wilhelm von Humboldt, and was formalized in 1957 by Noam Chomsky (see Chomsky 1957:v). The idea is very important. The evolution of life forms is based on rules, but the forms of life (kangaroos here, chimps there) are a set of unique outcomes. Every geological formation—every canyon and bluff—is unique, but we know that their formation and weathering are governed by rules. Every hurricane, every volcano eruption, and every battle is unique and, on the surface, chaotic. But we study hurricanes, volcano eruptions, and battles because we know that there are regularities across many unique events.

TRANSCRIPTIONS ♦

To identify turns and other features of conversations (like **adjacency pairs** and **repair sequences**, which we'll take up later), you need detailed records of actual talk-in-interaction. The tactic for signaling the intention to take a turn or to repair a broken turn sequence may be a word or a phrase, or it may be **prosodic features of speech** (intonation, length of vowels, stress, and so on), or breaths, tokens (like er, ummm, eh), gestures, body language, or gazes (Gardner 2001; Goodwin 1994).

Table 14.1 shows one widely used system, developed by Gail Jefferson (1983, 2004), for transcribing speech, including some of the basic prosodic features. (**Further Reading**: transcribing conversation)

Table 14.1 Conventions for Transcribing Text (After Jefferson 1983)

Symbol	Definition
ni::::ce	Indicates length of a consonant or vowel. More colons = more length.
>text<	Speech between angle brackets is faster than normal speech.
(text)	Text in parentheses means that the transcriber had doubts about it.
( )	Parens with no text means that transcriber could not make it out at all.
(1.6)	Numbers in parens indicate pauses, in seconds and tenths of a second.
(.)	A period in parens indicates an untimed and quick pause
((text))	Double parens contain comments by the researcher about people's gestures, gazes, and so on. Often in italics.
[ ]	Left square brackets indicate where one person interrupts another or talks simultaneously. Right square brackets mark the end of overlap.
–	An en-dash (longer than a hyphen) indicates an abrupt end in the middle of a word.

(Continued)

Table 14.1 (Continued)

Symbol	Definition
?	A question mark indicates rising intonation. It does not necessarily mean that a question is being asked.
.	A period indicates falling intonation. It does not necessarily mean the end of a sentence.
=	The equal sign indicates that a person takes a turn immediately as the previous turn ends.
°text°	Text between degree symbols is quieter speech than that surrounding it.
TEXT	Text in caps indicates louder speech than that surrounding it.
Text	Underlining means that the words are emphasized.
.hh and hh	These indicate inhaled (with period first) and exhaled (no period) breaths, as often occur in natural conversation.

SOURCE: After Jefferson (1983).

It takes six–eight hours to transcribe an hour of ordinary interviews. If you have 40 hours of recorded interviews, plan on working eight hours a day, every day for 30 days to convert them to text files. The real time may be several months. And if you have 100 hours of recorded interviews. . . . And if you are doing conversation analysis, the problem is much worse. It can take 20 hours or more to transcribe an hour of conversation with the level of detail required for this kind of work.

If you have the budget for it, the easiest and most pleasant choice is to turn your recordings over to a professional transcriber. If you are transcribing interviews yourself, be sure to invest in the right equipment. There are two choices: (1) a combination of transcription hardware and software and (2) voice recognition (VR) software.

1. With the transcription hardware and software option, you control the recording playback using a foot pedal or a set of hot keys on your keyboard. This lets you listen to a couple of seconds of recording at a time, type everything into the computer, and then move on to the next chunk. Using a foot pedal or a set of keys lets you go back and repeat chunks, all while keeping your hands on the keyboard. (You may also be able to use a mouse, but this takes more time.)

2. With VR software, you listen to an interview through a set of headphones and repeat the words—both your questions and your respondent's responses—out loud, in your own voice. The software listens to your voice and types out the words across the screen.

It can take months to train VR software to its maximum accuracy, depending on how much of a workout you put it through, but once the software is up to speed, it can convert digital text from voice with 95%–99% accuracy at about 100–120 word per minute—normal speech, in other words. With a 1%–5% error rate, you still have to go over every line of your work to find the errors—you may have to tell it that the word "bloat" should be "float," for instance—and you also have to tell the software where to put punctuation, paragraph breaks, and such. But once a VR program is fully trained, the total time for transcribing interviews can be reduced greatly, compared to regular transcription, especially if you're not a professional at the keyboard.

The built-in vocabularies are enormous—something like 250,000 words in English—but the programs still need to learn all the special vocabulary words you throw at them. If you say, "Freddie said he didn't want to be friends with me," you would have to spell out "Freddie"—literally, by saying F-R-E-D-D-I-E—and the software would add the word to its vocabulary. After that, the software would recognize the word "Freddie" when you said it out loud.

VR software is available in English, Spanish, French, German, Japanese, and Chinese, and there is VR software being developed for many other languages, like Swahili and Urdu. If you are working in a language for which there is no VR software, you can listen to a recording and read it back, aloud, in a language that the software understands.

VR programs are trained to one voice, but you can use them to transcribe focus groups by speaking each participant's part. If you do this, be sure to identify each participant by a pseudonym.

Taking Turns

We've known for a long time that there are regularities in conversations (Aristotle observed in Poetics IV that "conversational speech runs into iambic lines more frequently than into any other kind of verse"), but Harvey Sacks and his colleagues, Emmanuel Schegloff and Gail Jefferson, are widely credited for developing the systematic study of order in conversations (Jefferson 1973; Sacks et al. 1974; Schegloff 1968; Schegloff and Sacks 1973).

Among the basic rules they discovered is that the person who is speaking may (but does not have to) identify the next speaker to take a turn (Sacks et al. 1974:700ff). This is done with conversational devices—like "So what do you think, Jack?"—or with gazes or body language (Goodwin 1986, 1994). If the person speaking does not select the next speaker, then any other person in the conversation can self-select to take a turn.

Alternatively, the next speaker may jump in before a speaker has completed a turn, by anticipating the end of a turn—a supportive gesture—or by interrupting and trying to take away the speaker's turn by force—a hostile gesture. Big gaps occur so rarely in real conversations because speakers anticipate the end of turns so well. For example:

```
1   A: what a cute no::se.
2   B: all [babies ha-
3   A:      [no they don't
```

A takes a turn; B responds and then A says "No they don't" just as the syllable "ba" in "baby" registers. There is no gap at the end of B's turn because the end of B's turn is predictable to A. And even though A contradicts B, the interruption is supportive, in grammatical terms—i.e., it doesn't violate any rules—because it keeps the conversation going.

If the turn taking runs out of steam in a conversation, either because it becomes unpredictable or the content gets used up and no one jumps in to take a turn at the appropriate time, then the current speaker may (but does not have to) continue talking. If none of these things happen, there will be a gap in the conversation. Gaps don't usually last very long if the rules of conversation are followed.

The rules are often broken in real conversations. People often do interrupt each other unsupportively and don't wait to take their turns. People who get interrupted don't always push on, trying to finish their turn, but relinquish their turn instead, without finishing. On the other hand, people usually recognize when the preferred order of turn taking has not been adhered to and engage in what are called **repair tactics**. For example, Sacks et al. (1974) noted that when two people start talking over each other, one of them might just stop and let the other finish. Here's an example from conversation we overheard:

```
1   A: [It's not like we–
2   B:    [Some people are–
3   B: Sorry.
4   A: No, g'head
5   B: .hhhh I wus jus gonna say that some people aren't innerested in sports [at all.
6   A:                                                                         [right
```

This is a simple repair tactic that doesn't involve any serious content. Other repair tactics can be more complex. The result of this repair sequence could have come out differently. But in the study of hundreds of natural conversations between equals, we can uncover the rules governing how people open and close conversations, how they repair mistakes (e.g., when they break the rules of turn taking), and how they segue from one theme to another.

The **turn-taking sequence rules** can be suspended, of course, in the telling of jokes and stories. If you ask someone "Did you hear the one about ...?" and they say "No, tell me," then this suspends turn taking until you're finished with the joke. If they interrupt you in telling the joke, this breaks the rule for this conversation element.

And the same thing goes for storytelling. If you say "I was on the flight from Hell coming back from Detroit last week" and the person you're talking to responds by saying "What happened?" then you get to tell you the story all the way through. Certain kinds of interruptions are permitted—in fact, you expect people to say "Uh, huh" and other such supportive interruptions when you're on a roll—but sidetracking you completely from the story is not expected.

It's not expected, but it happens, and when sidetracking happens, one of several repair sequences might kick in. "Sorry, I got you off track. Then what happened?" is a repair sequence. We've all experienced the pain of never getting back to a story from which we were sidetracked in a conversation. When that happens, we might think badly of the person who did it or we might shrug it off—depending on the context and what's at stake. If you're in a job interview and the interviewer sidetracks you, you might think twice about insisting that the interviewer let you finish the story you were telling.

Adjacency Pairs

Among the first things that conversation analysts noticed when they started looking carefully at conversations was ordered pairs of expressions, like questions and greetings (Schegloff and Sacks 1973). Once the first part of a pair occurs, the second part is expected.

For example, as Schegloff pointed out (1968, 1979), if you say "Hello" and you get silence in return, you might take the absence of response as meaningful. If someone asks "How're you doing?" and you respond by saying "Great" but don't follow up with "And how about you?" then the other person might look for meaning in your tone of voice. Did you say "Great" with enthusiasm or with sarcasm? If the former, you might hear "I'm so glad to hear that," in return. But if it was the latter, you might hear "Sorry I asked" or "Excuse me for asking" with equal sarcasm. In other words, other people's interpretation of the content in your turn leads them to adjust the content of their next turn.

Sacks (1992:3ff) noticed that workers at a psychiatric hospital's emergency telephone line greeted callers by saying something like, "Hello. This is Mr. Smith. May I help you?" Most of the time, the response was "Hello, this is Mr. Brown," but on one occasion, the caller responded, "I can't hear you." When the worker repeated his greeting, "This is Mr. *Smith*," with an emphasis on Smith, the caller responded "Smith."

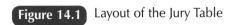
Figure 14.1 Layout of the Jury Table

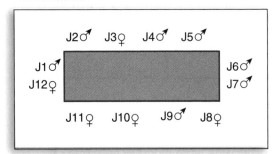

SOURCE: Manzo (1996).

Figure 14.1 shows the layout of the jury table, and Table 14.2 contains the data for one turn-taking sequence. At the start of the deliberations, the foreperson, J1, at the head of the table, on the left, proposed that each juror talk about how she or he felt about the case.

Manzo noticed that, at lines 10 and 12, both juror 2 and juror 12 chime in and support juror 1's suggestion about everyone making an opening statement. It takes 2.5 seconds for juror 2 to respond after juror 12 does, but the foreperson, juror 1, chooses juror 2 (to his left), rather than juror 12. Juror 2 launches right in, down to line 27.

Now, look closely at what happens next. At this juncture, it is still possible for juror 12 to be the next speaker. After all, she had signaled her interest back in line 10. But at the end of his statement, juror 2 turns his gaze toward juror 3, to his left, and then down to the table. Juror 3 cranes her head to see what the foreperson will do next. He nods to juror 3, and she launches into her statement (down to line 39).

The first turn for an opening statement was decided entirely by juror 1, who chose juror 2 over juror 12. The *second* turn, however, is a joint operation, involving three people: the foreperson and jurors 2 and 3. Juror 3's gaze, at the end of his statement, toward juror 3 sets things up; juror 3's craning her neck to see the foreperson is part of the operation; and juror 1's gaze toward juror 3 nails down that it is her turn.

By the time juror 3 completes her turn (at line 39), she only has to shift her weight to her left, for juror 4 to take up the next turn. At this point, the rule is established. No more gazes or instructions from juror 1 are needed.

A Final Word About Conversation Analysis

Conversation analysis is a highly empirical and highly inductive method, but nothing is 100% inductive, and in actual practice, it involves both induction and hypothesis testing. You start with a transcript and come at it with as few assumptions as you can and look for regularities in how people manage themselves during conversations. You look for indicator behaviors (gazes, phrases, postures) and, as you pick up clues about these things, you begin to look for repetitions of them.

The process is really hypothesis testing within a transcript. You discover what you think is a regularity, then look for it again to see if you're right. The procedure is the same as that in classical grounded theory, where you let themes emerge from initial narratives and then look for repetitions of those themes. (**Further Reading**: conversation analysis)

Table 14.2	Excerpt From a Criminal Jury

Line	Speaker	Text
1 2 3 4 5 6 7 8 9	J1	If I may make a suggestion? rather than- I know that juries uh um >like Mr. ( ) mentioned< like to take a vote right off the bat and..hh I think if we <u>do</u>:: that we'll probably end up discussing it anyhow so let's:: just go around the table discuss the case? and your:.hh views? and uh after:: everybody's said their piece us (.5) we can uh. take a vote on u what we think. if::: that's agreeable to everybody? (1.8)
10 11	J12	uh huh (2.5)
12	J2	sounds good=
13	J1	=so. *((turns to and smiles at J2))* you wanna start?
14 15 16 17 18 19 20 21 22 23 24 25 26 27 28 29 30	J2	mm okay?.hh I found three:: points. that the prosecutor. hadda prove? he proved.hh that the defendant did possess the gun >the defendant <u>knew</u> he possessed a gun<.hh and that uh: the defendant knew he was (.) a convicted felon at the time he uh: possessed a gun..hh however uh::. because of this case and because of uhm: (1.6) because of the:: record of the defendant uh I 'd have a re- I'd have a real <u>tough</u> time.h uh voting him guiltyu on this a:nduh:- I haven't made up my <u>mind</u> yet.hhh but I see both sides of- <u>both</u> sides of uhm:: <u>both</u> the cases BOTH of the cases as they've been laid out. and uh: rinow? I haven't made up my mind one uh >how I'm goin ta vote. (2.3) *((J2 directs gaze toward J3 and then down to table. J1 then nods in the direction of J3, and J3 cranes her neck in order to meet J1's gaze))*
31 32 33 34 35 36 37 38 39 40 41	J3	>Okay I feel the defendant is.< guilty. uh. on all three accusations <u>technically</u>. (.) but I I guess I feel that we should *also* take into consideration the fact that..h he du::z have a reading disability. as *well* as maybe some <u>other</u> disabilities >I'm not trying to pay on your <u>sympathies</u> or anything but. .h it is <u>something</u> that I have to consider tch and right now I haven't (.) determined whether I should name the defendant guilty or innocent. (3.0) *((Juror 3 produces a postural shift toward J4 without eye contact))*
42	J4	.hh I fee:l that . . .

SOURCE: J. Manzo, 1996. Taking turns and taking sides: Opening scenes from two jury deliberations. *Social Psychology Quarterly* 59:107–25.

♦ PERFORMANCE ANALYSIS: ETHNOPOETICS

In **performance analysis**, or **ethnopoetics**, the goal is to discover regularities in how people tell stories, whether in everyday life (Ochs and Capps 2001) or in classrooms (Juzwik 2004). The method is best known in folklore and linguistics and was heavily influenced by the work of Dell Hymes on narratives from the Chinookan languages of Oregon and Washington. We're going to go through Hymes's work in some detail. Because it deals with American Indian languages, it will seem very esoteric at first. But stay with us; its value for all discourse analysis is hard to exaggerate.

The Chinookan Texts

Chinookan is a family of American Indian languages with related but mutually unintelligible branches, like Shoalwater and Kathlemet and Wasco-Wishram. To get an idea of how these languages are related, think of languages, like Spanish, Italian, Rumanian, French, and Portuguese—all branches of (descended from) Latin.

Now, between 1890 and 1894, the anthropologist Franz Boas had run into an informant who was fluent in both Shoalwater and Kathlamet Chinook and had collected texts in both languages. Hymes examined those texts as well as texts from Clackamas Chinook (collected in 1930 and 1931 by Melville Jacobs) and in Wasco (Wishram) Chinook (collected by Edward Sapir in 1905, by Hymes in the 1950s, and by Michael Silverstein in the 1960s and 1970s).

What Hymes found was that features of Chinook that might have seemed idiosyncratic to the speakers of those three Chinook languages—Shoalwater, Kathlamet, and Clackamas Chinook—were actually "part of a common fabric of performance style," so that the three languages "share a common form of poetic organization" in which narratives are "organized in terms of lines, verses, stanzas, scenes, and what many call acts" (D. Hymes 1977:431). Hymes discovered the existence of verses, by recognizing repetition within a block of text. "Covariation between form and meaning," said Hymes, "between units with a recurrent Chinookan pattern of narrative organization, is the key" (1977:438).

This discovery had implications for a general theory of poetics and literature.

Finding Patterns in Performance

In some texts, Hymes found recurrent linguistic elements that made the task easy. Linguists who have worked with precisely recorded texts in Native American languages have noticed the recurrence of elements like "now," "then," "now then," and "now again" at the beginning of sentences. These kinds of things often signal the separation of verses. The trick is to recognize them, and the method is to look for "abstract features that co-occur with the use of initial particle pairs in the narratives" of other speakers who use initial particle pairs. The method, then, is a form of controlled comparison (1977:439) and it can be applied to the analysis of any set of texts.

In a series of articles and books (1976, 1977, 1980a, 1980b, 1981), Hymes showed that most Native American texts of narrative performance (going back to the early texts collected by Franz Boas and his students and continuing in today's narrative performance by American Indians as well) are organized into verses and stanzas that are aggregated into groups of either fives and threes or fours and twos. Boas and his students organized the narratives of American Indians into lines and this, according to Virginia Hymes, hid from view "a vast world of poetry waiting to be released by those of us with some knowledge of the languages" (V. Hymes 1987:65).

Dell Hymes's method, according to Virginia Hymes, involves "working back and forth between content and form, between organization at the level of the whole narrative and at the level of the details of lines within a single verse or even words within a line" (V. Hymes 1987:67–68). Gradually, an analysis emerges that reflects the analyst's understanding of the larger narrative tradition and of the particular narrator.

This emergent analysis doesn't just happen miraculously. It is, Virginia Hymes reminds us, only through close work with many narratives by many narrators that you develop an understanding of the narrative devices that people use in a particular language and the many ways they use those little devices (V. Hymes 1987).

Since Hymes's discovery, the method of ethnopoetics has been applied to many other Native American narrative texts, including Kuna Indian chants in Panama (Sherzer 1994) and modern Navajo poetry (Mitchell and Webster 2011), as well as to Japanese commercials (Kataoka 2012) and Kenyan gospel music (Lamont 2010).

Staat's Study of Mathematics Discourse in the Classroom

It has also been extended to the study of discourse in the classroom (Oslund 2012). In 1987, David Pimm reported on a lesson he was teaching about modular mathematics to high-school freshmen. (Modular mathematics deals with cycles of numbers and remainders that repeat themselves. The numbers on a clock, for example, repeat with a modulus of 12 [called mod 12]. So, at, say, 5:00 pm, "20 mod 12" would be 8 hours from the following 5:00 am, or 1:00 pm the next day.) The students in Pimm's class were picking up one of five different colored rods, and Pimm asked the students if they could tell which color rod a girl named Debbie was going to take.

David raised his hand and the teacher asked: "David did you want to say something?" Here is David's answer:

"Yes, cos every fifth one from William is going to be a white, and every fifth one from the next person on is going to be a red, and every fifth one from the next person is going to be a green, eh?" (Pimm 1987:57).

Susan Staats (2008) reanalyzed this brief discourse between a teacher and his student, applying Hymes's method of ethnopoetics—marking repetitions and parallels visually to illustrate how narrators build arguments.

David makes his observation using strong syntactic parallelism. One means of highlighting this parallelism relies on indentation (D. Hymes 1981):

```
 1   Yes
 2   Cos every fifth one
 3         from William
 4             is going to be
 5               a white,
 6   and every fifth one
 7         from the next person on
 8             is going to be
 9               a red
10   and every fifth one
11           from the next person
12             is going to be
13               a green
14   eh?
```
(From Staats 2008:26)

Note how Staats has rewritten the dialogue into three poetic lines, with the "yes" and "eh?' in lines 1 and 14 as bookends. In the first poetic line (lines 2–4 here), Staats shows how David, the student, establishes a pattern, which he will repeat in the next two lines. With this device, Staats says, David shows that he understands the principle of modular arithmetic. In fact, Staats says, "the discourse structure is identical to the mathematical argument" (p. 27).

Staats point out that the poetic line format reveals something less obvious, too. Lines 1 and 14 are a device that David uses to establish his grasp of the lesson. He answers "yes," to the teacher's question; he does, indeed, have something to say. And he ends with "eh?"— "a conversational QED," as Staats puts it—to show that he has nailed it. (**Further Reading**: ethnopoetics and performance analysis)

LANGUAGE IN USE ◆

This branch of discourse analysis is about how people use language to get things done. Studies in this area involve the detailed analysis of interaction—much like conversation analysis, but paying attention to the content and the motivations of speakers, not just to the structure of their interaction.

People around the world are very adept at using just the right language to find marriage partners (Gal 1978), at using jokes to engage in forbidden political discourse (Van Boeschoten 2006), at using subtle language cues to bribe border officials while giving everyone plausible deniability (Mele and Bello 2007).

One area of interest is **situational ethnicity**, or ethnic identity switching. This phenomenon—where people adopt different ethnicity markers, depending on the situation—has fascinated social scientists for years (Gluckman 1958 [1940]; Nagata 1974; Okamura 1981). People switch ethnicity by telling jokes, or by choosing particular foods when offered a choice, or by casually dropping cultural-insider phrases that signal ethnicity to others. They may do this to land a job, to get a better price in a bargaining situation, to get a better table in a restaurant, and so on.

Negrón's Study of Situational Ethnicity in New York

Rosalyn Negrón (2011) studied situational ethnicity among Puerto Rican American and other Hispanics in New York. Her work focused on how Spanish–English bilinguals use **code switching**—moving back and forth between two languages—as a marker for ethnic identity switching and for getting things they wanted in various interactions.

One of Negrón's informants was Roberto, a 36-year-old Venezuelan who grew up in New York in a neighborhood of Whites, Blacks, and Latinos. Roberto has blue eyes and white skin. He's married to a Puerto Rican women, and his step-mother is a black Haitian. He is completely fluent in Venezuelan Spanish, two dialects of Puerto Rican Spanish (standard and nonstandard), African American Vernacular English, and New York English.

Roberto sells equipment for street fairs—tables, chairs, canopies, and so on. In the interaction below, Roberto goes into a cellphone store and gives James, the store manager, a flyer about the street-fair business. Like Roberto, James is a Latino who looks European and who speaks English with no Spanish accent at all.

Dropping Hints and Doing Business

As they start to talk, neither one knows that the other is Latino, but both of them have business interests to pursue—Roberto to sell his street-fair merchandise; James to sell his cellphones. Negrón's recordings let us listen in:

1 R: H'you doing.

2 J: Alright.=

3 R: =You guys ah participating in the street fai(-r)z?

4 (0.7)

5 J: Yeah.

6 R: You are? (0.5) 'K. Just in case you need, ah, in

7 case you need canopies tables and chai(-r)z,

8 (1.0)

9 j's gimee a call.

10 J: Yeah. I don't know when the next one is I

11 haven't got [any-]

12 R: [May twenty-secon(-d).]

13 J: Rea:.lly?

14 R: That's the one with the Chamber and <Clearvie::wz

15 is in deh:: fawl>.

16 (1.0)

17 J: Mm, well I do the Clearview one over at at my

18 other store.

19 R: Ah, which store is [that-

20 J: [(By the), ah, Junction Boulevard.

21 R: On Junction?, yeah?

22 J: Yeah.

23 R: Well, I got the canopies, tables and chairs. I

24 used to work for Clearview. I worked for Clearview

25   for 8 yea(-r)z.

26 J: [°Ok.°]

27 R: [An'] um I started a canopy company (0.5)

28   that's (0.8) direct contact with dem, so whenever you

29   need one or if you need tables, chai®z whatever

30   you need,[j's give me a cawl ahead of time, let=

31 J: [°Ok.°

32 R: =me know what event, give me your spot nuhmbuh and

33   it will be there before you get der.

34   (1.0)

35 J: Ok.=

36 R: =And [it'll already be set up.

37 J: [( )=

38 R: =>Yah.<

(Negrón 2011:87–88)

Roberto is dropping clues all over the place that he's a New Yorker. There's the aw
sound (fawl and cawl in lines 15 and 30, instead of fall and call); the use of deh, der,

and dem instead of the, there, and them (lines 15, 28, 33); and the dropped r's in chairs, fairs, years, and numbers (lines 3, 7, 25, 29, 32). So, far, though, there's no hint that either of them is Latino. That soon changes. James looks at the flyer that Roberto gave him:

39	J:	Let me give you some information.
40		(5.0)
41	J:	*Roberto?!*
42	R:	Yeah.
43	J:	I had a couple of other customers that that(.) do
44		fairs and stuff.
45	R:	O?k.
46		(2.0)
47	J:	°Try to give you some info.°
48		(2.0)
49		((James searches for business card))
50	J:	°(Ok)° ((James hands Roberto business card))

(Negrón 2011:89)

In line 41, James reads Roberto's name from the flyer, using perfect Spanish pronunciation of the name. Then, in line 50, he hands Roberto his own business card.

51		(3.0)
52		((Roberto reads business card))
53	R:	*Cuchifrito* for Thought.
		('Puerto Rican soul food')
54		((Roberto laughs))
55	R:	I like that! [That's hot.]
56		((Roberto looking at business card))
57	J:	[(Yeah I),] I own an online magazine
58		called *Cuchifrito* for Thought, it's been around for 8
59		years.
60		R: O?k.
61	J:	Ahm, (2.0) I'm working with a company called
62		*Alianza Latina?*
		('Latino/a Alliance')
63		(.5)
64	J:	They did something really big in, ah, Flushing
65		Meadow Park last year.
66	R:	*No me diga/h/.=*
		('You don't say?')
67	J:	=Yeah and >it's all *Latino*(-s)< and [and from 21 countries?]
68	R:	[*O:h, coño, e(-s)ta (bien).*]
		('Oh, damn, that's good.')

69   J: >and they used a bunch [of canopies and stuff like that.]<=
70   R: [°Mm::::h, o?k.°]
(Negrón 2011:90–91)

There's a Lot Going on Here

In line 53, when Roberto reads James's card aloud, he uses perfect Spanish pronunciation for the word *cuchifrito*. Cuchifritos are small cubes of fried pork (usually tails,
ears, stomach, and tongue) and are a famous Spanish Caribbean dish. Any speaker of
Spanish who lives in a Puerto Rican or Dominican neighborhood in New York City
would know the word and its ethnic implications.

In line 58, when James repeats the word, he, too, uses the Spanish pronunciation.
He follows up by telling Roberto that he works for *Alianza Latina*, again code switching
from perfect English in line 61 to perfect Spanish in line 62.

A few lines later, in lines 66 and 68, Roberto nails it all down, by responding in
Spanish to James's discussion in English about an event in Flushing Meadow Park. And
it's not just any old Spanish. In lines 66 and 68, Roberto uses an unmistakably Puerto
Rican dialect.

In Negrón's work, we see again how important it is to be steeped in a culture to
do this kind of analysis. You have to know, for example, about cuchifritos; and you
have to know that the aspiration at the end of *diga/h/* in the expression *No me diga/h/*
in line 66 is a replacement for an s and that this is characteristic of Caribbean Spanish.
(**Further Reading**: code switching and ethnic identity)

◆ CRITICAL DISCOURSE ANALYSIS:
LANGUAGE AND POWER

The critical perspective in social science is rooted in Antonio Gramsci's discussion
(1994; and see Forgacs 2000) in the 1930s of what he called **cultural hegemony**.
Modern states, Gramsci observed, control the mass media and the schools, the structural mechanisms for shaping and transmitting culture. Marxist theory predicts that the
culture (the superstructure) follows the structure, and so the lower and middle classes
in modern states come to believe in—even advocate—the entrenched differences in
power that keep them subservient to the elite.

In critical discourse analysis, the idea is to show how these power differences—
between men and women, for example, or between doctors and patients, employers
and employees, and so on—are perpetuated, reinforced, and resisted. (**Further Reading**:
critical discourse analysis)

Gender and Discourse

Mattei (1998), for example, counted the number of times male and female witnesses in a U.S. Senate hearing were interrupted. These were panel hearings in the nomination of David H. Souter to the U.S. Supreme Court. There were 30 question periods in these panels, and Mattei counted 76 cases of overlap in the testimony. Thirteen cases of overlap were simply to ask the witness to speak louder or to ask a senator to clarify a question. The other 63 cases were interruptions—that is, cutting off a speaker and trying to take over a turn.

The distribution of these 63 cases is revealing. As we expect, senators (who are in a position of power) interrupted witnesses 41 times; witnesses interrupted senators 22 times. Also as expected, of the 41 interruptions by senators, 34 were against women and seven were against men. Women, however, were more assertive than men were when it came to interrupting senators: Of the 22 interruptions against senators by witnesses, 17 were by women (see Box 14.3).

Box 14.3

Gendered Interruption

Pioneering research by Zimmerman and West (1983 [1975]) showed that, in ordinary conversations, men interrupted women more often than women interrupted men. Later research by these same scholars and by many others has shown how complex the patterns are. Kennedy and Camden (1983), for example, showed that women sometimes interrupt more than men, and Kendall and Tannen (2001:552) showed that not all interruptions are equal: some are better characterized as overlapping where the purpose is really "to show support rather than to gain the floor." And West (1995:116) showed that in conversations with men, it is often women's response efforts that enable men to "produce 'something worth listening to' in the first place." (**Further Reading**: gendered interruption)

Doctor–Patient Interaction

Dozens of studies have established the asymmetry in the doctor–patient relation: Doctors use their knowledge to establish their authority and patients adopt a meek, accepting role.

Maynard (1991) analyzed how a doctor delivers bad news to a mother and father of a child who has developmental problems (particularly in language and speech).

The parents tell the doctor that their child, J, doesn't seem to be progressing normally in speaking. The doctor says that J is having a problem with language, which, he says, is different from speaking.

The parents don't understand the distinction, and the doctor says:

> Language are (*sic*) the actual words. Speech is how the words sound. Okay? J's speech is a very secondary consideration. It's the language which is her problem. When language goes into her brain, it gets garbled up, and doesn't make sense. ... It has something to do with the parts of her brain that control speech that control language, and it doesn't work. (Maynard 1991:454)

What's going on here? The parents are being taught that they don't control certain kinds of information and must therefore accept a subservient role in the interaction. Talcott Parsons had observed this patient–doctor dynamic in his discussion of roles (1951), but Maynard shows that patients don't necessarily come into the doctor's office with that role in mind. Instead, they develop the subservient role, *in cooperation with doctors*, during conversations about the illness.

Coding Doctor–Patient Interactions

Howard Waitzkin and his colleagues (Borges and Waitzkin 1995; Waitzkin et al. 1994) analyzed transcripts of 50 encounters between older patients and primary care internists. Analysis begins by coding the text for elements of interest in the research. In this case, coders were told to "flag instances when either doctors or patients made statements that conveyed ideologic content or expressed messages of social control" and nonverbal elements in the text—like interruptions or shifts in tone of voice or unresponsiveness to questions by patients—"that might clarify a deeper structure lying beneath the surface elements of discourse" (Borges and Waitzkin 1995:35).

When the coders finished their work, they produced a "preliminary structural outline or diagram that depicted how the medical discourse ... processed contextual issues" (Borges and Waitzkin 1995:35). Then members of the research group met together for several months to review annotated transcripts and preliminary outlines or diagrams. They looked at all the coded instances of instances of ideology and social control—the main topics that they had told the coders to flag—and chose texts to illustrate those and other themes, like gender roles and aging.

There were plenty of instances in which the members of the team disagreed about the meaning of a text. In those cases, they report, "we brainstormed to resolve our disagreements and tried to avoid the discussion's being dominated by one person's views" (Borges and Waitzkin 1995:35).

Recognizing that readers can have different interpretations of the same text, the researchers made all their original data available for reanalysis by filing them at University Microfilms International. Then they present their results, which consist of a series of excerpts from the texts and an analysis of the meaning of each excerpt. (**Further Reading**: doctor—patient interaction)

Presenting the Results

Borges and Waizkin's work is an example of a common method for presenting results of interpretive analysis: laying out conclusions that are instantiated by prototypical quotes from the transcripts.

For example, a woman visits her doctor complaining of multiple symptoms. The doctor reaches a diagnosis of what's called "suburban syndrome," an illness that affects women who try to do too much outside the home while maintaining all their responsibilities at home as well. The doctor prescribes rest; the patient says that she wants a prescription for tranquilizers.

The doctor resists at first, but then relents—and not only gives the patient a prescription, but a renewable one at that. He tries to reassure the patient that there is nothing wrong with her that withdrawing from a few activities wouldn't fix. Still, the patient returns to her concern about organic disease and the doctor cuts her off:

P: That's what I thought maybe you would give me a blood test
      today, see if I was anemic
D: [For what? Nah (words)
P: [I sometimes feel
      light-headed
D: I know.
P: And my mother, and my mother tends to be anemic.
D: Don't choose a diagnosis out of the blue. Buy a medical
      book and get a real *nice* diagnosis. Well, and you, I'll
      order them ((referring to the tranquilizers)). Which drug store do you use?
      (Borges and Waitzkin 1995:40–41)

Borges and Waitzkin comment on this section of text:

From the doctor's viewpoint, a search for an underlying physical disorder is fruitless. Such patients with diverse somatic symptoms can present diagnostic and therapeutic challenges for primary care physicians. The doctor concludes that the patient's physical symptoms reflect troubles in her social context, more than pathophysiology. Yet his attempts to persuade her on this point never quite succeed. ...

A college graduate with young children at home, the patient does not refer at any time to her own work aspirations or to her children, nor does the doctor ask. For the present and the indefinite future, one assumes, her work consists of the housewife's duties. ...

Although the doctor gives a contextual diagnosis, suburban syndrome, potentially important contextual issues arise in the conversation either marginally (brief allusions to the patient's husband) or not at all (work aspirations, child care arrangements, and social support network). Nevertheless, the doctor manages the patient's contextual difficulties by encouraging rest and prescribing a tranquilizer. Presumably the patient continues to accept the ideologic assumption that her social role as suburban homemaker is the proper one for her. She thus returns and consents to same social context as before, now with the benefit of medical advice and pharmacologic assistance. (Borges and Waitzkin 1995:41)

Here's another example from the same project—a snippet of interaction between a doctor (D) and his patient (P), an elderly woman who has come in for a follow-up of her heart disease:

P: Well I should—now I've got birthday cards to buy.
   I've got seven or eight birthdays this week—month. Instead
   of that I'm just gonna write 'em and wish them a happy
   birthday. Just a little note, my grandchildren.
D: Mm hmm.
P: But I'm not gonna bother. I just can't do it all, Dr. —
D: Well.
P: I called my daughters, her birthday was just, today's the third.
D: Yeah.
P: My daughter's birthday in Princeton was the uh first, and I
   called her up and talked with her. I don't know what time
   it'll cost me, but then, my telephone is my only indiscretion.
   (Waitzkin et al. 1994:330)

Then, the researchers comment:

At no other time in the encounter does the patient refer to her own family, nor does the doctor ask. The patient does her best to maintain contact, even though she does not mention anything that she receives in the way of day-to-day support. Compounding these problems of social support and incipient isolation, the patient recently has moved from a home that she occupied for 59 years. (Waitzkin et al. 1994:330)

And finally, Waitzkin et al. interpret the discourse:

This encounter shows structural elements that appear beneath the surface details of patient-doctor communication. ... Contextual issues affecting the patient include social isolation; loss of home, possessions, family, and community; limited resources to preserve independent function; financial insecurity; and physical deterioration associated with the process of dying. ... After the medical encounter, the patient returns to the same contextual problems that trouble her, consenting to social conditions that confront the elderly in this society.

That such structural features should characterize an encounter like this one becomes rather disconcerting, since the communication otherwise seems so admirable. ... The doctor manifests patience and compassion as he encourages a wide-ranging discussion of socioemotional concerns that extend far beyond the technical details of the patient's physical disorders. Yet the discourse does nothing to improve the most troubling features of the patient's situation. To expect differently would require redefining much of what medicine aims to do. (1994:335–36)

This interpretive analysis is done from a critical perspective, but the method is hermeneutic: You lay out a chunk of text, add running commentary about what you think is going on, and interpret the result.

Key Concepts in This Chapter

discourse analysis	lexemes	turn-taking
grammar beyond the sentence	syntax	sequence rules
	semantics	dynamic sequence
conversation analysis	discourse	performance analysis
ethnopoetics	talk-in-interaction	(ethnopoetics)
language in use	generative principle	situational ethnicity
critical discourse analysis	adjacency pairs	code switching
phonemes	repair sequences	cultural hegemony
schwa	prosodic features of	gendered interruption
phonology	speech	
morphology	repair tactics	

Summary

- Grammar beyond the sentence is about the rules that govern the construction and flow of naturally occurring speech, including narratives and conversations.
- Language in use focuses on how people pursue their goals in naturally occurring speech.
- The study of language and power, or critical discourse analysis, focuses on how the content of discourse establishes, reflects, or perpetuates power differences between actors in society.
- The study of grammar beyond the sentence is grounded in linguistics. Linguists recognize five levels of grammar: phonology, morphology, syntax, semantics, and discourse.

  o Phonology is the study of the basic sounds of a language (its phonemes) and the rules governing their use.
  o Morphology comprises the rules for making meaningful units, or lexemes, out of phonemes. Most lexemes are stand-alone words, but some (like un in unnatural) are always attached to others.
  o Syntax—what we usually think of as the grammar of a language—is the set of rules for stringing lexemes together to make phrases and sentences that native speakers recognize as well formed.
  o Semantics is the set of rules governing the variable meaning of words and phrases in context.
  o Finally, there's discourse, the part of the grammar beyond the sentence. Linguistics-based discourse analysis is the study of the rules governing the construction of whole conversations and narrative performances.

- Conversation analysis is the search for the grammar of ordinary discourse, or talk-in-interaction. It is the study of how people take turns in ordinary discourse—who talks first (and next, and next), who interrupts, who waits for a turn.

  o The grammatical rules of turn taking are, like the rules that govern the formation of sentences, known to native speakers of any language. But unlike the other rules of grammar, the rules for taking turns are flexible and allow turn taking to be negotiated, on the fly, by participants in a conversation.
  o There are special turn-taking rules for some institutions and occupations. Pilots, for example, almost never allow overlap in their conversations and allow one another to finish a sentence before responding.

- Detailed transcriptions are needed in order to study conversations.

  o It takes five–eight hours to transcribe an hour of ordinary interviews. It can take 20 hours or more to transcribe conversation with the level of detail required for this kind of work.

- o Transcription hardware and software, and voice recognition (VR) software can reduce but not eliminate the transcription burden.
- o VR programs are trained to one voice, but you can use them to transcribe focus groups by speaking each participant's part.

- The fact that there are patterns in conversations has been known since Aristotle, but Harvey Sacks and his colleagues, Emmanuel Schegloff and Gail Jefferson, are credited for developing the systematic study of order in conversations.

  - o Big gaps occur so rarely in real conversations because speakers anticipate the end of turns so well.

- The rules for turn taking are often broken in real conversations. This often results in repair tactics. "Sorry, I got you off track. Then what happened?" is a repair sequence.

  - o However, if you're in a job interview and the interviewer sidetracks you, you'd probably think twice about insisting that the interviewer let you finish the story you were telling.

- Among the first things that conversation analysts noticed when they started looking carefully at conversations were adjacency pairs—ordered pairs of expressions, like questions and greetings.

  - o In what is now a classic analysis, Sacks (1992:3ff) noticed that workers at a psychiatric hospital's emergency telephone line greeted callers by saying something like, "Hello. This is Mr. Smith. May I help you?" Most of the time, the response was "Hello, this is Mr. Brown," but on one occasion, the caller responded, "I can't hear you." When the worker repeated his greeting, "This is Mr. *Smith*," with an emphasis on Smith, the caller responded "Smith."
  - o In this case, the rule for an adjacency pair was being negotiated by both parties, on the fly, during the conversation. Mr. Smith, the suicide prevention worker, was trying to get the caller to give his name, and the caller was trying not to give his name.

- Real conversations are full of dynamic sequences rather than lock-step sequences. Dynamic sequences are negotiated on the fly and are very complicated.

  - o In the example of whether to order the Szechuan pork in a Chinese restaurant, two people, in a dynamic conversation among equals, worked together to make everything come out right.
  - o Conversation analysis is a highly empirical and highly inductive method, but in actual practice it involves both induction and hypothesis testing. As you study a transcript you discover what you think is a regularity and then you look for it again to see if you're right.

- In performance analysis, or ethnopoetics, the goal is to discover regularities in how people tell stories.

  o The method was developed in folklore and linguistics. Dell Hymes found that Native American texts of narrative performance are organized into verses and stanzas that are aggregated into groups of either fives and threes or fours and twos. The discovery that Native American languages shared a common form of poetics—i.e., ways of relating stories—had implications for a general theory of poetics and literature.

- Studies of language in use involve the detailed analysis of interaction—much like conversation analysis, but paying attention to the content and the motivations of speakers, not just to the structure of their interaction.

  o One area of interest is situational ethnicity, or ethnic identity switching, where people adopt different ethnicity markers in order to land a job, get a better price in a bargaining situation, or get a better table in a restaurant.
  o Rosalyn Negrón (2011) studied how Spanish–English bilinguals in New York use code switching—moving back and forth between two languages—as a marker for ethnic identity switching and for getting things they wanted in various interactions.
  o Doing this kind of work requires a deep knowledge of local culture and language.

- The critical perspective in social science is rooted in Antonio Gramsci's discussion (1994) in the 1930s of cultural hegemony, in which modern states control the mass media and the schools, the structural mechanisms for shaping and transmitting culture.

  o Marxist theory predicts that the culture (the superstructure) follows the structure, and so the lower and middle classes in modern states come to believe in—even advocate—the entrenched differences in power that keep them subservient to the elite.

- In critical discourse analysis, the idea is to show how these power differences—between men and women, for example, or between doctors and patients, employers and employees, and so on—are perpetuated, reinforced, and resisted.

  o Pioneering research by Zimmerman and West (1983 [1975]) showed that, in ordinary conversations, men interrupted women more often than women interrupted men. Much research since then has shown that gendered interruption is a complex phenomenon.
  o And dozens of studies have established the asymmetry in the doctor–patient relation: Doctors use their knowledge to establish their authority, and patients adopt a meek, accepting role.

Exercises

1. Transcribe one minute of ordinary conversation. Ask two friends or peers to allow you to record a few minutes of their conversation. Give them a topic to discuss—something that people around you are talking about. You only need a few minutes of real conversation for this exercise, which is to transcribe a single minute of the conversation.

2. Analyze the turn-taking behavior in the transcript from Exercise 1.

3. Go back to the recordings you made for Exercise 1 in Chapter 13 of several tellings of a well-known folktale in your native language. The task here is to do a performance analysis. Look for similarities across speakers as to how they present the story, not at the content.

4. If you are bilingual, you can do this yourself. If you are not bilingual, you'll need to enlist the help of one or more bilingual friends. The task is to keep track, for a few days, of the times when you (or your friends) switch ethnicity. Exactly what words were used to do this? In each case, what was the purpose of doing it?

5. Repeat Exercise 1, but this time work in a group, with other students. Have each student ask an opposite-sex pair of friends or peers and a same-sex pair to hold a conversation. If you have at least six people in your group, you can study the presence or absence of gendered information. Give each pair the same topic to discuss. No need to transcribe these conversations. Just video record them and document any interruptions. Then count the interruptions. Do men or women interrupt more? Does it depend on whether they are talking to someone of the same or opposite sex?

Further Reading

Reviews of discourse analysis. Fairclough (1995), Gee (2005), Gee and Handford (2012), Gumperz (1982), Schiffrin et al. (2001), Wodak and Reisigl (1999).

Transcribing conversation. Atkinson and Heritage (1984), Davidson (2010), Psathas (1979), Sacks et al. (1974).

Conversation analysis. Drew and Heritage (2006), Gafaranga (2001), Goodwin and Heritage (1990), Liddicoat (2011), Moerman (1988), Psathas (1995), Silverman (1993, 1998), ten Have (1999), Woofit (2005), Zeitlyn (2004).

Ethnopoetics and performance analysis. Bauman (1984, 1986), Blommaert (2006), D. Hymes (1981, 2003), Juzwik (2004), R. Moore (2013), Poveda (2002), Sammons and Sherzer (2003), Yamaguchi (2012).

Code-switching and ethnic identity. De Fina (2007), Finnis (2014), Fung and Carter (2007), Gafaranga (2001), García (2010), Nishimura (1995), Wei and Milroy (1995).

Critical discourse analysis. Fairclough (2010), Locke (2004), Rogers (2011), Wodak and Meyer (2011).

Gendered interruption. Anderson and Leaper (1998), Auer (2005), Garrett (2005), James and Clarke (1993), Leaper and Robnett (2011), Okamoto et al. (2002), Smith-Lovin and Brody (1989), Tannen (1984, 1994, 2012), ten Have (1991).

Doctor–patient interaction. Heath (1989), Heritage and Maynard (2005), Maynard and Heritage (2005), McHoul and Rapley (2005), Robinson (1998), Robinson and Heritage (2005), ten Have (1991), West (1984), West and Zimmerman (1983), Wodak (2006).

Visit the online resource site at study.sagepub.com/bernardaqd to access engaging and helpful digital content, like video tutorials on working with MAXQDA, presentation slides, MAXQDA keyboard shortcuts, datasets, stop list, and recommended readings.

CHAPTER **15**

ANALYTIC INDUCTION AND QUALITATIVE COMPARATIVE ANALYSIS

INTRODUCTION

Analytic induction is a qualitative method for building up causal explanations of phenomena from a close examination of a small number of cases. It flourished in the 1940s and 1950s with a series of books by scholars from the Chicago School of

Sociology—which emphasized participant observation fieldwork and the study of real human problems—but fell out of favor for several decades for reasons which we'll lay out below.

The method of analytic induction was formalized in 1987 with the publication of Charles Ragin's *The Comparative Method. Moving beyond Qualitative and Quantitative Strategies.* Since then, Ragin's method, called qualitative comparative analysis, or QCA, has been used in hundreds of studies. (QCA is a **Boolean** generalization of analytic induction, but more about that later).

◆ INDUCTION AND DEDUCTION—AGAIN

As we saw in Chapter 12, **induction** is reasoning from observation to formulate rules. It is contrasted with **deduction**, which involves reasoning from general rules to infer what should be out there and available for observation. For example, once we know that abject poverty causes despair, and that despair causes people to engage in destructive and self-destructive behavior, we can use those rules to infer that there is more child abuse, spouse abuse, and alcoholism and suicide (examples of destructive and self-destructive behavior) among people who are poor than among people who are not. Then we can collect data to test this deductively derived hypothesis.

By contrast, we would use inductive reasoning if we were at an earlier stage in research and were shopping for ideas about what causes some phenomenon in which we're interested. We might examine many cases of child abuse and look for what those cases have in common. If we notice that many cases involve despair, we'd formulate a hypothesis about the relationship between child abuse and despair and figure out a way to test it.

In practice, induction and deduction are used by all empiricists, whether they rely on qualitative or quantitative data. There is no way to decide if deduction or induction is better, but some branches of the social sciences rely more on one kind of inference than the other. For example, as we saw in Chapters 10 and 11, grounded theorists tend to be inductivists, and content analysts tend to be deductivists.

The Induction Tradition

Credit for the distinction between inductive and deductive reasoning (the "two ways of searching into and discovering truth") goes to Francis Bacon (1864 [1620]:71). Bacon's method of induction involved making and comparing lists of observations. One list would comprise examples of something we want to explain. Another would comprise things that are *like* those in the first list, but in which the thing we want to explain is absent.

For example, Bacon was interested in the phenomenon of heat and what caused it. In collecting many examples, he noticed that some animals are hotter than others and that the insides of animals were hotter than the outsides. He also noticed that animals were hotter after exercise. From these and many other observations, he concluded that motion was a cause of heat. Not a bad conclusion, considering he was writing in 1620 (Box 15.1).

Bacon did not tell us how we actually get from lists to conclusions about cause and effect. The rules for inductive logic—"the means which mankind possess for exploring the laws of nature by specific observation and experience"—were formalized by John Stuart Mill (1898:259). Two of Mill's rules—what he called the "**method of agreement**" and the "**method of difference**"—are the foundation of analytic induction.

The method of agreement states that if two or more cases of a phenomenon (like getting sick) are different in every way but have one thing in common (like eating a particular food), then that thing is the cause or the effect of the phenomenon. The method of difference states that if two cases of something (like getting sick) are alike in every respect, except for one thing (like not eating a particular food), then that thing is at least part of the cause or effect of the phenomenon (Mill 1898:255, 256).

Box 15.1

Bacon's Death

To Bacon goes the honor of being the first "martyr of empiricism." In March 1626, at the age of 65, Bacon was driving through a rural area north of London. He had an idea that cold might delay the biological process of putrefaction, so he stopped his carriage, bought a hen from a local resident, killed the hen, and stuffed it with snow. Bacon was right—the cold snow did keep the bird from rotting—but he himself caught bronchitis and died a month later (Lea 1980).

ANALYTIC INDUCTION ◆

Florian Znaniecki introduced the term "analytic induction" in 1934 in his book on sociological method (pp. 235ff), observing that the method had a long history, especially in the physical sciences. He contrasted the method with what he called **enumerative, or statistical induction** (pp. 221ff), and analytic induction has been part of the social science tool kit ever since (see Box 15.2).

Box 15.2

Statistical Induction

By the 1920s, with the development of things like the correlation coefficient and the *t*-test, statistical induction had become very popular in the social sciences. In statistical induction, you see if the distribution of two things (like age and weight) are related and you try to infer cause and effect. Many social scientists quickly noticed the flaw in statistical induction: Correlation does not *necessarily* mean cause and effect. The sales of ice cream and the number of drownings per day are correlated, but that doesn't mean that one of those things causes the other. They're both caused by what are called lurking variables: summer, nice weather, and lots of people at the beach. And some correlations are just plain coincidences. Still, with proper precaution, statistical induction is an excellent start in the search for rules governing social phenomena.

The idea of analytic induction is to formulate ironclad rules about the causes and effects of social phenomena—with none of the wishy-washy tendencies and associations that are the product of statistical analysis. (Think of the difference between saying: "Whenever you see X you will see Y" and "Whenever you see X, there is a 62% chance that you'll see Y.") Several qualitative methods—including grounded theory, schema analysis, and decision modeling—are based on the logic of analytic induction.

Robinson (1951) laid out the rules for the method. Here's the algorithm:

1. Start with a single case and develop a theory to account for that one case.

2. Then, look at a second case and see if the theory fits. If it does, go on to a third case.

3. Keep doing this until you run into a case that doesn't fit your theory. (If you see something called "negative case analysis" or "deviant case analysis," this is what it means; see Emigh 1997.)

4. At this point, you have two choices: Modify the theory or redefine the phenomenon you're trying to explain.

5. Repeat the process until your theory is stable—i.e., until it explains every new case you try (Robinson 1951:813). No fair explaining cases by declaring them all unique. That's an easy way out, but not an option of the method.

How many cases in a row do you need to explain before declaring victory? As in any science, the answer is that you're never home free. No matter how many cases your theory explains, there's always the possibility that the next one will fail the test. Still, if a theory is built on 10–20 cases, and it goes on to explain another, independent sample of 10–20 cases, that's strong evidence in any science that the theory should be accepted (see Box 15.3).

Box 15.3

Large and Small *Ns*

Some research problems demand a really big number of cases. Clinical studies around the world long ago confirmed that mothers who breastfeed their children are less likely to develop breast cancer than are mothers who don't. Clinical studies, though, are often on a small number of cases. Even with a few hundred cases, it's impossible to test for small but potentially important effects. For example, if women who breastfeed are more likely to avoid breast cancer, then do mothers who breastfeed longer have an even better chance?

It turns out that they do. For every year a mother breastfeeds her children, she cuts her risk of cancer by 4.3%, and for every baby she has, she cuts her risk by 7%. In countries where women have six or seven babies and breastfeed each of them for up to two years, the combined effect (more babies and longer breastfeeding of each one) lowers the lifetime risk of breast cancer from 6.3 per 100 women (the rate for the industrialized nations) to 2.7 per 100. But researchers couldn't detect this until they brought together studies from around the world with data on a total of about 150,000 women (Collaborative Group 2002).

On the other hand, many research problems in the social and behavioral sciences involve a really small number of cases. Freud, Piaget, and Skinner all produced their big theories— the theories of psychosexual development, cognitive development, and operant conditioning, respectively—from careful study of a few cases. Comparing the transcripts of clinical interviews from three or four schizophrenics can produce a lot of insight about the illness. Comparing the historical details of how four or five countries (like Chile, Taiwan, Uganda, and South Korea) changed from autocratic to democratic regimes yields a lot of insight about political processes.

Intensive case studies like these are important because they yield insight and understanding about how things work—information about process, not just about presence. They also typically produce hypotheses that can be tested on large samples of people or countries, or whatever.

An Example: Cressey's Study of Embezzlers

Among the best-known studies to use analytic induction is Donald Cressey's classic on embezzlers. Cressey (1950, 1953) interviewed 133 prisoners at the Illinois State

Penitentiary at Joliet—men who had been convicted of stealing money from their employers. This is the part of analytic induction where you define and redefine the phenomenon you want to study. Cressey could have defined the phenomenon as simply "stealing from employers," but he decided to focus only on men who had taken their jobs with no intention of becoming embezzlers. During a screening interview to find prisoners who were eligible for his study, Cressey listened carefully and chose men who said they had never intended to steal—that it just sort of happened (1950:740).

Cressey began with the hypothesis that men who were in positions of financial trust—like accountants—would become embezzlers if they came to believe, on the job, that taking money from their employers was just a "technical violation" and not really illegal (1950:741). Unfortunately, as soon as he started doing his interviews, real-life embezzlers told Cressey that they knew all along that what they were doing was illegal. So, Cressey formulated a second hypothesis: Men will embezzle when they have some need—like a family emergency or a gambling debt—that they can interpret as an emergency and that they can't see being met legally.

This hypothesis was abandoned when Cressey ran into two kinds of negative cases: men who reported having emergencies that did not drive them to steal and men who stole when they had no financial emergency. One of the prisoners told Cressey that no man would steal if he always confided in his wife about financial problems, but Cressey had to reject this hypothesis, too (1950:741).

Cressey was getting closer, though. His next hypothesis was that men who have the technical skill to embezzle would do so if they had any kind of problem (financial or otherwise) that they felt (1) could *not* be shared with anyone and (2) *could* be solved with an infusion of money.

Some men told Cressey that they had been in this situation and had not embezzled because the circumstances were not sufficiently clear to make stealing something they could reconcile with their values. That's when Cressey added the final piece of the theory: Men had to be able to square "their conceptions of themselves as trusted persons with conceptions of themselves as users of the entrusted funds or property" (1950:742).

This theory explained all 133 cases that Cressey collected. In fact, it also explained about 200 cases that had been collected by others in the 1930s (1950:740).

Another Example: Manning's Study of Abortions

Peter Manning used analytic induction in his study of 15 college women who sought and obtained abortions (Manning 1971). In 1969, when Manning did his study, abortion was illegal in the United States. Getting an abortion required getting information, finding an abortionist, and then making the decision to actually have the procedure.

Manning thought at first that the decision would be facilitated in cases in which women had a close relationship with the biological father who could encourage the woman to have the abortion. Women did not always have a close relationship with the biological father, so Manning reformulated the theory to "a network of supporting people who encourage the abortion, rather than the single potential father" (Manning 1982:292).

Just as Cressey had found two decades earlier in his study of embezzlers, the women in Manning's study had to "develop a self-conception as law-abiding people while making an exception" for their own illegal act. Here's the final theory in Manning's study, derived inductively, by trial and error:

> An abortion takes place when an unmarried woman defines herself as pregnant, is neither willing to marry at that time nor to rear a child, is advised by friends to solve the problem by abortion, neutralizes her self-concept as deviant, and finally is able to locate an abortionist. (Manning 1982:286)

This theory accounted for all the cases of abortion. If any of the conditions were false—if the woman married, for example, or did not come to terms with the problem of self-image—the result was no abortion.

Zeoli et al.'s Study of Abused Women

Zeoli et al. (2013) used analytic induction to develop a theory of how divorced women protected their children from physically abusive ex-husbands. This was pretty ambitious. After all, the outcome variable in Cressey's study and in Manning's study was binary: Men either embezzled or they didn't; women either had an abortion or they didn't. The range of outcome behaviors for women who are protecting themselves and their children from what they perceive to be potential harm by their ex-husbands is more complex.

Like grounded theory, analytic induction is often based on qualitative data, but unlike grounded theory, analytic induction can proceed deductively, from a hypothesis to a test of the hypothesis. From the literature, Zeoli et al. developed two hypotheses, which they called preliminary assertions:

> Assertion 1 In those cases where the ex-husband neglects or harms the child(ren), the mother will make efforts to protect them that may not be supported by the system (e.g., if she tries to legally change the custody determination, she will be denied).

Assertion 2 In those cases where the ex-husband attempts to maintain control over the mother, she will make efforts to set boundaries to limit her contact with him. (p. 548)

Next, Zeoli et al. did 19 in-depth interviews with mothers who had divorced their husbands between one and three years earlier. In all cases, the women had been subject to intimate partner violence (IPV) and feared for their safety and for that of their children. Interviewers probed to assess (1) IPV during the marriage and since the divorce; (2) whether women thought family court supported their efforts to protect them and their children from violent ex-husbands; and (3) women's responses to their ex-husbands' violence after the divorce.

Then, the interviews were coded for things like: physical and emotional abuse of mothers and children; women's concerns about the possibilities for physical harm or kidnapping of their children; and what women did to avoid any abuse.

Here is how Zeoli et al. describe their application of analytic induction:

When an assertion did not adequately capture a participant's experience or was disconfirmed, we undertook in-depth examinations of the contexts in which this occurred and, when appropriate, modified the assertion to accurately reflect a participant's experience. We then tested the modified assertion on all participants for final confirmation. However, we also allowed assertions to be disconfirmed without adjusting the assertion to fit the case when modification was not appropriate. (2013:550)

With only 19 cases, and a range of possible outcomes, these researchers were not able to develop a theory that covered *every* particular outcome in *every* case, so, as they make clear, they "allowed assertions to be disconfirmed without adjusting the assertion to fit the case when modification was not appropriate." As they analyzed the 19 interviews, two important new themes emerged (inductively) that they had not considered in their original, deductive formulation: (1) that the women were as concerned about future neglect and harm to their children as they were about events in the past and (2) that women had no faith that decisions in family court were in the best interests of children.

Zeoli et al. modified the two assertions as follows:

Assertion 1 In those cases where the ex-husband neglects or harms the child(ren) and/or there is a perceived likelihood of future neglect, physical harm, or parental kidnapping, the mother will perceive that family court does not make decisions that are in the best interests of the children. This will manifest in one of three different ways: 1) she will not go to family court for assistance; 2) she may attempt to use family court for assistance, but find that they do not support her; or 3) she may gain support from family court after extreme harm to the child occurs.

Assertion 2 In those cases where the ex-husband contacts the ex-wife, or uses times at which he has contact with her, to attempt to maintain control over her, she will make efforts to limit her contact with him. (2013:550)

Assertion 1 was applicable to 10 of the 19 respondents. (That is, the woman's ex-husband was reported to have neglected or physically harmed the child, etc.) For those 10 women, eight confirmed the assertion. Two of the 10 women believed that the family court had *initially* acted in the best interests of the children but would not continue to do so. All the women in the study experienced post-separation abuse, but a few experienced abuse outside the interaction with their ex-husbands. As a result, Assertion 2 was confirmed for 16 of the 19 women.

Like many good studies based on qualitative data and on a small number of respondents, the result of Zeoli et al.'s analytic induction is a set of highly credible hypotheses that can be tested with more cases. (**Further Reading**: analytic induction)

Critique of Analytic Induction

Analytic induction is a powerful, qualitative method, but sociologists in the 1950s were quick to point out its flaws (Robinson 1951; Turner 1953). The most obvious is that the method accounts for data you've already collected but does not allow prediction about individual cases.

Cressey could not predict, a priori—i.e., without data about actual embezzlers who had been arrested and jailed for their crime—which bank workers would violate the trust of their employers. Manning could not predict, a priori, which pregnant women would ultimately seek an abortion. And Zeoli et al. couldn't predict which mothers' behavior would not confirm their expectations.

Cressey's theory, however, was superb, a posteriori, as was Manning's—and Zeoli et al.'s did really well, considering that they had just 19 respondents and a complex outcome variable.

The critique, then, is that, much as in grounded theory, theories derived from analytic induction explain what's already known. This is not as strong a critique as it may appear. Retrospective understanding of a small set of cases, especially if achieved with systematic methods of data collection and analysis, allows us to make strong predictions about the set of uncollected cases yet to come.

In other words, analytic induction does not produce perfect knowledge for the prediction of individual cases, but it can do as well as statistical induction—the standard in social science—in predicting the outcome in aggregates of cases, and it does so with a relatively small number of cases.

It's true that collecting and analyzing case histories of phenomena is much more labor intensive than, say, collecting questionnaire data by telephone. But if you want

---

Box 15.5

Finding the Simplest Set, or Prime Implicants

To find the simplest set of features—the prime implicants—that account for the dependent variable (eating disorders) requires a systematic comparison of all pairs of configurations that produce eating disorders.

There are $n(n-1)/2$ pairs of anything. With three elements in a set, A, B, and C, there are $3(2)/2 = 6/2 = 3$ pairs. Here they are: AB, AC, BC. With four elements (cars, people, countries, whatever), there are $4(3)/2 = 12/2 = 6$ pairs. There are, then, $7(6)/2 = 21$ pairs of the seven configurations in the top panel of Table 15.3.

Pair 1 and 2, for example, is: CRUd and CRud

Pair 1 and 3 is: CRUd and cruD

And so on, down to pair 6 and 7: CrUD and CRUD

Notice that both C R U D and C r U D produce the same outcome (an eating disorder). This makes R superfluous. On the other hand, R is needed for the pair C R U d and C R u D, but in that case, U is superfluous (Haworth-Hoeppner 2000:219–20).

The method here is to examine all pairs of conditions and see if we can reduce the number of combinations that account for the outcomes in the truth table. Then we see if we can reduce the number of combinations again until we find the minimum number of variables and their combinations that account for a set of cases in a truth table. These are called the prime implicants in Boolean logic.

Haworth-Hoeppner gave these eight configurations new numbers and repeated the process. There are $8(7)/2 = 28$ pairs of eight configurations, but in the end, Haworth-Hoeppner found that only three combinations of variables (CD, CR, and ruD) were needed to account for the 21 cases of eating disorders in her data. Those configurations are shown in the right-hand column of the bottom panel of Table 15.3. The final result—the prime implicants for eating disorders—is expressed in the **Boolean formula**:

$$\text{Eating disorders} = CR + CD + ruD$$

We read this as: "Eating disorders are caused by the simultaneous presence of C AND R, AND by the simultaneous presence of C AND D, AND by the presence of D in the absence of R and U" (Haworth-Hoeppner 2000:219–20).

Note how U dropped out of the picture entirely. From the literature about eating disorders, Haworth-Hoeppner expected to find that unloving parents were a prime factor in creating the problem for women. But from the QCA, she learned that this feature was simply not needed to explain the cases in her sample. This sets up an entire agenda for future research.

Like classic content analysis and cognitive mapping, analytic induction and its Boolean incarnation QCA require that human coders read and code text and produce a matrix. The object of the analysis, however, is not to show the relationships between all codes but to find the minimal set of logical relationships among the concepts that account for a single dependent variable. With four binary independent variables, as in Haworth-Hoppner's data, there are 16 configurations to simplify. With each additional variable, the analysis becomes much more difficult. Computer programs are available to help with this for Boolean analyses. (**Further Reading**: QCA and computer programs for QCA)

AND FINALLY . . . ◆

By far, the most widely used method for analyzing text is content analysis, with 1.5 million hits on Google Scholar. Next is grounded theory, with 370,000 hits. Analytic induction and qualitative comparative analysis have about 7,000 hits each. As we saw in the studies by Cressey, by Manning, and by Zeoli et al., analytic induction is a powerful method for developing theory. Unlike grounded theory, analytic induction usually starts with a hypothesis, derived from observation or the literature. After that, the procedure overlaps with that of grounded theory and its reliance on negative case analysis: You modify the theory as it is challenged by data from new cases. In our view, analytic induction deserves a lot more attention.

Key Concepts in This Chapter

analytic induction	Mill's method of agreement and method of difference	qualitative comparative analysis or QCA
Boolean induction	enumerative or statistical induction	Boolean truth table
deduction		prime implicants
		Boolean formula

Summary

- Analytic induction is a qualitative method for building up causal explanations of phenomena from a close examination of a small number of cases.

  o With statistical reasoning, a common result might be: "Whenever you see X, there is a 62% chance that you'll see Y." Using the logic analytic induction the goal is to result like: "Whenever you see X you will see Y."

- o Several qualitative methods—including grounded theory, schema analysis, and decision modeling—are based on the logic of analytic induction.

- Analytic induction begins with a theory to account for one case of a phenomenon. The theory is applied to more cases until the theory no longer fits. The next step is to modify the theory or redefine the phenomenon you're trying to explain. The process continues until a theory explains every new case you try.

  - o No matter how many cases a theory explains, there's always the possibility that the next one will fail the test. Still, if a theory is built on 10–20 cases and it goes on to explain another independent sample of 10–20 cases, that's strong evidence in any science that the theory should be accepted.

- A classic example of analytic induction is Cressey's theory to explain the behavior of embezzlers—men who had been convicted of stealing money from their employers. Cressey's initial hypothesis was that men who were in positions of financial trust—like accountants—would become embezzlers if they came to believe, on the job, that taking money from their employers was just a "technical violation" and not really illegal.
- When real-life embezzlers told Cressey that they knew all along that what they were doing was illegal, Cressey reformulated the hypothesis: Men will embezzle when they have some need—like a family emergency or a gambling debt—that they can interpret as an emergency and that they can't see being met legally.

  - o When Cressey found cases of men who reported having emergencies that did not drive them to steal and men who stole when they had no financial emergency, he changed to hypotheses: Men who have the technical skill to embezzle would do so if they had any kind of problem (financial or otherwise) that they felt (1) could *not* be shared with anyone and (2) *could* be solved with an infusion of money.
  - o Some of Cressey's respondents said that they had been in this situation and had not embezzled because could not reconcile stealing with their values. Cressey added the final piece of the theory: Men had to be able to square "their conceptions of themselves as trusted persons with conceptions of themselves as users of the entrusted funds or property" (Cressey 1950:742).
  - o This theory explained all 133 cases that Cressey collected and about 200 cases that had been collected by others in the 1930s.

- Peter Manning used analytic induction in his study of 15 college women who sought and obtained abortions in 1969, when abortion was illegal in the United States. His theory, derived inductively, by trial and error, accounted for all the cases of abortion:

○ An abortion takes place when an unmarried woman defines herself as pregnant, is neither willing to marry at that time nor to rear a child, is advised by friends to solve the problem by abortion, neutralizes her self-concept as deviant, and finally is able to locate an abortionist. (Manning 1982:286)

○ If any of the conditions were false—if the woman married, for example, or did not come to terms with the problem of self-image—the result was no abortion.

• Zeoli et al. (2013) used analytic induction to develop a theory of how divorced women protected their children from physically abusive ex-husbands. Unlike the binary outcomes in Cressey's theory and in Manning's theory, women who are protecting themselves and their children from what they perceive to be potential harm by their ex-husbands engage in a range of behaviors.

○ Zeoli et al. analyzed 19 in-depth interviews with mothers who had divorced their husbands between one and three years earlier and induced two hypotheses:

○ In those cases where the ex-husband neglects or harms the child(ren) and/or there is a perceived likelihood of future neglect, physical harm, or parental kidnapping, the mother will perceive that family court does not make decisions that are in the best interests of the children. This will manifest in one of three different ways: (1) she will not go to family court for assistance; (2) she may attempt to use family court for assistance, but find that they do not support her; or (3) she may gain support from family court after extreme harm to the child occurs.

○ In those cases where the ex-husband contacts the ex-wife, or uses times at which he has contact with her, to attempt to maintain control over her, she will make efforts to limit her contact with him (Zeoli et al. 2013:550).

○ With just 19 respondents and a complex outcome, the analytically induced hypotheses wound up fitting many, but not all respondents.

• Analytic induction fell out of favor after the 1950s because the method accounts for data you've already collected but does not allow prediction about individual cases. While it does not produce perfect knowledge for the prediction of individual cases, it can do as well as statistical induction—the standard in social science—in predicting the outcome in aggregates of cases, and it does so with a relatively small number of cases.

• Charles Ragin formalized the logic of analytic induction using a Boolean approach. Ragin called the method he developed qualitative comparative analysis, or QCA (1987).

• Susan Haworth-Hoeppner (2000) used QCA in her study of why white, middle-class women develop eating disorders. She coded each of 30 interview transcripts for four concepts that were thought to make a woman prone to eating disorders: Did the woman live in a family where she was always being criticized for her appearance? Were her parents controlling? Were her parents unloving? Were they always going on about weight and appearance? Finally, she coded for the dependent variable: Was the woman herself bulimic or anorexic?

- o This produced a table with 30 lines, one for each person, and five columns (four independent variables and one dependent variable).Haworth-Hoeppner arranged her data in a Boolean truth table. With four hypothesized causal variables for which each can be present or absent (1 or 0), there are 2^4, or 16 possible combinations in this particular truth table.
- o Then, using Ragin's method, Haworth-Hoeppner cut the table down to its prime implicants by examining pairs of configurations (lines) and looking for terms that are unnecessary.
- o The final result—the prime implicants for eating disorders—was expressed in a Boolean formula: Eating disorders = the simultaneous presence of a critical family environment AND the simultaneous presence of a critical family environment AND a main family discourse on weight, AND by the presence of a main discourse on weight in the absence of controlling and unloving parents (Haworth-Hoeppner 2000:219–20).
- o From the literature about eating disorders, Haworth-Hoeppner expected to find that unloving parents were a prime factor in creating the problem for women. But from the QCA she learned that this feature was simply not needed to explain the cases in her sample.

- This kind of analysis is difficult to do, but computer programs are available to help with the analysis.

Exercises

1. Here are a few widely discussed issues on which people can have polar opposite positions:

   1. A woman's unfettered right to an abortion through the first two trimesters.
   2. The impact of humans on climate change.
   3. The right of animals to not be killed and eaten by humans.
   4. The importance of reducing taxation on businesses.
   5. The right of humans of all ages to health care.
   6. The right of women to get equal pay for equal work.

   The literature on political ideology indicates that people who have opposite scores on one of these issues will have opposite scores on most or all of these issues.
   Choose one of these issues as a dependent variable and interview people about their attitudes on the other five. If you are working alone, collect interviews from six

people, three of whom are one side the issue you choose and three of whom are on the other. (If you are working in a group, collect interviews from six people, half on one side the issue and half on the other.) The object is to develop a theory that accounts for the difference in people's position on one issue from their attitudes on the other issues in the list. During the interview, ask people if they consider themselves more liberal (or progressive) or more conservative, and why; ask if they consider themselves to be religious, and why. After the first interview, build a theory that explains the data you have in hand. Be prepared to change your theory as the data come in.

Note that all six of the issues above are in the realm of domestic social and economic values. If you add issues related to foreign policy, be prepared to change your theory even more.

Further Reading

Analytic induction. Crouch and McKenzie (2006), Hammersley (2010b), B. A. Jacobs (2004), S. I. Miller (1982), Tacq (2007).

Critiques of analytic induction and QCA. Goldenberg (1993), Hicks (1994), Lieberson (1991), Romme (1995).

Computer programs for QCA. AQUAD 7: Gürtler and Huber (2014); Huber and Gürtler (2013); FS/QCA: Ragin and Davey (2014); Kirq: Reichert and Rubinson (2014); Rubinson (2013); QCA with *R*: Duşa and Thiem (2014); Thiem and Duşa (2013a);Tosmana: Cronqvist (2007). See Thiem and Duşa (2013b) for a review of software for QCA.

QCA. Basurto and Speer (2012), Hicks et al. (1995), Hodson (2004), Kilburn (2004), Marx et al. (2014), Mollinga and Gondhelekar (2014), Rihoux (2003, 2006), Rihoux and Ragin (2008), Schneider and Wagemann (2010), Schweizer (1996), Smilde (2005), Williams and Farrell (1990).

Visit the online resource site at study.sagepub.com/bernardaqd to access engaging and helpful digital content, like video tutorials on working with MAXQDA, presentation slides, MAXQDA keyboard shortcuts, datasets, stop list, and recommended readings.

CHAPTER **16**

ETHNOGRAPHIC DECISION MODELS

IN THIS CHAPTER

INTRODUCTION

Ethnographic decision models (EDMs) are qualitative analyses that predict **episodic behaviors**. Any recurring decision—to buy or not buy a computer; to use (or demand the use of) a condom during sex; to attend or not attend an eight-o'clock class—can be modeled using the EDM method.

Authors' note: This chapter is adapted from Ryan and Bernard (2006). Used by permission, Society for Applied Anthropology.

Like analytic induction and qualitative comparative analysis (Chapter 15), EDMs are based on logic. Unlike analytic induction and qualitative comparative analysis, EDMs produce probabilities for behavioral outcomes: Given X, and Y, and Z, people are predicted to make a particular decision with a particular probability. So, EDMs take negative cases into account by incorporating them into a prediction.

EDMs are typically built from interviews with 20–60 people and are tested on a similarly small sample—just the sort of samples used by researchers who rely on qualitative data. Even with such small samples, EDMs typically predict 75%–90% of all outcomes (Box 16.1).

Box 16.1

EDMs and Binary Outcomes

EDMs are easiest to build for questions about behaviors that can be answered yes or no. Breslin et al. (2000), for example, applied the EDM method to referrals by clinicians of drug abuse patients for outpatient treatment. Their model accurately predicted 17 out of 20 (85%) of the informants' decisions. Beck (2000) used the method to model the decision by psychologists in British Columbia to report suspected cases of child abuse to the authorities. Both of these are yes–no decisions: to refer a patient for treatment or not; to report suspected abuse to the authorities or not.

EDMs are not limited, however, to binary decisions. Ryan and Martínez (1996) modeled the decision by mothers in a Mexican village of when to take their children to the doctor. In that case, there were four options: Do nothing; use various home remedies; engage the services of a curandera (local curer); or take the child to the doctor. The Ryan–Martínez model accounted for 15 out of 17 cases (88%) in their original model and 17 out of 20 cases (85%) in their test of the original model.

◆ HOW TO BUILD EDMS

Christina Gladwin (1989) made the method of ethnographic decision tree modeling widely accessible. Here are the steps: (1) Select a specific behavioral choice to model and elicit **decision criteria** from a convenience sample of respondents. (2) Further elaborate and verify the decision criteria on a purposive, heterogeneous sample of informants. (3) Use the ethnographic data from step 1 and the survey data from step 2 to build a **hierarchical decision model**. (4) Test the model on an independent and, if possible, representative sample from the same population.

We will add a fifth step: (5) Validate the model with responses from people about why they acted as they did.

Step 1. Selecting a Behavioral Choice to Model, and Eliciting the Decision Criteria for Recycling

In one of our projects (Ryan and Bernard 2006), we modeled people's decision to recycle (or not) the last aluminum beverage can they had in their hand. We chose this decision because: (1) it is very common; (2) the consequences are economically and ecologically great; and (3) a lot is already known about it. We wanted to know whether an EDM, based on a small, ethnographic sample, would reflect what has long been known, in general, about recycling, from large surveys: When it's convenient, people will do it. When it's not convenient, they won't.

To start, we did exploratory, free-ranging interviews with a convenience sample—some men, some women, some older, some younger—of 21 informants in Florida and North Dakota.

We asked each informant three questions: (1) Think about the last time you had a can of something to drink in your hand—soda, juice, water, beer, whatever. When was that? (2) What did you do with the can when you were done? (3) Why did you [didn't you] recycle?

The goal was to elicit as many possible reasons for why people recycled or not. By the time we got through 21 informants, there were few new rationales being mentioned, so we stopped. The results are shown in Table 16.1. Most people claimed to have recycled the last can they had in their hand, so there are more reasons for recycling than for not recycling. Of course, there is a **social desirability effect**—people want to make themselves look good when they answer survey questions—so we expect some people to claim to have recycled when they hadn't. This may affect the final results, but it doesn't affect the building of the model.

Step 2. Collecting Data for a Preliminary Model

In Step 2, we collected survey data from a new group of ethnographic informants and used these data to build a preliminary model of the behavior. Ethnographic informants are people who know about the behavior of interest and about the culture surrounding the behavior. That is, they can knowledgeably respond to questions about their own behavior (in this case, getting rid of an empty beverage can) and about their reasons for their behavior. The data collected from

Table 16.1 Reasons for Recycling or Not Recycling From 21 Informants

Reasons for Recycling	Reasons for Not Recycling
1. It's wasteful to just throw it away.	1. I was traveling and I had no place to recycle it.
2. The city has a recycling program. The garbage man picks it up.	2. Bins aren't around. I didn't have a recycling bin. There aren't enough recycling bins available.
3. To help save the environment.	
4. Recycling bins are conveniently located.	3. There's no recycling program where I live. No city recycling program
5. That's what Big Blue is for.	4. Because I don't have Big Blue.
6. My kid made a pact with a TV club so she now recycles.	5. I didn't think about it.
7. I'm concerned about the environment.	6. I gave it to kids who turn it in for money.
8. It's environmentally sound.	7. Forgot.
9. Land is not a renewable resource.	8. Recycling is not available to me.
10. I save cans to get money for them.	9. Laziness.
11. The people I'm staying with recycle, so I do, too.	10. The recycling bin was not conveniently located.
12. The bins were around.	11. Because I have to separate out cans from my garbage and that's a problem.
13. It's useful and can be used again.	
14. To keep the environment clean.	12. Lack of education.
15. Because of habit; we usually put it in Big Blue.	13. I don't have enough time.
16. Because I'm environmentally conscious.	
17. To preserve the environment for my kids.	
18. It's not biodegradable.	
19. It's no good in the landfill.	
20. Because it's just good to recycle.	
21. It's easy to do.	
22. Because it's the right thing to do.	
23. Because it's the big thing to do these days.	
24. Because someone told me to.	
25. We shouldn't cover the land up with garbage.	
26. To buy more beer.	
27. Because if you don't you have to pay a fee.	

SOURCE: Ryan and Bernard (2006). Material used with permission of the Society for Applied Anthropology.

these informants are survey data because every informant is asked the same set of questions.

We interviewed 70 informants, 37 in Florida and 33 in North Dakota. Here again, we purposefully selected a diverse group of informants (age range 18–71 years, education one–23 years, 48% male) in hopes that we could build a robust model that would account for can-recycling behavior across a wide range of people (see Box 16.2).

Box 16.2

Sample Size for EDMs

Our sample size was based on some crude calculations. We wanted enough cases to be able to build a **decision tree** (see Figures 16.2 and 16.4 below) that was at least three levels deep and where each endpoint would contain at least five people. Having at least five cases at each endpoint gives us confidence that the decision criteria are nontrivial. We calculate the minimum sample size for such a tree as follows:

$$\text{Minimum Sample Size} = \text{Minimum cases in each endpoint} \times 2^{(\text{\# of Levels})}$$

In our case, the minimum sample size would have been $(5 \times 2^3) = 40$. The reason this is a minimum is that our assumptions are met only if the cases bifurcate perfectly at each decision point in the tree. Our experience with decision trees, however, suggests that this rarely happens, so we try to more-or-less double the minimum sample size to insure that we wind up with some cases at each endpoint ... hence, our 70 survey cases for building the model.

We began our interviews with the same initial questions we had asked in Step 1: "Think about the last time you had a can of something to drink in your hand—soda, juice, water, beer, whatever. Did you recycle the can? Why [Why not?]" Then we asked each of those 70 people 31 questions derived from Table 16.1. The 31 questions are shown in Table 16.2.

Note that some of the questions are about general behavior ("Do you normally recycle cans at home?"); some are about structural conditions ("Was a recycling bin handy?"); and some are about attitudes ("Do you consider yourself environmentally conscious?"). Also note that questions 7–11 are expansions of the question "Where were you when you had that used beverage can in your hand?" into five binary questions. This ensures that all informants are given the same set of cues as the data are collected to build the preliminary model.

Table 16.2 Questions Asked in the Recycling Study

After asking about the last can and the reasons for recycling, ask each of the following:

1. Does your city have a recycling program?
2. Can you return aluminum cans for redemption in your town or city?
3. Did you live in a house or apartment?
4. If you live in a house, is there a special pickup for recycled materials (e.g., Big Blue)?
5. Are there special bins for recycled materials in your apartment building, etc.?
6. Are there recycling bins for cans where you work?

The last time you drank from an aluminum can were you:

7. at home?
8. at work?
9. driving in your car?
10. inside or outside?
11. at someone else's house?
12. The last time you drank from an aluminum can did you get the can from a vending machine?
13. The last time you drank from an aluminum can was there a recycling bin conveniently located nearby?
14. The last time you drank from an aluminum can were you busy?
15. The last time you drank from an aluminum can were there other people around when you finished your drink?
16. If so, do these people usually recycle cans?
17. If so, did anyone suggest that you recycle the can?
18. Do you have children?
19. Do you habitually recycle material such as cans, newspapers, and plastics at home?
20. Do you habitually recycle material such as cans, newspapers, and plastics at work?
21. Do you consider yourself environmentally conscious (not at all, a little, some, a lot)?
22. How much do you think that recycling helps to save the environment (not at all, a little, some, a lot)?
23. How much are you concerned about the environment (not at all, a little, some, a lot)?
24. How much do you think recycling helps to keep the environment clean (not at all, a little, some, a lot)?
25. How important is it for you to preserve the environment for children (not at all, a little, some, a lot)?
26. Do you think it's wasteful to throw away an aluminum can?
27. Do you think that there is a lot of social pressure nowadays to recycle?
28. Do you think that cans are bad for landfills?
29. Do you think that recycling aluminum cans is useful?
30. Do you recycle any materials besides cans?
31. If so, what other materials do you recycle?

SOURCE: Authors.

Step 3. Building the Preliminary Model

In Step 3, we looked for patterns among the decision criteria in Step 1 and the reported behaviors in Step 2 and built an explicit logical model to account for the behaviors.

This is the most difficult of the steps and the hardest to describe because it involves a lot of trial-and-error. There are formal approaches, but we use the method of analytic induction recommended by Gladwin (1989): Closely examine cases that do not fit the model and modify the model accordingly until it achieves some desired level of accuracy, say, at least 80% (see Box 16.3).

Box 16.3

Formal Approaches for Decision Modeling

One formal method is to produce **vignettes** that lay out all possible combinations of factors identified as important in a decision. For example:

You're [standing at a bus stop] [at home] [at work]. You're [alone] [not alone] and your children [are there] [not there]. You have a can of [soda][juice] [beer] in your hand. When you finish the can, you [throw it in the garbage] [put it in a recycle bin] [leave it anywhere that's handy, like a desk or on the ground].

The modal responses from vignettes like these can be used to generate the decision rules in the model.

The vignette method is attractive but, like all methods, it has its limitations. Even with just eight binary factors, there are $2^8 = 256$ combinations. In a **small-*n* study**—the kind usually done in exploratory research—each informant would have to see 256 vignettes. There is an alternative to this full-scale approach, called the **factorial survey**, in which informants see a random sample of vignettes, but this requires a large number of respondents to make sure that all combinations are seen by at least some people. (See Jasso [2006], Rossi and Noch [1982], and Stokes and Schmidt [2012] for more on this method.)

From the responses to our EDM survey of 70 informants in Florida and North Dakota, we drafted models of the decision process, trying different combinations of variables. The result was a preliminary model, shown in Figure 16.1.

We got to this first model by going through the questions in Table 16.2 one at a time and asking: How many errors (i.e., outcomes not predicted by the model) would this question produce? The idea is to find the one question that produces the fewest errors. That question then becomes the first branch of a proposed model.

Figure 16.1 Decision to Recycle Cans (first criterion)

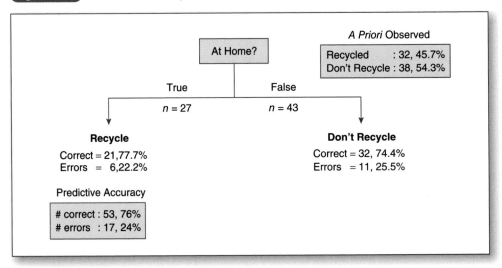

In examining the data, the question "Were you at home when you had that can in your hand?" produced the fewest errors (see Figure 16.1). Thus, guessing that everyone at home recycled and that everyone not at home did not recycle produces six errors (22% of the 27 cases) on the left-hand branch and 11 errors (26% of the 43 cases) on the right-hand branch, for a total of 17 errors and an accuracy rate of 53 out of 70 cases, or 76%.

Balancing the Advantages of Complexity and Simplicity

A slightly more complex model, shown in Figure 16.2, improves the results from 76% to 90%.

First, the left-hand branch of the model: Of the 27 informants who were at home, the best predictor of who did or who did not recycle was to ask whether they recycled any other products. Of the 23 who said they recycled other products, 21 (91.3%) recalled recycling the last can they had in their hand. All four of those who said they didn't recycle other products also recalled not recycling the can. The rule here is: For those at home who recycle other products, guess "recycled the can"; otherwise, guess "didn't recycle the can." This results in just two errors out of 27 cases, or 92.6% correct.

On the right-hand branch of the model, just guessing that nobody recycled produced 32 out of 43 correct answers, or 74.4% correct. This improves to 88.4% correct by distinguishing whether those not at home were at work or elsewhere, and then asking: "Was a recycling bin conveniently located nearby?"

Figure 16.2 Decision to Recycle Cans (Ethnographic Sample, *N* = 70)

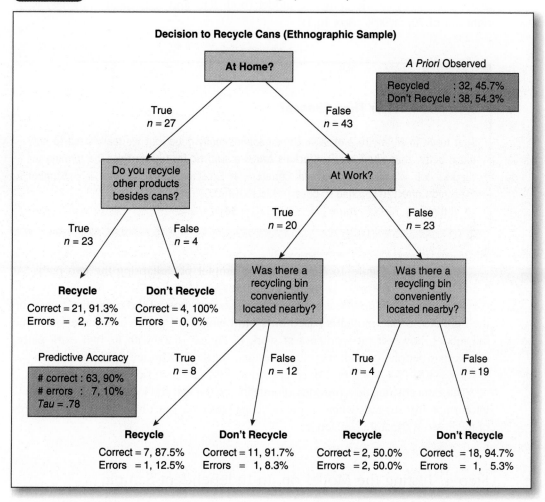

SOURCE: Ryan and Bernard (2006). Material used with permission of the Society for Applied Anthropology.

First, as shown in Figure 16.2, when bins were nearby, seven of the eight (87.5%) respondents who were at work recycled. When bins were not nearby, 11 of the 12 respondents (91.7%) who were at work said that they didn't recycle. This branch of the model gets 18 out of 20, or 90% correct. Second, among the 23 respondents who were neither at home nor at work, asking if a recycling bin was nearby produces a model with just three errors, or 87% correct.

Overall, on the right-hand branch, the model produces five errors (88.4% correct), and the accuracy of the complete model (both left- and right-hand branches) is 63 right out of 70, or 90% (Box 16.4).

Box 16.4

How Much Better Than Chance?

That result in Figure 16.2 of 90% correct sounds really good, but we really need to how much better than chance it is. **Klecka's** *tau* is a statistic for testing this. The formula for Klecka's *tau* is *tau* = (# Observed Correct − # Expected Correct)/(Total # − Number Expected Correct [if you had to guess]) (Klecka 1980:50−51).
  In this case, Klecka's *tau* = (63 − 38)/(70 − 38) = .78.

The model in Figure 16.2 can be made simpler by collapsing the two paths "At Work?" and "Not at Work?" as shown in Figure 16.3.

This change has no effect on the error rate, since most of the predictive power on the right side of the model is based on a bin being nearby. The extra criterion in the full model, however (at work–not at work in Figure 16.2), with its two extra paths, shows that people at work recycle more than do those who are neither at home nor at work—40% (7 + 1 = 8 of 20), compared to 13% (2 + 1 = 3 of 23).

The extra criterion thus provides information on the size and location of the problem—information that suggests where to put recycling bins if we don't have an unlimited supply of them. More about this in Step 4.

Step 4. Testing the Model on an Independent Sample

An accuracy rate of 90% (and a rate that's 78% better than chance) may seem high, but it's hardly a surprise when a model accounts for the data on which it is built. All we are doing in Figure 16.2 is representing graphically what people told us they did. Models, however, are hypotheses. Their validity doesn't depend on how they are derived but on how well they stand up to tests on an independent sample of people who were not involved in building the model in the first place.

To see how our model EDM did on a larger population, we tested it on a representative, national sample of 386 respondents in the United States. The results are in Figure 16.4 (Box 16.5).

Figure 16.3   Decision to Recycle Cans—Simplified Model (Ethnographic Sample, *N* = 70)

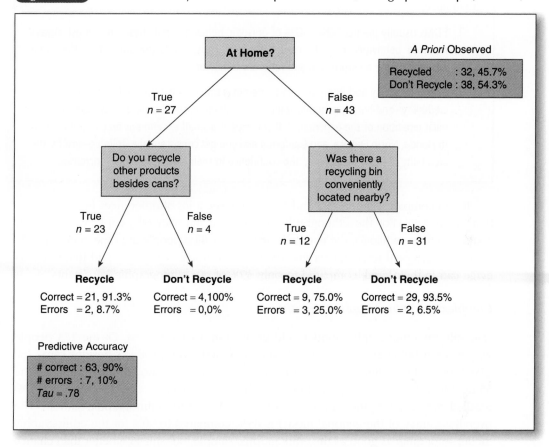

SOURCE: Ryan and Bernard (2006). Material used with permission of the Society for Applied Anthropology.

Box 16.5

Samples for Testing EDMs

Samples for testing EDMs are typically drawn from the same local populations that are used to build the models. Strong agreement between two, independently derived EDMs is the equivalent of repeating a laboratory experiment in terms of reliability and internal validity. There are two cautions here:

(Continued)

(Continued)

1. EDMs usually predict 80%–90% of episodic behaviors, but these are almost always reported behaviors, not observed behaviors. Thus, EDMs are subject to the same problem as are all studies of self-reported behavior.

2. Strong reliability and internal validity are not a proxy for external validity. However, the credibility—and hence, generalizability—of results from small experiments increases with each repetition of the experiment. If you repeat a small experiment on cultural content in Florida, North Dakota, and California and you get consistent—i.e., reliable—results, the credibility of those results—i.e., the confidence in their external validity—increases.

If you compare Figures 16.2 and 16.4, you'll see a lot of differences in the distribution of answers. For the ethnographic model, we interviewed people wherever we could find them, while for the national survey, we called people at home. Sure enough, 58% of the national respondents said they were at home when they had that last beverage can in their hand, compared to only 39% of our ethnographic informants.

Complexity Versus Simplicity Again

And still, the ethnographic model held up well in a national test. Of the 173 people who were at home and who also said they recycled other products besides cans, 160 (93%) recalled recycling the can, compared to 91% in the ethnographic sample. Of the 55 people at home who reported not recycling other products besides cans, 45 (82%) recalled not recycling the can, compared to 100% for the ethnographic sample. The overall accuracy of the national model is 85%, compared to 90% for the ethnographic model—not quite as good as the ethnographic sample, but still 45% better than chance (as indicated by Klecka's *tau*).

Just as with the ethnographic model, adding the question about where the behavior took place (at work vs. at home) has no effect on prediction power. It does, however, corroborate the policy-relevant information produced in the ethnographic model regarding where to put scarce resources if we want to increase recycling behavior. Of the 158 people in the national sample who said they were not at home when they had that last beverage can in their hands, 20% (20 + 1 = 21 out of 104 in Figure 16.4) said they didn't recycle if they also said they were at work. By contrast, 50% (25 + 2 = 27 out of 54 in Figure 16.4) of the not-home people said they didn't recycle if they also said they were not at work.

It may be tempting to go after the 50% error rate, but the not-home/not-at-work condition covers people who are at football games, or driving on the freeway, or visiting other people's houses, or window shopping. With so many conditions, and limited resources with which to put out recycling bins, it is going to be tough to have an impact on that 50% error rate. In the short term, it's easier to imagine incentives for getting employers to put out those bins.

Figure 16.4 Decision to Recycle Cans (National Sample, *N* = 386)

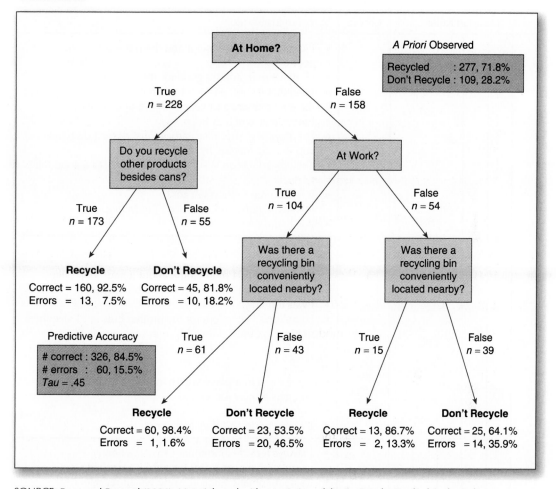

SOURCE: Ryan and Bernard (2006). Material used with permission of the Society for Applied Anthropology.

Step 5. Assessing the Validity of Ethnographic Decision Models

We can take the process one step further and bring qualitative information into assessing the model's validity. We asked 33 of our ethnographic informants to tell us, in their own words, why they recycled, *before* we asked systematically about their decision criteria. For these informants, we can examine the fit between their justifications of their choice to recycle or not and the model's predictions.

We do this by flowing individual recycling cases down the decision tree and examining the degree to which each end point in the tree (each final decision) corresponds to our informants' own accounts. The results are shown in Table 16.3.

Table 16.3 Verbatim Justifications for 33 Recycling Choices From an Ethnographic Sample

Decision Rules			Choice	Verbatim Justification
At home?	Recycle other things?			

Yes	Yes		Yes	• I know you can recycle it and the bin was easy to get to. • I believe in it, and it's good for the environment. • I feel that it's some form of token effort in trying to protect the environment and keep stuff out of landfills. • I recycle as much as I can. • For recycling—because garbage just doesn't disappear—if you recycle there is less garbage then. • They pick it up on Wednesday—because it's a good thing to do. • It is required to recycle cans. • It is mandatory, and I believe in recycling. • It is mandatory.
	No		No	*Correct* • I don't recycle. I didn't think about it and I don't like storing it around home because it brings pests. • I was too lazy. • Sometimes I keep 'em for my brother but. . . . I give them to him. . . . I just didn't this time. *Incorrect* • I take them to a place where they take aluminum cans and gets money for 'em. • I did it to recycle . . . no reason just to recycle. • It's easy to do and they pick 'em up.
No	At work	Yes — Bin nearby? Yes	Yes	• I always recycle aluminum cans. . . . I don't know . . . because I can, because it's available. • It's an automatic thing at work; we all recycle there. • I wasn't gonna mess with it—it was easy. • One of the operator collects them at work, and she takes the bag weekly to put it . . . to take in for recycling.
		No	No	• We're not allowed to keep cans on the job. • There was no recycling center nearby. • A lady at work collects them—so I put them in the bag to give to this one lady.
		Yes	Yes	*No examples available.*

Decision Rules						Choice	Verbatim Justification
At home	No	At work?	No	Bin nearby?	No	No	*Correct* • It wasn't convenient I guess. • There was no obvious place to put it for recycling. • I don't know—I didn't have a container to put it in. • I was not home—I was someplace in town. • I was at someone's house. • I was driving—I threw it out the window—it was a beer can—the environment—I'm down with it but there are too many rules—I threw it out so I wouldn't get caught with it in my car. • I wasn't at home—at home I would've put it in the recycling bucket—If it weren't illegal to put it in my car. . . . I'd've taken it home with me—more people would recycle if it weren't for those open container laws. *Incorrect* • Well I didn't know what to do with it. • That's better on the environment. • I take 'em in and turns 'em in for money. • I think it's a good thing—why use new things when you can reuse old things.

SOURCE: Ryan and Bernard (2006). Material used with permission of the Society for Applied Anthropology.

The top right-most cell of Table 16.3 contains the rationales from people who reported that they were at home and recycled other things besides cans. At home, only one person said it was *easy* to do. Three people, however, said it was a *good thing* to do or that it was *mandatory*. Nowhere else in the rationales do these latter two themes arise.

The next cell down shows the rationales from people who reported that they were at home but did *not* recycle other things. The model correctly predicted that the first three of the respondents would not recycle. Unlike those who had recycled, none of the three mentioned that it was important or good to recycle—or that it was mandatory. The three cases that were misclassified more closely resemble the rationales in the cell above.

The rationales for those at work are clearly divided between those respondents who reported having a recycling bin conveniently located nearby and those who did not. Those who had a bin nearby reported its availability and the ease with which one could recycle. Those who didn't have a bin spontaneously mentioned not being able to keep cans on the job or not having a recycling center.

The last cell shows the rationales for those who were not at home or at work and who did not have a recycling bin nearby. Of the eight cases that the model predicted correctly, half spontaneously mentioned either the lack of convenience or the lack of a recycling bin. The other half mentioned explicitly where they were and clearly implied that place had something to do with their behavior. The two people who said that they threw the can out of the car identified a factor we hadn't thought of before—laws against drinking and driving might have an impact on environmentally friendly behaviors.

Resolving Errors With Ethnography

Why do people recycle when the model predicts that they shouldn't and don't recycle when the model predicts that they should? Again, we turn to the verbatim comments of our informants. Those who recalled recycling a can despite not being at home or at work and not having a bin conveniently located were likely to justify their behavior by citing their beliefs in environmentalism or citing financial benefits for doing it. This may be the result of positive attitudes about recycling—attitudes that give people the extra impetus they need for recycling when bins aren't handy.

This is worth testing, but note that attitudes (or whatever else is at work) can account for no more than 10% of responses in the local sample (because the model predicts 90% of responses there) and no more than 15% of responses in the national sample (because the model predicts 85% of responses there).

We don't have ethnographic data to account for those not at home who reported not recycling a can despite having a recycling bin handy—because none of our 33 informants were in that category. In fact, only three out of 76 people in our national sample reported not recycling despite having a bin handy—just one out of the 61 who were at work and two of the 15 who were not at work.

Clearly, just putting a lot of recycling bins around will increase recycling behavior. This has been known for some time, of course, but the fact that we can validate a well-understood piece of information like this gives us confidence in the EDM method for answering questions that are not this obvious. (**Further Reading**: ethnographic decision modeling)

Key Concepts in This Chapter

episodic behaviors	social desirability	small-*n* study
decision criteria	effect	factorial survey
hierarchical decision model	decision tree	Klecka's *tau*
	vignettes	

Summary

- Ethnographic decision models (EDMs) are qualitative analyses that predict episodic behaviors. Any recurring decision—to buy or not buy a computer; to use (or demand the use of) a condom during sex; to attend or not attend an eight-o'clock class—can be modeled using the EDM method.

- Christina Gladwin (1989) laid out four steps for building and testing decision tree models: (1) Select a specific behavioral choice to model and elicit decision criteria from a convenience sample of respondents. (2) Further elaborate and verify the decision criteria on a purposive, heterogeneous sample of informants. (3) Use the ethnographic data from step 1 and the survey data from step 2 to build a hierarchical decision model. (4) Test the model on an independent and, if possible, representative sample from the same population.

  o We added a fifth step: (5) Validate the model with responses from people about why they acted as they did.

- Step 1. In one of our projects (Ryan and Bernard 2006), we modeled people's decision to recycle (or not) the last aluminum beverage can they had in their hand.

  o We did exploratory interviews with a convenience sample of 21 informants in Florida and North Dakota. We asked each informant three questions: (1) Think about the last time you had a can of something to drink in your hand—soda, juice, water, beer, whatever. When was that? (2) What did you do with the can when you were done? (3) Why did you [didn't you] recycle?
  o This produced a list of 31 reasons for why people recycled or not.

- Step 2. We collected survey data from 70 respondents, 37 in Florida and 33 in North Dakota. We asked each respondent the same initial questions from Step 1 and then asked 31 questions derived from the list of 31 reasons to recycle or not.

  o We wanted enough cases to be able to build a decision tree that was at least three levels deep and where each endpoint would contain at least five people.
  o Minimum Sample Size = Minimum cases in each endpoint x $2^{(\# \text{ of Levels})}$.
  o This would be $(5 \times 2^3) = 40$, which we try to double to ensure that we wind up with some cases at each endpoint.

- Step 3. Examine the decision criteria in Step 1 and the reported behaviors in Step 2 and, with trial and error, build a logical model to account for the behaviors.

  o The idea is to find the one question that produces the fewest errors and make that question the first branch of a proposed model. In our data, "Were you at home when you had that can in your hand?" produced the fewest errors. Guessing that everyone at home recycled and that everyone not at home did not recycle produce an accuracy rate of 53 out of 70 cases, or 76%.

- Step 4. To see how our model EDM did on a larger population, we tested it on a representative, national sample of 386 respondents in the United States. The ethnographic model predicted 84.5% of responses on that sample.

- Cautions: EDMs usually predict 80%–90% of episodic behaviors, but these are almost always reported behaviors, not observed behaviors. Thus, EDMs are subject to the same problem as are all studies of self-reported behavior. Strong reliability and internal validity are not a proxy for external validity.

  ○ However, the credibility—and hence, generalizability—of results from small experiments increases with each repetition of the experiment. If you repeat a small experiment on cultural content in Florida, North Dakota, and California and you get consistent—i.e., reliable—results, the credibility of those results—i.e., the confidence in their external validity—increases.

- Step 5. We can take the process one step further and bring qualitative information into assessing the model's validity. We asked 33 of our ethnographic informants to tell us, in their own words, why they recycled, *before* we asked systematically about the decision criteria. We can examine the fit between the justifications of these 33 informants to recycle or not and compare that to the model's predictions.

  ○ We do this by flowing individual recycling cases down the decision tree and examining the degree to which each end point in the tree (each final decision) corresponds to our informants' own accounts.
  ○ Those who recalled recycling a can despite not being at home or at work and not having a bin conveniently located were likely to justify their behavior by citing their beliefs in environmentalism or citing financial benefits for doing it. This is interesting: We know that attitudes (or whatever else is at work) can account for no more than 10% of responses in the local sample (because the model predicts 90% of responses there) and no more than 15% of responses in the national sample (because the model predicts 85% of responses there).

- The results show that just putting a lot of recycling bins around will increase recycling behavior. This has been known for some time. But the fact that we can validate a well-understood piece of information like this gives us confidence in the EDM method for answering questions that are not this obvious.

Exercises

1. With several colleagues, build and test an ethnographic decision model. If you are at a college or university that has early classes, you might start with the question: Do you have an 8 o'clock class? If the respondent does have an 8 o'clock class, then ask: Did you go to that class the last time it met? Why [why not]? Do this until you have no more than one new reason in the full list of reasons for three respondents in a row. Convert all the reasons into questions.

For example, "I was too tired" becomes "Were you too tired?" and "I never miss that class. It's calculus and I can't afford to fall behind" becomes "Is that class calculus?" Next, ask 30 people who have an 8 o'clock class the same original question and then ask all the questions from the earlier step. Build the decision model and then test it on another 30 people.

Further Reading

Ethnographic decision modeling. Bauer and Wright (1996), Chang and Fang (2012), Dy et al. (2005), Fairweather (1999), Heemskerk (2000), Hill (1998), Hurwicz (1995), Mathews and Hill (1990), B. W. Miller et al. (2014), Montbriand (1994), Morera and Gladwin (2006), Ryan and Martínez (1996), Weller et al. (1997), Young and Garro (1994 [1981]).

Visit the online resource site at study.sagepub.com/bernardaqd to access engaging and helpful digital content, like video tutorials on working with MAXQDA, presentation slides, MAXQDA keyboard shortcuts, datasets, stop list, and recommended readings.

CHAPTER **17**

KWIC ANALYSIS AND WORD COUNTS

INTRODUCTION ◆

Most qualitative data come in the form of free-flowing texts. There are four major types of analysis for this latter kind of data. In one, the text is segmented into chunks that conform to a set of themes and the themes are analyzed qualitatively or quantitatively. This is the basis for grounded theory, content analysis, and analytic induction—the subjects of Chapters 10, 11, and 15.

In the second type, the entire text is examined closely for patterns. This is the basis for schema analysis, narrative analysis, and discourse analysis—the subjects of Chapters 12, 13, and 14.

Third, there are mixed methods, like ethnographic decision modeling, the subject of Chapter 16.

In the fourth major type of analysis, the text is segmented into its most fundamental components: words. This is the basis for KWIC (key-word-in-context) analysis, word counts, and semantic network analysis. We'll treat KWIC analysis and word counts in this chapter. Semantic network analysis will have to wait until Chapter 19, after we discuss the use of proximity matrices for analyzing relational data.

♦ KWIC—KEY WORD IN CONTEXT

The **key-word-in-context** method is summed up in J. R. Firth's famous aphorism: "You shall know a word by the company it keeps" (1957:11). In other words, to understand a concept, look at how it is used.

The term **KWIC** was coined by an IBM engineer (Luhn 1960), but the general method has a very long history. Since at least the 13th century (see Busa 1971:595), students of the Old and New Testaments have produced **concordances**, or lists of every substantive word in those texts, each with its associated sentence, so that people might study the meaning of each word in all its contexts. Concordances have been done on sacred texts from other religions (see Kassis [1983] on the Koran), on famous works of literature from Euripides (Allen and Italie 1954), to Beowulf (Bessinger and Smith 1969), to Dylan Thomas (Farringdon and Farringdon 1980), and on bureaucratic documents governing science education in public schools (Tenam-Zemach et al. 2014).

Today, any digitized work essentially contains its own concordance. When you search for a word, you see it in context and if you keep searching for the same word, you see it in all its contexts. KWIC software and concordance programs simply automate this process, searching a text for every use of a particular word or phrase and printing out all the hits, within their contexts. (KWIC is available as a feature of many text analysis programs, and there is lots of specialized software—including freeware—for doing concordances.)

If you run a KWIC program on all the substantive words in a text and then arrange the hits in alphabetical order, by substantive words, you've got a classic concordance.

♦ AN EXAMPLE OF KWIC

The concept of "deconstruction" is an abstract term used by social scientists, literary critics, and journalists. Jacques Derrida, who coined the term, did not define it.

To Derrida, the meaning of any text is inherently unstable and variable. As an exercise, we wondered if we could understand the term by looking at how one author actually used it.

We downloaded an interesting article titled "Deconstructing Development Theory: Feminism, the Public/Private Dichotomy and the Mexican Maquiladoras," by Joanne Wright (1997) and used KWIC software for each use of the word "deconstruction." There were 19 hits, shown in Table 17.1.

In doing a KWIC analysis, you have to decide on the form of the word that you search for. We searched for the complete word, "deconstruction" or its plural "deconstructions." Had we used a **wild card** approach and looked for "deconstruct*" we would have captured words like "deconstructs" and "deconstructing." Our analysis

Table 17.1   KWIC Table for the Word *Deconstruction* in Wright (1997)

1	This varied group of postmodern thinkers employs the tool of *deconstruction* to critically evaluate—indeed, to peel back the discursive layers of—development's assumptions: capitalist economics, progress, modernity and rationality.
2	Their *deconstructions* reveal development's asymmetric dichotomization of the world into modern, Westernized societies on the one hand and traditional, "backward" societies on the other.
3	It will be the purpose of this article to utilize the deconstructive tool from a feminist perspective, to carry the postmodern theorists' *deconstructions* one step further to unravel the elements of development theory that carry Western gender biases regarding proper roles for women and men based on their "true nature."
4	This process of feminist *deconstruction* correlates with a contemporary trend in feminist analysis, that of deconstructing institutions such as the state and law, and discourses of democratic theory and international relations theory, to expose their reliance upon, and infusion with, gender.
5	Feminist *deconstruction*, then, is distinct from the earlier empirical project that enumerates women's experiences with development.
6	Feminist *deconstruction* is "not simply about women," but about the interdependent constructions of masculine and feminine, and about shifting feminist analysis from the margin to the centre.
7	The first step in this exercise is to briefly describe the postmodern approach to Western development theory, following which a theoretical feminist *deconstruction* can be carried out.
8	It will be instructive, as well, to apply this *deconstruction* to an example of development in practice, the maquiladora project of Mexico.

(Continued)

Table 17.1 (Continued)

9	*Deconstruction* will be used here to refer to a critical method, a conceptual tool, with which the ideological layers of development are peeled back and examined.
10	The process of *deconstruction* is part of the larger postmodern project, which is to de-naturalize some of the dominant features of our way of life; to point out that those entities that we unthinkingly experience as "natural" (they might even include capitalism, patriarchy, liberal humanism) are in fact "cultural"; made by us, not given to us (Hutcheon 1989:2).
11	Postmodern *deconstructions* of development recognize that world cultures have always been mutually influencing and that there exists no such thing as a "pure" culture to be preserved and cloistered away.
12	A viable *deconstruction* of development can be commenced without relying on the binarism of universal/relative.
13	What *deconstruction* does show is that development has, from its inception, posited a Western model as "the most successful way of life mankind [*sic*] has ever known" (Ayres 1978: xxxii–xxxiii) and that the implementation of this assumption through development has proved destructive to viable and vital cultures and societies.
14	It is this gap in postmodern theorizing that necessitates a specifically feminist *deconstruction* of the development paradigm.
15	Moreover, a feminist *deconstruction* of development theory takes as axiomatic the idea that women, in practice, transgress the border between public and private.
16	Just as postmodern theory finds the dichotomies of developed/underdeveloped, modern/traditional, and so forth to be central features of development thought, a feminist *deconstruction* reveals that development theory is phallocentric as it organizes social life along the lines of the dichotomies of man/woman, public/private, reason/emotion and knowledge/experience.
17	Rather than trying to reconcile these dichotomies, as women and development theory has tried to do, a feminist *deconstruction* recognizes them as instrumental to the Westernizing project of development.
18	Feminist *deconstruction*, then, must involve changing the parameters of who can know and who can produce theory; it must involve relocating the site of knowledge and theory creation.
19	Derrida, who coined the term, refuses to define *deconstruction*, arguing that any attempt to define it is also subject to the process of deconstruction.

SOURCE: Wright, J. 1997. Deconstructing development theory: feminism, the public/private dichotomy, and the Mexican maquiladoras. *Canadian Journal of Sociology and Anthropology* 34:71–91. Table source: Authors.

might be different with more uses of words that contain the stem "deconstruct." Also, we decided to pull only the sentence in which the word "deconstruction" was found. Here again, our analysis might have been different if we had increased the context and pulled the sentences before and after the sentence in which the word was found—or even the entire paragraph.

To continue our KWIC analysis, we printed each of the sentences that contained the word "deconstruction" on a separate note card and sorted the cards into piles of sentences that we thought somehow "go together." This method taps into the various meanings that we carry around for the word "deconstruction."

The KWIC method gives us a way to deconstruct the meaning of the word "deconstruction," as used by one author. It seems to us that Wright uses it to mean a tool, a process of analysis, the results of an analysis, and a theory. We can see whether our interpretation is idiosyncratic or is shared by others by asking colleagues to sort the 19 statements in Table 17.1 into piles and to explain why they think various statements go together. We can also systematically compare Wright's use of the term "deconstruction" with its use by others by creating tables like 17.1 for other articles.

Finally, we can apply the KWIC method to any word or phrase that we want to analyze. To get an understanding of what the phrase "corporate culture" means, for example, we could examine its use in articles from the *Wall Street Journal* and the *Financial Times of London*. (**Further Reading**: KWIC and concordance)

WORD COUNTS ♦

Like so many simple things, it's easy to lose sight of how much we can learn from just counting words in a text. Although it's not a perfect relationship, words and phrases that appear more often in a text tend to be more salient to the writer or speaker who produced the text. Jasienski (2006) found that natural scientists use the word "unexpected" to describe their findings 2.3 times more often than do scholars in the social sciences and humanities. "One might think," says Jasienski, "that academic machismo or realism would cause scientists to downplay their surprise, but, on the other hand, overstating the level of astonishment may occur when striving for media attention" (2006:1112).

Word counts have been used to trace the ebb and flow of support for political figures over time (Danielson and Lasorsa 1997; de Sola Pool 1952); to estimate the amount of time that graduate students spend reading for an online course (Brown and Green 2009); and to test whether gender of author affects the evaluations of medical students (Isaac et al. 2011).

In a classic study, Mosteller and Wallace (1964) compared the use of words common to the writings of James Madison and Alexander Hamilton and concluded that

Madison and not Hamilton had written 12 of the *Federalist Papers*. You'd be surprised at what we can learn from counting words. (**Further Reading**: authorship studies)

♦ WORDS AND MATRICES

At the heart of word count analysis is the conversion of text into either a **respondent-by-word matrix** or a **word-by-respondent matrix**. To illustrate, we asked 15 university students the following:

> Please recall the last time that you had a cold or the flu. Take a moment and think about this illness episode. Try to remember as many details as you can. After you have thought about the illness, please describe it in as much detail as possible.

Figure 17.1 displays the results for five of the respondents, and Figure 17.2 shows how we converted the data into a word-by-respondent matrix.

Stop Lists

Before we convert these texts into matrices, we give the software what's called a **stop list**—a list of common words (like prepositions, conjunctions, and articles) that we don't want counted in the matrix. This is shown in the middle column of Figure 17.2.

Deciding what goes into the stop list is a crucial part of the analysis. We use a list compiled by Fox (1989–90) and modify for each project we run. For example, words that are only used once in a corpus of texts can't co-occur, by definition, so they are dropped from analysis. We use a concordance program to count up the words in each corpus of text, identify the ones that are used just once, and then add those words to Fox's basic stop list.

Most researchers also ignore common words, like prepositions. Some researchers recode synonyms so they are not counted twice. We always make sure that there are no misspellings and that orthographic differences are ignored (e.g., we combine behavior and behaviour).

Many researchers lump singular and plural forms of the same word (e.g., product and products), and some lump words with the same root (e.g., partial and partially). Fox's list contains words in English that are usually semantically neutral.

After eliminating the words in the stop list, the software goes through each text and counts each use of each word.

Figure 17.1 Five Texts From Students About a Recent Experience With a Cold or Flu

#1

I waited till after finals were over to seek care. Had cough, drainage, runny nose, increased wheezing/asthmatic problems. Had symptoms/signs for about three days before going to health center. Receive antibiotics symptoms/signs progressed until almost end of antibiotics. worsened in the middle of illness. Illness lasted for about two and a half to three weeks. Cause fatigue and general run down feeling but did not interfere with life other than mild inconvenience. When symptoms/signs started took home remedy of antihistamine/decongestant and started using inhaler more to help control illness.

#2

I know I'm getting sick by first feeling "puny," you know, weak and tired like you don't want to lift your arms. If I'm really sick it will later be accompanied with "hot flashes." My voice will drop about two octaves (which can be fun since this participant happens to be a girl). Last time I was sick was spring break, I had a terrible congestive cough that would rack my body and wake me up at night, not to mention I would wake up my roommates too. Other than the cough I didn't have too many other symptoms. (Except after coughing a lot I would get dizzy.)

#3

Freshman year, I caught the flu for the first time in three years. I definitely didn't miss not being sick. It started when I began having trouble walking, my body became very weak. Everything on me hurt, and I didn't want to move. After about three hours of laying in bed, I felt like I was going to throw up. Fortunately, I had someone bring up a bucket to my room, however. I threw up repeatedly. When I was finished, I had to brush my teeth, and I figured since I was up, I would take a shower. This was a relieving feeling for me as I sat in the shower for about an hour. This spell of aching body and stomach flu continued for about two days, so I had about twelve hours to study for a test that I hadn't even begun studying for. Everything worked out fine; I guess it was a case of food poisoning or the twenty-four hour flu.

#4

I got the flu last January right before my twenty-first birthday. I took Advil, Tylenol, whatever pain medicine I could find. But it got worse and by two days before my birthday, I went to see a doctor. I wanted to make sure I got well by my birthday so I could party and get my free drinks. Well, it turn out that I had some sort of bad infection of the sinus, and the doctor prescribed for me to take antibiotics for the next ten days, even if I felt better. And because of the antibiotics, I could not drink any alcohol. So I had to wait at least eight days after my birthday before I could drink . . . so after those eight days, I drank up like there was no tomorrow.

#5

The last time I had a cold/flu was in Feb 98. I laid in bed for two days with a headache, a stomach ache, fever, body pain. I had spells of dizziness and nausea. I pretty much slept for most of forty-eight hours. I was still tired and worn out for a couple of days beyond the initial illness.

SOURCE: Authors.

Figure 17.2 Converting Texts to Matrices

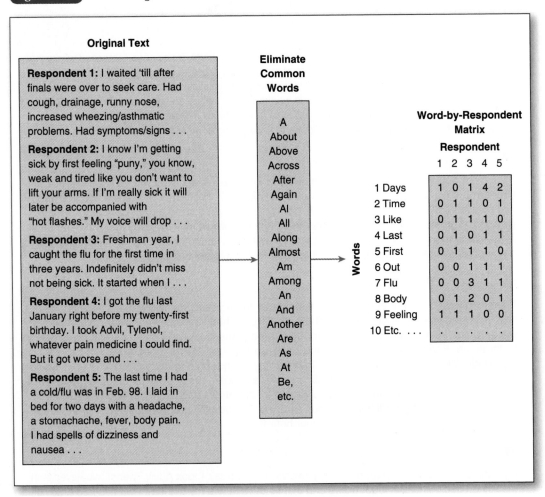

Results of Analyzing the Data in Figure 17.1

The five respondents whose texts are shown in Figure 17.1 used a total of 555 words, but they only used 268 different words. Our stop list contained 65 words, and the five informants used 44 of them. So, not counting those 44 words, the five informants used 224 different words. However, they used 187 of those 224 words just once. Limiting the words in the corpus to those used by two or more informants, we're left with the 224–187=37 words in Table 17.2 (see Box 17.1).

Box 17.1

Words as Variables

Table 17.2 is a profile matrix of five people by the 37 words used at least twice in the corpus of texts. The units of analysis in Table 17.2 are the five respondents, shown in the columns. The variables in Table 17.2 are the 37 words the five respondents used in their texts. The columns show the number of times each word was used by each of the five respondents.

   Table 17.2 is a profile matrix. Here, each of the five respondents is "profiled" by her or his use of or non-use of the words in the text. The usual way to represent profile matrices is with the units of analysis in the rows and the variables in the columns. When we do word counts, however, we may wind up with too many variables to display. That's why, in Table 17.2, the matrix is portrayed with the people (the units of analysis) in the columns and the variables (the words) in the rows.

Inspecting Table 17.2, we see that the word "days" was mentioned once by persons 1 and 3, twice by person 5, four times by person 4, and never by person 2.

   Figure 17.3 is a **scree plot** showing the distribution of the 224 unique words in the five texts and labeling the 37 words used by at least two people. ("Scree" refers to the rubble that piles up at the base of a mountain. A scree plot is a visualization of items in a list that are important in an analysis, plus all the items that don't—the rubble—which can be ignored.)

Table 17.2 Words Used at Least Twice in Five Texts Shown in Figure 17.1

ID	WORD	RESP1	RESP2	RESP3	RESP4	RESP5
1	two	1	1	1	1	1
2	not	1	1	1	1	0
3	days	1	0	1	4	2
4	after	1	1	1	2	0
5	first	0	1	1	1	0
6	me	0	1	2	1	0
7	feeling	1	1	1	0	0
8	flu	0	0	3	1	1

(Continued)

Table 17.2 (Continued)

ID	WORD	RESP1	RESP2	RESP3	RESP4	RESP5
9	body	0	1	2	0	1
10	time	0	1	1	0	1
11	my	0	3	3	5	0
12	last	0	1	0	1	1
13	took	1	0	0	1	0
14	since	0	1	1	0	0
15	sick	0	3	1	0	0
16	stomach	0	0	1	0	1
17	weak	0	1	1	0	0
18	pain	0	0	0	1	1
19	cough	1	2	0	0	0
20	bed	0	0	1	0	1
21	going	1	0	1	0	0
22	three	2	0	2	0	0
23	twenty	0	0	1	1	0
24	want	0	1	1	0	0
25	take	0	0	1	1	0
26	illness	3	0	0	0	1
27	symptoms	3	1	0	0	0
28	get	0	1	0	1	0
29	started	2	0	1	0	0
30	hours	0	0	2	0	1
31	didn't	0	1	2	0	0
32	before	1	0	0	3	0
33	felt	0	0	1	1	0
34	eight	0	0	0	2	1
35	antibiotics	2	0	0	2	0
36	tired	0	1	0	0	1
37	even	0	0	1	1	0

Figure 17.3 Scree Plot of the 224 Unique Non-Stopped Words in Figure 17.1

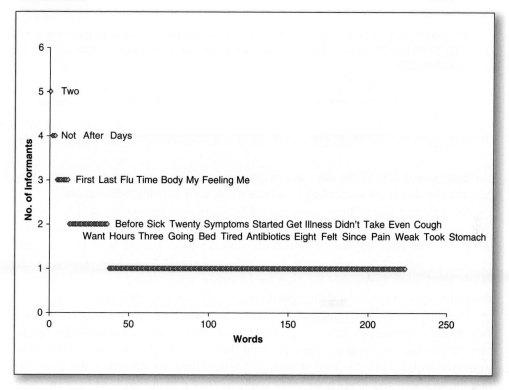

PERSONAL ADS ♦

Back in Chapter 11, on content analysis, we went over the pioneering work of Elizabeth Hirschman on personal ads. Classic content analysis, like that done by Hirschman, involves identifying themes in a set of texts, coding the texts for occurrences of those themes, and then doing statistical analysis of the text-by-theme matrix. We applied the word-count-matrix method to a set of personal ads, just to see how much we could learn from that simple method. As we suspected, you can learn a lot.

Figure 17.4 shows two typical ads, one from a man and one from a woman, pieced together from ads we found online.

These ads have their own vocabulary: SWF means "single white female," DBPM means "divorced black professional male," ISO means "in search of," LTR means "long-term relationship," and HWP stands for "height and weight proportionate," which is code for "no fat." These abbreviations developed when people were charged by the word for

Figure 17.4 Some Typical Personal Ads

> SWF (HWP), 5'6," sandy hair, hazel eyes, fun, adventurous, sensual, passionate, ISO SWM (HWP), 35–40, fun, sexy, and intelligent, for all kinds of outdoor fun and possible, LTR.
>
> DBPM, 31, 6'1," 185 lbs, intelligent, employed, ambitious, creative. I like sports, dancing, movies, books, and stimulating conversation. ISO an intelligent SF with similar interests.

placing personal ads. These days, ads online personal ads are either free or very low cost, but the shorthand vocabulary continues to be used in many personal ads.

We collected 380 of these personal ads—146 placed by women, 234 by men—from an Internet website in 1998. Table 17.3 shows the 22 words used most frequently by the men and the 21 words most used by the women who placed these ads as they *offered* features about themselves to others. Table 17.4 shows the 21 words used most frequently by men and women who placed these ads as they *sought* features in potential dating partners.

Men and women are about equally likely to mention their hair and eye color when they describe themselves (the differences in percentages are not statistically significant). Some women explicitly seek tall men, but, overall, men are more likely than women to seek a particular kind of body in women (they use adjectives like attractive, slim, fit, slender), and women are more likely to offer a particular kind of body (they use adjectives like full-figured and attractive).

Men and women alike describe themselves in terms of their interests and their physical and personal attributes. But what they seek in others is based primarily on personal attributes, such as honesty, sincerity, caring, and humor—though women are more likely to seek honesty than men are. Men and women both mention their financial status, but women are more likely than men to seek someone who is financially secure.

These findings about what men and women offer each other in personal ads in the United States have been remarkably stable since Hirschman's work, 30 years ago.

Things may be changing, though. In a study done in Spain, Gil-Burmann et al. (2002) found that, as expected, men of all ages in Spain sought physical attractiveness in women and women over 40 sought financial resources. Women under 40, however, sought physical attractiveness in men. Gil-Burmann et al. interpret this shift in behavior among younger women to economic development in Spain and the participation of women in the workforce. And in an Internet survey about mate preferences of 1,851 English-speaking, heterosexual women, those who were financially independent tended to prefer good looks over good financial prospects (F. R. Moore et al. 2006). (**Further Reading**: personal ads)

Table 17.3 What Men and Women *Offer* in Personal Ads

		Women			Men	
		Frequency (n = 146)	Percentage		Frequency (n = 234)	Percentage
1	Hair	68	46.6	Hair	102	43.6
2	Eyes	64	43.8	Eyes	92	39.3
3	Movies	38	26.0	Employed	76	32.5
4	Brown	37	25.3	Brown	72	30.8
5	Employed	36	24.7	Likes	55	23.5
6	Mom	34	23.3	Fishing	46	19.7
7	Dancing	30	20.5	Movies	43	18.4
8	Outgoing	27	18.5	Camping	43	18.4
9	Reading	26	17.8	Sports	42	17.9
10	Music	23	15.8	Out	37	15.8
11	Likes	22	15.1	Outgoing	34	14.5
12	Blue	22	15.1	Blue	34	14.5
13	Out	20	13.7	Music	27	11.5
14	Full figured	19	13.0	Blond	26	11.1
15	Blonde	19	13.0	Outdoors	23	9.8
16	Gardening	17	11.6	Humorous	23	9.8
17	Attractive	17	11.6	Biking	22	9.4
18	Outdoors	16	11.0	Hobbies	21	9.0
19	Fishing	15	10.3	Fun	20	8.5
20	Fun	15	10.3	Shy	20	8.5
21	Dining	15	10.3	Working	20	8.5
22				Easygoing	20	8.5

Table 17.4 What Men and Women *Seek* in Personal Ads

		Women			Men	
		Frequency (n = 146)	Percentage		Frequency (n = 234)	Percentage
1	Honest	61	41.8	Honest	74	31.6
2	Caring	21	14.4	Sincere	23	9.8
3	Humorous	18	12.3	Relationship	23	9.8
4	Loving	13	8.9	Caring	22	9.4
5	Sincere	13	8.9	Attractive	21	9.0
6	Employed	11	7.5	Fun Loving	18	7.7
7	Secure	11	7.5	Interests	17	7.3
8	Respectful	10	6.8	Possible	15	6.4
9	Interests	9	6.2	Slim	15	6.4
10	Kind	9	6.2	Similar	14	6.0
11	Similar	9	6.2	Compatible	14	6.0
12	Tall	8	5.5	Fit	13	5.6
13	Romantic	7	4.8	Loving	12	5.1
14	Outgoing	6	4.1	Intelligent	12	5.1
15	Good	6	4.1	Slender	12	5.1
16	Life	6	4.1	Humorous	11	4.7
17	Nice	6	4.1	Kind	11	4.7
18	Sensitive	6	4.1	Outgoing	11	4.7
19	Intelligent	6	4.1	Good	11	4.7
20	Meet	6	4.1	Nice	9	3.8
21	Financially	6	4.1	Trustworthy	9	3.8

DESCRIBING CHILDREN ♦

Here's one more. As part of a longitudinal study of families in Los Angeles, Ryan and Weisner (1996) asked 82 fathers and 82 mothers of teenagers: "What is your teenager like now? Does she or he have any special qualities or abilities?" Parents all used the same social science questionnaire schema to answer the questions—writing a series of terse phrases and words for a minute or so.

Figure 17.5 shows three of the responses.

Using a word processor, Ryan and Weisner made sure that each thought (phrase or sentence) was separated by a period. Then they used their word processor and a KWIC program to do some simple counts, shown in Table 17.5 (see Box 17.2).

Figure 17.5 Examples of Parents' Descriptions of Their Children

---

ID-009 (Father's description of son) Loving. Obedient. Maintains own identity. Likes being home. Independent. Anxious to go to California to school.

ID-016. (Father's description of son) Smart. Energetic. Arrogant. Dependent. Slick. Passive. Lack of imagination. Attraction to inner-city lifestyle.

ID124. (Mother's description of daughter) Great kid. Willing to communicate with parents. Listens. Motivated in school. Helpful around the house. Healthy. Active. Lots of friends. She tends to play it safe.

SOURCE: Adapted from Ryan, G. W. and T. Weisner. (1996). Analyzing words in brief descriptions: Fathers and mothers describe their children. *Cultural Anthropology Methods Journal, 8*(2), 13–16. Copyright © 1996 Sage Publications.

Box 17.2

Using Word Processors for Basic Counts

In Table 17.5, to get the average number of characters per word, we just divided the number of characters (including spaces) in the document by the number of words. The number of words and the number of characters are part of a document's basic description in word processors, like MS-Word, OpenOffice Writer, and WordPerfect. WordPerfect also counts sentences, but MS-Word counts paragraphs.

(Continued)

(Continued)

To count sentences in MS-Word, just make a copy of your document and make each sentence a paragraph by putting a hard return after each period. If you're comfortable with writing macros in MS-Word, use the following macro for counting sentences in MS-Word.

```
Sub MAIN
   StartOfDocument
   Count = 0
   While SentRight(1, 1) < > 0
      If Right$(Selection$(), 1) < > Chr$(13) Then count = count +1
   Wend
   MsgBox "Number of sentences in document:" + Str$(count)
End Sub
```

Many KWIC programs, as well as major text analysis programs, count the number of unique words.

The data in Table 17.5 reveal similarities and differences in the way these mothers and fathers describe their children. Dividing the number of characters by the number of words in Table 17.5 shows that mothers and fathers use roughly the same size words (about 5.7 characters each). Mothers and fathers also use roughly the same number of words per phrase (3.20 vs. 3.27), and with 666 unique words in a corpus of 1,692 words, mothers have a **type-token ratio** of (666/1692) = 0.39, or 39%, almost identical to that for fathers at (548/1346) = 0.41 (41%).

On the other hand, mothers used 28% more sentences (528 sentences compared to 411 sentences for fathers) and 26% more words (1,692 compared to 1,346). We can't tell from this if fathers have less to say about their children or they just have less to say about all topics, but the type-token ratio shows that men's vocabulary for describing children is as rich as women's vocabulary. The type-token ratio is one of a whole family of **measures of lexical richness** (see Box 17.3).

Box 17.3

Measures of Lexical Richness

The type-token ratio (TTR) is widely used in linguistics-based text analysis and in bilingual education. Tang and Nesi (2003), for example, used the TTR to assess the difference in lexical richness between two secondary schools in China where the children were learning English.

There is a well-known problem with the TTR: You can get misleading results if the texts on which it is calculated are of very different lengths. Assuming that the mothers and fathers in Ryan and Weisner's sample had similar vocabularies—i.e., they were working with more or less the same number of words with which to talk about their children—longer texts could have lower type-token ratios. In this case they don't, and so we conclude that the mothers have a slightly richer vocabulary than the fathers do—at least when they talk about their children. We won't go into them here, but there are many competing measures of **text concentration** (for a review of these, see Daller et al. 2003).

We lose a lot of information when we examine unique words. Unlike a KWIC analysis, we do not know the context in which the words occurred, nor whether informants used words negatively or positively. Nor do we know how the words were related to each other. But **text distillations** like TTRs introduce very little investigator bias (though we do have to choose what words to leave out of the analysis), and they can help us identify constructs, or themes.

Table 17.5 Text Statistics for Ryan and Weisner's Data

	Mothers (N = 82)	Fathers (N = 82)	Total (N = 164)
1. Characters	9,748	7,625	17,373
2. Word count	1,692	1,346	3,038
3. Average word length in characters	5.76	5.66	5.72
4. Sentence count	528	411	939
5. Average sentences/phrases per person	6.44	5.01	5.72
6. Average words per sentence	3.20	3.27	3.24
7. Maximum words per sentence	14	17	
8. Number of unique words	666	548	
9. Type-token ratio	0.39	0.41	

SOURCE: From Ryan, G. W. and T. Weisner. (1996). Analyzing words in brief descriptions: Fathers and mothers describe their children. *Cultural Anthropology Methods Journal, 8*(2), 13–16. Copyright © 1996 Sage Publications.

Table 17.6 shows an abbreviated list of the mothers' and fathers' words—the 37 words most used by mothers out of their 666 unique words and 30 words most used by fathers out of their 548 unique words. Mothers mentioned the words "good,"

Table 17.6 Mothers' and Fathers' Word Lists in Describing Their Children

\#	Count/Word	\#	Count/Word
	Mothers' Descriptions		Fathers' Descriptions
1	22 good	1	23 good
2	12 friends	2	16 school
3	11 loving	3	11 hard
4	11 out	4	9 intelligent
5	11 people	5	8 bright
6	10 doesn't	6	8 independent
7	10 hard	7	8 out
8	10 school	8	8 well
9	9 responsible	9	7 doesn't
10	9 sense	10	7 lack
11	8 caring	11	7 loving
12	8 intelligent	12	7 people
13	8 lacks	13	7 sensitive
14	8 sensitive	14	7 sports
15	7 bright	15	7 student
16	7 honest	16	6 caring
17	7 others	17	6 does
18	7 self	18	6 life
19	7 time	19	6 others
20	7 well	20	6 work
21	7 work	21	5 ability
22	6 creative	22	5 enjoys
23	6 does	23	5 great
24	6 great	24	5 lacks
25	6 mature	25	5 likes

Mothers' Descriptions		Fathers' Descriptions	
26	6 sports	26	5 mature
27	5 academically	27	5 own
28	5 artistic	28	5 sense
29	5 cares	29	5 social
30	5 concerned	30	5 wants
31	5 goals	. . .	
32	5 going	548	1 zero
33	5 humor		
34	5 independent		
35	5 other		
36	5 social		
37	5 times		
. . .			
666	1 zest		

SOURCE: From Ryan, G. W. and T. Weisner. (1996). Analyzing words in brief descriptions: Fathers and mothers describe their children. *Cultural Anthropology Methods Journal* 8(2), 13–16. Copyright © 1996 Sage Publications.

"friends," "loving," "out," and "people" at least 11 times and "zest" (the last word on the mothers' list) just once. Fathers mentioned the words "good," "school," "hard," and "intelligent" at least nine times and "zero" (the last word on the fathers' list) just once.

Word Clouds

Word cloud programs offer a fast and easy way to visualize word frequencies and especially to spot potentially important concepts in a set of texts. Many word cloud programs can be used free of cost.

The analysis underlying word clouds is a word count, like the one from which Table 17.6 was extracted. (Remember: The full word-count table has 666 unique words used by mothers and 548 unique words used by fathers.) In a word cloud, each word is displayed only once, no matter how often it appears in the text, but words that appear more frequently are displayed in larger and bolder type.

Prompting

As in any kind of interviewing, people respond with more information if you learn how to probe for it. Brewer (2002:112) found that **semantic cueing** increased the recall of items in a free list by over 40%. When informants finish giving you a list, ask them to: "Think of all the kinds of X [the domain] that are like Y," where Y is the first item on their initial list. If the informant responds with more items, you take it another step: "Try to remember other types of X that are like Y and tell me any new ones that you haven't already said."

Do this until the informant says there are no more items like Y. Then you repeat the exercise for the second item on the informant's initial list, and the third, and so on (see Box 18.1).

Box 18.1

Other Prompts

Brewer tested three other kinds of probes for free lists: **redundant questioning, nonspecific prompting,** and **alphabetic cueing.** Here's the redundant question that Brewer and his colleagues asked a group of IV-drug users:

> Think of all the different kinds of drugs or substances people use to get high, feel good, or think and feel differently. These drugs are sometimes called recreational drugs or street drugs. Tell me the names of all the kinds of these drugs you can remember. Please keep trying to recall if you think there are more kinds of drugs you might be able to remember. (Brewer et al. 2002:347)

In nonspecific prompting you ask people "What other kinds of X are there?" after they've responded to your original question. You keep asking this question until people say they can't think of any more Xs.

And in alphabetic cueing, you ask informants "What kinds of X are there that begin with the letter A ". . . ."With the letter B" And so on.

People who are very knowledgeable about the contents of a cultural domain usually provide longer lists than others. Some items will be mentioned over and over again, but eventually, if you keep asking people to list things, you get a lot of repeat items and all the new items are unique—i.e., mentioned by only one informant.

This happens quickly with **well-specified domains** like names of African animals—often by the time you've interviewed 15 or 20 informants. With somewhat

fuzzy domains, like "names of ethnic groups," you might still be eliciting new items after interviewing 30 or 40 people. With really fuzzy domains, like "things that mothers do," you might be eliciting new items after interviewing 40 or 50 people.

Long lists don't necessarily mean that people know a lot about the things they name. In fact, in modern societies, people can often name a lot more things than they can recognize in the real world (see Box 18.2).

Box 18.2

Loose Talk

John Gatewood (1983) interviewed 40 adult Pennsylvanians and got free lists of names of trees. He asked each informant to go through his or her list and check the trees that they thought they could actually recognize. Thirty-four out of the 40 informants listed "pine," and 31 of the 34 said that they could recognize a pine.

Orange trees were another matter. Twenty-seven people listed "orange," but only four people said they could recognize an orange tree (without oranges hanging all over it, of course). On average, these 40 Pennsylvanians said they could recognize half of the trees they listed, a phenomenon that Gatewood called "loose talk."

Gatewood and his students (1983) asked 54 university students, half of them women and half of them men, to (1) list all the musical instruments, fabrics, hand tools, and trees they could think of; and (2) check off the items in each of their lists that they thought they would recognize in a natural setting.

Gatewood chose musical instruments with the idea that there would be no gender difference in the number of items listed or recognized; that women might name more kinds of fabrics than would men; and that men would name more kinds of hand tools than would women. He chose the domain of trees to see if his earlier findings would replicate. There were no surprises: All the hypotheses—and stereotypes—were supported (Gatewood 1984).

PLOTTING FREE LISTS ♦

We asked 34 people: "Please write down the names of all the fruits you can think of." Because free list data are texts, they have to be cleaned up before you can analyze them. Only 10 people listed grapes, but another 22 (for a total of 32 out of 34 people) listed grape (in the singular). Before counting up the frequency for each item in the free lists, we had to combine all mentions of grapes and grape. It doesn't matter whether you change grapes into grape or vice versa, so long as you make all the required changes.

Then there are spelling mistakes. In our data, three people listed bananna (wrong spelling), and 27 people listed banana (right spelling); three people listed avacado (wrong), one listed avocato (wrong), and six people listed avocado (right). Cantaloupe was hopeless, as was pomegranate. We got eight cantaloupes (the preferred spelling in the dictionary), six cantelopes, two cantelopes, and three canteloupes. We got 17 listings for guava and one for guayaba, which happens to be the Spanish term for guava. We got 10 listings for passion fruit and one for passion-fruit, with a hyphen (when computers list word frequencies, they see those two listings as different).

Once the data were cleaned, we plotted how often each fruit was mentioned. The result is the **scree plot** in Figure 18.1. (We saw scree plots in Chapter 17. Recall that "scree" refers to the rocks that pile up at the base of a cliff and the telltale L-shape of the pile.)

Figure 18.1 Scree Plot of Free List of 143 Fruits From 34 Informants

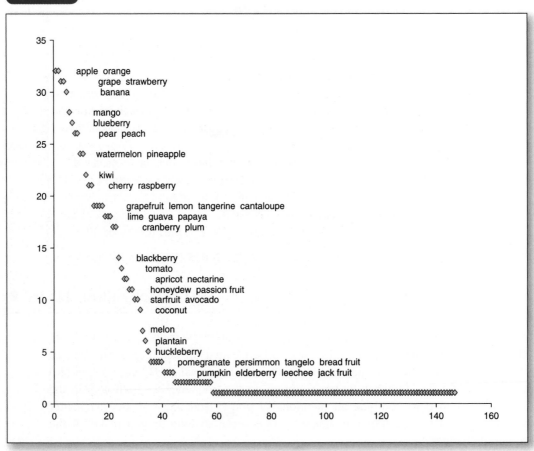

The shape of the curve in Figure 18.1 is typical for a well-defined domain, like fruits: The 34 informants named a total of 147 different fruits, but 88 of those fruits were named by just one person (prickly pear and quince, for example) and almost everyone named a few items (apple and orange, for example). Compare that to the results for lists of "things that mothers do." For this domain, 34 informants named 554 items, of which 515 were named by just one person and only a handful (love, clean, cook) were named by five or more people.

The difference is that fruits (and animals and emotions) are very well defined, but things that mothers do (and things that people can do to help the environment, and things that people might do on a weekend) are much less well-defined cultural domains. Many of the most interesting domains are things that people don't have easy lists for.

Selecting Items From a Free List for Further Study

We use scree plots to choose the set of items that we want to study in more depth. For example, by counting the dots in Figure 18.1, we see that: (1) 14 fruits were mentioned by 20 or more of our 34 informants; and (2) 58 items were mentioned by at least two of our informants. All the other fruits were mentioned just once.

How many items should we choose from these data as representing the contents of the domain? There is no formal rule here, but a good general rule is to select items that are mentioned by at least 10% of your informants. If you have 40 informants, then choose items that were mentioned by at least four of them. If this still produces too many items, then move up to 15% of informants or more.

There is nothing forcing you to take every item that's mentioned a lot, especially if you already know something about the domain you're studying. If you want to study, say, 40 items in depth, you can choose some that are mentioned frequently and others that are mentioned less frequently—or even by no one at all.

An item mentioned once is usually not a good candidate to include for further work on the structure of the domain. The whole idea of a cultural domain, as contrasted with an individual cognitive domain, is that the content is shared (Borgatti 1999).

On the other hand, we often want to know where a particular item fits within a cultural domain. In the late 1990s, we studied the domain of green behaviors in the United States—things that people believe they can do to help the environment—under a contract from a motor vehicle manufacturer (Bernard et al. 2009). We collected free list data from 43 people across the United States but nobody, not a single person, mentioned buying an electric or a hybrid car.

At the time, there were no electric or hybrid cars on the market, but our client wanted to know where Americans might place the behavior of "buying an electric car" within the domain of green behaviors, so we put that item into the pile-sort task of the study (more on that in a minute).

triad tests [see Weller 2014]. On triad tests, see pages 170–72.) (**Further Reading**: **paired comparisons** and **triad tests**)

Pile sorts are a simple and fun way for informants to identify relationships among items in a domain. Begin by writing the name of each item on a single card (index cards cut in thirds work nicely). Label the back of each card with the number from 1 to n (where n is the total number of items in the domain). Spread the cards out randomly on a large table with the item-side up and the number-side down. Ask each informant to sort the cards into piles according to "which items belong together."

Informants often ask three things when we do pile sorts: (1) What do you mean by "belong together"? (2) How many piles should I make? (3) Can I put something in more than one pile? The answer to the first question is that you're really, really interested in what the informant thinks and that there are no right or wrong answers. The answer to the second is that they can make lots of piles, but they can't put every item into its own separate pile and they can't put all the cards in one big pile.

One answer to the third question is that each item can only belong to one pile. This simplifies the analysis, but may not reflect the complexity of people's thinking about items in a domain. For example, in a study of consumer electronics, someone might want to put a DVD player in one pile with TVs and in another pile with camcorders, but might not want to put camcorders and TVs in the same pile. To handle this problem, you can hand people duplicate cards when they want to put an item into more than one pile, though this complicates the data analysis.

When they're done sorting the cards, ask informants to name each pile and describe it in their own words. Record the names and the criteria for each pile in your notes. When you are done, turn the cards over. On a separate line, record all the numbers for each pile.

Recording the Data From Pile Sorts

Table 18.2 shows the pile sort data for one male informant who sorted the names of 18 fruits. The 18 fruits are listed at the top of the table. The bottom of the table shows the five piles that the informant made and which fruits went in each pile. For example, the informant put orange, lemon, and grapefruit in pile #1, and blueberry and strawberry in pile #4.

Importing the Data From Pile Sorts

We use ANTHROPAC (Borgatti 1992; appendix) to get pile-sort data into a computer for analysis, although there are other options.

Table 18.2 Pile-Sort Data for One Person for 18 Fruits

1. Apple	10. Strawberry
2. Orange	11. Lemon
3. Papaya	12. Cantaloupe
4. Mango	13. Grapefruit
5. Peach	14. Plum
6. Blueberry	15. Banana
7. Watermelon	16. Avocado
8. Pineapple	17. Fig
9. Pear	18. Cherry

One Person's Sorting of 18 Fruits

Pile #1: 2, 11, 13

Pile #2: 1, 5, 9, 14, 17, 18

Pile #3: 3, 4, 8, 15, 16

Pile #4: 6, 10

Pile #5: 7, 12

Whichever program you use will convert the raw pile-sort data into an **item-by-item similarity matrix**, shown in Table 18.3.

This similarity matrix is similar to the one we saw in Chapter 7. When the informant put items 2, 11, and 13 (orange, lemon, grapefruit) into a pile, he did so because he thought the items were similar. To indicate this, there is a 1 in the matrix where items 2 and 11 intersect; another 1 in the cell where items 2 and 13 intersect; and another 1 in the cell where 11 and 13 intersect.

And similarly for Pile #2: There is a 1 in the 1-5 cell, the 1-9 cell, the 1-14 cell, and so on. There are 0s in all the cells that represent no similarity of a pair of items (for this informant) and 1s down the diagonal (since items are similar to themselves). Also, notice that if 11 is similar to 13, then 13 is similar to 11, so this is a **symmetric matrix**. In a symmetric matrix, the bottom and top halves (above and below the diagonal of 1s) are identical (see Box 18.4). (**Further Reading**: pile sorts)

Table 18.3 Similarity Matrix From One Person's Pile Sorting of the 18 Fruits

		1 AP	2 OR	3 PA	4 MA	5 PE	6 BL	7 WA	8 PI	9 PE	10 ST	11 LE	12 CA	13 GR	14 PL	15 BA	16 AV	17 FI	18 CH
1	APPLE	1	0	0	0	1	0	0	0	1	0	0	0	0	1	0	0	1	1
2	ORANGE	0	1	0	0	0	0	0	0	0	0	1	1	1	0	0	0	0	0
3	PAPAYA	0	0	1	1	0	0	0	1	0	0	0	0	0	0	1	1	0	0
4	MANGO	0	0	1	1	0	0	0	1	0	0	0	0	0	0	1	1	0	0
5	PEACH	1	0	0	0	1	0	0	0	1	0	0	0	0	1	0	0	1	1
6	BLUEBERRY	0	0	0	0	0	1	0	0	0	1	0	0	0	0	0	0	0	0
7	WATERMELON	0	0	0	0	0	0	1	0	0	0	0	1	0	0	0	0	0	0
8	PINEAPPLE	0	0	1	1	0	0	0	1	0	0	0	0	0	0	1	1	0	0
9	PEAR	1	0	0	0	1	0	0	0	1	0	0	0	0	1	0	0	1	1
10	STRAWBERRY	0	0	0	0	0	1	0	0	0	1	0	0	0	0	0	0	0	0
11	LEMON	0	1	0	0	0	0	0	0	0	0	1	1	0	0	0	0	0	0
12	CANTALOUPE	0	0	0	0	0	0	1	0	0	0	0	1	0	0	0	0	0	0
13	GRAPEFRUIT	0	1	0	0	0	0	0	0	0	0	1	0	1	0	0	0	0	0
14	PLUM	1	0	0	0	1	0	0	0	1	0	0	0	0	1	0	0	1	1
15	BANANA	0	0	1	1	0	0	0	0	0	0	0	0	0	0	1	1	0	0
16	AVOCADO	0	0	1	1	0	0	0	1	0	0	0	0	0	0	1	1	0	0
17	FIG	1	0	0	0	1	0	0	0	1	0	0	0	0	1	0	0	1	1
18	CHERRY	1	0	0	0	1	0	0	0	1	0	0	0	0	1	0	0	1	1

Box 18.4

Getting Pile Sort Data Into the Computer

A major headache in all computer-based data analysis—whether you're analyzing quantitative or qualitative data—is **file compatibility**. All major statistics programs can import data from a variety of sources. SPSS for example, can import data from Microsoft Excel. SPSS and Excel do not share file structures, but SPSS will take Excel data and convert them to a file that SPSS can read.

Statistics programs, however, cannot easily import the kinds of data—like free lists and pile sorts—used in cultural domain analysis. FLAME (Free-List Analysis Under Microsoft Excel) is a free Excel plug-in program for analyzing free lists (see the appendix and http://tinyurl.com/free-list-analysis). Instructions for installing FLAME in Excel are in the appendix online and at http://tinyurl.com/domain-analysis. ANTHROPAC (Borgatti 1992), available free from analytictech.com, can be used to import pile sorts. ANTHROPAC was written for DOS machines (the ancient PC operating system before Windows), but you can run DOS programs with a free utility from dosbox.com. Instructions for running DOSBOX and ANTHROPAC are also at http://tinyurl.com/domain-analysis.

UCINET is a Windows-based program for doing network analysis. It shares a file structure with ANTHROPAC, so any data you import with ANTHROPAC are available to UCINET for analysis. You can also import pile-sort data with UCINET. Instructions for importing pile-sort data into UCINET are also at http://tinyurl.com/domain-analysis. UCINET exports data as an Excel file, so you can use the data in most statistics programs.

ANALYZING PILE SORT DATA: MDS ◆

If you examine it carefully, you'll see that, despite the 1s and 0s, there is not a shred of math in Table 18.3. It contains nothing more than the information in the bottom half of Table 18.2, displayed as 1s and 0s, and there is nothing numerical about those 1s and 0s. They simply stand for whether oranges and papayas and so on were put in the same pile or not. But by substituting 1s and 0s for the relationship between the items, we can use software to look for patterns in the informant's pile sort data.

Figure 18.2 is a multidimensional scaling, or MDS, of the data in Table 18.3. MDS is one of a family of **visualization methods**—widely used in all the sciences—that look for patterns in numerical data and display those patterns graphically. The MDS in Figure 18.2, then, shows how one informant sees the similarities among the 18 fruits (see Box 18.5).

Figure 18.2 Multidimensional Scaling of 18 Fruits From One Pile Sort

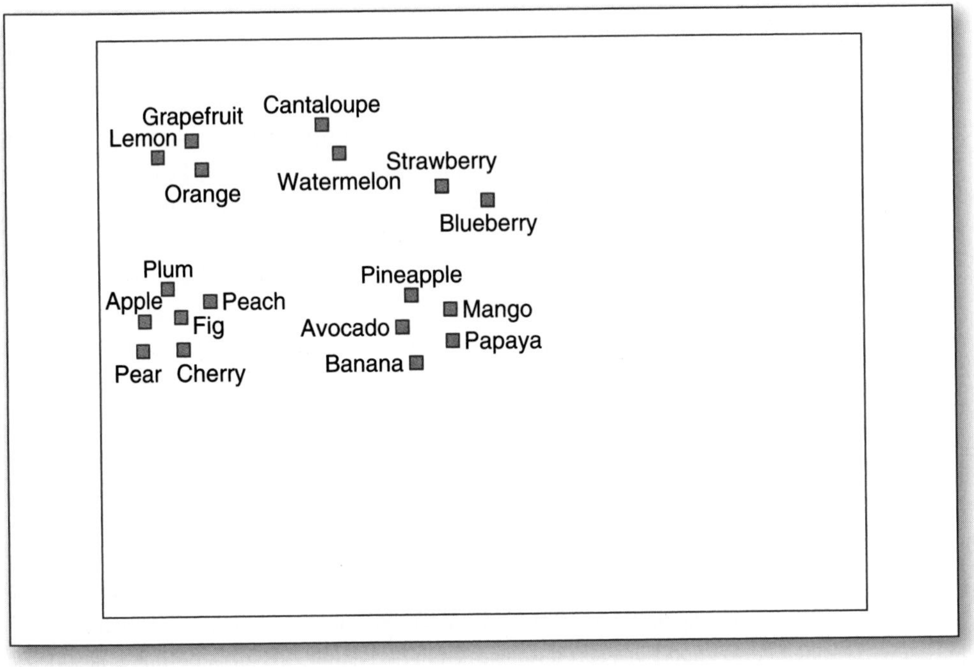

How MDS Works

Multidimensional scaling maps the relations among numbers in a matrix. Look carefully at Table 18.3. There are 1s in the cells 2-11, 2-13, and 11-13. This is because the informant put orange (2), lemon (11), and grapefruit (13) in one pile and nothing else in that pile. This behavior is presented graphically in Figure 18.2 with the orange-lemon-grapefruit cluster shown separated from other clusters.

It's convenient to think of the MDS graph in Figure 18.2 as a sort of **mental map**—that is, it represents what the informant was thinking when he pile sorted those fruits. We say "sort of mental map" because MDS graphs of pile-sort data are not one-to-one maps of what's going on inside people's heads. We treat them, however, as a rough proxy for what people were thinking when they made piles of cards or words or whatever.

You'll sometimes see MDS called **smallest-space analysis**. That's because MDS programs work out the best spatial representation of a set of objects that are represented by a set of similarities.

Suppose, for example, that you measure the distance, in miles, among three cities, A, B, and C. The matrix for these cities is in the inside box of Table 18.4.

Table 18.4   Distances Among Four Cities

	City A	City B	City C	City D
City A	0	50	40	110
City B	50	0	80	65
City C	40	80	0	100
City D	110	65	100	0

Figure 18.3   Two-Dimensional Plot of the Distance Among Three Cities (a) and Among Four Cities (b).

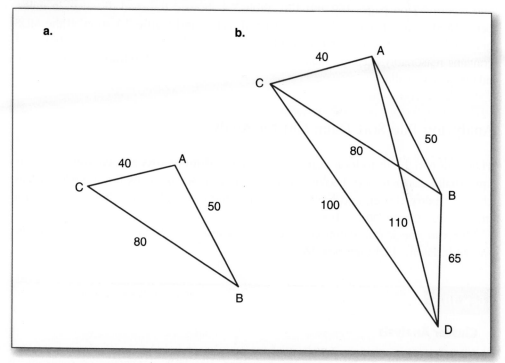

Clearly, cities A and C are closer to one another than are A and B, or B and C. You can represent this with a triangle, as in Figure 18.3a.

In other words, we can place points A, B, and C on a plane in some position relative to each other. The distance between A and B is longer than that between A and C (reflecting the difference between 50 and 40 miles), and the distance between B and C is longer than that between A and C (reflecting the difference between 40 and 80 miles). Figure 18.3a contains precisely the same information as the inside box of Table 18.4, but in graphic form. *You can see in Figure 18.3a that the physical distance (in inches) between B and C is twice that of A and C.*

If we add a fourth city, things get considerably more complicated. With four items, there are six relations to cope with: AB, AC, AD, BC, BD, and CD. These relations are shown in the complete box of Table 18.4. With measurements like distance (in inches or miles) it's easier to plot a set of relations. It's more difficult when we're trying to graph the relations among a set of concepts or themes and smallest-space solutions are likely to be a bit distorted.

MDS programs produce a statistic that measures this distortion, or **stress**, as it's called, which tells us how far off the graph is from one that would be perfectly pro-portional. The lower the stress, the better the solution. Go back and look at Table 7.4 and Figure 7.1 on pages 169 and 170. Table 7.4 showed the road distance, in miles, between all pairs of nine cities in the United States, and Figure 7.1 showed the MDS graph of those nine cities. That graph has a stress of close to zero because Table 7.4 contains reasonably accurate measures of a physical reality. (**Further Reading**: mul-tidimensional scaling)

Analyzing Pile Sort Data: Cluster Analysis

There are two things to look at in an MDS graph: **dimensions** and **clusters**. Clusters are usually easier to see. Looking at Figure 18.2, it seems to us that there's a citrus cluster, a berry cluster, and a melon cluster at the top, with a fruit tree cluster and a tropical fruit cluster on the bottom.

We can check our intuition about these clusters by running a cluster analysis, shown in Figure 18.4 (see Box 18.5).

Box 18.5

Cluster Analysis

Cluster analysis is another visualization method. Like MDS, it operates on similarity matrices, like that in Table 18.3. However, the **algorithms** (the sets of instructions) for finding clusters in matrices are very different from those used in MDS. With MDS, the program tries to find the best **spatial fit** of a set of similarities. In other words, an MDS graph is a map.

> In cluster analysis, the object is to partition a set of similarities into subgroups (clusters), where the members of each subgroup are more like each other than they are like members of other subgroups.
>
> Clusters can simply be listed, but they are commonly represented graphically in the form of a tree, or **dendrogram**, like the ones shown in Figures 18.4 and 18.6. (**Further Reading**: cluster analysis)

Read Figure 18.4 as follows: At the first **level of clustering**, the informant put 7 (watermelon) and 12 (cantaloupe) together, and he put 6 (blueberry) and 10 (strawberry) together. These two clusters together form a cluster at the second level. And the same goes for the other clusters: They come together at the second level and all form one big cluster.

Because there is just one informant, there can only be two levels. The first level is the level at which the informant made the separate piles. The second is the entire set of fruits. We've taken you through what looks like a trivial exercise to show you how to read the cluster diagram (dendrogram) and the MDS picture. As we'll see next, things get more interesting when we add informants.

Figure 18.4   Cluster Analysis of 18 Fruits From One Pile Sort

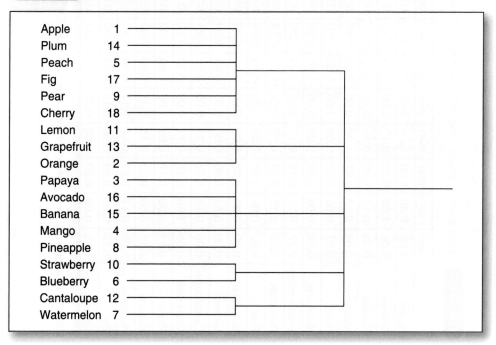

MDS and Cluster Analysis of the Aggregate Matrix

Figure 18.5 shows the MDS plot of the data in Table 18.5. It looks pretty much like Figure 18.2, but there are some differences. Averaging across the six informants, figs and cherries now appear to be in a separate cluster and to be a bridge between the berry group (strawberries and blueberries) and the major tree-fruit group (apples, plums, peaches, and pears). Furthermore, banana, which was in the tropical fruit cluster for our first informant, now appears to be a bridge between the tropical fruit cluster (mangos, papayas, pineapples, and avocados) and the traditional tree-fruit cluster (apples, plums, peaches, and pears) (see Box 18.6).

Box 18.6

Clusters and Bridges

What does it mean to say that "figs and cherries appear to be a bridge between the berry group and major tree-fruit cluster" or that "banana appears to be a bridge between tropical fruits and traditional tree fruits"? When we interviewed people about why they put various fruits together, some people who put figs and cherries with apples and pears said "These all grow on trees." People who put figs and/or cherries into other piles said things like "Figs are more exotic, but not like mangoes" or "Cherries grow on trees, but they are small and clumpy."

Some informants said that banana was a tropical fruit and "went with papaya," but others said it was unique and belonged in a group by itself. One person said it belonged with apples and pears "because you can mix them together to make fruit salad."

We always ask people to explain their pile choices. Later, when we see figs and cherries in an MDS graph lying between a berries cluster and traditional tree-fruit cluster, we have some basis for interpreting the graph.

The cluster analysis on the data in Table 18.5 is shown in Figure 18.6. It confirms that our informants saw cherries and figs as related to strawberries and blueberries and saw all four of these fruits as more closely related to apples, plums, peaches, and pears than to all the other fruits. It isn't that our first informant was anomalous or idiosyncratic. In fact, there is a lot of consensus across the six informants about what goes with what. But the consensus isn't perfect; there is **intracultural variation**.

This is, of course, well known to all qualitative researchers, but MDS and cluster analysis let us examine the variation and the consensus more systematically (see Box 18.7).

Figure 18.6   Cluster Analysis of the Data in Table 18.5 From Six Pile Sorts

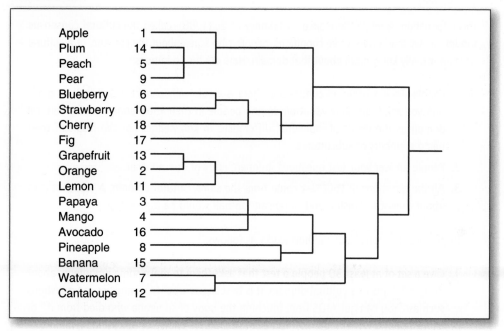

SOURCE: H. R. Bernard and G. W. Ryan, *Social Research Methods: Qualitative and Quantitative Approaches.*
Thousand Oaks, Second Edition CA: Sage Publications. 2012.

Box 18.7

Consensus Analysis

There is a formal method for measuring consensus, which we'll describe only briefly here. The method is based on the observation that people who know a lot about something tend to agree with one another (Boster 1986). If you give a test about the rules of baseball to a group of serious fans and a group who never watch the game, you'd find that: (1) The fans will agree on the answers more often than will the nonfans; and (2) the serious fans will get the answers right more often than will the nonfans.

This is pretty much like any test you might take in a class. The instructor makes up the test and an answer key with the correct answers. Your job is to match your answers with those on the answer key.

But what if there were no answer key? That's what happens when we ask people to, say, rate the social status of others in a community. We wind up with a lot of opinions about social status, but we don't have an answer key to tell whether informants are accurate in their reporting of

(Continued)

(Continued)

this information. A model developed by Romney et al. (1986)—called the **cultural consensus model**—shows that, under three conditions, people who agree about the contents of a cultural domain actually know more about that domain. Here are the conditions:

1. People share a common culture and there is a culturally correct answer to any question you ask them. Any variation among people in their knowledge about a cultural domain is the result of individual differences in knowledge, not the result of their being members of subcultures.

2. People answer your test questions independently of one another.

3. All the questions in your test come from the same cultural domain. A test that asks about American kinship and American football would be a poor test.

In practice, the consensus method works as follows:

1. Give a set of at least 30 people a test that asks them to make some judgments about 30 to 40 items in a cultural domain. It is best to use true–false and yes–no questions such as: "You can get AIDS from touching the body of someone who died from it," or "A field goal is worth 7 points." You can use multiple-choice or open-ended, fill-in-the-blank questions, but this makes the analysis tougher.

2. Produce a **person-by-person agreement matrix** of the answers. If 100 students take a 40-question, true–false test, then each pair of students could agree 40 times, irrespective of whether they got the answer to each question right or wrong. We count the agreement for each pair of students (1 and 2, 1 and 3, 1 and 4, and so on, down to student 39 and 40) and we divide each count by 40. This produces a 100-by-100, student-by-student agreement matrix.

3. Do factor analysis on the agreement matrix. Factor analysis is based on the simple and compelling idea that if things we observe are correlated with each other, they must have some underlying thing in common.

Factor analysis refers to a set of techniques for identifying and interpreting those underlying variables. If the first factor in the analysis of the agreement matrix is at least three times the size of the second factor, then: (1) The first factor is knowledge about the domain (because agreement equals knowledge under conditions of the model); and (2) the individual factor scores are a measure of knowledge for each person who takes the test.

Can you really lose the answer key to a test and recover it by analyzing the matrix of agreements among the test takers? We tested this with data from 160 students in a real introduction to anthropology class. The correlation between the percentage of questions they got right, according to the answer key, and their scores on the first factor of the agreement matrix was 0.96—nearly perfect.

In other words, as long as the three conditions of the model hold, you can apply consensus analysis to tests of people's responses about who hangs out with whom in an organization, or what people think are proper foods to give infants, or ways to avoid getting AIDS, and so on. (**Further Reading**: consensus analysis)

FOLK TAXONOMIES ◆

A **taxonomy** is a list of things (music, foods, vehicles, electronic gadgets, countries) and a set of rules for organizing those things into related sets. We're all familiar with scientific taxonomies for plants and animals, but listen carefully to ordinary speech and you'll hear people invoking taxonomic rules all the time (see Box 18.8).

Overheard at the supermarket:

"Where's the barley?"

"It's with the rice, over on aisle 4."

You'll also hear people *negotiating* the taxonomic rules.

Overheard at the zoo:

"What's that monkey doing?"

"Actually, it's an ape, not a monkey."

"Really? What's the diff?"

Overheard on a college campus:

"I can't tell if I like Shania Twain because her music is country or pop, I just know I like her."

The conversation that followed that last snippet was about blended genres (think New Age–Latin and Reggae-Blues) and about artists who succeed in more than one genre. The people who were having that conversation were relying on the fact that they shared a taxonomy. Every once in a while, they would renegotiate the rules for the taxonomy.

"Glenn Campbell was never really a country singer."

"What do you mean? Of course he was."

Box 18.8

Scientific and Folk Taxonomies

A folk taxonomy is one that is accepted by a community of speakers of a language. A scientific taxonomy is one that is accepted by a community of scholars. Carl Linnaeus, the Swedish botanist, spent years developing the classification system that bears his name. When he published the first version of it, in 1735, it was one man's ideas about how natural organisms are related. The scheme was quickly recognized as a useful way of classifying living organisms, but new theory and new data changed the system over time.

In a sense, then, all taxonomies begin as folk taxonomies and some folk taxonomies develop into scientific ones.

In the social sciences, scholars of ethnobotany and ethnozoology are interested in how people in different cultural groups organize their knowledge of the natural world. Ethnobotanical and ethnozoological taxonomies usually don't mirror scientific taxonomies, but the whole point of folk taxonomic research is to understand cultural knowledge on its own terms.

◆ HOW TO MAKE A TAXONOMY: LISTS AND FRAMES

The most widely used methods for building folk taxonomies are pile sorts, cluster analysis, and **frame substitution tasks** (Frake 1964).

Ask a native speaker of American English the following: "List the kinds of foods you know?" A typical list would include things like: "meat, fish, pasta, fruits, vegetables, snacks. . . ."

After the first round, ask the following: "What kinds of meats are there?" and "What kinds of fruits are there?" "What kinds of snacks are there?" . . . and so on. The idea here is to be systematic. That is, take every item the informant named in the first round and ask the follow-up question to expand the list one level down in the informant's taxonomy.

As we get further down into any folk taxonomy, people mix and drop **levels of contrast**. Here, the informant mentioned chicken and turkey, which are both kinds of poultry, but she didn't mention poultry at all. Poultry is a dropped level of contrast, but it may take several informants to discover the level of contrast called "poultry" in the American English taxonomy of meats. On the other hand, that the informant mentioned both venison and game. Here, the informant slipped in two levels of contrast because venison is a type of game.

At this point, you would ask: "What kinds of beef [lamb] [chicken] [etc.] are there?" Do this with several people and you'll discover that beef is divided into steak, chops, hamburger, and so on and that steak is divided into T-bone and Porterhouse and filet mignon and so on, and you'll find that vegetarians don't make as many distinctions as carnivores do about kinds of meat.

These questions get you the list of items in the domain—in this case, the list of foods—and some idea about the major types.

The next step is to find out about overlaps. For example, some foods, like avocados, get classified as fruits by some people and as vegetables by others. Some people think of peanuts as a source of protein; others think of them as a snack. In fact, in real folk taxonomies, you'll find people classifying items differently, depending on the circumstances. You can learn about the possible overlaps in folk categories by using **substitution frames**:

Is _____ a kind of _____?

Is _____ a part of _____?

Once you have a list of terms in a domain, and a list of categories, you can use substitution frames for all possible combinations. Are marshmallows a kind of meat? A kind of fish? A kind of snack? This can get really tedious, but discovering levels of contrast—magenta is a kind of red; cashews are a kind of nut; alto is a kind of sax; ice cream is a kind of dessert—just takes plain hard work. (**Further Reading**: frame substitution tasks)

Unless you're a child, in which case all this discovery is just plain fun. In fact, one object of this kind of research is to discover the kind of cultural knowledge that every 10 year old knows about her or his culture.

Displaying Taxonomies

A common way to display folk taxonomies is with a **branching tree diagram**. Figure 18.7 shows a tree diagram for part of a folk taxonomy of passenger cars, elicited in Morgantown, West Virginia, from Jack in 1976 (we saw Jack's taxonomy of cars in Figure 8.13 [page 194] in the chapter on kinds of models).

Things to Look for in Folk Taxonomies

There are five important points to make about the taxonomy shown in Figure 18.7:

1. Intracultural variation is common in folk taxonomies. That is, different people may use different words to refer to the same category of things. Sometimes, in fact, terms can be almost idiosyncratic. Jack distinguished among what he called "regular cars," "station wagons," and "vans." The term "regular cars" is not one you normally see in automobile ads, or hear from a salesperson on a car lot.

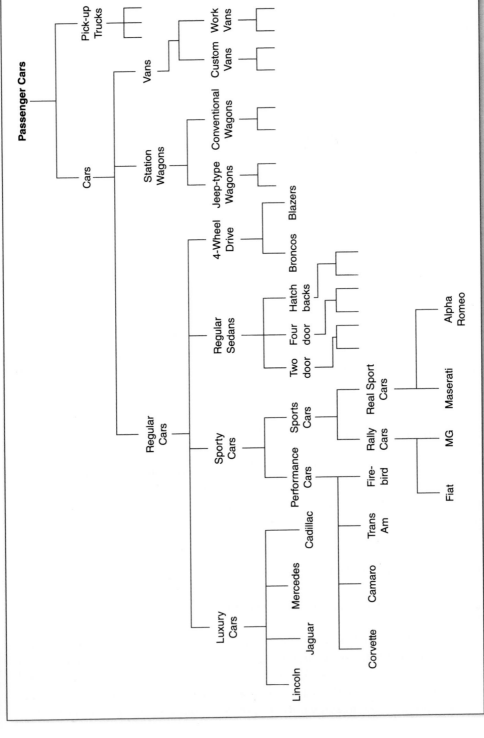

Figure 18.7 Part of Jack's Taxonomy of Cars and Trucks

SOURCE: H. R. Bernard. (2011). *Research Methods in Anthropology: Qualitative and Quantitative Approaches.* 5th Edition. AltaMira Press.

2. Category labels can run from single words to complex phrases. In West Virginia, the category labeled "4-wheel drive" vehicles in Figure 18.6 was sometimes called "off-road vehicles" in 1976, or even "vehicles you can go camping in or tow a horse trailer with." Jack said that Jeep station wagons were both wagons and 4-wheel-drive cars you can go camping in.

3. Categories and their labels change over time. By the 1990s, the cars that Jack had called "vehicles you can go camping in or tow a horse trailer with" back in 1976 were being called "utes" by some people—short for "sport utility vehicle." Today, most people in the United States call them SUVs, though small SUVs are sometimes called "cute utes" or "crossovers" and In 2015, Autoweb.com had an article comparing 14 cute utes.

4. Always look for **covert categories**—that is, categories of things that are real but not named (Whorf 1945). Some people insist that Corvettes, Camaros, and Maseratis are part of a single category, which they find difficult to name (one informant suggested "sporty cars" as a label). Others, like Jack, separate "performance cars" from "sports cars" and even subdivide sports cars into "true sports cars" and "rally cars."

   Many native speakers of English understand that wolves and foxes and dogs are somehow related, just as they understand that lions and tigers and housecats are all related. But, as D'Andrade points out (1995:98), you can say, "look at that cat" when you're referring to a tiger, but you couldn't say "look at that dog" if you're talking about a fox. The category of "cats" is named, while the category of "animals related to the dog family" is covert. This doesn't make the latter category any less real for speakers of English. It does make it harder to discover, however.

5. Even when there are consistent labels for categories, the categories may represent multiple dimensions, each of which has its own levels of contrast. For example, many native speakers of American English recognize a category of "foreign cars" that cuts across the taxonomy in Figure 18.7. There are foreign sports cars, foreign luxury cars, foreign regular cars, and so on. (**Further Reading**: folk taxonomies)

AND FINALLY... ◆

Cultural domain analysis is a set of methods for mapping and understanding information that people use every day. The method comes from cognitive anthropology, but it has long been used in consumer research (J. C. Johnson et al. 1987; Stefflre 1972). We expect CDA to become increasingly popular as scholars in many disciplines seek to understand the production of local knowledge.

- Once the items in a cultural domain are identified, the next step is to examine how the items are related to each other. To do this, informants are asked to make similarity judgments among the items.
- Pile sorts are an effective method for collecting these judgments.

  o Write the name of each item on a single card. Write the numbers of the items on the back of the cards. Spread the cards out randomly on a large table with the item-side up and the number-side down. Ask each informant to sort the cards into piles according to "which items belong together."

  o When they're done sorting the cards, ask informants to name each pile and describe it in their own words. Record the names and the criteria for each pile in your notes. When you are done, turn the cards over. On a separate line, record all the numbers for each pile. Use ANTHROPAC or UCINET to import these data and convert them into an item-by-item similarity matrix. You can visualize the relations among the pile-sorted items with multidimensional scaling (MDS) and cluster analysis.

- In the example for the chapter (kinds of fruit), the MDS plot showed that figs and cherries appeared to be a bridge between a berry group (strawberries and blueberries) and the traditional tree-fruit group (apples, plums, peaches, and pears). Banana appeared to be a bridge between the tropical fruit cluster (mangos, papayas, pineapples, and avocados) and the traditional tree-fruit cluster (apples, plums, peaches, and pears).

  o Cluster analysis confirms that informants saw cherries and figs as related to strawberries and blueberries and saw all four of these fruits as more closely related to apples, plums, peaches, and pears than to all the other fruits.

- A taxonomy is a list of things (music, foods, vehicles, electronic gadgets, countries) and a set of rules for organizing those things into related sets.

  o A scientific taxonomy is one that is accepted by a community of scholars. When Linnaeus developed the classification system that bears his name, it was a folk taxonomy but developed into a scientific one over time.

  o In the social sciences, scholars of ethnobotany and ethnozoology are interested in how people in different cultural groups organize their knowledge of the natural world. Ethnobotanical and ethnozoological taxonomies usually don't mirror scientific taxonomies, but the whole point of folk taxonomic research is to understand cultural knowledge on its own terms.

- The most widely used methods for building folk taxonomies are pile sorts, cluster analysis, and frame elicitation.

  o Ask a native speaker of American English the following: "List the kinds of foods you know?" A typical list would include things like: "meat, fish, pasta, fruits, vegetables, snacks. . . ." After the first round, ask the following: "What kinds of meats are there?" and "What kinds of fruits are there?" "What kinds of snacks are there?" . . . and so on.

o The idea here is to be systematic. That is, take every item the informant named in the first round and ask the follow-up question to expand the list one level down in the informant's taxonomy.

o These questions get you the list of items in the domain—in this case, the list of foods—and some idea about the major types.

• The next step is to find out about overlaps. For example, some foods, like avocados, get classified as fruits by some people and as vegetables by others. Some people think of peanuts as a source of protein; others think of them as a snack. In fact, in real folk taxonomies, you'll find people classifying items differently, depending on the circumstances.

• You can learn about the possible overlaps in folk categories by using substitution frames:

Is _____ a kind of _____?

Is _____ a part of _____?

• Once you have a list of terms in a domain, and a list of categories, you can use this substitution frame for all possible combinations. Are marshmallows a kind of meat? A kind of fish? A kind of snack? This can get really tedious, but discovering levels of contrast—magenta is a kind of red; cashews are a kind of nut; alto is a kind of sax; ice cream is a kind of dessert—just takes plain hard work.

o Unless you're a child, in which case all this discovery is just plain fun. In fact, one object of this kind of research is to discover the kind of cultural knowledge that every 10 year old knows about her or his culture.

o A common way to display folk taxonomies is with a branching tree diagram, like the one Figure 8.13 in the chapter on kinds of models.

• Some things to remember about folk taxonomies

1. Intracultural variation is common.

2. Category labels can run from single words to complex phrases.

3. Categories and their labels change over time.

4. There may be covert categories—that is, categories of things that are real but not named. Many native speakers of English think of dogs and wolves as belonging to a single category and if people to name the category they may say something like "It's things in the dog family."

5. Even when there are consistent labels for categories, the categories may represent multiple dimensions, each of which has its own levels of contrast. For example, many native speakers of American English recognize a category of "foreign cars" that cuts across sports cars, luxury cars, SUVs, and so on.

Exercises

1. Collect free lists for any cultural domain you like. The object here is to compare the results across domains or across men and women or across subcultural groups. If you are working alone, you can collect lists from, say, 10 men and 10 women. If you are working with other students, you can each collect 20 lists. Import and analyze data using FLAME a free plug-in for Excel (http://tinyurl.com/free-list-analysis), or ANTHROPAC (analytictech.com). ANTHROPAC is free, but it requires a DOS emulator to run on today's computers. DOSBOX is free at dosbox.com (see Box 18.4).

2. After running the free lists, choose a set of 20–30 terms for pile sorts. Import the data, using ANTHROPAC or UCINET, and then run multidimensional scaling and cluster analysis on the aggregate proximity matrix. Write up your interpretation of the results. How would you label the clusters?

Further Reading

Cultural domain analysis. Borgatti (1992, 1999), Borgatti et al. (2004), Borgatti and Halgin (2013), Collins and Dressler (2008), Dressler et al. (2007), Eyre and Milstein (1999), J. C. Johnson and Weller (2001), Rosch (1975), Rosch and Mervis (1975), Ross et al. (2002), Spradley (1972, 1979), Weller (2014).

Free lists. Brewer (1995), Dong and Chick (2012), Furlow (2003), Ginon et al. (2014), Henley (1969), Karlawish et al. (2011), Longfield (2004), Parr and Lashua (2004), Quinlan (2005), Rödlach et al. (2012), Ryan et al. (2000), Schrauf and Sanchez (2008), J. J. Smith and Borgatti (1997), Thomson et al. (2012), E. C. Thompson and Juan (2006).

Measuring salience. For measures in free lists, see Quinlan (2005), Robbins and Nolan (1997, 2000), J. J. Smith (1993), Sutrop (2001).

Paired comparisons and triad tests. Bernard (2012), Borgatti (1999), Boster et al. (1987), Brewer (1995), Burton (2003), Durrenberger (2003), Durrenberger and Erem (2005), Furlow (2003), Nyamongo (2002), Reyes-Garcia et al. (2004), Ross et al. (2005), Weller and Romney (1988).

Pile sorts. Alvarado (1998), Bibeau et al. (2012), Ensign and Gittelsohn (1998), Harman (2001), Nyamongo (1999, 2002), Singer et al. (2011), Trotter and Potter (1993), Verma et al. (2001).

Multidimensional scaling. Borgatti (1997), Bradway et al. (2010), E. H. Cohen and Valencia (2008), DeJordy et al. (2007), Kruskal and Wish (1978), Marcussen (2014), Mugavin (2008), Pinkley et al. (2005), Shepard et al. (1972).

Cluster analysis. Aldenderfer and Blashfield (1984), Biedenweg and Monroe (2013), Borgatti (1994), Ginon et al. (2014), Karademir-Hazir (2014), Windsor (2013).

Consensus analysis. Carothers et al. (2014), Caulkins (2001), Crona et al. (2013), de Munck et al. (2002), Dressler et al. (2005), Furlow (2003), Gibson (2014), Harvey and Thorburn Bird (2004), Horowitz (2007), Jaskyte and Dressler (2004), M. Miller et al. (2004), Schnegg et al. (2014), Snodgrass et al. (2013), Swora (2003), Weller (2007).

Frame substitution. D'Andrade et al. (1972), Garro (1986), Hruschka et al. (2008), Metzger and Williams (1966), Weller and Romney (1988).

Folk taxonomies. Atran (1998), Beaudreau et al. (2011), Kaplan and Levine (1981), Salman and Kharusi (2014), Shawyer et al. (1996).

Visit the online resource site at study.sagepub.com/bernardaqd to access engaging and helpful digital content, like video tutorials on working with MAXQDA, presentation slides, MAXQDA keyboard shortcuts, datasets, stop list, and recommended readings.

CHAPTER 19

SEMANTIC NETWORK ANALYSIS

INTRODUCTION ♦

In Chapter 18, we introduced multidimensional scaling (MDS) and cluster analysis—two methods for **visualizing relations** among items in a cultural domain. These same methods can be used to analyze relations among *any set of things that are connected or related to one another* in some way—in other words, a **network**.

If the things that are connected to each other are resistors and capacitors and such, you have an electrical network. If the things are roads and bridges, you have a transportation network. If the things are people, you have a social network. And if the things are words or themes, you have a **semantic network**.

Figure 19.1 Converting a Word-by-Respondent Matrix Into Two Kinds of Similarity Matrices

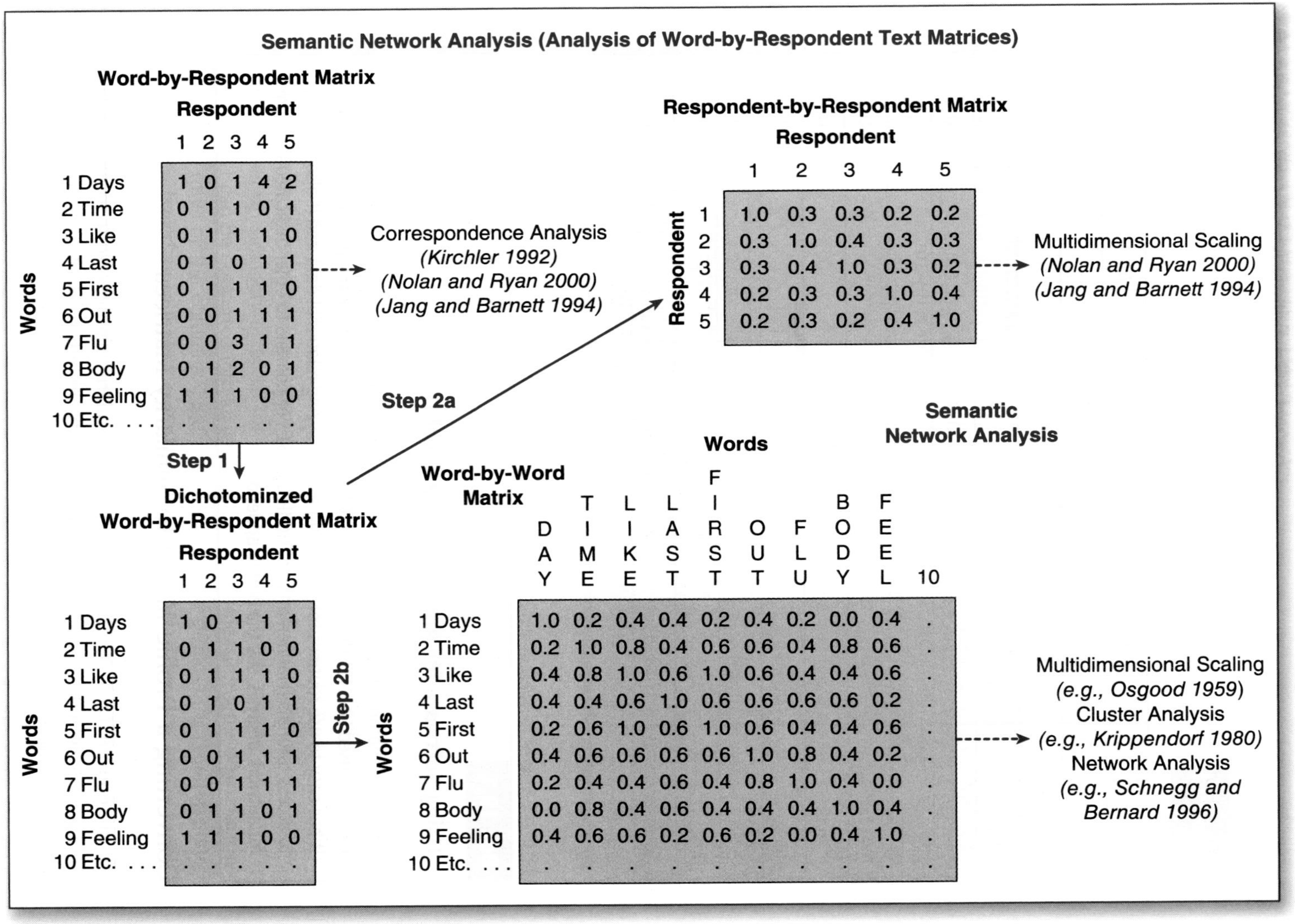

Table 19.2 The Data in Table 19.1, Dichotomized

Word	Inf.1	Inf.2	Inf.3	Inf.4	Inf.5
two	1	1	1	1	1
not	1	1	1	1	0
days	1	0	1	1	1
after	1	1	1	1	0
first	0	1	1	1	0
me	0	1	1	1	0
feeling	1	1	1	0	0
flu	0	0	1	1	1
body	0	1	1	0	1
time	0	1	1	0	1
my	0	1	1	1	0
last	0	1	0	1	1

Table 19.3 shows the first kind. Each cell in Table 19.3 contains the percentage of times that each of the words in the 66 pairs of words are both present or both absent in the five texts. (Remember: There are $n(n-1)/2$ pairs of anything; here, $12(11)/2=66$). For example:

1) The words "two" and "days" in Table 19.2 co-occur in four texts (texts 1, 3, 4, and 5), which is 80% of the five texts available. Thus, the number 0.80 appears in the first line of Table 19.3, below, where the words "two" and "days" intersect.

2) The word "feeling" is used in texts 1, 2, and 3, and the word "flu" is used in texts 3, 4, and 5, so there's a 0.20 (20%) in the cell where "feeling" and "flu" intersect in Table 19.3.

3) The words "body" and "time" are *both* used by informants 2, 3, and 5, and *neither* word is used by informants 1 and 4. The 1s and 0s in the rows for "body" and "time" in Table 19.2 match perfectly, so there is a 1.00 in the body–time cell of Table 19.3.

Summarizing so far: For this set of 12 words in five texts, the pair two-days is 80% alike; the pair feeling-flu is 20% alike; and the pair body-time is 100% alike.

Table 19.3 Percentage of Times Each Pair of Words Co-Occurs in the Set of Five Texts

	two	not	days	after	first	me	feeling	flu	body	time	my	last
two	1.00	0.80	0.80	0.80	0.60	0.60	0.60	0.60	0.60	0.60	0.60	0.60
not	0.80	1.00	0.60	1.00	0.80	0.80	0.80	0.40	0.40	0.40	0.80	0.40
days	0.80	0.60	1.00	0.60	0.40	0.40	0.40	0.80	0.40	0.40	0.40	0.40
after	0.80	1.00	0.60	1.00	0.80	0.80	0.80	0.40	0.40	0.40	0.80	0.40
first	0.60	0.80	0.40	0.80	1.00	1.00	0.60	0.60	0.60	0.60	1.00	0.60
me	0.60	0.80	0.40	0.80	1.00	1.00	0.60	0.60	0.60	0.60	1.00	0.60
feeling	0.60	0.80	0.40	0.80	0.60	0.60	1.00	0.20	0.60	0.60	0.60	0.20
flu	0.60	0.40	0.80	0.40	0.60	0.60	0.20	1.00	0.60	0.60	0.60	0.60
body	0.60	0.40	0.40	0.40	0.60	0.60	0.60	0.60	1.00	1.00	0.60	0.60
time	0.60	0.40	0.40	0.40	0.60	0.60	0.60	0.60	1.00	1.00	0.60	0.60
my	0.60	0.80	0.40	0.80	1.00	1.00	0.60	0.60	0.60	0.60	1.00	0.60
last	0.60	0.40	0.40	0.40	0.60	0.60	0.20	0.60	0.60	0.60	0.60	1.00

| Table 19.4 | A 5-by-5, Informant-by-Informant Matrix for the Data in Table 19.2 |

Informant	1	2	3	4	5
1	1.00	0.42	0.50	0.50	0.42
2	0.42	1.00	0.75	0.58	0.33
3	0.50	0.75	1.00	0.67	0.42
4	0.50	0.58	0.67	1.00	0.42
5	0.42	0.33	0.42	0.42	1.00

Two more things about Table 19.3: (1) There is a 1.00 in every cell down the diagonal, signifying that each word universally co-occurs with itself. (2) The table is **symmetric**. The numbers above and below the 1.00s in the diagonal mirror one another: Thus, on the first line, there is a 0.60 in the cell for "two" and "me," and there is a 0.60 in the first column where "me" and "two" intersect.

Table 19.4 shows the second kind of similarity matrix we can derive from Table 19.2: the 5-by-5, informant-by-informant similarity matrix. The cells in the informant-by-informant matrix show the percentage of words that a pair of people used in common. As a rule, the more words two people use in common, the more similar their texts are. If you look down columns 1 and 2 in Table 19.2, you'll see 1s in the cells for "two," "not," "after," and "feeling," and 0s in the cells for "flu."

This means that informants 1 and 2 used four words in common and *did not use* one word in common. The two informants are 42% similar on this measure (4 words-in-common + 1 word-that-neither-used = 5/12=0.42). Informants 2 and 4 used seven words in common, and no words that neither of them used, so informants 2 and 4 are 7/12=0.58 or 58% similar in Table 19.4 (see Box 19.2).

Box 19.2

How to Count the Hits in Table 19.2

Tables 19.3 and 19.4 are both similarity matrices, and the numbers in the tables are **measures of similarity**. That's what it means to say that the words "two" and "days" are 80% alike or that informants 4 and 2 are 58% alike. We can measure similarity in many ways, and, as in all aspects of research, the decision on what kind of similarity measure you use has consequences.

(Continued)

(Continued)

In Table 19.3, we used a **match coefficient of similarity**: If any pair of cells has the same value, then it was a match. With just 1s and 0s in Table 19.2, if two cells have 0s or if two cells have 1s, that counts as a match.

If we decide that two people *not* using a word should *not* count as a match, we need a different measure of similarity. **Jaccard's coefficient of similarity** is a useful measure of similarity when you only want matching 1s to count and not matching 0s. Table 19.5 is the result of applying Jaccard's coefficient of similarity to the rows of data in Table 19.2.

Table 19.5 Applying Jaccard's Coefficient of Similarity to the Rows in Table 19.2

WORD	two	not	days	after	first	me	feeling	flu	body	time	my	last
two	1.00	0.80	0.80	0.80	0.60	0.60	0.60	0.60	0.60	0.60	0.60	0.60
not	0.80	1.00	0.60	1.00	0.75	0.75	0.75	0.40	0.40	0.40	0.75	0.40
days	0.80	0.60	1.00	0.60	0.40	0.40	0.40	0.75	0.40	0.40	0.40	0.40
after	0.80	1.00	0.60	1.00	0.75	0.75	0.75	0.40	0.40	0.40	0.75	0.40
first	0.60	0.75	0.40	0.75	1.00	1.00	0.50	0.50	0.50	0.50	1.00	0.50
me	0.60	0.75	0.40	0.75	1.00	1.00	0.50	0.50	0.50	0.50	1.00	0.50
feeling	0.60	0.75	0.40	0.75	0.50	0.50	1.00	0.20	0.50	0.50	0.50	0.20
flu	0.60	0.40	0.75	0.40	0.50	0.50	0.20	1.00	0.50	0.50	0.50	0.50
body	0.60	0.40	0.40	0.40	0.50	0.50	0.50	0.50	1.00	1.00	0.50	0.50
time	0.60	0.40	0.40	0.40	0.50	0.50	0.50	0.50	1.00	1.00	0.50	0.50
my	0.60	0.75	0.40	0.75	1.00	1.00	0.50	0.50	0.50	0.50	1.00	0.50
last	0.60	0.40	0.40	0.40	0.50	0.50	0.20	0.50	0.50	0.50	0.50	1.00

In Table 19.2, we see that informants 2, 3, and 4 used the words "not" and "me," so there are 1s in the not-me cell for those three informants. Informant 1 used the word "not" but did not use the word "me," so we see a 1 and a 0 in the "not" and "me" cell, respectively, for informant 1. Informant 5 used neither the word "not" nor the world "me," so we see 0s in both the "not" and "me" cell for informant 5. If we don't count the matching 0s, we have only four possible hits in this case, not 5. Three hits (informants 2, 3, and 4) out of four is 75%, and we see 0.75 in the not-me cell in Table 19.5.

JANG AND BARNETT'S STUDY OF CEO LETTERS ♦

Once you have a similarity matrix, like Table 19.3 or Table 19.5, you can examine it with **multidimensional scaling** and **cluster analysis**. Ha-Yong Jang (1995) used this method to examine whether there is a national culture discernible in the annual letters to stockholders from the CEOs of American and Japanese corporations. He selected 35 Fortune 500 companies, including 18 American and 17 Japanese firms, matched by type of business. For example, Ford was matched with Honda, Xerox with Canon, and so on.

All of these firms are traded on the New York Stock Exchange, and each year stockholders receive an annual message from either the CEO or the president of these companies. (Japanese firms that trade on the New York Exchange send the annual letters in English to their U.S. stockholders.) Jang downloaded the 1992 annual letters to shareholders and (applying a stop list of 60 common words) isolated 94 words that occurred at least 26 times across the corpus of 35 letters (Jang 1995:49).

Then Jang created a 94-by-35 matrix, where the rows are the 94 words and the columns are the 35 companies. The cells in this matrix contained a number from 0 to 25, 25 being the largest number of times any word ever occurred in *one* of the letters. (The word was "company," and it occurred 25 times in the letter from General Electric.)

Next, Jang correlated the columns of the matrix. This produced a 35-by-35, company-by-company **co-occurrence matrix**—that is, a similarity matrix based on the co-occurrence of words in their letters to stockholders. Jang analyzed that matrix with multidimensional scaling and the result is shown in Figure 19.2 (from Jang and Barnett 1994).

No doubt about it: Figure 19.2 shows that there are real differences in the way American and Japanese CEOs communicated with their companies' stockholders. Jang and Barnett (1994) found that 13 words were most associated with the American group of companies: board, chief, leadership, president, officer, major, position, financial, improved, good, success, competitive, and customer. From their reading of all the texts and their knowledge of corporate culture, Jang and Barnett saw these 13 words as representing two themes: financial information and organizational structure.

Six words were more associated with the Japanese companies: income, effort, economy, new, development, and quality. To Jang and Barnett, these words represented organizational operations and reflected Japanese concern for the development of new, quality products in order to compete in the U.S. business environment.

NOLAN AND RYAN'S STUDY OF HORROR FILMS ♦

Here's another example. Nolan and Ryan (2000) asked 60 undergraduates (30 women and 30 men) to name and describe the "most frightening slasher film they could recall" (p. 42). They ran a word count—applying a **stop list** (see page 382) and

Figure 19.2 Multidimensional Scaling of Jang and Barnett's Company-by-Company Data

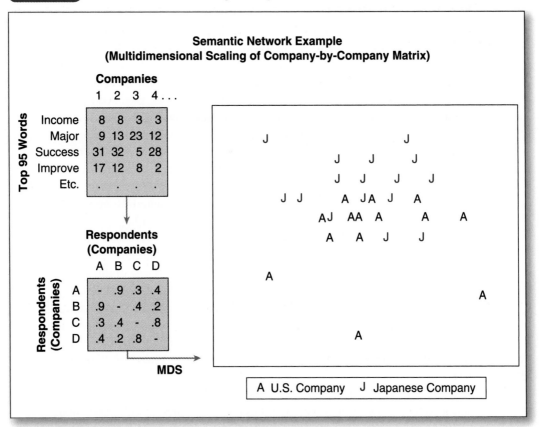

SOURCE: Jang and Barnett (1994).

isolated the adjectives, verbs, and nouns used at least three times across all the descriptions of the films. They eliminated words that referred to the tasks of actually watching the movie and describing it—words like movie, watching, recalling, and so on—and they collapsed word pairs, like rape–raped, violent–violence, and blood–bloody.

This left a list of 40 descriptive words. Next, Nolan and Ryan produced a 60-by-40, person-by-word matrix. They ran several kinds of analysis on this matrix to look for differences in how men and women describe slasher films. First, they arranged the word list as shown in Table 19.6 so that differences between men and women would be easy to spot. The words at the top of the table were used mostly by men, while the words at the bottom were used mostly by women—and the words in the middle were used more or less equally by women and men.

| Table 19.6 | Frequency of Mention of Descriptive Image Words for Men and Women (*N* = 60) |

Words	Total		Men		Women		Difference
	Frequency	Percent	Frequency	Percent	Frequency	Percent	Men–Women
Teenagers	10	16.7	10	33.3	0	0.0	33.3
Violent/ce	10	16.7	9	30.0	1	3.3	26.7
Disturbing	20	33.3	14	46.7	6	20.0	26.7
Rural	6	10.0	6	20.0	0	0.0	20.0
Dark	8	13.3	7	23.3	1	3.3	20.0
Tension	6	10.0	6	20.0	0	0.0	20.0
Country	4	6.7	4	13.3	0	0.0	13.3
Blood/y	9	15.0	6	20.0	3	10.0	10.0
Chainsaw	3	5.0	3	10.0	0	0.0	10.0
Hillbillies	3	5.0	3	10.0	0	0.0	10.0
Sickening	3	5.0	3	10.0	0	0.0	10.0
Texas	3	5.0	3	10.0	0	0.0	10.0
Killer	12	20.0	7	23.3	5	16.7	6.7
Horrible	6	10.0	4	13.3	2	6.7	6.7
Rape/d	6	10.0	4	13.3	2	6.7	6.7
City	4	6.7	3	10.0	1	3.3	6.7
Death	4	6.7	3	10.0	1	3.3	6.7
Massacre	4	6.7	3	10.0	1	3.3	6.7
Kid	3	5.0	2	6.7	1	3.3	3.3
Night	3	5.0	2	6.7	1	3.3	3.3
Scary	13	21.7	7	23.2	6	20.0	3.3
Kidnapped	4	6.7	2	6.7	2	6.7	0.0
Children	9	15.0	4	13.3	5	16.7	−3.3
Pretty	5	8.3	2	6.7	3	10.0	−3.3

(Continued)

Table 19.6 (Continued)

Words	Total		Men		Women		Difference
	Frequency	Percent	Frequency	Percent	Frequency	Percent	Men–Women
Woman	5	8.3	2	6.7	3	10.0	−3.3
Far	3	5.0	1	3.3	2	6.7	−3.3
Parents	3	5.0	1	3.3	2	6.7	−3.3
Religious	4	6.7	1	3.3	3	10.0	−6.7
Victims	4	6.7	1	3.3	3	10.0	−6.7
Girl/s	15	25.0	6	20.0	9	30.0	−10.0
Frightening	11	18.3	4	13.3	7	23.3	−10.0
Terrible	7	11.7	2	6.7	5	16.7	−10.0
Father	4	6.7	0	0.0	4	13.3	−13.3
Horror	15	25.0	5	16.7	10	33.3	−16.7
Evil	13	21.7	4	13.3	9	30.0	−16.7
Devil	5	8.3	0	0.0	5	16.7	−16.7
Young	12	20.0	3	10.0	9	30.0	−20.0
Little	8	13.3	1	3.3	7	23.3	−20.0
Boy	6	10.0	0	0.0	6	20.0	−20.0
Possess/ ed/ion	6	10.0	0	0.0	6	20.0	−20.0

SOURCE: Nolan, J. M. and G. Ryan (2000). Fear and loathing at the cineplex: Gender differences in descriptions and perceptions of slasher films. *Sex Roles* 42(1–2):39–56.

Notice that *some men—but no women*—mentioned rural and hillbillies; and that *some women—but no men*—mentioned the devil and possession. To explore this further, Nolan and Ryan correlated the columns of the 40-by-60, word-by-person matrix. This gave them a 60-by-60 similarity matrix of their informants, which they analyzed with multidimensional scaling. Figure 19.3 shows the result.

Though there is some overlap, it's pretty clear that men and women use different sets of words to describe horror films. Nolan and Ryan next used **correspondence analysis** to examine the words that men and women were more likely to use in the texts. Figure 19.4 shows the result (Box 19.3).

Figure 19.3 MDS of Words Used in Men's and Women's Description of Horror Films

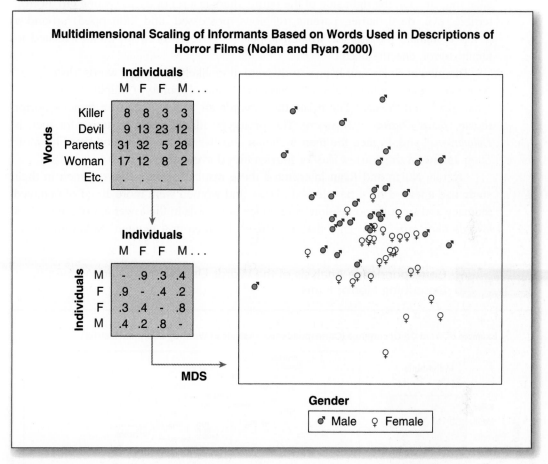

SOURCE: Nolan, J. M. and G. Ryan (2000). Fear and loathing at the cineplex: Gender differences in descriptions and perceptions of slasher films. *Sex Roles* 42(1–2):39–56.

Box 19.3

Correspondence Analysis

Like MDS, correspondence analysis produces a map but it scales the rows and columns of a profile matrix simultaneously, so you can see the relation between the objects in a study (the rows of a profile matrix) and the variables that describe those objects (the columns). Here, the profile matrix is the 60-by-40 person-by-word matrix.

The closer things are to one another on a correspondence analysis map, the more alike they are. On the right side of the figure, there is a set of terms (young girl, horror, terrible, evil, devil, father, parents, religious, possessed, and kidnapped) around a group of female informants. Women appear to have focused on themes related to family, terror, and the occult.

The men in Nolan and Ryan's study were more likely to use the words "disturbing," "violence," "dark," killer," "death," "teenager," "rural," "country," "hillbilly," "massacre," "chainsaw," and "Texas." These last three words are a reference to a famous horror movie, *Texas Chainsaw Massacre*. The prototype film about rural terror for men is *Deliverance*, and, in fact, the men in Nolan and Ryan's sample named that film most often as one of the scariest slasher movies they'd ever seen.

Overall, Nolan and Ryan interpreted these results to mean that the men in their study had a fear of rural people and places, and women were more afraid of betrayed intimacy and spiritual possession. And notice the words in the lower left of Figure 19.4 (words like "rape" and "far") that are shared by men and women. Nolan and Ryan

| **Figure 19.4** | Correspondence Analysis of the Words Used by Men and Women in Describing Horror Films |

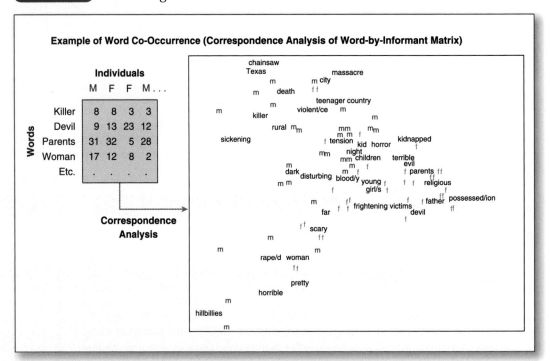

SOURCE: Nolan, J. M. and G. Ryan (2000). Fear and loathing at the cineplex: Gender differences in descriptions and perceptions of slasher films. *Sex Roles* 42(1–2):39–56.

interpreted this to be a semantic extension of the rural terror theme and reflecting what Clover (1992) called the "rape–revenge" motif in slasher films. (**Further Reading**: semantic network analysis)

SOME CAUTIONS ABOUT ALL THIS ◆

One really appealing thing about analyzing word-by-word co-occurrence matrices is that it's done entirely by computer. In fact, the initial analyses can only be done with a computer. This may make it tempting to let the computer do all the work, but in the end it still takes a thoroughly human, interpretive method to make sense of numerical data.

Jang and Barnett, for example, interpreted their results as showing a split between Japanese corporate concern with product innovation and quality versus an American concern with finance and organization. Nolan and Ryan interpreted their results as showing gender differences in what Americans fear. This is the work of cell B in Figure 1.1: the qualitative search for and presentation of meaning in the results of quantitative data processing. No study, no matter how sophisticated the numerical processing, is complete without this step. Don't quit early.

Computer processing of matrices also means that that you have to be especially vigilant about bias going in. One source of bias is the choice of which words to keep in a matrix. This choice begins with the building of a stop list. The bigger the list, the more choices you've made about the analysis—and, as we've seen time and time again, every choice in methods introduces potential bias.

Another choice is the number of words to analyze. Jang chose the top 94 words— words that were all used at least 26 times each across the 35 CEO letters. We re-ran Jang's data, using the top 100 words and the top 200 words. Our findings were substantially the same, but they might not have been. Always check this potential source of bias.

How to check? We introduce bias on purpose to see if we can clobber our findings when we use these methods. If we can't, that gives us more confidence that we're seeing something meaningful in the results.

For example, we took Jang's data and removed two really important concept words from his top 94: United States and Japan. What if the dramatic picture in Figure 19.2 was simply the result of the Japanese executives referring a lot to Japan and the U.S. executives referring a lot to the United States? When we removed the words from Jang's data and re-ran the analysis, the plot showing the split between Japanese and U.S. companies became even more dramatic—with one exception. Mitsubishi wound up squarely among the American companies.

Was Mitsubishi trying to become more like an American company? Only further analysis can get at this, but that's the nature of research (see Box 19.4).

> **Box 19.4**
>
> **Bibliometrics and Semantic Network Analysis**
>
> Bibliometrics is an area of study that focuses on the analysis of academic books and articles. One of its core methods, citation analysis, traces co-citation relationships (that is, who cites whom) across these texts. Bibliometricians also use the tools of semantic network analysis to trace the use of words, themes, and concepts across publications. Bibliometrics is a good field to follow if you are interested in learning about the latest methodological developments in semantic network analysis.

◆ SEMANTIC NETWORK ANALYSIS OF THEMES

Another way to perform semantic network analysis is on themes, not words. To begin, you need to identify themes, whether inductively or deductively (see Chapter 5 for a review). Once you identify the themes, you'll need to select the ones you want to pursue in a systematic analysis. The next step is to develop codes, which define and operationalize themes, and a codebook that contains these code definitions plus instructions about how to code the text (see Chapter 6 for a review). From there, you'll need to systematically code the texts.

After you've completed the coding, you can create a respondent-by-code matrix. You'll want to think about how to count the codes. Are you interested in knowing *how many times* a theme occurred within a text, or is it enough to know whether or not a theme *ever occurred* in that text? If you need to know how many times the theme occurred in each text, use interval-level counts. If you just need to know if the theme ever occurred in each text, use nominal measures of presence and absence. Text analysis programs like MAXQDA or NVivo will automatically count how many times you've used a code, and they will also let you create variables that keep track of theme occurrence (with an option to specify interval or nominal type variables) in each text.

Once you have the respondent-by-code matrix, you can proceed directly to doing a correspondence analysis (using the same process as Nolan and Ryan's (2000) analysis of the word-by-informant matrix in Figure 19.4) or a network analysis (discussed below). If you want to do a multidimensional scaling analysis or cluster analysis (like Jang and Barnett's [1994] analysis of CEO letters in Figure 19.2 or Nolan and Ryan's [2000] gender analysis in Figure 19.3), you'll have to go one step further and create a similarity matrix (using a process similar to the one illustrated in Figure 19.1).

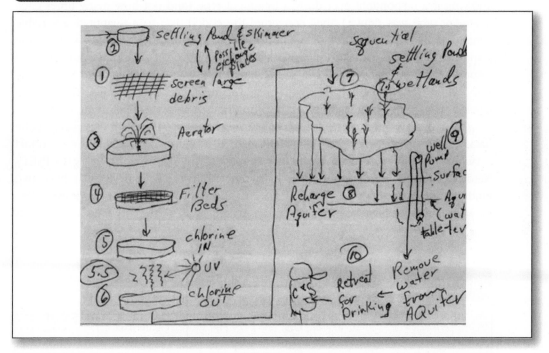

Figure 19.5 U.S. Respondent's Hand-Drawn Depiction of a Wastewater Treatment Path

Here's an example. Wutich and colleagues (2015) wanted to understand cross-cultural views on acceptable wastewater treatment techniques. They selected four field sites—in Guatemala, Fiji, the United States, and Spain—to represent a continuum from low to high levels of wastewater treatment technology. In each site, they asked around 60–80 community members: "Please draw the treatment path that you think wastewater should take so that it can become drinkable again." In all, they interviewed 279 people across the four field sites. Respondents drew pictures like the one in Figure 19.5, above, from the United States.

The respondents drew dozens of different wastewater treatments. But Wutich and colleagues wanted to know how these drawings matched up against real treatments that engineers would actually use to treat wastewater. Since the responses were hand-drawn images, they could not easily do a word-based analysis. Instead, they developed 13 codes for common wastewater treatments: filtration, purification, sterilization, sedimentation, and so forth (Table 19.6 contains the full list, in the first column). Following the techniques covered in Chapters 6 and 11, they tested interrater reliability and revised the codebook until Cohen's kappa for each code was $k \geq .80$.

Then, they coded the data. For example, one U.S. respondent's drawing, shown in Figure 19.5, contained the following themes: filtration, sedimentation, UV treatment, aeration, and chemical disinfection. Since the researchers were only interested in knowing if a respondent ever drew a treatment type (and not how many times each treatment type was drawn), they converted the coded data to a quantitative variable containing nominal measures of theme presence or absence. Then, they created the respondent-by-code matrix shown partially in Table 19.7. The columns contained 279 respondents from research sites in the United States, Fiji, Guatemala, and Spain (one respondent from each site is shown here). The rows are the 13 codes. The column labeled "U.S. Resp." contains the data for the drawing shown in Figure 19.5.

Once the drawings were coded, the researchers brought the full version of the dataset (partially shown in Table 19.7) into UCINET. There, they were able to conduct a **two-mode network analysis** of the respondent-by-code matrix using UCINET's Netdraw network visualization tool. In two-mode network analysis, you have two kinds of nodes (in this case, respondents and codes). The program then draws a line between any nodes that the dataset says are linked (in this case, any time a theme was

Table 19.7 Respondent-by-Code Matrix for a Cross-Cultural Study of Wastewater Treatment

Code	U.S. Resp.	Fiji Resp.	Guatemala Resp.	Spain Resp.
Filtration	1	1	0	0
Purification	0	0	1	1
Sterilization	0	0	0	0
Sedimentation	1	1	0	1
UV Treatment	1	0	0	1
Ozonation	0	0	0	0
Reverse Osmosis	0	0	0	0
Distillation	0	0	0	0
Boiling	0	0	0	0
Aeration	1	0	0	0
Testing	0	0	0	1
Chemical Disinfection	1	0	1	1
Chemical Additive	0	0	0	0

present in a respondent's drawing). Further, you can import an attribute dataset, which is a respondent-by-attribute profile matrix that tells you something about the nodes (in this case, whether each respondent was from a high-technology or low-technology site). You can use the attribute data to control the shape, size, and color of the nodes. The results are shown in Figure 19.6.

The researchers were interested in comparing wastewater treatments that were drawn in low-technology sites (Guatemala and Fiji, in the white square-shaped nodes) and high-technology sites (United States and Spain, in the white circle-shaped nodes). As the results show, many wastewater treatments, such as testing, were drawn more by respondents in high-technology sites. For only one treatment, boiling, was there no difference between drawings collected in high-technology and low-technology sites. And none of the 13 wastewater treatment themes appeared more often in the drawings from low-technology sites, as compared to high-technology sites.

Semantic network analysis offers many tools for exploring patterning in coded texts. In the wastewater treatment study, for instance, the researchers could go on to make a code-by-code similarity matrix to explore patterning in themes. Alternatively, they could create a respondent-by-respondent similarity matrix to explore patterns across respondents. Once you know how to use coded texts to create profile and similarity matrices, you have a range of new methods at your fingertips (Box 19.5).

Figure 19.6 Semantic Network Analysis of Wastewater Treatment Codes (black diamond-shaped nodes), Based on Drawings Collected From Respondents in Low-Technology Sites (white square-shaped nodes) and Respondents in High-Technology Sites (white circle-shaped nodes)

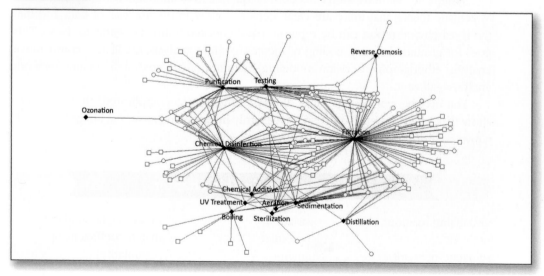

Box 19.5

Big Data, Automated Coding, and Semantic Network Analysis

Scholars have been excited by the idea of big data—huge datasets that have to be processed computationally due to their sheer size—since the 1960s. But only recently has our ability to collect and analyze big textual datasets made this relatively easy to do. With the popularization of the Internet, the creation of user-generated textual content (such as blogs) has grown exponentially. Analysts, sitting in their own offices, can now grab hundreds of thousands of tweets from around the world in one swipe. Using sophisticated word-based analyses, they can auto-code the data for words and themes.

Many big data specialists use semantic network analysis to analyze the coded data. For some, this kind of analysis raises serious privacy concerns. For others, it represents an opportunity to capture and study text at a scale never before possible. For those of us who are trained to carefully and slowly develop codes, iteratively revise them, and hand-code interview data we collected ourselves, it raises a troubling question: Does all this effort get us any further than the latest big data analysis techniques? This question is one that text analysts working in the social sciences will need to consider carefully in coming years.

◆ AND FINALLY . . .

Let's end by going back to the beginning of this book. Think again about the title: Analyzing Qualitative Data: Systematic Approaches.

Systematic methods aren't necessarily quantitative, although certainly some are. Systematic means that there are clear steps to follow in the analysis of data and that the research you report can be replicated and checked if anyone wants to do so. This goes for grounded theory, coding of themes, content analysis, qualitative comparative analysis, ethnographic decision modeling, cultural domain analysis, semantic network analysis—all of it.

You may be wondering: "How did *qualitative* get so complicated?" It just goes to show that, while systematic doesn't necessarily mean quantitative, the analysis of qualitative data doesn't mean wimpy, either.

Key Concepts in This Chapter

visualizing relations	covariation	measures of similarity
network	dichotomize	match coefficient of
semantic network	symmetric	similarity

Jaccard's coefficient of
  similarity

multidimensional scaling
cluster analysis
co-occurrence matrix
stop list

correspondence analysis
two-mode network
  analysis

Summary

- Any set of things that are connected or related to one another in some way is a network. If the things are people, it's a social network. If the things are words or concepts, it's a semantic network. Semantic network analysis is the application of methods from the study of relations (network analysis) to text.

  ○ This treats words in a text as actors. Texts that share many words—and the people or organizations that produce the words—are more like each other than are texts that share few words.
  ○ The same analysis can also be done with codes.

- Semantic network analysis begins by calculating the similarity between all pairs of rows or all pairs of columns in a text-by-word profile matrix—where each text is the equivalent of a respondent in a survey and words are the variables in the columns. This is spelled out in Figure 19.1.

  ○ We can measure similarity among rows of data in many ways. With valued data, we might use a correlation coefficient. In many cases, we begin by dichotomizing the data—turning all the numbers in a matrix into 1s and 0s and applying a simple match coefficient or a Jaccard's coefficient to measure similarity among pairs of rows.
  ○ With a match coefficient, if any pair of cells has the same measure—either a 1 or a 0—then it is a match. If a matrix has a lot of 0s, this will inflate the similarity. Jaccard's coefficient is a useful measure of similarity when you only want matching 1s to count and not matching 0s.

- Multidimensional scaling and cluster analysis are useful methods for analyzing similarity matrices. Jang (1995) downloaded the 1992 annual letters to shareholders from the CEOs of 18 American and 17 Japanese corporations. After applying a stop list of 60 common words, Jang created a 94-by-35 matrix, where (1) the rows were the 94 words used at least 26 times across the letters; (2) the columns were the 35 companies; and (3) the cells contained the number of times any word occurred in one of the letters.

  ○ Jang correlated the columns of the matrix to produce a 35-by-35, company-by-company co-occurrence matrix—that is, a similarity matrix based on the co-occurrence of words in their letters to stockholders. Jang analyzed this matrix with multidimensional scaling.

Run the word count program on: (1) the first illness description; (2) all the descriptions together; (3) all the women's descriptions (#1Female through #10Female; and (4) all the mens' descriptions (#1Male – #10Male). Describe the differences you see in the four outputs.

2. Go to the website for this book and download the word-by-respondent Excel spreadsheet. Look at the file in Excel. It is derived from the 20 short illness descriptions (10 female and 10 male) from Exercise 1. The columns represent the respondents, and the rows represent the 41 words that were mentioned by at least five of the 20 respondents.

Download a trial version of UCINET from analytictech.com. (The trial version is free.) Import the Excel spreadsheet into UCINET (*Input Excel/Matrices*) and name the file ILLNESS. Next dichotomize the data by going to *Tools/Dichtomize*. Select ILLNESS as your input dataset. UCINET will automatically name your output data set ILLNESS_GT_0 (which means *greater than 0*). This new data set has a 1 if the person mentioned the word and 0 otherwise.

To see how similar the illness descriptions were to each other, create a similarity matrix by going to *Similarities & Differences*. Select ILLNESS_GT_0 as your input file. For your similarity measure, select *Matches* and for the mode select *Columns* (the respondents). UCINET will automatically name ILLNESS_GT_0-Mat-R and it will produce a 20-respondent-by-20-respondent measure filled with numbers between 0 and 1.

Now use MDS (*Tools/Scaling-Decomposition/Non-Metric MDS*) and cluster analysis (Tools/Cluster Analysis) to explore how similar the illness descriptions were to each other. Look at the output from these two and interpret what it means. Next go back and repeat the steps, but instead of using *Matches* for your similarity measure, select *Jaccard* and run MDS and cluster analysis on the resulting similarity matrix. How do these analyses look different from your previous analyses? Finally, repeat the process by creating and analyzing word-by-word (*rows*) similarity matrices.

Further Reading

Semantic network analysis. Danowski (1982, 2009), Doerfel (1998), Doerfel and Barnett (1999), Fitzgerald and Doerfel (2004), Kirchler (1992), Kwon et al. (2009), Maynard (1997), Rice and Danowski (1993), Roberts (1997), Schnegg and Bernard (1996), Siregar et al. (2011), R. A. Smith and Parrott (2012).

Visit the online resource site at study.sagepub.com/bernardaqd to access engaging and helpful digital content, like video tutorials on working with MAXQDA, presentation slides, MAXQDA keyboard shortcuts, datasets, stop list, and recommended readings.

Appendix

RESOURCES FOR ANALYZING QUALITATIVE DATA ◆

More resources for *Analyzing Qualitative Data*: *Systematic Approaches*, Second Edition (AQD2) are at study.sagepub.com/bernardaqd.

That site has (1) lectures designed to match up with many of the chapters in AQD2; (2) two of the sample datasets discussed in the book (Illnesses and Personals Ads); and (3) hands-on activities.

You will need to register for a username and password before you can access these materials. Registration can be found on the lower right side of the screen.

TRANSCRIPTION AND VOICE RECOGNITION SOFTWARE ◆

Express Scribe (http://www.nch.com.au/scribe/) and HyperTranscribe (http://www.researchware.com/products/hypertranscribe.html) support transcription of both audio and video files. The makers of the Express Scribe also sell a foot pedal. HyperTranscribe uses keyboard controls. Many of the most widely used text analysis packages also support transcription.

A widely used voice recognition (VR) program for text is Dragon® Naturally Speaking (http://www.nuance.com/dragon/index.htm). VR software can be used as a transcription device. You listen with earphones to an interview, for example, and you repeat the content, as you hear it, word for word. This can save a lot of time, once the software is fully up to speed. It can take many hours of practice before VR software reaches its maximum accuracy (around 90%, or greater). Speech recognition is developing quickly in mobile devices, and that technology should lead to increasing accuracy in VR software for text.

A discussion forum on VR software and transcription hardware and software is here: http://www.knowbrainer.com/forums/forum/index.cfm

♦ KWIC (KEY WORD IN CONTEXT) AND CONCORDANCE SOFTWARE AND WORD LIST SOFTWARE

Several programs are available free, including Simple Concordance Program (http://www.textworld.com/scp/) and TextQuest (http://www.textquest.de/pages/en/analysis-of-texts/concordances-kwic.php?lang=EN), and Concordance (http://www.concordancesoftware.co.uk). Commercial programs include WordSmith Tools (http://www.lexically.net/wordsmith/) and Concordance Suite (http://www.lexisnexis.ca/en-ca/products/concordance-suite.page).

♦ SEMANTIC NETWORK ANALYSIS

Several programs are available for doing semantic network analysis, including ConText (http://context.lis.illinois.edu), WORDij (http://wordij.net/), and Tapor (http://tapor-test.artsrn.ualberta.ca/home). Semantic network analysis can also be done with network analysis packages, like UCINET (http://www.analytictech.com), Pajek (http://mrvar.fdv.uni-lj.si/pajek), and ORA (http://www.casos.cs.cmu.edu). DNA Discourse Network Analyzer (https://github.com/leifeld/dna/wiki) produces matrices that can be analyzed with network analysis software.

♦ WORD CLOUD SOFTWARE

Free online programs include Wordle (http://www.wordle.net), WordItOut (http://worditout.com), TagCrowd (http://tagcrowd.com), and Tagul (https://tagul.com).

♦ THE OUTLINE OF CULTURAL MATERIALS

This is available at The Human Relations Area Files (http://hraf.yale.edu) and see Ember and Ember 2009.

♦ CAQDAS AND TEXT ANALYSIS SOFTWARE

CAQDAS stands for "computer-assisted qualitative data analysis." For a review of major CAQDAS software packages, see Lewins and Silver (2014). The following provide information on dozens of programs for text analysis and are updated frequently.

http://textanalysis.info/

https://en.wikipedia.org/wiki/Computer-assisted_qualitative_data_analysis_software

Many programs today will handle written text, audio files, and video files. The CAQDAS networking project (at http://caqdas.soc.surrey.ac.uk) provides "practical support, training and information in the use of a range of software programs designed to assist qualitative data analysis."

CONTENT ANALYSIS ♦

For information resources about content analysis: http://www.content-analysis.de/. For automated content analysis, see: http://gking.harvard.edu/readme and http://gking .harvard.edu/category/research-interests/applications/automated-text-analysis. Text mining and data mining software is developing very quickly, and dozens of software packages are competing for the attention of users. Several sites try to keep up with these developments, including: http://www.kdnuggets.com/software/text.html; http:// www.predictiveanalyticstoday.com/top-free-data-mining-software/

COURSES ON TEXT ANALYSIS ♦

Short courses on text analysis are offered at the following:

Essex Summer School in Social Science Data Analysis (http://www.essex.ac.uk/ summerschool/).

Summer Institute in Survey Research Techniques at the University of Michigan (http://si.isr.umich.edu/).

European Consortium for Political Research at the University of Ljubljana (http:// ecpr.eu/Default.aspx).

The Qualitative Data Analysis Program (QDAP) at the University of Pittsburgh has online tutorials and software for coding and managing text. The main QDAP site is at http://www.qdap.pitt.edu/. QDAP developed coding software, called CAT (Coding Analysis Toolkit). Information of CAT is at http://cat.texifter.com/

CULTURAL DOMAIN ANALYSIS ♦

Software for cultural domain analysis includes ANTHROPAC and UCINET (http:// www.analytictech.com/) and FLAME. ANTHROPAC is a full-featured suite of programs for collecting cultural domain analysis data (free-lists, pile sorts, triad tests, paired comparisons) and for getting those data into the computer for analysis. The disadvantage of ANTHROPAC is that it was written for DOS computers (before Windows) and is therefore entirely command driven. For free lists, FLAME is a better resource (http://www.mae.u-paris10.fr/lesc/spip.php?article63). Pile-sort data can be imported into UCINET, a Windows program. For instructions on how to import pile-sort data into UCINET, go to http://tinyurl.com/pkgpna2. Analysis chores for CDA data can be done in ANTHROPAC but are better done in UCINET (which was originally developed for network analysis).

◆ QCA: QUALITATIVE COMPARATIVE ANALYSIS

For computer programs and other resources for QCA, see the COMPASSS resource site for small-n research: http://www.compasss.org/. Some computer programs for analyzing truth tables include fs/QCA (Ragin 2008; http://www.u.arizona.edu/~cragin/fsQCA/software.shtml), and Kirq (Reichert and Rubinson 2014; http://grundrisse.org/qca/docs/kirq.html).

◆ JOURNALS

Increasingly, scholarly journals in the social sciences publish research based on the collection and analysis of qualitative data. Many journals, however, are devoted to publishing papers in the qualitative tradition and papers in the mixed-methods tradition. A few examples:

Forum Qualitative Sozialforschung / Forum: Qualitative Social Research (online and free at http://www.qualitative-research.net/index.php/fqs/index)

Journal of Mixed Methods Research

International Journal of Qualitative Studies in Education

Journal of Qualitative and Ethnographic Research

Journal of Contemporary Ethnography

Journal of Qualitative Criminal Justice & Criminology

International Journal of Qualitative Studies on Health and Well-Being

Qualitative Health Research

Qualitative Inquiry

Qualitative Psychology

Qualitative Social Work

Qualitative Market Research

Qualitative Report

Qualitative Research

Qualitative Research Journal

Qualitative Research in Accounting and Management

Qualitative Research in Organizations and Management

Qualitative Research Reports in Communication

Qualitative Social Work

Qualitative Sociology

Qualitative Sociology Review

Qualitative Studies in Education

Studies in Qualitative Methodology

Global Qualitative Nursing Research

References

Abdul-Rahman, M. S. 2003. *Islam: Questions and Answers*, Vol. 4, *The Hadeeth and Its Sciences*. London: MSA Publications Ltd.

Abele, A. E., and D. Spurk. 2011. The dual impact of gender and the influence of timing of parenthood on men's and women's career development: Longitudinal findings. *International Journal of Behavioral Development* 35:225–32.

Abelson, R. P., and A. Levi. 1985. Decision making and decision theory. In *The Handbook of Social Psychology*, Vol. 1, L. Gardener and E. Aronson, eds., 231–309. New York: Random House.

Addison, R. B. 1992. Grounded hermeneutic research. In *Doing Qualitative Research*, B. F. Crabtree and W. L. Miller, eds., 110–24. Newbury Park, CA: Sage.

Adriansen, H. K. 2012. Timeline interviews: A tool for conducting life history research. *Qualitative Studies* 3:40–55.

Agar, M. H. 1973. *Ripping and Running: A Formal Ethnography of Urban Heroin Addicts*. New York: Seminar Press.

Agar, M. H. 1979. Themes revisited: Some problems in cognitive anthropology. *Discourse Processes* 2:11–31.

Agar, M. H. 1980. *The Professional Stranger*. New York: Academic Press.

Agar, M. H. 1983. Political talk: Thematic analysis of a policy argument. *Policy Studies Review* 2:601–14.

Agar, M. H. 1996. *The Professional Stranger: An Informal Introduction to Ethnography*, 2d ed. San Diego: Academic Press.

Agar, M. H., and J. MacDonald. 1995. Focus groups and ethnography. *Human Organization* 54:78–86.

Agresti, A., and C. Franklin. 2007. *Statistics: The Art and Science of Learning from Data*. Upper Saddle River, NJ: Pearson Prentice Hall.

Alali, A. O. 1993. Management of death and grief in obituary and in memorium pages of Nigerian newspapers. *Psychological Reports* 73:835–42.

Aldenderfer, M. S., and R. K. Blashfield. 1984. *Cluster Analysis*. Beverly Hills, CA: Sage.

Alkon, A. H. 2004. Place, stories, and consequences. Heritage narratives and the control of erosion on Lake County, California, vineyards. *Organization and Environment* 17:145–69.

Al-Krenawi A., and R. Wiesel-Lev. 1999. Attitudes toward and perceived psychosocial impact of female circumcision as practiced among the Bedouin-Arabs of the Negev. *Family Process* 38:431–43.

Allan, C. 2007. Exploring natural resource management with metaphor analysis. *Society and Natural Resources* 20:351–62.

Allen, J. T., and G. Italie. 1954. *A Concordance to Euripides*. Berkeley: University of California Press.

Allwood, C. M. 2012. The distinction between qualitative and quantitative research is problematic. *Quality and Quantity* 46:1417–29.

Alterovitz, S. R., and G. A. Mendelsohn. 2013. Relationship goals of middle-aged, young-old, and old-old Internet daters: An analysis of online personal ads. *Journal of Aging Studies* 27:159–65.

Altheide, D. L., and C. J. Schneider. 2012. *Qualitative Media Analysis*, 2d ed. Thousand Oaks, CA: Sage.

Alvarado, N. 1998. A reconsideration of the structure of the emotion lexicon. *Motivation and Emotion* 22:329–44.

An, S. K., and K. K. Gower. 2009. How do the news media frame crises? A content analysis of crisis news coverage. *Public Relations Review* 35:107–12.

Anderson, K. J., and C. Leaper. 1998. Meta-analyses of gender effects on conversational interruption: Who, what, when, where, and how. *Sex Roles* 39:225–52.

Anderson, T., K. Daly, and L. Rapp. 2009. Clubbing masculinities and crime: A qualitative study of Philadelphia nightclub scenes. *Feminist Criminology* 4:302–32.

Angrosino, M. V. 1989. *Documents of Interaction: Biography, Autobiography, and Life History in Social Science Perspective*. Gainesville: University of Florida Press.

Andriotis, K. 2010. Brits behaving badly—Template analysis of newspaper content. *International Journal of Tourism Anthropology* 1:15–34.

Aquilino, W. S. 1993. Effects of spouse presence during the interview on survey responses concerning marriage. *Public Opinion Quarterly* 57:358–76.

Aquilino, W. S. 1994. Interview mode effects in surveys of drug and alcohol use: A field experiment. *Public Opinion Quarterly* 58:210–40.

Aquilino, W. S., D. L. Wright, and A. J. Supple. 2000. Response effects due to bystander presence in CASI and paper-and-pencil surveys of drug use and alcohol use. *Substance Use and Misuse* 35:845–67. Special issue: *Methodological Issues in the Measurement of Drug Use*.

Aristotle. N.d. *Poetics*. The Internet Classics Archive. Copyright (C) 1994–2009, D. C. Stevenson, Web Atomics.http://classics.mit.edu/Aristotle/poetics.3.3.html (accessed January 29, 2016).

Aristotle. N.d. *Rhetoric*. The Internet Classics Archive. Copyright (C) 1994–2000, D. C. Stevenson, Web Atomics. http://classics.mit.edu/Aristotle/rhetoric.html (accessed March 24, 2009).

Aronsky, D., M. Fiszman, W. W. Chapman, and P. J. Haug. 2001. Combining decision support methodologies to diagnose pneumonia. *Annual Proceedings of the American Medical Informatics Association*, pp. 12–16.

Arthur, H., G. Johnson, and A. Young. 2007. Gender differences and color: Content and emotion of written descriptions. *Social Behavior and Personality* 35:827–34.

Ascher, G. J. 2001. Sephardic songs, proverbs, and expressions: A continuing tradition. *Shofar: An Interdisciplinary Journal of Jewish Studies* 19:19–39.

Ashworth, G. J. 2004. Tourism and the heritage of atrocity: Managing the heritage of South African apartheid for entertainment. In *New Horizons in Tourism. Strange Experience and Stranger Practices*, T. V. Singh, ed., 95–108. Cambridge, MA: CABI Publishers.

Atkinson, J. M., and J. Heritage, eds. 1984. *Structures of Social Action: Studies in Conversation Analysis*. New York: Cambridge University Press.

Atkinson, R. 1998. *The Life Story Interview*. Thousand Oaks, CA: Sage.

Atkinson, R. 2002. The life story interview. In *Handbook of Interview Research*, J. F. Gubrium and J. A. Holstein, eds., 121–40. Thousand Oaks, CA: Sage.

Atran, S. 1998. Folk biology and the anthropology of science: Cognitive universals and cultural particulars. *Behavioral and Brain Sciences* 21:547–609.

Atran, S., and D. L. Medin. 2008. *The Native Mind and the Cultural Construction of Nature*. Boston: MIT Press.

Attardo, S., L. Pickering, and A. Baker. 2011. Prosodic and multimodal markers of humor in conversation. *Pragmatics and Cognition* 19:224–47.

Auer, P. 2005. A postscript: Code-switching and social identity. *Journal of Pragmatics* 37:403–10.

Auerbach, C. F., and L. B. Silverstein. 2003. *Qualitative Data: An Introduction to Coding and Analysis*. New York: New York University Press.

Axinn, W. G., and L. D. Pearce 2006. *Mixed Method Data Collection Strategies*. New York: Cambridge University Press.

Ayres, C. E. 1978. *The Theory of Economic Progress: A Study of the Fundamentals of Economic Development and Cultural Change*, 3d ed. Kalamazoo: New Issues Press, Western Michigan University.

Bacon, F. 1864 [1620]. *The Works of Francis Bacon*, Vol. 3, J. Spedding, R. L. Ellis, and D. D. Heath, eds. New York: Hurd and Houghton. (Full text on books.google.com. accessed May 3, 2008.)

Badahdah, A. M., and K. A. Tiemann. 2005. Mate selection criteria among Muslims living in America. *Evolution and Human Behavior* 26:432–40.

Baker, R. 1996a. PRA with street children in Nepal. *PLA Notes* 25:56–60. London: International Institute for Environment and Development.

Baker, R., with C. Panter-Brick and A. Todd. 1996b. Methods used in research with street children in Nepal. *Childhood* 3:171–93.

Baker-Ward, L. E., K. L. Eaton, and J. B. Banks 2005. Young soccer players' reports of a tournament win or loss: Different emotions, different narratives. *Journal of Cognition and Development* 6:507–27.

Baksh, M., C. G. Neumann, M. Paolisso, R. M. Trostle, and A. A. J. Jansen. 1994. The influence of reproductive status on rural Kenyan women's time use. *Social Science and Medicine* 39:345–54.

Ball, M. S., and G. W. H. Smith. 1992. *Analyzing Visual Data*. Newbury Park, CA: Sage.

Bantum, E. O., and J. E. Owen. 2009. Evaluating the validity of computerized content analysis programs for identification of emotional expression in cancer patients. *Psychological Assessment* 21:79–88.

Barber, N. 1998. Ecological and psychosocial correlates of male homosexuality: A cross-cultural investigation. *Journal of Cross-Cultural Psychology* 29:387–401.

Barbour, R. 2007. *Doing Focus Groups*. London: Sage.

Bareiss, W. 2014. "Mauled by a Bear": Narrative analysis of self-injury among adolescents in US news, 2007–2012. *Health* 18:279–301.

Barkin, S., G. W. Ryan, and L. Gelberg. 1999. What pediatricians can do to further youth violence prevention—A qualitative study. *Injury Prevention* 5:53–58.

Barnes, J. H., B. F. Banahan, III, and K. E. Fish. 1995. The response effect of question order in computer-administered questioning in the social sciences. *Social Science Computer Review* 13:47–63.

Barnett, G. A., and J. Danowski. 1992. The structure of communication: A network analysis of the international communication association. *Human Communication Research* 19:164–285.

Barroso, J. 1997. Reconstructing my life: Becoming a long-term survivor of AIDS. *Qualitative Health Research* 7:57–74.

Barroso, J., and M. Sandelowski. 2003. Sample reporting of qualitative studies of women with HIV infection. *Field Methods* 15:386–404.

Bartlett, F. 1964 [1932]. *Remembering: A Study in Experimental and Social Psychology*. Cambridge: Cambridge University Press.

Basturkman, H. 1999. A content analysis of ELT textbook blurbs: Reflections of theory in use. *RELC Journal* 30:18–38.

Basurto, X., and J. Speer. 2012. Structuring the calibration of qualitative data as assets for qualitative comparative analysis (QCA). *Field Methods* 24:155–74.

Bauer, M. W. 2000. Classical content analysis: A review. In *Qualitative Researching with Text Image and Sound*, M. W. Bauer and G. Gaskell, eds., 131–51. Thousand Oaks, CA: Sage.

Bauer, M. W., and A. L. Wright. 1996. Integrating qualitative and quantitative methods to model infant feeding behavior among Navajo mothers. *Human Organization* 55:183–92.

Bauman, R. 1984. *Verbal Art as Performance*. Long Grove, IL: Waveland Press.

Bauman, R. 1986. *Story, Performance, and Event. Contextual Studies of Oral Narrative*. New York: Cambridge University Press.

Bauman, Z. 1978. *Hermeneutics and Social Science*. New York: Columbia University Press.

Beaudreau, A. H., P. S. Levin, and K. C. Norman. 2011. Using folk taxonomies to understand stakeholder perceptions for species conservation. *Conservation Letters* 4:451–63.

Beck, K. A. 2000. A decision making model of child abuse reporting. Ph.D. dissertation, University of British Columbia.

Beck, M. 2007. Dinner preparation in the modern United States. *British Food Journal* 109:531–47.

Becker, H. S. 1970. *Sociological Work. Method and Substance. Essays by Howard Becker*. New Brunswick, NJ: Transaction Publishers.

Becker, H. S. 1993. How I learned what a crock was. *Journal of Contemporary Ethnography* 22:28–35.

Becker, H. S. 1998. *Tricks of the Trade: How to Think about Your Research while You're Doing It*. Chicago: University of Chicago Press.

Beegle, K., C. Calogero, and K. Himelein. 2012. Reliability of recall in agricultural data. *Journal of Development Economics* 98:34–41.

Behar, R. 1990. Rage and redemption: Reading the life story of a Mexican marketing woman. *Feminist Studies* 16:223–58.

Behr, D., L. Kaczmirek, W. Bandilla, and M. Braun. 2012. Asking probing questions in web surveys. Which factors have an impact on the quality of responses? *Social Science Computer Review* 30:487–98.

Bem, S. L. 1981. Gender schema theory: A cognitive account of sex typing. *Psychological Review* 88:354–64.

Bem, S. L. 1983. Gender schema theory and its implications for child development: Raising gender-aschematic children in a gender-schematic society. *Signs* 8:598–616.

Bem, S. L. 1985. Androgyny and gender schema theory: A conceptual and empirical integration. In *Psychology and Gender*, T. B. Sonderegger, ed., 179–226. Lincoln: University of Nebraska Press.

Bender, A., and S. Beller. 2011. The cultural constitution of cognition: Taking the anthropological perspective. *Frontiers in Psychology* 2:16.

Bennett, L. 2012. Patterns of listening through social media: Online fan engagement with the live music experience. *Social Semiotics* 22:545–57.

Benoit, W. L. 2011. Content analysis in political communication. In *The Sourcebook for Political Communication Research. Methods, Measures, and Analytical Techniques*, E. P. Bucy and R. L. Holbert, eds., 268–79. New York: Routledge.

Berelson, B. 1952. *Content Analysis in Communication Research*. Glencoe, IL: Free Press.

Bernard, H. R. 1987. Sponge fishing and technological change in Greece. In *Technology and Social Change*, 2d ed., H. R. Bernard and P. J. Pelto, eds., 167–206. Prospect Heights, IL: Waveland.

Bernard, H. R. 1996. Qualitative data, quantitative analysis. *Cultural Anthropology Methods Journal* 8(1):9–11.

Bernard, H. R. 2011. *Research Methods in Anthropology: Qualitative and Quantitative Approaches*, 5th ed. Thousand Oaks, CA: Sage.

Bernard, H. R. 2012. *Social Research Methods: Qualitative and Quantitative Approaches*, 2d ed. Thousand Oaks, CA: Sage.

Bernard, H. R., and P. D. Killworth. 1993. Sampling in time allocation research. *Ethnology* 32:207–15.

Bernard, H. R., P. D. Killworth, L. Sailer, and D. Kronenfeld. 1984. The problem of informant accuracy: The validity of retrospective data. *Annual Review of Anthropology* 13:495–517.

Bernard, H. R., P. J. Pelto, D. Romney, C. Ember, A. Johnson, O. Werner, J. Boster, A. K. Romney, A. Johnson, C. R. Ember, and A. Kasakoff. 1986. The construction of primary data in cultural anthropology. *Current Anthropology* 27:382–96.

Bernard, H. R., G. W. Ryan, and S. P. Borgatti. 2009. Green cognition and behavior: A cultural domain analysis. In *Networks, Resources, and Economic Action. Ethnographic Case Studies in Honor of Hartmut Lang*, C. Greiner and W. Kokot, eds., 189–215. Berlin: Dietrich Reimer Verlag.

Bernard, H. R., and J. Salinas Pedraza 1989. *Native Ethnography: A Mexican Indian Describes His Culture*. Newbury Park, CA: Sage.

Berra, Y., and J. Garagiola. 1998. *The Yogi Book: "I Really Didn't Say Everything I Said."* New York: Workman Publishing.

Bessinger, J. B., and P. H. Smith. 1969. *A Concordance to Beowulf*. Ithaca, NY: Cornell University Press.

Best, D. L., A. S. House, A. E. Barnard, and B. S. Spicker. 1994. Parent–child interactions in France, Germany, and Italy: The effects of gender and culture. *Journal of Cross-Cultural Psychology* 25:181–93.

Bialostok, S. 2002. Metaphors for literacy: A cultural model of white, middle-class parents. *Linguistics and Education* 13:347–71.

Bibeau, W. S., B. I. Saksvig, J. Gittelsohn, S. Williams, L. Jones, and D. R. Young. 2012. Perceptions of the food marketing environment among African American teen girls and adults. *Appetite* 58:396–99.

Biedenweg, K. A., and M. Monroe. 2013. Cognitive methods and a case study for assessing shared perspectives as a result of social learning. *Society and Natural Resources: An International Journal* 26:931–44. DOI: 10.1080/08941920.2012.725455

Biernacki, P., and D. Waldorf. 1981. Snowball sampling: Problems, techniques, and chain referral sampling. *Sociological Methods and Research* 10:141–63.

Binongo, J. N. G. 2012. Who wrote the 15th book of Oz? An application of multivariate analysis to authorship attribution. *Chance* 16:9–17.

Birks, M., and J. Mills. 2011. *Grounded Theory: A Practical Guide*. Thousand Oaks, CA: Sage.

Black, E. 1992. *Parallel Realities: A Jewish/Arab History of Israel/Palestine*. Boulder, CO: Paradigm.

Blair, E. 1979. Interviewing in the presence of others. In *Improving Interview Method and Questionnaire Design: Response Effects to Threatening Questions in Survey Research*, N. M. Bradburn and Seymour Sudman, eds., 134–46. San Francisco: Jossey-Bass.

Blair-Loy, M. 2003. *Competing Devotions: Career and Family among Women Executives*. Cambridge, MA: Harvard University Press.

Blau, P. M. 1964. *Exchange and Power in Social Life*. New York: John Wiley and Sons.

Bletzer, K., and M. P. Koss. 2006. After-rape among three populations in the Southwest. *Violence Against Women* 12:5–29.

Blix, B. H., T. Hamran, and H. K. Normann. 2013. Struggles of being and becoming: A dialogical narrative analysis of the life stories of Sami elderly. *Journal of Aging Studies* 27:264–75.

Blommaert, J. 2006. Applied ethnopoetics. *Narrative Inquiry* 16:181–90.

Bloom, F. R. 2001. "New beginnings": A case study in gay men's changing perceptions of quality of life during the course of HIV infection. *Medical Anthropology Quarterly* 15:38–57.

Blum-Kulka, S. 1993. "You gotta know how to tell a story": Telling, tales, and tellers in American and Israeli narrative events at dinner. *Language in Society* 22:361–402.

Blustein, D. L., S. Kozan, and A. Connors-Kellgren. 2013. Unemployment and underemployment: A narrative analysis about loss. *Journal of Vocational Behavior* 82:256–65.

Boas, F. 1901. *Kathlamet Texts*. Bureau of American Ethnology Bulletin 26. Washington, DC: U.S. Government Printing Office.

Boeije, H. R. 2002. A purposeful approach to the constant comparative method in the analysis of qualitative interviews. *Quality and Quantity* 36:391–409.

Boeije, H. R. 2004. And then there were three: Why third persons are present in interviews and the impact on the data. *Field Methods* 16:3–32.

Boelen, W. A. M. 1992. Street corner society. Cornerville revisited. *Journal of Contemporary Ethnography* 21:11–51.

Bogdan, R. C. 1972. *Participant Observation in Organizational Settings*. Syracuse, NY: Syracuse University Press.

Bogdan, R. C., and S. K. Biklen. 1982. *Qualitative Research for Education: An Introduction to Theory and Methods*. Boston: Allyn and Bacon.

Bogdan, R. C., and S. J. Taylor. 1975. *Introduction to Qualitative Research Methods*. New York: John Wiley & Sons.

Bohenmeyer, J. 2003. Invisible time lines in the fabric of events: Temporal coherence in Yucatec narratives. *Journal of Linguistic Anthropology* 13:139–62.

Bondas, T., and K. Eriksson. 2001. Women's lived experience of pregnancy: A tapestry of joy and suffering. *Qualitative Health Research* 11:824–40.

Boonen, A. J. H., M. van der Schoot, F. vanWesel, M. H. de Vries, and J. Jolles. 2013. What underlies successful world problem solving? A path analysis in sixth grade students. *Contemporary Educational Psychology* 38:271–79. doi:10.1016/j.cedpsych.2013.05.001

Borgatti, S. P. 1992. *Anthropac 4.8*. Columbia, SC: Analytic Technologies. http://www.analytictech.com/ (accessed September 22, 2008).

Borgatti, S. P. 1994. Cultural domain analysis. *Journal of Quantitative Anthropology* 4:261–78.

Borgatti, S. P. 1997. Consensus analysis. http://www.analytictech.com/borgatti/consensu.htm (accessed January 28, 2016).

Borgatti, S. P. 1999. Elicitation techniques for cultural domain analysis. In *Enhanced Ethnographic Methods: Audiovisual Techniques, Focused Group Interviews, and Elicitation Techniques*, J. J. Schensul, M. D. LeCompte, B. K. Nastasi, and S. P. Borgatti, eds., 115–51. (*Ethnographer's Toolkit*, Vol. 3.) Walnut Creek, CA: AltaMira.

Borgatti, S. P. 2015. FLAME (version 1.1). CNRS, 2012. *Field Methods* 27:199–205. http://www.mae.u-paris10.fr/lesc/spip.php?article63 (accessed January 29, 2016).

Borgatti, S. P., M. G. Everett, and L. C. Freeman. 2002. UCINET for Windows. Harvard, MA: Analytic Technologies. http://www.analytictech.com/ (accessed December 12, 2009).

Borgatti, S. P., M. G. Everett, and L. C. Freeman. 2004. *UCINET 6.69*. Harvard, MA: Analytic Technologies.

Borgatti, S. P., and D. S. Halgin. 2013. Elicitation techniques for cultural domain analysis. In *Specialized Ethnographic Methods. A Mixed Methods Approach*, J. J. Schensul and M. D. LeCompte, eds., 80–116. Lanham, MD: Rowman and Littlefield.

Borgers, N., J. Hox, and D. Sillel. 2004. Response effects in surveys on children and adolescents: Options, negative wording, and neutral mid-point. *Quality and Quantity* 38:17–33.

Borges, S., and H. Waitzkin. 1995. Women's narratives in primary care medical encounters. *Women and Health* 23:29–56.

Boruch, R. F., and J. S. Cecil, eds. 1983. *Solutions to Ethical and Legal Problems in Social Research*. New York: Academic Press.

Bosk, C. 2004. The ethnographer and the IRB: Comment on Kevin D. Haggerty, "Ethics creep: Governing social science research in the name of ethics." *Qualitative Inquiry* 27:417–20.

Boster, J. S. 1986. Exchange of varieties and information between Aguaruna manioc cultivators. *American Anthropologist* 88:428–36.

Boster, J. S., and J. C. Johnson. 1989. Form or function: A comparison of expert and novice judgments of similarity among fish. *American Anthropologist* 91:866–89.

Boster, J. S., J. C. Johnson, and S. C. Weller. 1987. Social position and shared knowledge: Actors' perceptions of status, role, and social structure. *Social Networks* 9:375–87.

Bourgois, P. I. 1990. Confronting anthropological ethics: Ethnographic lessons from Central America. *Journal of Peace Research* 27:43–54.

Bowen, G. A. 2008. Naturalistic inquiry and the saturation concept: A research note. *Qualitative Research* 8:137–52.

Boyatzis, R. E. 1998. *Transforming Qualitative Information. Thematic Analysis and Code Development*. Thousand Oaks, CA: Sage.

Bradburn, N. M. 1979. Interviewing in the presence of others. In *Improving Interview Method and Questionnaire Design*, N. M. Bradburn and S. Sudman, eds., 135–46. San Francisco: Jossey-Bass.

Bradburn, N. M. 1983. Response effects. In *Handbook of Survey Research*, P. H. Rossi, J. D. Wright, and A. B. Anderson, eds., 289–328. New York: Academic Press.

Bradburn, N. M., and S. Sudman and associates. 1979. *Improving Interview Method and Questionnaire Design: Response Effects to Threatening Questions in Survey Research*. San Francisco: Jossey-Bass.

Bradley, E. H., L. A. Curry, and K. J. Devers. 2007. Qualitative data analysis for health services research: Developing taxonomy, themes, and theory. *Health Service Research* 42:1758–72.

Bradway, C., B. Dahlberg, and F. K. Barg. 2010. How women conceptualize urinary incontinence: A cultural model. *Journal of Women's Health* 19:1533–41.

Brailey, C. D. 2007. A critical analysis of black preachers' sermons in the electronic-digital age (1980 to 2005): A quest for social change. Ph.D. dissertation, Howard University.

Brajer, V., and A. Gill. 2010. Yakity-yak: Who talks back? An email experiment. *Social Science Quarterly* 91:1007–24.

Bramley, N., and V. Eatough. 2005. The experience of living with Parkinson's disease: An interpretative phenomenological analysis case study. *Psychology and Health* 20:223–35.

Brand, L. A. 2010. National narratives and migration: Discursive strategies of inclusion and exclusion in Jordan and Lebanon. *International Migration Review* 44:78–110.

Brenneis, D. 1988. Telling troubles: Narrative, conflict, and experience. *Anthropological Linguistics* 30:279–91.

Breslin, F. C., C. H. Gladwin, D. Borsoi, and J. A. Cunningham. 2000. De facto client-treatment matching: How clinicians make referrals to outpatient treatments for substance use. *Evaluation and Program Planning* 23:281–91.

Brewer, D. D. 1995. Cognitive indicators of knowledge in semantic domains. *Journal of Quantitative Anthropology* 5:107–28.

Brewer, D. D. 2002. Supplementary interviewing techniques to maximize output in free listing tasks. *Field Methods* 14:108–18.

Brewer, D. D., S. B. Garrett, and G. Rinaldi. 2002. Free-listed items are effective cues for eliciting additional items in semantic domains. *Applied Cognitive Psychology* 16:343–58.

Brewer, W. F. 2000. Bartlett's concept of the schema and its impact on theories of knowledge representation in contemporary cognitive psychology. In *Bartlett, Culture and Cognition*, A. Saito, ed., 69–89. Hove, UK: Psychology Press.

Brewer, W. F., and J. C. Treyens. 1981. Role of schemata in memory for places. *Cognitive Psychology* 13:207–30.

Brewis, A., and S. Lee. 2010. Children's work, earnings, and nutrition in urban Mexican shantytowns. *American Journal of Human Biology* 22:60–68.

Bridger, J. C., and D. R. Maines. 1998. Narrative structures and the Catholic church closings in Detroit. *Qualitative Sociology* 21:319–40.

Bridges, J. S. 1993. Pink or blue: Gender-stereotypic perceptions of infants as conveyed by birth congratulations cards. *Psychology of Women Quarterly* 17:193–206.

Brown, A. H., and T. Green. 2009. Time students spend reading threaded discussions in online graduate courses requiring asynchronous participation. *International Review of Research in Open and Distance Learning* 10:51–64.

Browne, K. E. 2001. Female entrepreneurship in the Caribbean: A multisite, pilot investigation of gender and work. *Human Organization* 60:326–42.

Browne, K. E. 2005. Snowball sampling: Using social networks to research non-heterosexual women. *International Journal of Social Research Methodology* 8:47–60.

Bryant, A., and K. Charmaz, eds. 2007. *The Sage Handbook of Grounded Theory*. London: Sage.

Bryman, A. 1984. The debate about quantitative and qualitative research: A question of method or epistemology? *British Journal of Sociology* 35:75–92.

Bryman, A. 1988. *Quantity and Quality in Social Research*. London: Routledge.

Bryman, A., and R. G. Burgess, eds. 1994. *Analyzing Qualitative Data*. London: Routledge.

Bulmer, M. 1979. Concepts in the analysis of qualitative data. *Sociological Review* 27:651–77.

Burgess, R. G. 1989. *The Ethics of Educational Research*. London: Falmer.

Burke, T. 1998. Cannibal margarine and reactionary Snapple: A comparative examination of rumors about commodities. *International Journal of Cultural Studies* 1:253–70.

Burton, M. L. 2003. Too many questions? The uses of incomplete cyclic designs for paired comparisons. *Field Methods* 15:115–30.

Busa R. 1971. Concordances. In *Encyclopedia of Library and Information Science*, Vol. 5A, K. Lancur and H. Lancour, eds., 592–604. New York: Marcel Dekker.

Buss, D. M. 1985. Human mate selection. *American Scientist* 73:47–51.

Butler-Smith P., S. Cameron, and A. Collins. 1998. Gender differences in mate search effort: An exploratory economic analysis of personal advertisements. *Applied Economics* 30:1277–85.

Byrne, D. 2015. Response to Fugard and Potts: Supporting thinking on sample sizes for thematic analyses: A quantitative tool. *International Journal of Social Research Methodology*. DOI: 10.1080/13645579.2015.1005455

Cachia, P. 2006. Pulp stories in the repertoire of Egyptian folk singers. *British Journal of Middle Eastern Studies* 33:117–29.

Calder, N. 1993. *Studies in Early Muslim Jurisprudence*. New York: Oxford University Press.

Calfano, B. R., and P. A. Djupe. 2009. God talk religious cues and electoral support. *Political Research Quarterly* 62:329–39.

Cambon de Lavalette, B. C. Tijus, S. Poitrenaud, C. Leproux, J. Bergeronc, and J.-P. Thouez. 2009. Pedestrian crossing decision-making: A situational and behavioral approach. *Safety Science* 47:1248–53.

Cameron S., and A. Collins. 1998. Sex differences in stipulated preferences in personal advertisements. *Psychological Reports* 82:119–23.

Campbell, D. T. 1988. Qualitative knowing in action research. In *Methodology and Epistemology for Social Science: Selected Papers*, E. S. Overman, ed., 360–76. Chicago: University of Chicago Press.

Cannell, C. F., and R. L. Kahn. 1968. Interviewing. In *The Handbook of Social Psychology*, Vol. 2, *Research Methods*, G. Lindzey and E. Aronson, eds., 526–95. Reading, MA: Addison-Wesley.

Capello, M. 2005. Photo interviews: Eliciting data through conversations with children. *Field Methods* 17:170–82.

Carballo-Diéguez, A., and J. Bauermeister. 2004. "Barebacking": Intentional condomless anal sex in HIV-risk contexts. Reasons for and against it. *Journal of Homosexuality* 47:1–16.

Carbon, C. C., and S. Albrecht. 2012. Bartlett's schema theory: The unreplicated "portrait d'homme" series from 1932. *Quarterly Journal of Experimental Psychology* 65:2258–70.

Carey, J. W., and D. Gelaude. 2008. Systematic methods for collecting and analyzing multidisciplinary team-based qualitative data. In *Handbook for Team-based Qualitative Research*, G. Guest and K. M. MacQueen, eds., 227–74. Lanham, MD: AltaMira.

Carey, J. W., M. Morgan, and M. J. Oxtoby. 1996. Intercoder agreement in analysis of responses to open-ended interview questions: Examples from tuberculosis research. *Cultural Anthropology Methods Journal* 8:1–5.

Carey, M. A. 2012. *Focus Group Research*. Walnut Creek, CA: Left Coast Press, Inc.

Carley, K. 1988. Formalizing the social expert's knowledge. *Sociological Methods and Research* 17:165–232.

Carlson, R. G., J. Wang, and H. A. Siegal. 1994. An ethnographic approach to targeted sampling: Problems and solutions in AIDS prevention research among injection drug and crack-cocaine users. *Human Organization* 53:278–86.

Carlson, T. A., G. Alvarez, D. A. Wu, and F. J. J. Verstraten. 2010. Rapid assimilation of external objects into the body schema. *Psychological Science* 21:1000–5.

Caron, C. D., and B. J. Bowers. 2003. Deciding whether to continue, share or relinquish caregiving: Caregiver views. *Qualitative Health Research* 13:1252–71.

Carothers, C., C. Brown, K. J. Moerlein, J. A. López, D. B. Andersen, and B. Retherford. 2014. Measuring perceptions of climate change in northern Alaska: Pairing ethnography with cultural consensus analysis. *Ecology and Society* 19:27. http://dx.doi.org/10.5751/ES-06913-190427 (accessed November 6, 2014).

Casagrande, J. B., and K. L. Hale. 1967. Semantic relationships in Papago folk-definitions. In *Studies in Southwestern Ethnolinguistics: Meaning and History in the Languages of the American Southwest*, D. H. Hymes and W. E. Bittle, eds., 165–93. Paris: Mouton.

Caspi, A., T. E. Moffitt, J. Morgan, M. Rutter, A. Taylor, L. Arseneault, L. Tully, C. Jacobs, J. Kim-Cohen, and M. Polo-Thomas. 2004. Maternal expressed emotion predicts children's antisocial behavior problems: Using monozygotic-twin differences to identify environmental effects on behavioral development. *Developmental Psychology* 40:149–61.

Casson, R. 1983. Schemata in cultural anthropology. *Annual Review of Anthropology* 12:429–62.

Catania, J. A., D. Binson, J. Canchola, L. M. Pollack, W. Hauck, and T. J. Coates. 1996. Effects of interviewer gender, interviewer choice, and item wording on responses to questions concerning sexual behavior. *Public Opinion Quarterly* 60:345–75.

Caulkins, D. D. 2001. Consensus, clines, and edges in Celtic cultures. *Cross-Cultural Research* 35:109–26.

Cavanaugh, J. R. 2007. Making salami, producing Bergamo: The transformation of value. *Ethnos* 72:149–72.

Chang, C., and K. Fang. 2012. Use of ontology-based ethnographic decision tree model to explore MMORPGs. In *Information Science and Service Science and Data Mining (ISSDM), 2012 6th International Conference on New Trends in Information Science, Service Science and Data Mining* (pp. 755–59). IEEE. Taipei, October 23–25, pp. 755–59.

Chaplin, E. 1994. *Sociology and Visual Representation*. London: Routledge.

Charmaz, K. 1987. Struggling for a self: Identity levels of the chronically ill. In *The Experience and Management of Chronic Illness. Research in the Sociology of Health Care*, Vol. 6, J. A. Roth and P. Conrad, eds., 283–307. Greenwich, CT: JAI.

Charmaz, K. 1990. "Discovering" chronic illness: Using grounded theory. *Social Science and Medicine* 30:1161–72.

Charmaz, K. 1991. *Good Days, Bad Days: The Self in Chronic Illness and Time*. New Brunswick, NJ: Rutgers University Press.

Charmaz, K. 1995a. Grounded theory. In *Rethinking Methods in Psychology*, J. A. Smith, R. Harré, and L. van Langenhove, eds., 27–49. London: Sage.

Charmaz, K. 1995b. Body, identity, and self: Adapting to impairment. *Sociological Quarterly* 36:657–80.

Charmaz, K. 2000. Grounded theory: Objectivist and constructivist methods. In *The Handbook of Qualitative Research*, 2d ed., N. K. Denzin and Y. S. Lincoln, eds., 507–35. Thousand Oaks, CA: Sage.

Charmaz, K. 2002. Qualitative interviewing and grounded theory analysis. In *Handbook of Interview Research*, J. F. Gubrium and J. A. Holstein, eds., 675–94. Thousand Oaks, CA: Sage.

Charmaz, K. 2006. *Constructing Grounded Theory: A Practical Guide through Qualitative Analysis.* Thousand Oaks, CA: Sage.

Charmaz, K. 2014. *Constructing Grounded Theory: A Practical Guide through Qualitative Analysis*, 2d ed. Thousand Oaks, CA: Sage.

Chatterjee, I. 2007. Packaging of identity and identifiable packages: A study of women-commodity negotiation through product packaging. *Gender, Place and Culture* 14:293–316.

Chen, Y., C. Latkin, D. C. Celentano, X. Yang, X. Li, G. Xia, J. Miao, and P. J. Surkan. 2012. Delineating interpersonal communication networks: A study of the diffusion of an intervention among female entertainment workers in Shanghai, China. *AIDS Behavior* 16:2004–14.

Chen, Y.-N. K. 2010. Examining the presentation of self in popular blogs: A cultural perspective. *Chinese Journal of Communication* 3:28–41.

Cho, G. E., T. L. Sandel, P. J. Miller, and S.-H. Wang. 2005. What do grandmothers think about self-esteem? American and Taiwanese folk theories revisited. *Social Development* 14:701–21.

Chomsky, N. 1957. *Syntactic Sructures.* Series Janua Linguarum, number 4. s-Gravenhage: Mouton.

Christopherson, N., M. Janning, and E. D. McConnell. 2002. Two kicks forward, one kick back: A content analysis of media discourses on the 1999 women's World Cup soccer championship. *Sociology of Sport Journal* 19:170–88.

Churchill, S. L., V. L. Plano Clark, K. Prochaska-Cue, J. W. Creswell, and L. Ontai-Grzebik. 2007. How rural low-income families have fun: A grounded theory study. *Journal of Leisure Research* 39:271–94.

Citro, C. F., D. R. Ilgen, and C. B. Marrett, eds. 2003. *Protecting Participants and Facilitating Social and Behavioral Sciences Research. Panel on Institutional Review Boards, Surveys, and Social Science Research, Committee on National Statistics and Board on Behavioral, Cognitive, and Sensory Sciences, Division of Behavioral Sciences and Education, National Research Council of the National Academies.* Washington, DC: National Academies Press.

Clark, G. K. 1967. *The Critical Historian.* London: Heinemann Educational Books.

Clark, L., and L. Zimmer. 2001. What we learned from a photographic component in a study of Latino children's health. *Field Methods* 13:303–28.

Clover, C. J. 1992. *Men, Women, and Chainsaws: Gender in the Modern Horror Film.* Princeton, NJ: Princeton University Press.

Coffey, A., and P. Atkinson. 1996. *Making Sense of Qualitative Data: Complementary Research Strategies.* Thousand Oaks, CA: Sage.

Cohen, E. H., and J. Valencia. 2008. Political protest and power distance. *Bulletin of Sociological Methodology* 99:54–72.

Cohen, J. 1960. A coefficient of agreement for nominal scales. *Educational and Psychological Measurement* 20:37–48.

Cohen, N., and T. Arieli. 2011. Field research in conflict environments: Methodological challenges and snowball sampling. *Journal of Peace Research* 48:423–35.

Colby, B. N. 1966. The analysis of culture content and the patterning of narrative concern in texts. *American Anthropologist* 68:374–88.

Cole, A. L., and J. G. Knowles. 2001. *Lives in Context: The Art of Life History Research*. Walnut Creek, CA: AltaMira.

Collaborative Group on Hormonal Factors in Breast Cancer. 2002. Breast cancer and breastfeeding: Collaborative reanalysis of individual data from 47 epidemiological studies in 30 countries, including 50,302 women with breast cancer and 96,973 women without the disease. *The Lancet* 360:187–95.

Colley, S. K., and A. Neal. 2012. Automated text analysis to examine qualitative differences in safety schema among upper managers, supervisors and workers. *Safety Science* 50:1775–85.

Collier, J., Jr., and M. Collier. 1986 [1967]. *Visual Anthropology: Photography as a Research Method*, rev. and expanded ed. Albuquerque: University of New Mexico Press.

Collings, P. 2009. Participant observation and phased assertion as research strategies in the Canadian arctic. *Field Methods* 21:133–53.

Collins, A., and D. Gentner. 1987. How people construct mental models. In *Cultural Models in Language and Thought*, D. Holland and N. Quinn, eds., 243–65. Cambridge: Cambridge University Press.

Collins, C. C., and W. W. Dressler. 2008. Cultural models of domestic violence: Perspectives of social work and anthropology students. *Journal of Social Work Education* 44:53–73.

Collins, R. L. 2011. Content analysis of gender roles in media: Where are we now and where should we go? *Sex Roles* 64:290–98.

Conrad, C. F. 1978. A grounded theory of academic change. *Sociology of Education* 51:101–12.

Conrad, F. G., and M. F. Schober. 2010. New frontiers in standardized survey interviewing. In *Handbook of Emergent Methods*, S. N. Hesse-Biber and P. Leavy, eds., 173–188. New York: Guilford Press.

Converse, J. M., and H. Schuman. 1974. *Conversations at Random: Survey Research as the Interviewers See It*. New York: John Wiley.

Coombes, A. 1994. *Reinventing Africa. Museums, Material Culture, and Popular Imagination in Late Victorian and Edwardian England*. New Haven, CT: Yale University Press.

Corbin, J., and A. Strauss. 2008. *Basics of Qualitative Research*, 3d ed. Thousand Oaks, CA: Sage.

Cornell, L. L. 1984. Why are there no spinsters in Japan? *Journal of Family History* 9:326–39.

Cornwell, G., and M. Atia. 2012. Imaginative geographies of Amazigh activism in Morocco. *Social and Cultural Geography* 13:255–74.

Corti, L., and G. Backhouse. 2005. Acquiring qualitative data for secondary analysis. *Forum: Qualitative Social Research* 6(2). http://www.qualitative-research.net/index.php/fqs/article/view/459 (accessed April 26, 2015).

Côté-Arsenault, D., D. Bidlack, and A. Humm. 2001. Women's emotions and concerns during pregnancy following perinatal loss. *MCN: The American Journal of Maternal Child Nursing* 26:128–34.

Cowan, G., and M. O'Brien. 1990. Gender and survival vs. death in slasher films: A content analysis. *Sex Roles* 23:187–96.

Coyne, I. T. 1997. Sampling in qualitative research. Purposeful and theoretical sampling: Merging or clear boundaries? *Journal of Advanced Nursing* 26:623–30.

Crabtree, B. F., and W. L. Miller, eds. 1999. *Doing Qualitative Research*, 2d ed. Thousand Oaks, CA: Sage.

Crane, D., and L. Bovone. 2006. Approaches to material culture: The sociology of fashion and clothing. *Poetics* 34:319–33.

Cressey, D. R. 1950. The criminal violation of financial trust. *American Sociological Review* 15:738–43.

Cressey, D. R. 1953. *Other People's Money: A Study in the Social Psychology of Embezzlement*. Glencoe, IL: Free Press.

Creswell, J. W. 1998. *Qualitative Inquiry and Research Design: Choosing among Five Traditions*. Thousand Oaks, CA: Sage.

Creswell, J. W. 2003. *Research Design: Qualitative, Quantitative and Mixed Methods Approaches*. Thousand Oaks, CA: Sage.

Creswell, J. W., and V. L. Plano Clark. 2011. *Designing and Conducting Mixed Methods Research*, 2d ed. Thousand Oaks, CA: Sage.

Crona, B., A. Wutich, A. Brewis, and M. Gartin. 2013. Perceptions of climate change: Linking local and global perceptions through a cultural knowledge approach. *Climatic Change* 119:519–31.

Cronqvist, L. 2007. Tosmana—Tool for small-*n* analysis [Version 1.3]. Marburg, Germany. http://www.compasss.org/software.htm#tosmana (accessed October 8, 2014).

Crouch, M., and H. McKenzie. 2006. The logic of small samples in interview-based qualitative research. *Social Science Information* 45:483–99.

Crume, T. L., C. DiGiuseppe, T. Byers, A. P. Sirotnak, and C. J. Garrett. 2002. Underascertainment of child maltreatment fatalities by death certificates, 1990–1998. *Pediatrics* 110:e18. http://pediatrics.aappublications.org/cgi/reprint/110/2/e18 (accessed August 25, 2013).

Cunningham, G. B., M. Sagas, M. L. Sartore, M. L. Amsden, and A. Schellhase. 2004. Gender representation in the NCAA News: Is the glass half or half empty? *Sex Roles* 50:861–70.

Curle, L., and H. Keller. 2010. Resident interactions at mealtime: An exploratory study. *European Journal of Ageing* 7:189–200.

Curtis, S., W. Gesler, G. Smith, and S. Washburn. 2000. Approaches to sampling and case selection in qualitative research: Examples in the geography of health. *Social Science and Medicine* 50:1001–14.

Cutliffe, J. R. 2005. Adapt or adopt: Developing and transgressing the methodological boundaries of grounded theory. *Journal of Advanced Nursing* 51:421–28.

Daller, H, R. Van Hout, and J. Treffers-Daller. 2003. Lexical richness in the spontaneous speech of bilinguals. *Applied Linguistics* 24:197–222.

Daly, M., and M. Wilson. 1988. *Homicide*. New York: Aldine de Gruyter.

Daly, M., and M. Wilson. 1998. *The Truth about Cinderella*. New Haven, CT: Yale University Press.

D'Andrade, R. G. 1991. The identification of schemas in naturalistic data. In *Person Schemas and Maladaptive Interpersonal Patterns*, M. J. Horowitz, ed., 279–301. Chicago: University of Chicago Press.

D'Andrade, R. G. 1995. *The Development of Cognitive Anthropology*. Cambridge: Cambridge University Press.

D'Andrade, R. G., N. Quinn, S. B. Nerlove, and A. K. Romney. 1972. Categories of disease in American English and Mexican Spanish. In *Multidimensional Scaling,* Vol. 2, *Applications,* A. K. Romney, R. Shepard, and S. B. Nerlove, eds., 9–54. New York: Seminar Press.

D'Andrade, R. G., and C. Strauss, eds. 1992. *Human Motives and Cultural Models.* New York: Cambridge University Press.

Danielson, W. A., and D. L. Lasorsa. 1997. Perceptions of social change: 100 years of frontpage content in the *New York Times* and the *Los Angeles Times.* In *Text Analysis for the Social Sciences: Methods for Drawing Statistical Inferences from Texts and Transcripts,* C. W. Roberts, ed., 103–15. Mahwah, NJ: Lawrence Erlbaum.

Daniulaityte, R. 2004. Making sense of diabetes: Cultural models, gender, and individual adjustment to Type 2 diabetes in a Mexican community. *Social Science and Medicine* 59:1899–912.

Danowski, J. 1982. Computer-mediated communication: A network-based content analysis using a CBBS conference. In *Communication Yearbook,* R. Bostrom, ed., 905–25. New Brunswick, NJ: Transaction Books.

Danowski, J. 1993. Network analysis of message content. In *Progress in Communication Science,* W. M. Richards and G. A. Barnett, eds., 197–222. Norwood, NJ: Ablex.

Danowski, J. 2009. WORDij 3.0. Chicago: University of Illinois. http://wordij.net (accessed January 28, 2016).

Dant, T. 2005. *Materiality and Society.* Maidenhead, Berks, England: Open University Press.

Dant, T. 2006. *Material Civilization: Things and Society.* British Journal of Sociology 57:289–308.

Dardis, F. E. 2006. Marginalization devices in U.S. press coverage of Iraq war protest: A content analysis. *Mass Communication and Society* 9:117–35.

Davidson, C. 2010. Transcription matters. Transcribing talk and interaction to facilitate conversation analysis of the taken-for-granted in young children's interactions *Journal of Early Childhood Research* 8:115–31.

Davies, C. E. 2006. Gendered sense of humor as expressed through aesthetic typifications. *Journal of Pragmatics* 38:96–113.

Davis, R. E., M. P. Couper, N. K. Janz, C. H. Caldwell, and K. Resnicow. 2010. Interviewer effects in public health surveys. *Health Education Research* 25:14–26.

Deaner, R. O., and B. A. Smith. 2013. Sex differences in sports across 50 societies. *Cross-Cultural Research* 47:268–309.

De Chesnay, M. 2015. *Nursing Research Using Life History: Qualitative Designs and Methods in Nursing.* New York: Springer.

DeCuir-Gunby, J. T., P. L. Marshall, and A. W. McCulloch. 2010. Developing and using a codebook for the analysis of interview data: An example from a professional development research project. *Field Methods* 23:136–55.

DeCuir-Gunby, J. T., P. L. Marshall, and A. W. McCulloch. 2012. Using mixed methods to analyze video data: A mathematics teacher professional development example. *Journal of Mixed Methods Research* 6:199–216.

De Fina, A. 1997. An analysis of Spanish bien as a marker of classroom management in teacher–student interaction. *Journal of Pragmatics* 28:337–54.

De Fina, A. 2007. Code-switching and the construction of ethnic identity in a community of practice. *Language and Society* 36:371–92.

DeJordy, R., S. P. Borgatti, and C. Roussin. 2007. Visualizing proximity data. *Field Methods* 19:239–63.

Demarest, J., and J. Garner. 1992. The representation of women's roles in women's magazines over the past 30 years. *Journal of Psychology: Interdisciplinary and Applied* 126:357–68.

de Munck, V., N. Dudley, and J. Cardinale. 2002. Cultural models of gender in Sri Lanka and the United States. *Ethnology* 41:225–61.

Denney, A. S., and R. Tewksbury. 2013. Characteristics of successful personal ads in a BDSM on-line community. *Deviant Behavior* 34:153–68.

Dennis, W. 1940. Does culture appreciably affect patterns of infant behavior? *The Journal of Social Psychology* 12:305–17.

Denzin, N. 1970. *The Research Act*. Englewood Cliffs, NJ: Prentice Hall.

DeRocher, J. E., M. S. Miron, S. M. Patton, and C. S. Pratt. 1973. *The Counting of Words: A Review of the History, and Theory of Word Counts with Annotated Bibliography*. Springfield, VA: National Technical Information Service, ERIC Document Number ED098814.

de Sousa Campos, L. O. Emma, and J. de Oliveira Siqueira. 2002. Sex differences in mate selection strategies: Content analyses and responses to personal advertisements in Brazil. *Evolution and Human Behavior* 23:395–406.

De Swert, K. 2012. Calculating inter-coder reliability in media content analysis using Krippendorff's Alpha. http://tinyurl.com/pxm2et6 (accessed April 28, 2015).

Devine, E. B., W. Hollingworth, R. N. Hansen, N. M. Lawless, J. L.Wilson-Norton, D. P. Martin, D. K. Blough, and S. D. Sullivan. 2010. Electronic prescribing at the point of care: A time–motion study in the primary care setting. *Health Services Research* 45:152–71.

de Vreese, C. H., and H. G. Boomgaarden. 2006. Media effects on public opinion about the enlargement of the European Union. *Journal of Common Market Studies* 44:419–36.

de Vries, B., and J. Rutherford. 2004. Memorializing loved ones on The World Wide Web. *Omega: Journal of Death and Dying* 49:5–26.

DeWalt, B. R. 1979. *Modernization in a Mexican Ejido*. New York: Cambridge University Press.

DeWalt, K. M., and B. R. DeWalt. 2011. *Participant Observation: A Guide for Fieldworkers*. Lanham, MD: Rowman and Littlefield.

Dewey, J. 1910. Systematic inference: Induction and deduction. In *How We Think*, J. Dewey, ed., 79–100. Lexington, MA: D. C. Heath.

Dey, I. 1993. *Qualitative Data Analysis: A User Friendly Guide for Social Scientists*. London: Routledge and Kegan Paul.

Dey, I. 1999. *Grounding Grounded Theory: Guidelines for Qualitative Inquiry*. San Diego: Academic Press.

Díaz de Rada, V. 2005. The effect of follow-up mailings on the response rate and response quality in mail surveys. *Quality and Quantity* 39:1–18.

Dickerson, S. S., M. A. Neary, and M. Hyche-Johnson. 2000. Native American graduate nursing students' learning experiences. *Journal of Nursing Scholarship* 32:89–196.

Dickson, D. B., J. Olsen, P. F. Dahm, and M. S. Wachtel. 2005. Where do you go when you die? A cross-cultural test of the hypothesis that infrastructure predicts individual eschatology. *Journal of Anthropological Research* 61:53–79.

Dijkstra, W., and J. van der Zouwen. 1982. *Response Behaviour in the Survey Interview*. New York: Academic Press.

Dilthey, W. 1989 [1883]. *Introduction to the Human Sciences*. Princeton, NJ: Princeton University Press.

Dilthey, W. 1996. *Hermeneutics and the Study of History*, R. A. Makkreel and F. Rodi, eds. Princeton, NJ: Princeton University Press.

Dittmar, H. 1991. Meanings of material possessions as reflections of identity: Gender and socio-material position in society. *Journal of Social Behavior and Personality* 6:165–86.

Dittmar, H. 1994. Material possessions as stereotypes: Material images of different socio-economic groups. *Journal of Economic Psychology* 15:561–85.

Doerfel, M. L. 1998. What constitutes semantic network analysis? A comparison of research methodologies. *Connections* 21:16–26.

Doerfel, M. L., and G. A. Barnett. 1999. A semantic network analysis of the International Communication Association. *Human Communication Research* 25:589–603.

Dong, E., and G. Chick. 2012. Leisure constraints in six Chinese cities. *Leisure Sciences: An Interdisciplinary Journal* 34:417–435. DOI: 10.1080/01490400.2012.714702

Donnenworth, G. V., and U. G. Foa. 1974. Effects of resource class on retaliation to injustice in interpersonal exchange. *Journal of Personality and Social Psychology* 29:785–93.

Dordick, G. A. 1996. More than refuge. *Journal of Contemporary Ethnography* 24:373–404.

Doucet, L., and K. A. Jehn. 1997. Analyzing harsh words in a sensitive setting: American expatriates in communist China. *Journal of Organizational Behavior* 18:559–82.

Doyle, K. O. 2001. Meanings of wealth in European and Chinese fairy tales. *American Behavioral Scientist* 45:191–204.

Draucker, C. B., D. S. Martsolf, R. Ross, and T. B. Rusk. 2007. Theoretical sampling and category development in grounded theory. *Qualitative Health Research* 17:1137–48.

Drazin, A., and D. Frolich. 2007. Good intentions: Remembering through framing photographs in English homes. *Ethnos* 72:51–76.

Dressler, W. W., M. C. Balieiro, R. P. Ribeiro, and J. E. dos Santos. 2007. A prospective study of cultural consonance and depressive symptoms in urban Brazil. *Social Science and Medicine* 65:2058–69.

Dressler, W. W., C. D. Borges, and M. C. Balierio. 2005. Measuring cultural consonance: Examples with special reference to measurement theory in anthropology. *Field Methods* 17:331–55.

Drew, P., and J. Heritage, eds. 2006. *Conversation Analysis*. Thousand Oaks, CA: Sage.

Dunbar, R. and L. Barrett, eds. 2007. *Oxford Handbook of Evolutionary Psychology*. Oxford: Oxford University Press.

Dundes, A. 1965. *The Study of Folklore*. Englewood Cliffs, NJ: Prentice Hall.

Dundes, A. 1980. *Interpreting Folklore*. Bloomington: Indiana University Press.

Dundes, A., ed. 1982. *Cinderella. A Folklore Casebook*. New York: Garland.

Dundes, A. 1989. *Folklore Matters*. Knoxville: University of Tennessee Press.

Durrenberger, E. P. 2003. Using paired comparisons to measure reciprocity. *Field Methods* 15:271–88.

Durrenberger, E. P., and S. Erem. 2005. Checking for relationships across domains measured by triads and paired comparisons. *Field Methods* 17:150–69.

Duşa, A., and A. Thiem. 2014. QCA: Qualitative Comparative Analysis. R Package Version 2.1 http://cran.r-project.org/web/packages/QCA/index.html (accessed April 21, 2016).

Dy, S. M., H. R. Rubin, and H. P. Lehman. 2005. Why do patients and families request transfers to tertiary care? A qualitative study. *Social Science and Medicine* 61:1846–53.

Eastman K. L., R. Corona, G. W. Ryan, A. L. Warsofsky, and M. A. Schuster. 2005. Developing a worksite-based program for parents of adolescents to promote healthy sexual development: A qualitative study. *Perspectives on Sexual and Reproductive Health* 37:62–69.

Ebbinghaus, H. 1913. *Memory: A Contribution to Experimental Psychology*, H. A. Ruger and C. E. Bussenius, trans. New York: Teachers College, Columbia University.

Eby, J., P. Kitchen, and A. Williams. 2012. Perceptions of quality life in Hamilton's neighbourhood hubs: A qualitative analysis. *Social Indicators Research* 10:299–315.

Ecocultural Scale Project. 2001. *The Ecocultural Family Interview. Codebook. Final Version*. Los Angeles: UCLA Center for Culture and Health.

Edgell, P., and D. Docka. 2007. Beyond the nuclear family? Familism and gender ideology in diverse religious communities. *Sociological Forum* 22:25–50.

Edwards, S. L., M. L. Slattery, and K.-N. Ma. 1998. Measurement errors stemming from nonrespondents present at in-person interviews. *Annals of Epidemiology* 8:272–77.

Eerola, T., J. Louhivuori, and E. Lebaka. 2009. Expectancy in Sami Yoiks revisited: The role of data-driven and schema-driven knowledge in the formation of melodic expectations. *Musicae Scientiae* 13:231–72.

Elahi, B., and G. Cos. 2005. An immigrant's dream and the audacity of hope: The 2004 convention addresses of Barack Obama and Arnold Schwarzeneger. *American Behavioral Scientist* 49:454–65.

El Guindi, F. 2004. *Visual Anthropology: Essential Method and Theory*. Walnut Creek, CA: AltaMira.

Ember, C. R., M. Ember, A. Korotayev, and V. de Munck. 2005. Valuing thinness or fatness in women. Reevaluating the effect of resources scarcity. *Evolution and Human Behavior* 26:257–70.

Emerson, R. W. 1907. Essays. E. H. L. Turin, ed. New York: Charles E. Merrill Co. http://www.gutenberg.org/files/1664/16643-h/16643-h.htm#SELF-RELIANCE (accessed January 29, 2016).

Emigh, R. J. 1997. The power of negative thinking: The use of negative case methodology in the development of sociological theory. *Theory and Society* 5:649–84.

Emmel, N. 2015. Themes, variables, and the limits to calculating sample size in qualitative research: A response to Fugard and Potts. *International Journal of Social Research Methodology* 18:685–86. DOI: 10.1080/13645579.2015.1005457

Ensign, J., and J. Gittelsohn. 1998. Health and access to care: Perspectives of homeless youth in Baltimore City, U.S.A. *Social Science and Medicine* 47:2087–99.

Escobar, M., and H. Roman. 2011. Presentation of self in cyberspace: An analysis of self-definitions in blogs and social networks. *Revista de Psicología Social* 26:207–22.

Ess, C., and Association of Internet Researchers (AoIR). 2002. Ethical decision-making and Internet research. Recommendations from the AoIR Ethics Working Committee. www.aoir.org/reports/ethics.pdf (acessed February 27, 2015).

Evers, A., and M. Sieverding. 2014. Why do highly qualified women (still) earn less? Gender differences in long-term predictors of career success. *Psychology of Women Quarterly* 38:93–106.

Eyre, S. L., and S. G. Milstein. 1999. What leads to sex? Adolescent preferred partners and reasons for sex. *Journal of Research on Adolescence* 9:277–307.

Eyssel, F., and G. Bohner. 2011. Schema effects of rape myth acceptance on judgments of guilt and blame in rape cases: The role of perceived entitlement to judge. *Journal of Interpersonal Violence* 26:1579–605.

Fairclough, N. 1995. *Critical Discourse Analysis: The Critical Study of Language*. London: Longman.

Fairclough, N. 2010. *Critical Discourse Analysis: The Critical Study of Language*, 2d ed. Harlow, UK: Longman.

Fairweather, J. R. 1999. Understanding how farmers choose between organic and conventional production: Results from New Zealand and policy implications. *Agriculture and Human Values* 16:51–63.

Fan, D. P., and C. L. Shaffer. 1990. Use of open-ended essays and computer content analysis to survey college students' knowledge of AIDS. *College Health* 38:221–29.

Fangman, T. D., J. P. Ogle, M. C. Bickle, and D. Rouner. 2004. Promoting female weight management in 1920s print media: An analysis of *Ladies' Home Journal* and *Vogue* magazines. *Family and Consumer Sciences Research Journal* 32:213–53.

Farmer, P. 1994. AIDS-talk and the constitution of cultural models. *Social Science and Medicine* 36:801–9.

Farr, D. 2011. Online women-seeking-women personal ads and the deployment of "tomboy" identities. *Journal of Lesbian Studies* 15:493–506.

Farringdon, J. M., and M. G. Farringdon. 1980. *A Concordance and Word-lists to the Poems of Dylan Thomas*. Swansea, UK: Ariel House.

Feinberg, J. 2014. Wordle. http://www.wordle.net/ (accessed January 29, 2016).

Fenno, R. 1990. *Watching Politicians: Essays on Participant Observation*. Berkeley: Institute of Governmental Studies, University of California at Berkeley.

Fernández, J. 1967. Revitalized words from "the parrot's egg" and "the bull that crashes in the kraal": African cult sermons. In *Essays on the Verbal and Visual Arts. Proceedings of the 1966 Annual Meeting of the American Ethnological Society*, J. Helm, ed., 45–63. Seattle: University of Washington Press.

Fielding, N. 2004. Getting the most from archived qualitative data: Epistemological, practical and professional obstacles. *International Journal of Social Research Methodology: Theory and Practice* 7:97–104.

Fielding, N., and R. Lee. 1996. Diffusion of a methodological innovation: Computer-assisted qualitative data analysis in the UK. *Current Sociology* 44:242–58.

Finkel, S. E., Guterbock, T. M., and M. J. Borg. 1991. Race-of-interviewer effects in a preelection poll: Virginia 1989. *Public Opinion Quarterly* 55:313–30.

Finnis, K. A. 2014. Variation within a Greek–Cypriot community of practice in London: Code-switching, gender, and identity. *Language in Society* 43:287–310.

Firth, J. R. 1935. The technique of semantics. *Transactions of the Philological Society for 1935* 34:36–72. Reprinted in Firth 1957, pp. 7–33.

Firth, J. R. 1957. *Papers in Linguistics 1934–1951*. London: Oxford University Press.

Fitzgerald, G. A., and M. L. Doerfel. 2004. The use of semantic network analysis to manage customer complaints. *Communication Research Reports* 21:231–42.

Fjellman, S. M., and H. Gladwin. 1985. Haitian family patterns of migration to South Florida. *Human Organization* 44:301–12.

Flaxman, S. M., and P. W. Sherman. 2000. Morning sickness: A mechanism for protecting mother and embryo. *The Quarterly Review of Biology* 75:113–48.

Fleisher, M. 1998. *Dead End Kids*. Madison: University of Wisconsin Press.

Flick, U. 2002. *An Introduction to Qualitative Research*, 2d ed. London: Sage.

Flores-Macias, F., and C. Lawson. 2008. Effects of interviewer gender on survey responses: Findings from a household survey in Mexico. *International Journal of Public Opinion Research* 20:100–10.

Fluehr-Lobban, C. 1996. Rejoinder to Wax and Herrera. *Human Organization* 55:240. (See also entries for Wax [1996] and for Herrera [1996].)

Fluehr-Lobban, C. 2008. Anthropology and ethics in America's declining imperial age. *Anthropology Today* 24:18–22.

Ford, J. M., T. A. Stetz, M. M. Bott, and B. S. O'Leary. 2000. Automated content analysis of multiple-choice test item banks. *Social Science Computer Review* 18:258–71.

Forgacs, D., ed. 2000. *The Gramsci Reader: Selected Writings 1916–1935*. New York: New York University Press.

Forster, M. 2008. *Friedrich Daniel Ernst Schleiermacher. The Stanford Encyclopedia of Philosophy* (Fall 2008 ed.), E. N. Zalta, ed. http://plato.stanford.edu/archives/fall2008/entries/schleiermacher (accessed April 26, 1015).

Forte, M. C. 2011. The Human Terrain System and anthropology: A review of ongoing public debates. *American Anthropologist* 113:149–53.

Fowler, L. D. 2008. Examination and critique of codebook for textual analysis. In *Proceedings of the Seventh Annual College of Education Research Conference: Urban and International Education Section*, M. S. Plakhotnik and S. M. Nielsen, eds., 38–45. Miami: Florida International University.

Fox, C. 1989–90. A stop list for general text. *Newsletter* ACM SIGIR Forum Homepage archive 24:19–21. New York: ACM.

Frake, C. O. 1964. How to ask for a drink in Subanum. In *Directions in Sociolinguistics*, J. Gumperz and D. Hymes, eds., 127–32. New York: Holt, Rinehart and Winston.

Francis, J. J., M. Johnston, C. Robertson, L. Glidewell, V. Entwistle, M. P. Eccles, and J. M. Grimshaw. 2010. What is an adequate sample size? Operationalising data saturation for theory-based interview studies. *Psychology and Health* 25:1229–45.

Frankel, M. S., and S. Siang. 1999. *Ethical and Legal Aspects of Human Subjects Research on the Internet*. Washington, DC: American Association for the Advancement of Science.

Freelon, D. 2013. ReCal OIR: Ordinal, interval, and ratio intercoder reliability as a web service. *International Journal of Internet Science* 8:10–16.

Freilich, M., ed. 1977. *Marginal Natives at Work: Anthropologists in the Field*, 2d ed. Cambridge, MA: Schenkman.

Fugard, A. J., and H. W. Potts. 2015. Supporting thinking on sample sizes for thematic analyses: A quantitative tool. *International Journal of Social Research Methodology* 18:669–84. DOI: 10.1080/13645579.2015.1005453

Fung, L., and R. Carter. 2007. Cantonese e-discourse: A new hybrid variety of English. *Multilingua* 26:35–66.

Gluckman, M. 1958 [1940]. The analysis of a social situation in modern Zululand. *African Studies* 14:1–30, 147–74. (Reprinted as Rhodes-Livingston Paper No. 28. Manchester, UK: Manchester University Press, 1958.)

Goffman, E. 1959. *The Presentation of Self in Everyday Life.* Garden City, NY: Doubleday.

Goffman, E. 1967. *Interaction Ritual.* Garden City, NY: Anchor Books.

Goffman, E. 1974. *Frame Analysis.* New York: Harper & Row.

Goffman, E. 1979. *Gender Advertisements.* New York: Harper and Row.

Golani, M., and A. Manna. 2012. *Two Sides of the Coin. Independence and Nakba 1948. Two Narratives of the War of 1948 and Its Outcome.* Dordrecht, Netherlands: Republic of Letters Publishing, The Institute for Historical Justice and Reconciliation Series.

Goldenberg, S. 1993. Analytic induction revisited. *The Canadian Journal of Sociology* 18:161–76.

Goldsen, J. M. 1947. Analyzing the contents of mass communication: A step toward inter-group harmony. *International Journal of Opinion and Attitude Research* 1:81–92.

Gomes do Espiritu Santo, M. E., and G. D. Etheredge. 2002. How to reach clients of female sex workers: A survey "by surprise" in brothels in Dakar, Senegal. *Bulletin of the World Health Organization* 80:709–13.

González, R. J. 2007. Towards mercenary anthropology? The new US Army counterinsurgency manual *FM 3-24* and the military-anthropology complex. *Anthropology Today* 23:14–19.

Goode, E. 1996. Gender and courtship entitlement: Responses to personal ads. *Sex Roles* 34:141–69.

Goodwin, C. 1981. *Conversational Organization: Interaction between Speakers and Hearers.* New York: Academic Press.

Goodwin, C. 1986. Gesture as a resource for the organization of mutual orientation. *Semiotica* 62:29–49.

Goodwin, C. 1994. Recording human interaction in natural settings. *Pragmatics* 3:181–209.

Goodwin, C., and J. Heritage. 1990. Conversation analysis. *Annual Review of Anthropology* 19:283–307.

Gorden, R. L. 1987. *Interviewing: Strategy, Techniques, and Tactics,* 4th ed. Homewood, IL: Dorsey.

Gordon, S. 1991. *The History and Philosophy of Social Science.* London: Routledge.

Gottschalk, L. A., and R. J. Bechtel. 1993. *Psychologic and Neuropsychiatric Assessment. Applying the Gottschalk-Gleser Content Analysis Method to Verbal Sample Analysis Using the Gottschalk-Bechtel Computer Scoring System.* Palo Alto, CA: Mind Garden.

Govrin, A. 2006. When the underdog schema dominates the we-ness schema: The case of radical leftist Jewish-Israelis. *Psychoanalytic Review* 93:623–54.

Gramsci, A. 1994. *Letters from Prison,* F. Rosengarten, ed., R. Rosenthal, trans. New York: Columbia University Press.

Graves, T. D., and C. A. Lave. 1972. Determinants of urban migrant Indian wages. *Human Organization* 31:47–61.

Greckhamer, T., and M. Koro-Ljungberg. 2005. The erosion of a method: Examples from grounded theory. *International Journal of Qualitative Studies in Education* 18:729–50.

Green, E. C. 2001. Can qualitative research produce reliable quantitative findings. *Field Methods* 13:3–19.

Greene, J. C. 2007. *Mixed Methods in Social Inquiry*. San Francisco: Jossey-Bass.

Greene, J. C. 2008. Is mixed methods social inquiry a distinctive methodology? *Journal of Mixed Methods Research* 2:17–22.

Greenhalgh, S.1994. Controlling births and bodies. *American Ethnologist* 21:3–30.

Gribble, J. N., H. G. Miller, and S. M. Rogers. 1999. Interview mode and measurement of sexual behaviors: Methodological issues. *Journal of Sex Research* 36:16–24.

Grimmer, J., and B. M. Stewart. 2013. Text as data: The promise and pitfalls of automatic content analysis. Methods for political texts. *Political Analysis* 21:267–97.

Groom, C. J., and J. W. Pennebaker. 2005. The language of love: Sex, sexual orientation, and language use in online personal advertisements. *Sex Roles: A Journal of Research* 52:447–61.

Gross, D. R. 1984. Time allocation: A tool for the study of cultural behavior. *Annual Review of Anthropology* 13:519–58.

Guba, E. G., and Y. S. Lincoln. 1981. *Effective Evaluation*. San Francisco: Jossey-Bass.

Guba, E. G., and Y. S. Lincoln. 1994. Competing paradigms in qualitative research. In *Handbook of Qualitative Research*, N. K. Denzin and Y. S. Lincoln, eds., 105–17. Thousand Oaks, CA: Sage.

Gubrium, J. F., and J. A. Holstein. 2002. *Handbook of Interview Research: Context and Method*. Thousand Oaks, CA: Sage.

Gubrium, J. F., and J. A. Holstein. 2009. *Analyzing Narrative Reality*. Thousand Oaks, CA: Sage.

Gudelunas, D. 2005. Online personal ads: Community and sex, virtually. *Journal of Homosexuality* 49:1–33.

Guest, G. 2015. Sampling and selecting participants in field research. In *Handbook of Methods in Cultural Anthropology*, 2d ed., H. R. Bernard and C. Gravlee, eds., 215–50. Lanham, MD: Rowman & Littlefield.

Guest, G., A. Bunce, and L. Johnson. 2006. How many interviews are enough? An experiment with data saturation and variability. *Field Methods* 18:59–82.

Guest, G., E. Namey, and K. McKenna. In press. How many focus groups are enough? An(other) experiment with data saturation and variability. *Field Methods* 29.

Guignon, C. B., ed. 2006. *The Cambridge Companion to Heidegger*, 2d ed. New York: Cambridge University Press.

Gummesson, E. 2000. *Qualitative Methods in Management Research*, 2d ed. Thousand Oaks, CA: Sage.

Gumperz, J. J. 1982. *Discourse Strategies*. Cambridge: Cambridge University Press.

Gürtler L., and G. L. Huber. 2014. *AQUAD 7 Manual—R Integration*. Tübingen, Germany: Günter Huber Softwarevetrieb. www.aquad.de/materials/manual_aquad7/AQUAD_R-e.pdf (accessed October 12, 2014).

Gustafson, J. 2012. Journalistic judgment calls: A grounded theory exploring journalists' coverage of environmental and climate news. Ph.D. dissertation, Northern Arizona University.

Guthrie, T. H. 2007. Good words: Chief Joseph and the production of Indian speech(es), texts, and subjects. *Ethnohistory* 54:509–46.

Habibi, M. R., M. Laroche, and M.-O. Richard. 2014. The roles of brand community and community engagement in building brand trust on social media. *Computers in Human Behavior* 37:152–61.

Hadaway, C. K., and P. L. Marler. 2005. How many Americans attend worship each week? An alternative approach to measurement. *Journal for the Scientific Study of Religion* 44:307–22.

Hagaman, A., and A. Wutich. In press. How many interviews are enough to identify metathemes in multi-sited and cross-cultural research? Another perspective on Guest, Bunce, and Johnson's (2006) landmark study. *Field Methods* 29.

Hak, T., and T. Bernts. 1996. Coder training: Theoretical training or practical socialization? *Qualitative Sociology* 19:235–57.

Haldrup, M., and J. Larsen. 2007. Material cultures of tourism. *Leisure Studies* 25:275–89.

Hale, A. 2001. Representing the Cornish: Contesting heritage interpretation in Cornwall. *Tourist Studies* 1:185–96.

Halford, G. S. 1993. *Childrens's Understanding: The Development of Mental Models*. Hillsdale, NJ: Lawrence. Erlbaum.

Hamilton, L., C. Geist, and B. Powell. 2011. Marital name change as a window into gender attitudes. *Gender and Society* 25:145–75.

Hamlet, J. D. 1994. Religious discourse as cultural narrative: A critical analysis of African-American sermons. *Western Journal of Black Studies* 18:11–17.

Hammersley, M. 2004. Towards a usable past for qualitative research. *International Journal of Social Research Methodology* 7:19–27.

Hammersley, M. 2009. Against the ethicists: On the evils of ethical regulation. *International Journal of Social Research Methodology* 12:211–25.

Hammersley, M. 2010a. Can we re-use qualitative data via secondary analysis? Notes on some terminological and substantive issues. *Sociological Research Online* 15. http://www.socre sonline.org.uk/15/1/5.html (accessed September 7, 2013).

Hammersley, M. 2010b. A historical and comparative note on the relationship between analytic induction and grounded theorising. *Forum: Qualitative Social Research* 10:Article 4.

Hammersley, M. 2015. Sampling and thematic analysis: A response to Fugard and Potts. *International Journal of Social Research Methodology*. In press:1–2. DOI:10.1080/13645579. 2015.1056578

Handloff, R. 1982. Prayers, amulets and charms: Health and social control. *African Studies Review* 25:185–94.

Handwerker, W. P. 2003. Sample design. In *Encyclopedia of Social Measurement*, K. Kempf-Leonard, ed., 429–36. San Diego: Academic Press.

Handwerker, W. P., J. Hatcherson, and J. Herbert. 1997. Sampling guidelines for cultural data. *Cultural Anthropology Methods Journal* 9:7–9.

Hanneman, R. A., and M. Riddle. 2005. Introduction to social network methods. Riverside: University of California. http://faculty.ucr.edu/~hanneman/ (accessed December 26, 2014).

Hanson, B. 2008. Whither qualitative/quantitative? Grounds for methodological convergence. *Quality and Quantity* 42:97–111.

Hardesty, J. L., and L. H. Ganong. 2006. How women make custody decisions and manage co-parenting with abusive former husbands. *Journal of Social and Personal Relationships* 23:543–63.

Hardré, P. L., and D. W. Sullivan. 2008. Teacher perceptions and individual differences: How they influence rural teachers' motivating strategies. *Journal of Social and Personal Relationships* 23:543–63.

Harman, R. C. 2001. Activities of contemporary Mayan elders. *Journal of Cross Cultural Gerontology* 16:57–77.

Harper, D. 2012. *Visual Sociology*. New York: Routledge.

Harris, R. 2005. Wang Luobin: Folk song king of the Northwest or song thief? *Modern China* 31:381–408.

Hart, R. P., and J. P. Childers. 2005. The evolution of candidate Bush: A rhetorical analysis. *American Behavioral Scientist* 49:180–97.

Hartmann, P. 1994. Interviewing when the spouse is present. *International Journal of Public Opinion Research* 6:298–306.

Harvey, S. M., and S. Thorburn Bird. 2004. What makes women feel powerful? An exploratory study of relationship power and sexual decision-making with African Americans at risk for HIV/STDs. *Women and Health* 39:1–18.

Hatch, J. A., and R. Wisniewski, eds. 1995. *Life History and Narrative*. Washington, DC: Falmer Press.

Hattori, K., and D. N. Ishida. 2012. Ethnographic study of a good death among elderly Japanese Americans. *Nursing and Health Sciences* 14:488–94.

Haworth-Hoeppner, S. 2000. The critical shapes of body image: The role of culture and family in the production of eating disorders. *Journal of Marriage and the Family* 62:212–27.

Hayes, A. F. 2005. SPSS macro for computing Krippendorff's alpha. http://tinyurl.com/pey65hu (accessed April 18, 2014).

Hayes, A. F., and K. Krippendorff. 2007. Answering the call for a standard reliability measure for coding data. *Communication Methods and Measures* 1:77–89.

Haynes, J., and D. Jones. 2012. A tale of two analyses: The use of archived qualitative data. *Sociological Research Online* 17:1–9. DOI: 10.5153/sro.2523

Heath, C.1989. Pain talk: The expression of suffering in the medical consultation. *Social Psychology Quarterly* 52:113–25.

Heaton, J. 2008. Secondary analysis of qualitative data: An overview. *Historical Social Research* 33:33–45.

Heckathorn, D. D. 1997. Respondent-driven sampling: A new approach to the study of hidden populations. *Social Problems* 44:174–99.

Heckathorn, D. D. 2002. Respondent-driven Sampling II: Deriving valid population estimates from chain-referral samples of hidden populations. *Social Problems* 49:11–34.

Heckathorn, D. D., and J. Jeffri. 2001. Finding the beat: Using respondent-driven sampling to study jazz musicians. *Poetics* 28:307–29.

Hedley, M. 2002. The geometry of gendered conflict in popular film: 1986–2000. *Sex Roles* 47:201–17.

Heemskerk, M. 2000. Driving forces of small-scale gold mining among the Ndjuka Marroons: A cross-scale socioeconomic analysis of participation in gold mining in Suriname. Ph.D. dissertation, University of Florida.

Hektner, J. M., J. A. Schmidt, and M. Csikszentmihalyi. 2007. *Experience Sampling Method: Measuring the Quality of Everyday Life*. Thousand Oaks, CA: Sage.

Henley, N. M. 1969. A psychological study of the semantics of animal terms. *Journal of Verbal Learning and Verbal Behavior* 8:176–84.

Henry, S. G., and M. D. Fetters. 2012. Video elicitation interviews: A qualitative research method for investigating physician–patient interactions. *Annals of Family Medicine* 10:118–25.

Heritage, J., and D. Maynard. W. 2005. *Communication in Medical Care: Interactions between Primary Care Physicians and Patients*. Cambridge: Cambridge University Press.

Herman, D., ed. 2007. *The Cambridge Companion to Narrative*. Cambridge: Cambridge University Press.

Herrera, C. D. 1996. Informed consent and ethical exemptions. *Human Organization* 55:235–37. (See entries for Wax [1996] and for Fluehr-Lobban [1996].)

Herrmann, F. W. von. 1991. *Hermeneutics and Reflection: Heidegger and Husserl on the Concept of Phenomenology*. Toronto: University of Toronto Press.

Herzfeld, M. 1977. Ritual and textual structures: The advent of spring in rural Greece. In *Text and Context*, R. K. Jain, ed., 29–45. Philadelphia: Institute for the Study of Human Issues.

Hesse-Biber, S. N. 2010. *Mixed Methods Research: Merging Theory with Practice*. New York: Guilford Press.

Hewitt, M. 2002. Attitudes toward interview mode and comparability of reporting sexual behavior by personal interview and audio computer-assisted self-interviewing: Analyses of the 1995 National Survey of Family Growth. *Sociological Methods and Research* 31:3–26.

Hicks, A. 1994. Qualitative comparative analysis and analytic induction: The case of the emergence of the social security state. *Sociological Methods and Research* 23:86–113.

Hicks, A., J. Misra, and T. N. Ng. 1995. The programmatic emergence of the social security state. *American Sociological Review* 60:329–49.

Hilden, P. P., and S. M. Huhndorf. 1999. Performing "Indian" in the National Museum of the American Indian. *Social Identities* 5:161–83.

Hill, C. E. 1998. Decision modeling: Its use in medical anthropology. In *Using Methods in the Field: A Practical Introduction and Casebook*, V. C. de Munck and E. J. Sobo, eds., 137–59. Walnut Creek, CA: AltaMira.

Hinck, S. 2004. The lived experience of oldest-old rural adults. *Qualitative Health Research* 14:779–91.

Hirschman, E. C. 1987. People as products: Analysis of a complex marketing exchange. *Journal of Marketing* 51:98–108.

Hobhouse, L. T. 1891. Induction and deduction. *Mind* 16:507–20.

Hockings, P. 2003. *Principles of Visual Anthropology*, 3d ed. New York: Mouton de Gruyter.

Hodson, R. 1999. *Analyzing Documentary Accounts*. Thousand Oaks, CA: Sage.

Hodson, R. 2004. A meta-analysis of workplace ethnographies: Race, gender, and employee attitudes and behaviors. *Journal of Contemporary Ethnography* 33:4–38.

Hoffman, K. E. 2002. Generational change in Berber women's Song of the Anti-Atlas Mountains, Morocco. *Ethnomusicology* 46:510–40.

Hoggett, P., P. Beedell, L. Jimenez, M. Mayo, and C. Miller. 2006. Identity, life history and commitment to welfare. *Journal of Social Policy* 35:689–704.

Hogue, C. J., R. Menon, A. L. Dunlop, and M. R. Kramer. 2011. Racial disparities in preterm birth rates and short inter-pregnancy interval: An overview. *Acta Obstetricia et Gynecologica Scandinavica* 90:1317–24.

Holland, D. 1985. From situation to impression: How Americans get to know themselves and one another. In *Directions in Cognitive Anthropology*, J. Dougherty, ed., 389–412. Urbana: University of Illinois Press.

Holland, D., and D. Skinner. 1987. Prestige and intimacy: The cultural models behind Americans' talk about gender types. In *Cultural Models in Language and Thought*, D. Holland and N. Quinn, eds., 78–111. New York: Cambridge Univesity Press.

Holly, D. H., Jr., and C. E. Cordy. 2007. What's in a coin? Reading the material culture of legend tripping and other activities. *Journal of American Folklore* 120:335–54.

Holmes, J. 2006. Sharing a laugh: Pragmatic aspects of humor and gender in the workplace. *Journal of Pragmatics* 38:26–50.

Holstein, J. A., and J. F. Gubrium. 1995. *The Active Interview*. Thousand Oaks, CA: Sage.

Holsti, O. R. 1969. *Content Analysis for the Social Sciences and Humanities*. Reading, MA: Addison-Wesley.

Homans, G. C. 1961a. Social behavior as exchange. *American Journal of Sociology* 63:597–606.

Homans, G. C. 1961b. *Social Behavior: Its Elementary Forms*. New York: Harcourt, Brace, and World.

Hopkins, P. D. 2010. Using narrative analysis and discourse analysis to determine patterns of meaning in the sermon language of women preachers. Ph.D. dissertation, East Carolina University.

Horizon Research, Inc. 2001. September. 2001–2002 Local Systemic Change. 2001–2002 Core Evaluation Manual: Classroom Observation Protocol. http://www.horizon-research.com/instruments/lsc/cop.pdf (accessed September 7, 2013).

Horowitz, D. M. 2007. Applying cultural consensus analysis to marketing. Ph.D. dissertation, Florida State University.

Houston, M. J., and S. Sudman. 1975. A methodological assessment of the use of key informants. *Social Science Research* 4:151–64.

Howard, D. C. P. 1994. Human–computer interactions: A phenomenological examination of the adult first-time computer experience. *Qualitative Studies in Education* 7:33–49.

Howe, K. R. 1988. Against the quantitative–qualitative incompatibility thesis or dogmas die hard. *Educational Researcher* 17:10–16.

Hruschka, D. J., L. M. Sibley, N. Kalim, and J. K. Edmonds. 2008. When there is more than one answer key: Cultural theories of postpartum hemorrhage in Matlab, Bangladesh. *Field Methods* 20:315–37.

Hsiao, A. F., G. W. Ryan, R. D. Hays, I. D. Coulter, R. M. Andersen, and N. S. Wenger. 2006. Variations in provider conceptions of integrative medicine. *Social Science and Medicine* 62:2973–87.

Hudak, M. A. 1993. Gender schema theory revisited: Men's stereotypes of American women. *Sex Roles: A Journal of Research* 28:279–93.

Huber, G. L., and L. Gürtler. 2013. *AQUAD 7. Manual: The Analysis of Qualitative Data*. Tübingen, Germany: Ingeborg Huber Verlag. www.aquad.de/materials/manual_aquad7/manual-e.pdf (accessed October 12, 2014).

Huddy, L., J. Billig, J. Bracciodieta, L. Hoeffler, P. J. Moynihan, and P. Pugliani. 1997. The effect of interviewer gender on the survey response. *Political Behavior* 19:197–220.

Huhman, B. A., and J. J. Argo. 2011. Gender role and social power in African and North American Advertisements. In *Advertising in Developing and Emerging Countries. The Economic, Political and Social Context*, E. C. Alozie, ed., 271–85. Burlington, VT: Gower.

Hurwicz, M.-L. 1995. Physicians' norms and health care decisions of elderly medicare recipients. *Medical Anthropology Quarterly* 9:211–35.

Husserl, E. 1964 [1907]. *The Idea of Phenomenology*, W. P. Alston and G. Nakhnikian, trans. The Hague: Nijhoff.

Husserl, E. 1989 [1913]. *Ideas Pertaining to a Pure Phenomenology and to a Phenomenological Philosophy*, R. Rojcewicz and A. Schuwer, trans. Dordrecht, Netherlands: Kluwer Academic.

Hutchins, E. 1995. *Cognition in the Wild*. Cambridge, MA: MIT Press.

Hyams, M. 2002. "Over there" and "back then": An odyssey in national subjectivity. *Environment and Planning D-Society and Space* 4:459–76.

Hyman, H. H. (with W. J. Cobb et al.). 1975. *Interviewing in Social Research*. Chicago: University of Chicago Press.

Hymes, D. 1976. Louis Simpson's "The Deserted Boy." *Poetics* 5:119–55.

Hymes, D. 1977. Discovering oral performance and measured verse in American Indian narrative. *New Literary History* 8:431–57.

Hymes, D. 1980a. Verse analysis of a Wasco text: Hiram Smith's "At'unaqa." *International Journal of American Linguistics* 46:65–77.

Hymes, D. 1980b. Particle, pause, and pattern in American Indian narrative verse. *American Indian Culture and Research Journal* 4:7–51.

Hymes, D. 1981. *In Vain I Tried to Tell You: Essays in Ethnopoetics*. Philadelphia: University of Pennsylvania Press.

Hymes, D. 1985. Language, memory, and selective performance: Cultee's "Salmon's Myth" as twice told to Boas. *The Journal of American Folklore* 98:391–434.

Hymes, D. 2003. *Now I Know Only So Far: Essays in Ethnopoetics*. Lincoln: University of Nebraska Press.

Hymes, V. 1987. Warm Springs Sahaptin narrative analysis. In *Native American Discourse: Poetics and Rhetoric*, J. Sherzer and A. Woodbury, eds., 62–102. Cambridge: Cambridge University Press.

Ignatow, G. 2004. Speaking together, thinking together? Exploring metaphor and cognition in a shipyard union dispute. *Sociological Forum* 19:405–33.

Impedovo, M. A., G. Ritella, and M. B. Ligorio. 2013. Developing codebooks as a new tool to analyze atudents' ePortfolios. *International Journal of ePortfolio* 3:161–76.

Isaac, C., J. Chertoff, B. Lee, and M. Carnes. 2011. Do students' and authors' genders affect evaluations? A linguistic analysis of medical student performance evaluations. *Academic Medicine* 86:59–66.

Izugbara, C. O. 2005. Local erotic songs and chants among rural Nigerian adolescent males. *Sexuality and Culture* 9:53–76.

Jackson, S., and S. Gee. 2005. "Look Janet," "No you look John": Constructions of gender in early school reader illustrations across 50 years. *Gender and Education* 17:115–28.

Jacobs, B. A. 2004. A typology of street criminal retaliation. *Journal of Research in Crime and Delinquency* 41:295–323.

Jacobs, J. K., H. Hollingsworth, and K. B. Givvin. 2007. Video-based research made "easy": Methodological lessons learned from the TIMSS video studies. *Field Methods* 19:284–99.

Jacobs, L. 1995. *The Jewish Religion: A Companion*. New York: Oxford University Press.

James, D., and S. Clarke. 1993. Women, men and interruptions: A critical review of research. In *Gender and Conversational Interaction*, D. Tannen, ed., 281–312. New York: Oxford University Press.

Jamieson, P. E., and D. Romer. 2010. Trends in U.S. movie tobacco portrayal since 1950: A historical analysis. *Tobacco Control* 19:179–84.

Jang, H.-Y. 1995. Cultural differences in organizational communication and interorganizational networks: A semantic network analysis. Ph.D. dissertation, State University of New York at Buffalo.

Jang, H.-Y., and G. A. Barnett. 1994. Cultural differences in organizational communication: A semantic network analysis. *Bulletin de Methodologie Sociologique* 44:31–59.

Jasienski, M. 2006. Letter to the editor. *Nature* 440:1112.

Jaskyte, K., and W. W. Dressler. 2004. Studying culture as an integral aggregate variable: Organizational culture and innovation in a group of nonprofit organizations. *Field Methods* 16:265–84.

Jasso, G. 2006. Factorial survey methods for studying beliefs and judgments. *Sociological Methods and Research* 34:334–423.

Javeline, D. 1999. Response effects in polite cultures. *Public Opinion Quarterly* 63:1–28.

Javidi, M. N., and L. W. Long. 1989. Teachers' use of humor, self-disclosure, and narrative activity as a function of experience. *Communications Research Reports* 6:47–52.

Jefferson, G. 1973. A case of precision timing in ordinary conversation: Overlapped tag-positioned address terms in closing sequences. *Semiotica* 9:47–96.

Jefferson, G. 1983. *Issues in the Transcription of Naturally-occurring Talk. Caricature versus Capturing Pronunciation Particulars*. Tilburg Papers on Language and Literature. Tilburg, Netherlands: University of Tilburg.

Jefferson, G. 2004. Glossary of transcript symbols with an introduction. In *Conversation Analysis*, G. H. Lernered, ed., 13–31. Philadelphia: John Benjamins.

Jehn, K. A., and L. Doucet. 1996. Developing categories from interview data: Text analysis and multidimensional scaling. Part I. *Cultural Anthropology Methods Journal* 8(2):15–16.

Jehn, K. A., and L. Doucet. 1997. Developing categories for interview data: Consequences of different coding and analysis strategies in understanding text. Part 2. *Cultural Anthropology Methods Journal* 9(1):1–7.

Jobe, J. B., D. M. Keler, and A. F. Smith. 1996. Cognitive techniques in interviewing older people. In *Answering Questions: Methodology for Determining Cognitive and Communicative Processes in Survey Research*, N. Schwarz and S. Sudman, eds., 197–219. San Francisco: Jossey-Bass.

Johnson, A. 1975. Time allocation in a Machiguenga community. *Ethnology* 14:301–10.

Johnson, E. 1996. Word lengths, authorship, and four-letter words. *TEXT Technology* 6:15–23.

Johnson, J. C. 1990. *Selecting Ethnographic Informants*. Newbury Park, CA: Sage.

Johnson, J. C., D. C. Griffith, and J. D. Murray. 1987. Encouraging the use of underutilized marine fishes by southeastern U.S. anglers. Part I: The Research. *Marine Fisheries Review* 49:122–37.

Johnson, J. C., and S. C. Weller. 2001. Elicitation techniques for interviewing. In *Handbook of Interview Research*, J. F. Gubrium and J. A. Holstein, eds., 491–514. Thousand Oaks, CA: Sage.

Johnson, R. B., ed. 2006. *New Directions in Mixed Methods Research*. Special Issue of Research in the Schools. http://www.msera.org/rits_131.htm (accessed September 22, 2008).

Johnson, R. B., and A. J. Onwuegbuzie. 2004. Mixed methods research: A research paradigm whose time has come. *Educational Researcher* 33:14–26.

Johnson, R. K., P. Driscoll, and M. I. Goran. 1996. Comparison of multiple-pass 24-hour recall estimates of energy intake with total energy expenditure determined by the doubly labeled water method in young children. *Journal of the American Dietetic Association* 96:1140–44.

Johnson-Laird, P. N. 1983. *Mental Models: Toward a Cognitive Science of Language, Inference, and Consciousness.* Cambridge, MA: Harvard University Press.

Johnson-Laird, P. N. 2010. Mental models and human reasoning. *Proceedings of the National Academy of Sciences* 107:18243–50.

Johnston, J., and C. Walton. 1995. Reducing response effects for sensitive questions: A computer-assisted self-interview with audio. *Social Science Computer Review* 13:304–19.

Joinson, A. N., C. Paine, T. Buchanan, and U.-D. Reips. 2008. Measuring self-disclosure online: Blurring and non-response to sensitive items in web-based surveys. *Computers in Human Behavior* 24:2158–71.

Jones, D. 2003. The generative psychology of kinship: Part 2. Generating variation from universal building blocks with optimality theory. *Evolution and Human Behavior* 24:320–50.

Jones, D. 2004. The universal psychology of kinship: Evidence from language. *TRENDS in Cognitive Science* 18:211–15.

Jones, E. K., J. R. Jurgenson, J. M. Katzenellenbogen, and S. C. Thompson. 2012. Menopause and the influence of culture: Another gap for Indigenous Australian women? *BMC Women's Health* 12:43. DOI: 10.1186/1472-6874-12-43

Jones, N. A., and J. Bullock. 2012. The two or more races population: 2010. *United States Census Bureau.* https://www.census.gov/newsroom/releases/archives/race/cb12-182.html (accessed March 2, 2014).

Juzwik, M. M. 2004. What rhetoric can contribute to an ethnopoetics of narrative performance in teaching: The significance of parallelism in one teacher's narrative. *Linguistics and Education* 15:359–86.

Kadushin, C. 1968. Power, influence and social circles: A new methodology for studying opinion makers. *American Sociological Review* 33:685–99.

Kagan, S., and G. L. Zahn. 1975. Field-dependence and school achievement gap between Anglo-American and Mexican-American children. *Journal of Educational Psychology* 67:643–50.

Kahn, R. L., and C. F. Cannell. 1957. *The Dynamics of Interviewing.* New York: John Wiley.

Kane, E. W., and L. J. Macaulay. 1993. Interviewer gender and gender attitudes. *Public Opinion Quarterly* 57:1–28.

Kaplan, A. 1964. *The Conduct of Inquiry.* San Francisco: Chandler.

Kaplan, F. S., and D. M. Levine. 1981. Cognitive mapping of a folk taxonomy of Mexican pottery: A multivariate approach. *American Anthropologist* 83:868–84.

Karademir-Hazır, I. 2014. How bodies are classed: An analysis of clothing and bodily tastes in Turkey. *Poetics* 44:1–21.

Karlawish, J., F. K. Barg, D. Augsburger, J. Beaver, A. Ferguson, and J. Nunez. 2011. What Latino Puerto Ricans and non-Latinos say when they talk about Alzheimer's disease. *Alzheimer's and Dementia* 7:161–70.

Kassis, H. 1983. *A Concordance of the Qur'an.* Berkeley: University of California Press.

Kataoka, K. 2012. Toward multimodal ethnopoetics. *Applied Linguistics Review* 3:101–30.

Kaufman, G., and P. Voon Chin. 2003. Is ageism alive in date selection among men? Age requests among gay and straight men in Internet personal ads. *Journal of Men's Studies* 11:225–35.

Kearney, M. H. 1996. Reclaiming normal life: Women's experiences of quitting drugs. *Journal of Obstetric, Gynecologic, and Neonatal Nursing* 25:761–68.

Kearney, M. H. 1998. Truthful self-nurturing: A grounded formal theory of women's addiction recovery. *Qualitative Health Research* 8:495–512.

Kearney, M. H., S. Murphy, K. Irwin, and M. Rosenbaum. 1995. Salvaging self: A grounded theory of pregnancy on crack cocaine. *Nursing Research* 44:208–13.

Keith-Spiegel, P., and G. P. Koocher. 2005. The IRB paradox: Could the protectors also encourage deceit? *Ethics and Behavior* 15:339–49.

Kelly, E. F., and P. J. Stone. 1975. *Computer Recognition of English Word Senses*. Amsterdam: North-Holland Publishing Company.

Kempton, W. 1987. Two theories of home heat control. In *Cultural Models in Language and Thought*, D. Holland and N. Quinn, eds., 222–42. Cambridge: Cambridge University Press.

Kendall, C., L. R. Kerr, R. C. Gondim, G. L. Werneck, R. H. M. Macena, M. K. Pontes, L. G. Johnston, K. Sabin, and W. McFarland. 2008. An empirical comparison of respondent-driven sampling, time location sampling, and snowball sampling for behavioral surveillance in men who have sex with men, Fortaleza, Brazil. *AIDS and Behavior* 12:S97–S104.

Kendall, S., and D. Tannen. 2001. Discourse and gender. In *The Handbook of Discourse Analysis*, D. Schiffrin, D. Tannen, and H. E. Hamilton, eds., 548–67. Oxford: Blackwell.

Kennedy, C. W., and C. Camden. 1983. A new look at interruptions. *Western Journal of Speech Communication* 47:45–58.

Kern, D. W., K. E. Wroblewski, L. P. Schumm, J. M. Pinto, and M. K. McClintock. 2014. Field survey measures of olfaction: The Olfactory Function Field Exam (OFFE). *Field Methods* 26:421–34.

Khaw, L., and J. L. Hardesty. 2007. Theorizing the process of leaving: Turning points and trajectories in the stages of change. *Family Relations* 56:413–25.

Kilburn, H. W. 2004. Explaining U.S. urban regimes: A qualitative comparative analysis. *Urban Affairs Review* 39:633–51.

Kilcullen, D. 2007. Ethics, politics and nonstate warfare. A response to González in this issue. *Anthropology Today* 23:20.

Kim, A. I. 1985. Korean color terms: An aspect of semantic fields and related phenomena. *Anthropological Linguistics* 27:425–36.

King, A. 1996. The fining of Vinnie Jones. *International Review for the Sociology of Sport* 31:119–34.

King, G., R. O. Keohane, and S. Verba. 1994. *Designing Social Inquiry*. Princeton, NJ: Princeton University Press.

Kirchler, E. 1992. Adorable woman, expert man: Changing gender images of women and men in management. *European Journal of Social Psychology* 22:363–73.

Kirk, J., and M. Miller. 1986. *Reliability and Validity in Qualitative Research*. Beverly Hills, CA: Sage.

Klecka, W. R. 1980. *Discriminant Analysis*. Beverly Hills, CA: Sage.

Knigge, L., and M. Cope. 2006. Grounded visualization: Integrating the analysis of qualitative and quantitative data through grounded theory and visualization. *Environment and Planning A* 38:2021–37.

Koven, M. 2002. An analysis of speaker role inhabitance in narratives of personal experience. *Journal of Pragmatics* 34:167–217.

Kral, A. H., M. M. Malekinejad, J. Vaudrey, A. N. Martinez, J. Lorvick, W. McFarland, and H. F. Raymond. 2010. Comparing respondent-driven sampling and targeted sampling methods of recruiting injection drug users in San Francisco. *Journal of Urban Health* 87:839–50.

Krippendorff, K. 1980. *Content Analysis: An Introduction to Its Methodology*. Beverly Hills, CA: Sage.

Krippendorff, K. 2004a. *Content Analysis: An Introduction to Its Methodology*, 2d ed. Thousand Oaks, CA: Sage.

Krippendorff, K. 2004b. Reliability in content analysis. Some common misconceptions and recommendations. *Human Communication Research* 30:411–33.

Krippendorff, K. 2013. *Content Analysis: An Introduction to Its Methodology*, 3d ed. Thousand Oaks, CA: Sage.

Krippendorff, K., and M. A. Bock. 2009. *The Content Analysis Reader*. Thousand Oaks, CA: Sage.

Kroeber, A. L. 1919. On the principle of order in civilization as exemplified by changes in women's fashions. *American Anthropologist* 21:235–63.

Krueger, R. A., and M. A. Casey. 2009. *Focus Groups: A Practical Guide for Applied Research*, 4th ed. Thousand Oaks, CA: Sage.

Kruskal, J. B., and M. Wish. 1978. *Multidimensional Scaling*. Beverly Hills, CA: Sage.

Kurasaki, K. S. 1997. Ethnic identify and its development among third-generation Japanese Americans. Ph.D. dissertation, DePaul University.

Kurasaki, K. S. 2000. Intercoder reliability for validating conclusions drawn from open-ended interview data. *Field Methods* 12:179–94.

Kuzel, A. J. 1999. Sampling in qualitative inquiry. In *Doing Qualitative Research*, 2d ed., B. F. Crabtree and W. L. Miller, eds., 33–45. Newbury Park, CA: Sage.

Kvale, S., and S. Brinkmann. 2009. *InterViews: Learning the Craft of Qualitative Research Interviewing*, 2d ed. Thousand Oaks, CA: Sage.

Kwon, K., G. A. Barnett, and H. Chen. 2009. Assessing cultural differences in translations: A semantic network analysis of the Universal Declaration of Human Rights. *Journal of International and Intercultural Communication* 2:107–38.

Labov, W., and J. Waletzky. 1997. Narrative analysis: Oral versions of personal experience. *Journal of Narrative and Life History* 7:3–38.

Lakoff, G., and M. Johnson. 2003 [1980]. *Metaphors We Live By*. Chicago: University of Chicago Press.

Lakoff, G. and Z. Kövecses. 1987. The cognitive model of anger in American English. In *Cultural Models in Language and Thought*, D. Holland and N. Quinn, eds., 195–221. Cambridge: Cambridge University Press.

Lamont, M. 2010. Lip-synch gospel: Christian music and the ethnopoetics of identity in Kenya. *Africa* 80:473–96.

Lampert, M. D., and S. M. Ervin-Trip. 1993. Structured coding for the study of language and social interaction. In *Talking Data; Transcription and Coding in Discourse Research*, J. A. Edwards and M. D. Lampert, eds., 169–206. Hillsdale, NJ: Lawrence Erlbaum.

Lampert, M. D., and S. M. Ervin-Trip. 2006. Risky laughter: Teasing and self-directed joking among male and female friends. *Journal of Pragmatics* 38:51–72.

Lance, L. M. 1998. Gender differences in heterosexual dating: A content analysis of personal ads. *Journal of Men's Studies* 6:297–305.

Landis, J. R., and G. G. Koch. 1977. The measurement of observer agreement for categorical data. *Biometrics* 33:159–74.

Lanzieri, N., and T. Hildebrandt. 2011. Using hegemonic masculinity to explain gay male attraction to muscular and athletic men. *Journal of Homosexuality* 58:275–93.

Lasswell, H. D. 1949. Why be quantitative? In *Studies in Quantitative Semantics*, H. D. Lasswell, N. Leites, and associates, eds., 40–52. New York: George Stewart. [Reprinted 1965, Cambridge, MA: MIT Press.]

Laubach, M. 2005. Consent, informal organization and job rewards: A mixed methods analysis. *Social Forces* 83:1535–65.

Laver, M., and J. Garry. 2000. Estimating policy positions from political texts. *American Journal of Political Science* 44:619–34.

Lawson, K. 2012. The real power of parental reading aloud: Exploring the affective and attentional dimensions. *Australian Journal of Education* 56:257–72.

Lawson, V., and J. Wardle. 2013. A qualitative exploration of the health promotion effects of varying body size in photographs analyzed using interpretative phenomenological analysis. *Body Image* 10:85–94.

Lea, K. L. 1980. Francis Bacon. *Encyclopaedia Britannica*, Vol. 2. Chicago: Encyclopaedia Britannica Inc.

Leaper, C., and R. D. Robnett. 2011. Women are more likely than men to use tentative language, aren't they? A meta-analysis testing for gender differences and moderators. *Psychology of Women Quarterly* 35:129–42.

LeCompte, M. D. 2000. Analyzing qualitative data. *Theory Into Practice* 39:146–54.

LeCompte, M. D., and J. Schensul. 2013. *Analysis and Interpretation of Ethnographic Data. A Mixed Methods Approach*, 2d. ed. Lanham, MD: Rowman and Littlefield.

Ledema, R., A. Flabouris, S. Grant, and C. Jorm. 2006. Narrativizing errors of care: Critical incident reporting in clinical practice. *Social Science and Medicine* 62:134–44.

Leighton Dawson, B., and W. D. McIntosh. 2006. Sexual strategies theory and Internet personal advertisements. *CyberPsychology and Behavior* 9:614–17.

Lévi-Strauss, C. 1963. *Structural Anthropology*. New York: Basic Books.

Levy, R., and D. Hollan. 1998. Person-centered interviewing and observation. In *Handbook of Methods in Cultural Anthropology*, H. R. Bernard, ed., 333–64. Walnut Creek, CA: AltaMira.

Levy, R., and D. Hollan. 2014. Person-centered interviewing and observation. In *Handbook of Methods in Cultural Anthropology*, 2d ed., H. R. Bernard and C. C. Gravlee, eds., 314–42. Lanham, MD: AltaMira.

Lewins, A., and C. Silver. 2014. *Using Software in Qualitative Research. A Step by Step Guide*, 2d ed. London: Sage.

Lewis, A. T. E. Hall, and A. Black. 2011. Career stages in wildland firefighting: Implications for voice in risky situations. *International Journal of Wildland Fire* 20:115–24.

Li, J. 2004. Parental expectations of Chinese immigrants: A folk theory about children's school achievement. *Race, Ethnicity and Education* 7:167–83.

Liddicoat, A. 2011. *An Introduction to Conversation Analysis*. New York: Continuum.

Lieberson, S. 1991. Small Ns and big conclusions: An evaluation of the reasoning in comparative studies based on a small number of cases. *Social Forces* 70:307–20.

Lightcap, J. L., J. A. Kurland, and R. L. Burgess. 1982. Child abuse: A test of some predictions from evolutionary theory. *Ethology and Sociobiology* 3:61–67.

Lincoln, Y. S., and E. G. Guba. 1985. *Naturalistic Inquiry*. Newbury Park, CA: Sage.

Linnekin, J. 1987. Categorize, cannibalize? Humanistic quantification in anthropological research. *American Anthropologist* 89:920–26.

Locke, T. 2004. *Critical Discourse Analysis*. New York: Continuum.

Lofland, J., L. Anderson, D. Snow, and L. H. Lofland. 2006. *Analyzing Social Settings. A Guide to Qualitative Observation and Analysis*. Belmont, CA: Wadsworth/Thompson Learning.

Loftus, E. F., and W. Marburger. 1983. Since the eruption of Mt. St. Helens, has anyone beaten you up? Improving the accuracy of retrospective reports with landmark events. *Memory and Cognition* 11:114–20.

Lomax. A. 1968. *Folk Song Style and Culture*. Washington, DC: American Association for the Advancement of Science, Publication number 88.

Lomax, A. 2003. *Alan Lomax. Selected Writings*, R. D. Cohen, ed. New York: Routledge.

Lomax, H., J. Fink, N. Singh, and C. High. 2011. The politics of performance: Methodological challenges of researching children's experiences of childhood through the lens of participatory video. *International Journal of Social Research Methodology* 14(Special Issue): 231–43.

Lombard, M., J. Snyder-Duch, and C. Campanella Bracken. 2004. A call for standardization in content analysis reliability. *Human Communications Research* 30:434–37.

Lombard, M., J. Snyder-Duch, and C. Campanella Bracken. 2005. Practical resources for assessing and reporting intercoder reliability in content analysis research projects. http://www.temple.edu/sct/mmc/reliability/ (accessed March 31, 2008).

Long, T., and M. Johnson. 2000. Rigour, reliability and validity in qualitative research. *Clinical Effectiveness in Nursing* 4:30–37.

Longfield, K. 2004. Rich fools, spare tyres, and boyfriends: Partner categories, relationship dynamics and Ivorian women's risk for STIs and HIV. *Culture, Health and Sexuality* 66:483–500.

Loughran, T., and B. McDonald. 2011. When is a liability not a liability? Textual analysis, dictionaries, and 10-Ks. *The Journal of Finance* 64:35–65.

Luborsky, M. R., and R. L. Rubinstein. 1995. Sampling in qualitative research: Rationale, issues and methods. *Research on Aging* 17:89–113.

Luc, H., and B. Vervaeck. 2005. *Handbook of Narrative Analysis*. Lincoln: University of Nebraska Press.

Luhn, H. P. 1960. Keyword-in-context index for technical literature. *American Documentation* 11:288–95.

Lun, J., B. Mesquita, and B. Smith. 2011. Self- and other-presentational styles in the southern and northern United States: An analysis of personal ads. *European Journal of Social Psychology* 41:435–45.

Lyman, S. M. 1989. *The Seven Deadly Sins: Society and Evil*, rev. and expanded ed. Dix Hills, NY: General Hall.

Lynd, R. S., and H. M. Lynd. 1929. *Middletown. A Sudy in Contemporary American Culture*. New York: Harcourt, Brace & Company.

MacDougall, K., Y. Beyene, and R. D. Nachtigall. 2013. Age shock: Misperceptions of the impact of age on fertility before and after IVF in women who conceived after age 40. *Human Reproduction* 28:350–56.

MacQueen, K. M., E. McLellan, K. Kelly, and B. Milstein. 1998. Code book development for team-based qualitative analysis. *Cultural Anthropology Methods Journal* 10:31–36.

MacQueen, K. M., E. McLellan, K. Kelly, and B. Milstein. 2008. Team-based codebook development: Structure, process, and agreement. In *Handbook for Team-based Qualitative Research*, G. Guest and K. M. MacQueen, eds., 119–35. Lanham, MD: AltaMira.

Magnarella, P. J. 1986. Anthropological fieldwork, key informants, and human bonds. *Anthropology and Humanism Quarterly* 11:33–37.

Mahaffy, K. A. 1996. Cognitive dissonance and its resolution: A study of lesbian Christians. *Journal for the Scientific Study of Religion* 35:392–402.

Maines, D. R., and J. C. Bridger. 1992. Narratives, community and land use decisions. *The Social Science Journal* 29:363–80.

Malhotra, N. 2008. Completion time and response order effects in web surveys. *Public Opinion Quarterly* 72:914–34.

Malimabe-Ramagoshi, R. M., J. G. Maree, D. Alexander, and M. M. Molepo. 2007. Child abuse in Setswana folktales. *Early Child Development and Care* 177:433–48.

Malkin, A. R., K. Wornian, and J. C. Chrisler. 1999. Women and weight: Gendered messages on magazine covers. *Sex Roles* 40:647–55.

Mandler, J. M. 1984. *Stories, Scripts, and Scenes: Aspects of Schema Theory*. Hillsdale, NJ: Lawrence Erlbaum.

Mann, S. 2007. Understanding farm succession by the objective hermeneutics method. *Sociologia Ruralis* 47:369–83

Manning, P. K. 1971. Fixing what you feared: Notes on the campus abortion search. In *The Sociology of Sex*, J. M. Henslin, ed., 137–63. New York: Appleton-Century-Crofts.

Manning, P. K. 1982. Analytic induction. In *Handbook of Social Science Methods*, Vol. 2, *Qualitative Methods*, R. Smith and P. K. Manning, eds., 273–302. New York: Harper.

Manzo, J. 1996. Taking turns and taking sides: Opening scenes from two jury deliberations. *Social Psychology Quarterly* 59:107–25.

Marcussen, C. 2014. Multidimensional scaling in tourism literature. *Tourism Management Perspectives* 12:31–40.

Margolis, M. 1984. *Mothers and Such*. Berkeley: University of California Press.

Marham, A., and E. Buchanan. 2012. Ethical decision-making and Internet research. Recommendations from the AoIR Ethics Working Committee (Version 2.0). http://www.aoir .org/reports/ethics2.pdf (accessed February 27, 2015).

Markovic, M. 2006. Analyzing qualitative data: Health care experiences of women with gynecological cancer. *Field Methods* 18:413–29.

Markovic, M., L. Manderson, N. Wray, and M. Quinn. 2004. "He's telling us something." Women's experiences of cancer disclosure and treatment decision-making in Australia. *Anthropology and Medicine* 3:327–41.

Martin, C. L., and S. Parker. 1995. Folk theories about race and sex differences. *Personality and Social Psychology Bulletin* 21:45–57.

Martin, J. L., and L. Dean. 1993. Developing a community sample of gay men for an epidemiological study of AIDS. In *Researching Sensitive Topics*, C. M. Renzetti and R. M. Lee, eds., 82–100. Newbury Park, CA: Sage.

Martindale, C., and D. McKenzie. 1995. On the utility of content analysis in author attribution: The Federalist. *Computers and the Humanities* 29:259–70.

Martins, N., A. J. Weaver, D. Yeshua-Katz, N. H. Lewis, N. E. Tyree, and J. D. Jense. 2013. A content analysis of print news coverage of media violence and aggression research. *Journal of Communication* 63:1070–87.

Martsolf, D. S., T. J. Courey, T. R. Chapman, C. B. Drauker, and B. L. Mims. 2006. Adaptive sampling: Recruiting a diverse community sample of survivors of sexual violence. *Journal of Community Health Nursing* 23:169–82.

Marx, A., B. Rihoux, and C. Ragin. 2014. The origins, development, and application of qualitative comparative analysis: The first 25 years. *European Political Science Review* 6:115–42.

Mastin, T., A. Coe, S. Hamilton, and S. Tarr. 2004. Product purchase decision-making behavior and gender role stereotypes: A content analysis of advertisements in *Essence* and *Ladies' Home Journal*, 1990–1999. *Howard Journal of Communications* 15:229–43.

Matarazzo, J. D., M. Weitman, G. Saslow, and A. N. Wiens. 1963. Interviewer influence on durations of interviewee speech. *Journal of Verbal Learning and Verbal Behavior* 1:451–58.

Matarazzo, J. D., A. N. Wiens, G. Saslow, B. V. Allen, and M. Weitman. 1964a. Interviewer mm-humm and interviewee speech duration. *Psychotherapy: Theory, Research and Practice* 1:109–14.

Matarazzo, J. D., A. N. Wiens, G. Saslow, M. Weitman, and B. V. Allen. 1964b. Interviewer head nodding and interviewee speech durations. *Psychotherapy: Theory, Research and Practice* 1:54–63.

Mathews, H. F. 1992. The directive force of morality tales in a Mexican community. In *Human Motives and Cultural Models*, R. D'Andrade and C. Strauss, eds., 127–62. New York: Cambridge University Press.

Mathews, H. F., and C. Hill. 1990. Applying cognitive decision theory to the study of regional patterns of illness treatment choice. *American Anthropologist* 91:155–70.

Mattei, L. R. W. 1998. Gender and power in American legislative discourse. *The Journal of Politics* 60:440–61.

Maxwell, J. A. 1996. *Qualitative Research Design: An Interactive Approach*. Thousand Oaks, CA: Sage.

Maynard, D. W. 1991. Interaction and asymmetry in clinical discourse. *American Journal of Sociology* 97:448–95.

Maynard, D. W., and J. Heritage. 2005. Conversation analysis, doctor–patient interaction, and medical communication. *Medical Education* 39:428–35.

Maynard, M. L. 1997. Opportunity in paid vs. unpaid public relations internships: A semantic network analysis. *Public Relations Review* 23:377–90.

McCarroll, J. E., A. S. Blank, and K. Hill. 1995. Working with traumatic material: Effects on Holocaust Memorial Museum staff. *American Journal of Orthopsychiatry* 65:66–75.

McCarty, C., M. House, J. Harman, and S. Richards. 2006. Effort in phone survey response rates: The effects of vendor and client controlled factors. *Field Methods* 18:172–88.

McColl, R. W. 1982. Personal icons and amulets: Reflections of culture values and human/land relationships. *The Professional Geographer* 34:447–50.

McCracken, G. D. 1988. *Culture and Consumption: New Approaches to the Symbolic Character of Consumer Goods and Activities*. Bloomington: University of Indiana Press.

McCracken, G. D. 2005. *Culture and Consumption II: New Approaches to the Symbolic Character of Consumer Goods and Activities*. Bloomington: University of Indiana Press.

McCreaddie, M. 2010. Harsh humour: A therapeutic discourse. *Health and Social Care in the Community* 18:633–42.

McFate, M. 2005. Anthropology and counterinsurgency: The strange story of their curious relationship. *Military Review* 85:24–38.

McHoul, A., and R. Rapley. 2005. A case of attention-deficit/hyperactivity disorder diagnosis: Sir Karl and Francis B. slug it out on the consulting room floor. *Discourse and Society* 16:419–49.

McKelvey, M. M. 2014. The other mother: A narrative analysis of the postpartum experiences of nonbirth lesbian mothers. *Advances in Nursing Science* 37:101–16.

McKenna, S. A., and D. S. Main. 2013. The role and influence of key informants in community-engaged research: A critical perspective. *Action Research* 11:113–24.

McNamara, M. S. 2005. Knowing and doing phenomenology: The implications of the critique of "nursing phenomenology" for a phenomenological inquiry: A discussion paper. *International Journal of Nursing Studies* 42:695–704.

McVee, M. B., K. Dunsmore, and J. R. Gavelek. 2005. Schema theory revisited. *Review of Educational Research* 75:531–66.

Means, B., A. Nigam, M. Zarrow, E. F. Loftus, and M. S. Donaldson. 1989. *Autobiographical Memory for Health-related Events*. National Center for Health Statistics, Vital and Health Statistics, ser. 6, no. 2. Washington, DC: U.S. Government Printing Office.

Medin, D. L., and S. Atran. 2004. The native mind: biological categorization, reasoning and decision making in development across cultures. *Psychological Review* 111:960–83.

Mehta, R., and R. W. Belk. 1991. Artifacts, identity, and transition: Favorite possessions of Indians and Indian immigrants to the United States. *Journal of Consumer Research* 17:398–411.

Mele, M. M., and B. M. Bello. 2007. Coaxing and coercion in roadblock encounters on Nigerian highways. *Discourse and Society* 18:437–52.

Merriam, S. B. 1998. *Qualitative Research and Case Study Applications in Education*, rev. and expanded. San Francisco: Jossey-Bass.

Mertens, D. M. 2005. *Research and Evaluation in Education and Psychology: Integrating Diversity with Quantitative, Qualitative, and Mixed Methods*. Thousand Oaks, CA: Sage.

Mertens, D. M., and P. E. Ginsberg, eds. 2009. *The Handbook of Social Research Ethics*. Thousand Oaks, CA: Sage.

Merton, R. K., M. Fiske, and P. L. Kendall. 1956. *The Focused Interview: A Manual of Problems and Procedures*. Glencoe, IL: Free Press.

Messer, E., and M. Bloch. 1985. Women's and children's activity profiles: A comparison of time allocation and time allocation methods. *Journal of Comparative Family Studies* 16:329–43.

Messner, B. A., A. Jipson, P. J. Becker, and B. Byers. 2007. The hardest hate: A sociological analysis of country hate music. *Popular Music and Society* 30:513–31.

Metzger, D. G., and G. E. Williams. 1966. Procedures and results in the study of native categories: Tseltal firewood. *American Anthropologist* 68:389–407.

Miles, M. B. 1979. Qualitative data as an attractive nuisance: The problem of analysis. *Administrative Science Quarterly* 24:590–601.

Miles, M. B., and A. M. Huberman. 1994. *Qualitative Data Analysis: An Expanded Sourcebook*. Thousand Oaks, CA: Sage.

Miles, M. B., A. M. Huberman, and J. Saldaña. 2013. *Qualitative Data Analysis: A Methods Sourcebook.* Thousand Oaks, CA: Sage.

Mill, J. S. 1898. A *System of Logic, Ratiocinative and Inductive: Being a Connected View of the Principles of Evidence and the Methods of Scientific Investigation,* People's ed. London: Longmans, Green and Co.

Millar, M. M., and D. Dillman. 2011. Improving response to web and mixed-mode surveys. *Public Opinion Quarterly* 75:249–69.

Miller, B. W., P. W. Leslie, and J. T. McCabe. 2014. Coping with natural hazards in a conservation context: Resource-use decisions of Maasai households during recent and historical droughts. *Human Ecology* 42:753–68.

Miller, D. 1987. *Material Culture and Mass Consumption.* Oxford: Blackwell.

Miller, M., J. Kaneko, P. Bartram, J. Marks, and D. D. Brewer. 2004. Cultural consensus analysis and environmental anthropology: Yellowfin tuna fishery management in Hawaii. *Cross-Cultural Research* 38:289–314.

Miller, S. I. 1982. Quality and quantity: Another view of analytic induction as a research technique. *Quality and Quantity* 16:281–95.

Mishler, E. G. 1986. *Research Interviewing: Context and Narrative.* Cambridge, MA: Harvard University Press.

Mitchell, B., and A. K. Webster. 2011. "We don't know what we become": Navajo ethnopoetics and an expressive feature in a poem by Rex Lee Jim. *Anthropological Linguistics* 5:259–86.

Mitchell, R. 1965. Survey materials collected in the developing countries: Sampling, measurement, and interviewing obstacles to intra- and international comparisons. *International Social Science Journal* 17:665–85.

Moerman, M. 1988. *Talking Culture: Ethnography and Conversation Analysis.* Philadelphia: University of Pennsylvania Press.

Mollinga, P. P., and D. Gondhelekar. 2014. Finding structure in diversity: A stepwise small-*N*/medium-*N* qualitative comparative analysis approach for water resources management research. *Water Alternatives* 7:178–98.

Montbriand, M. J. 1994. Decision heuristics of patients with cancer: Alternative and biomedical choices. Ph.D. dissertation, University of Saskatchewan, Saskatoon.

Moor, N., W. Ultee, and A. Need. 2009. Analogical reasoning and the content of creation stories. Quantitative comparisons of preindustrial societies. *Cross-Cultural Research* 43:91–122.

Moore, C. C., A. K. Romney, T.-L. Hsia, and C. D. Rusch. 1999. The universality of the semantic structure of emotion terms: Methods for the study of inter- and intra-cultural variability. *American Anthropologist* 101:529–46.

Moore, F. R., C. Cassidy, M. J. L. Smith, and D. I. Perrett. 2006. The effects of female control of resources on sex-differentiated mate preferences. *Evolution and Human Behavior* 27:193–205.

Moore, N. 2007. (Re)using qualitative data, *Sociological Research Online* 12:3. http://www.socresonline.org.uk/12/3/1.html (accessed September 7, 2013).

Moore, R. 2013. Reinventing ethnopoetics. *Journal of Folklore Research* 50:13–39.

Moore, R. S., J. P. Lee, S. E. Martin, M. Todd, and B. C. Chu. 2009. Correlates of persistent smoking in bars subject to smokefree workplace policy. *International Journal of Environmental Research and Public Health* 6:1341–57.

Moran, D. 2000. *Introduction to Phenomenology*. London: Routledge.

Morera, M. C., and C. H. Gladwin. 2006. Does off-farm work discourage soil conservation? Incentives and disincentives throughout two Honduran hillside communities. *Human Ecology* 34:355–78.

Moret, M., R. Reuzel, G. J. Van Der Wilt, and J. Grin. 2007. Validity and reliability of qualitative data analysis: Interobserver agreement in reconstructing interpretative frames. *Field Methods* 19:24–39.

Morgan, D. L. 1997. *Focus Groups as Qualitative Research*, 2d ed. Thousand Oaks, CA: Sage.

Morgan, D. L., and R. Krueger. 1998. *The Focus Group Kit*, 6 vols. Thousand Oaks, CA: Sage.

Morgan, M. G., B. Fischoff, A. Bostrom, and C. J. Atman. 2002. *Risk Communication: A Mental Models Approach*. New York: Cambridge University Press.

Morine-Dershimer, G. 2006. Classroom management and classroom discourse. In *Handbook of Classroom Management: Research, Practice, and Contemporary Issues*, C. M. Evertson and C. S. Weinstein, eds., 127–56. Mahwah, NJ: Lawrence Erlbaum.

Morris, M. W., and A. Mok. 2011. Isolating effects of cultural schemas: Cultural priming shifts Asian-Americans' biases in social description and memory. *Journal of Experimental Social Psychology* 47:117–26.

Morrow, K. M., S. Vargas, R. K. Rosen, A. L. Christensen, L. Salomon, L. Shulman, C. Barroso, and J. L. Fava. 2007. The utility of non-proportional quota sampling for recruiting at-risk women for microbicide research. *AIDS and Behavior* 11:586–95.

Morse, J. M., ed. 1994. *Critical Issues in Qualitative Research Methods*. London: Sage.

Morse, J. M. 2003. Principles of mixed methods and multimethod research design. In *Handbook of Mixed Methods in Social and Behavioral Research*, A. Tashakkori and C. Teddlie, eds.,189–208. Thousand Oaks, CA: Sage.

Morse, J. M. 2007. Sampling in grounded theory research. In *Handbook of Grounded Theory*, T. Bryant and K. Charmaz, eds., 229–44. London: Sage.

Morse, J. M., and L. Niehaus. 2009. *Mixed Method Design. Principles and Procedures*. Walnut Creek, CA: Left Coast Press, Inc.

Morse, J. M., P. N. Stern, J. Corbin, B. Bowers, K. Charmaz, and A. E. Clarke. 2009. *Developing Grounded Theory: The Second Generation*. Walnut Creek, CA: Left Coast Press, Inc.

Moser, C. A., and A. Stuart. 1953. An experimental study of quota sampling. *Journal of the Royal Statistical Society*, Series A (General) 116:349–405.

Moss, B. J. 1994. Creating a community: Literacy events in African American churches. In *Literacy across Communities*, B. Moss, ed., 147–78. Cresskill, NJ: Hampton Press.

Mosteller, F., and D. L. Wallace. 1964. *Inference and Disputed Authorship: The Federalist Papers*. Reading, MA: Addison-Wesley.

Moustakas, C. 1994. *Phenomenological Research Methods*. Thousand Oaks, CA: Sage.

Mugavin, M. E. 2008. Multidimensional scaling: A brief overview. *Nursing Research* 57:64–68.

Muñoz Leiva, F., F. J. Montoro Ríos, and T. L. Martínez. 2006. Assessment of interjudge reliability in the open-ended questions coding process. *Quality and Quantity* 40:519–37.

Murdock, G. P., C. S. Ford, A. E. Hudson, R. Kennedy, L. W. Simmons, and J. W. M. Whiting. 2004 [1961]. *Outline of Cultural Materials*, 5th ed., with modifications. New Haven, CT: Human Relations Area Files.

Murphy, J. M., and M. E. Stuckey. 2002. Never cared to say goodbye: Presidential legacies and vice presidential campaigns. *Presidential Studies Quarterly* 32:46–66.

Murray, C. 2012. Young people's perspectives: The trials and tribulations of going straight. *Criminology and Criminal Justice* 12:25–40.

Murray, N. M., and S. B. Murray. 1996. Music and lyrics in commercials: A cross-cultural comparison between commercials run in the Dominican Republic and in the United States. *Journal of Advertising* 25:51–63.

Mustonen, A., and L. Pulkkinen. 1997. Television violence: A development of a coding scheme. *Journal of Broadcasting and Electronic Media* 41:168–89.

Nagata, J. 1974. What is Malay? Situational selection of ethnic identity in a plural society. *American Ethnologist* 1:331–50.

Namenwirth, J. Z., and R. P. Weber. 1987. *Dynamics of Culture*. Winchester, MA: Allen and Unwin.

Narayan, S., and J. A. Krosnick. 1996. Education moderates some response effects in attitude measurement. *Public Opinion Quarterly* 60:58–88.

Necheles, J, E., E. Q. Chung, J. Hawes-Dawson, G. W. Ryan, L. B. Williams, H. N. Holmes, K. B. Wells, M. E. Vaiana, and M. A. Schuster. 2007. The teen photovoice project: A pilot study to promote health through advocacy. *Progress in Community Health Partnerships: Research, Education, and Action* 1:221–29.

Neely, T. B. 2013. Language matters: Status loss and achieved status distinctions in global organizations. *Organization Science* 24:476–97.

Negrón, R. 2007. Switching of ethnic identification among New York City Latinos. Ph.D. dissertation, University of Florida.

Negrón, R. 2011. *Ethnic Identification among Urban Latinos: Language and Flexibility*. The New Americans: Recent Immigration and American Society Series. El Paso, TX: LFB Scholarly Publishing.

Neto, F., and A. Furnham. 2005. Gender-role portrayals in children's television advertisements. *International Journal of Adolescence and Youth* 12:69–90.

Neuendorf, K. A. 2002. *The Content Analysis Guidebook*. Thousand Oaks, CA: Sage.

Nevile, M. 2007. Talking without overlap in the airline cockpit: Precision timing at work. *Text and Talk* 27:225–49.

Nguyen, H.-H. D., C. Smith, G. L. Reynolds, and B. Freshman. 2015. The effect of acculturation on obesity among foreign-born Asians residing in the United States. *Journal of Immigrant Minority Health* 17:389–99.

Niebel, B. W. 1982. *Motion and Time Study*, 7th ed. Homewood, IL: Irwin.

Nightingale, F. 1871. *Introductory Notes on Lying-in Institutions; Together with a Proposal for Organising an Institution for Training Midwives and Midwifery Nurses*. London: Longmans, Green & Co.

Nikitina, S. 2003. Stories that stayed "under the skin." *Qualitative Studies in Education* 16:251–65.

Nishimura, M. 1995. A functional-analysis of Japanese English code-switching. *Journal of Pragmatics* 23:157–81.

Nolan, J. M., and G. W. Ryan. 2000. Fear and loathing at the cineplex: Gender differences in descriptions and perceptions of slasher films. *Sex Roles* 42:39–56.

Noll, J., D. Seichter, and S. Beecham. 2013. Can automated text classification improve content analysis of software project data? ACM/IEEE International Symposium on Empirical Software Engineering and Measurement (ESEM), pp. 300–303. DOI:10.1109/ESEM.2013.52

Nolle, A. P., L. Gulbs, J. A.Kuhlberg, and L. H. Zayas. 2012. Sacrifice for the sake of the family: Expressions of familism by Latina teens in the context of suicide. *American Journal of Orthopsychiatry* 82:319–27.

Norrick, N. R. 2001. On the conversational performance of narrative jokes: Toward an account of timing. *Humor* 14:255–74.

Nyamongo, I. K. 1999. Home case management of malaria: An ethnographic study of lay people's classification of drugs in Suneka division, Kenya. *Tropical Medicine and International Health* 4:736–43.

Nyamongo, I. M. 2002. Assessing intracultural variability statistically using data on malaria perceptions in Gusii, Kenya. *Field Methods* 14:148–60.

Oaten, M., R. J. Stevenson, and T. I. Case. 2009. Disgust as a disease-avoidance mechanism. *Psychological Bulletin* 135:303–21.

Ochs, E., and C. L. Capps. 2001. *Living Narrative: Creating Lives in Everyday Storytelling.* Cambridge, MA: Harvard University Press.

Ogilvie, D. M., P. J. Stone, and E. S. Schneidman. 1966. Some characteristics of genuine versus simulated suicide notes. In *The General Inquirer: A Computer Approach to Content Analysis*, P. J. Stone, D. C. Dunphy, M. S. Smith, and D. M. Olgivie, eds., 527–35. Cambridge, MA: MIT Press.

O'Halloran, S. 2005. Symmetry in interaction in meetings of Alcoholics Anonymous: The management of conflict. *Discourse and Society* 16:535–60.

Okamoto, D. G., L. S. Rashotte, and L. Smith-Lovin. 2002. Measuring interruption: Syntactic and contextual methods of coding conversation. *Social Psychology Quarterly* 65:38–55.

Okamura, J. Y. 1981. Situational ethnicity. *Ethnic and Racial Studies* 4:452–65.

Olmstead, S. P., S. Negash, K. Pasley, and F. D. Fincham. 2013. Emerging adults' expectations for pornography use in the context of committed romantic relationships: A qualitative study. *Archives of Sexual Behavior* 42:625–35.

Onwuegbuzie, A., and N. L. Leech. 2007. Sampling designs in qualitative research: Making the sampling process more public. *The Qualitative Report* 12:238–54.

Opler, M. E. 1945. Themes as dynamic forces in culture. *American Journal of Sociology* 51:198–206.

Osgood, C. 1959. The representational model and relevant research methods. In *Trends in Content Analysis*, I. de Sola Pool, ed., 33–88. Urbana: University of Illinois Press.

Oslund, J. A. 2012. Mathematics-for-teaching: What can be learned from the ethnopoetics of teachers' stories? *Educational Studies in Mathematics* 79:293–309.

Ostrander, S. A. 1980. Upper-class women: Class consciousness as conduct and meaning. In *Power Structure Research*, G. W. Domhoff, ed., 73–96. Beverly Hills, CA: Sage.

Otterbein, K. F. 1969. Basic steps in conducting a cross-cultural study. *Behavior Science Notes* 4:221–36.

Otterbein, K. F. 1986. *The Ultimate Coercive Sanction: A Cross-cultural Study of Capital Punishment.* New Haven, CT: HRAF Press.

Owen, W. F. 1984. Interpretive themes in relational communication. *Quarterly Journal of Speech* 70:274–87.

Öztürkmen, A. 2003. Remembering through material culture: Local knowledge of past communities in a Turkish Black Sea town. *Middle Eastern Studies* 39:179–93.

Sandelowski, M. 1995a. Sample size in qualitative research. *Research in Nursing and Health* 18:179–83.

Sandelowski, M. 1995b. Qualitative analysis: What it is and how to begin. *Research in Nursing and Health* 18:371–75.

Sandelowski, M., C. I. Voils, J. Leeman, and J. L. Crandell. 2012. Mapping the mixed-methods research synthesis terrain. *Journal of Mixed Methods Research* 6:317–31.

Sayles, J. N., G. W. Ryan, J. S. Silver, and W. E. Cunningham. 2007. Experiences of social stigma and implications for healthcare among a diverse population of HIV positive adults. *Journal of Urban Health* 84:814–28.

Scelza, B. A. 2009. The grandmaternal niche: Critical caretaking among Martu Aborigines. *American Journal of Human Biology* 21:448–54.

Schaeffer, N. C., J. Dykema, and D. W. Maynard. 2010. Interviewers and interviewing. In *Handbook of Survey Research*, 2d ed., P. D. Marsden and J. D. Wright, eds., 437–70. Bingley, UK: Emerald Group Publishing.

Schank, R., and R. Abelson. 1977. *Scripts, Plans, Goals and Understanding: An Inquiry into Human Knowledge Structures*. Hillsdale, NJ: Lawrence Erlbaum.

Schegloff, E. A. 1968. Sequencing in conversational openings. *American Anthropologist* 70:1075–95.

Schegloff, E. A. 1979. Identification and recognition in telephone conversation openings. In *Everyday Language: Studies in Ethnomethodology*, G. Psathas, ed., 23–78. New York: Irvington.

Schegloff, E. A., and H. Sacks. 1973. Opening up closings. *Semiotica* 7:289–327.

Schifflett, B., and R. Revelle. 1994. Gender equity in sports and media coverage: A review of the NCAA News. *Journal of Sport and Social Issues* 18:144–50.

Schiffrin, D., D. Tannen, and H. E. Hamilton. 2001. Introduction. In *The Handbook of Discourse Analysis*, D. Schiffrin, D. Tannen, and H. E. Hamilton, eds., 1–10. Malden, MA: Blackwell.

Schlau, J. 2004. I did not die, I just can't hear—A grounded theory study of acquired deafness. Ph.D. dissertation, Hofstra University.

Schleiermacher, F. 1998. *Hermeneutics and Criticism: And Other Writings*, A. Bowie, tr. and ed. Cambridge: Cambridge University Press.

Schmitt, R. 2005. Systematic metaphor analysis as a method of qualitative research. *Qualitative Report* 10:358–94.

Schnegg, M., and H. R. Bernard. 1996. Words as actors: A method for doing semantic network analysis. *Cultural Anthropology Methods Journal* 8(2):7–10.

Schnegg, M., R. Rieprich, and M. Pröpper. 2014. Culture, nature, and the valuation of ecosystem services in northern Namibia. *Ecology and Society* 19:26. http://dx.doi.org/10.5751/ES-06896-190426 (accessed January 29, 2016).

Schneider, C. Q., and C. Wagemann. 2010. Standards of good practice in qualitative comparative analysis (QCA) and fuzzy-sets. *Comparative Sociology* 9:1–22.

Schonhardt-Bailey, C. 2008. The congressional debate on partial-birth abortion: Constitutional gravitas and moral passion. *British Journal of Political Science* 38:383–410.

Schrauf, R. W., and J. Sanchez. 2008. Using freelisting to identify, assess, and characterize age differences in shared cultural domains. *Journal of Gerontology: Social Sciences* 63B:S385–S393.

Schuman. H. 2008. *Method and Meaning in Polls and Surveys*. Cambridge, MA: Harvard University Press.

Schuman, H. 2009. Context effects and social change. *Public Opinion Quarterly* 73:172–79.

Schuster, M. A., N. Duan, M. Regalado, and D. J. Klein. 2000. Anticipatory guidance: What information do parents receive? What information do they want? *Archives of Pediatric and Adolescent Medicine* 154:1191–98.

Schuster, M. A., N. Halfon, and D. L. Wood. 1998. African American mothers in south central Los Angeles. Their fears for their newborn's future. *Archives of Pediatric and Adolescent Medicine* 152:264–68.

Schwarz, N. 1999. Self-reports. How the questions shape the answers. *American Psychologist* 54:93–105.

Schweizer, T. 1996. Actor and event orderings across time: Latice representation and Boolean analysis of the political disputes in Chen Village, China. *Social Networks* 18:247–66.

Scott, S. B., C. S. Bergeman, A. Verney, S. Logenbaker, M. A. Markey, and T. L. Bosconti. 2007. Social support in widowhood: A mixed methods study. *Journal of Mixed Methods Research* 1:242–66.

Scotton, C. M., and W. Ury. 1977. Bilingual strategies: The social functions of code-switching. *International Journal of the Sociology of Language* 13:5–20.

Seale, C. 2011. Secondary analysis of qualitative data. In *Qualitative Research*, 3d ed., D. Silverman, ed., 347–64. London: Sage.

Seale, C., J. Charteris-Black, C. Dumelow, L. Locock, and S. Ziebland. 2008. The effect of joint interviewing on the performance of gender. *Field Methods* 20:107–28.

Sefcek, J. A., B. H. Brumbach, and G. Vasquez. 2007. The evolutionary psychology of human mate choice: How ecology, genes, fertility, and fashion influence mating strategies. *Journal of Psychology and Human Sexuality* 18:125–82.

Shanahan, E. A., M. K. McBeth, P. L. Hathaway, and R. J. Arnell. 2008. Conduit or contributor? The role of media in policy change theory. *Policy Sciences* 41:115–38.

Shapiro, G., and J. Markoff. 1997. A matter of definition. In *Text Analysis for the Social Sciences: Methods for Drawing Statistical Inferences from Texts and Transcripts*, C. W. Roberts, ed., 9–34. Mahwah, NJ: Lawrence Erlbaum.

Sharifian, F., and M. Jamarani. 2011. Cultural schemas in intercultural communication: A study of the Persian cultural schema of sharmandegi "being ashamed." *Intercultural Pragmatics* 8:227–51.

Shawyer, R. J., A. Sani Bin Gani, A. N. Punufimana, and N. Kamuta Fualaga Seuseu. 1996. The role of clinical vignettes in rapid ethnographic research: A folk taxonomy of diarrhoea in Thailand. *Social Science and Medicine* 42:111–23.

Shelley, G. A. 1992. The social networks of people with end-stage renal disease: Comparing hemodialysis and peritoneal dialysis patients. Ph.D. dissertation, University of Florida.

Shepard, R. N., A. K. Romney, and S. B. Nerlove, eds. 1972. *Multidimensional Scaling: Theory and Applications in the Behavioral Sciences*. New York: Seminar Press.

Sherzer, J. 1994. The Kuna and Columbus: Encounters and confrontations of discourse. *American Anthropologist* 96:902–25.

Shostak, S., J. Freese, B. G. Link, and J. C. Phelan. 2009. The politics of the gene: Social status and beliefs about genetics for individual outcomes. *Social Psychology Quarterly* 72:77–93.

Silva, E. B. 2007. What's [yet] to be seen? Re-using qualitative data. *Sociological Research Online* 12(3). http://www.socresonline.org.uk/12/3/4.html (accessed April 16, 2015).

Silverman, D. 1993. *Interpreting Qualitative Data: Methods of Analyzing Talk, Text, and Interaction*. Thousand Oaks, CA: Sage.

Silverman, D. 1998. *Harvey Sacks: Social Science and Conversation Analysis*. New York: Oxford University Press.

Silverman, D. 2011. *Interpreting Qualitative Data: Methods of Analyzing Talk, Text, and Interaction*, 4th ed. Thousand Oaks, CA: Sage.

Silverman, E., S. Woolshin, L. M. Schwartz, S. J. Byram, H. G. Welch, and B. Fischoff. 2001. Women's views on breast cancer risk and screening mammography: A qualitative interview study. *Medical Decision Making* 21:231–40.

Silverman, H., ed. 1991. *Gadamer and Hermeutics*. New York: Routledge.

Singer, E., and S. Presser. 1989. *Survey Research Methods: A Reader*. Chicago: University of Chicago Press.

Singer, M., S. Clair, M. Malta, F. I. Bastos, N. Bertoni, and C. Santelices. 2011. Doubts remain, risks persist: HIV prevention knowledge and HIV testing among drug users in Rio de Janeiro, Brazil. *Substance Use and Misuse* 46:511–22.

Singh, S., and L. Richards. 2003. Missing data: Finding "central" themes in qualitative research. *Qualitative Research Journal* 3:5–17.

Siregar, S. L., G. B. Dagnino, and F. Garraffo. 2011. Content analysis and social network analysis: A two-phase methodology in obtaining fundamental concepts of coopetition. *Jurnal Ilmiah Ekonomi Bisnis* 14:103–13.

Slaughter, V. 2005. Young children's understanding of death. *Australian Psychologist* 40:179–86.

Smilde, D. 2005. A qualitative comparative analysis of conversion to Venezuelan evangelicism: How networks matter. *American Journal of Sociology* 111:757–96.

Smith, A. 2000. "Safety" in gay men's personal ads, 1985–1996. *Journal of Homosexuality* 39:43–48.

Smith, C. A., J. A. Konik, and M. V. Tuve. 2011. In search of looks, status, or something else? Partner preferences among butch and femme lesbians and heterosexual men and women. *Sex Roles* 64:658–68.

Smith, C. A., and S. Stillman. 2002a. Butch/femme in the personal advertisements of lesbians. *Journal of Lesbian Studies* 6:45–51.

Smith, C. A., and S. Stillman. 2002b. What do women want? The effects of gender and sexual orientation on the desirability of physical attributes in the personal ads of women. *Sex Roles* 46:337–342.

Smith, C. D., and W. Kornblum. 1996. *In the Field. Readings on the Research Experience*. New York: Praeger.

Smith, J. J. 1993. Using ANTHROPAC 3.5 and a spreadsheet to compute a freelist salience index. *Cultural Anthropology Methods Newsletter* 5(3):1–3.

Smith, J. J., and S. P. Borgatti. 1997. Salience counts—and so does accuracy: Correcting and updating a measure for free-list item salience. *Journal of Linguistic Anthropology* 7:208–9.

Smith, P. K., A. Kupferberg, J. A. Mora-Merchan, M. Samara, S. Bosley, and R. Osborn. 2012. A content analysis of school anti-bullying policies: A follow-up after six years. *Educational Psychology in Practice: Theory, Research and Practice in Educational Psychology* 28:47–70.

Smith, R. A., and R. Parrott. 2012. Mental representations of HPV in Appalachia: Gender, semantic network analysis, and knowledge gaps. *Journal of Health Psychology* 17:917–28.

Smith, T. M. F. 1983. On the validity of inferences from non-random samples. *Journal of the Royal Statistical Society*, Series A:146:394–403.

Smith, T. W. 1997. The impact of the presence of others on a respondent's answers to questions. *International Journal of Public Opinion Research* 9:33–47.

Smith-Lovin, L., and C. Brody. 1989. Interruptions in group discussions: The effect of gender and group composition. *American Sociological Review* 54:424–35.

Snodgrass, J. G., H. J. F. Dengah, II, M. G. Lacy, and J. Fagan. 2013. A formal anthropological view of motivation models of problematic MMO play: Achievement, social, and immersion factors in the context of culture. *Transcultural Psychiatry* 50:235–62.

Sobal, J. 2001. Sample extensiveness in qualitative nutrition education research. *Journal of Nutrition Education* 33:184–93.

Sokolowski, R. 2000. *Introduction to Phenomenology*. New York: Cambridge University Press.

de Sola Pool, I. 1952. *Symbols of Democracy* (with the collaboration of H. Lasswell, P. H. Odegard, and D. Lerner). Stanford, CA: Stanford University Press.

de Sola Pool, I. 1959. Trends in content analysis today: A summary. In *Trends in Content Analysis*, I. de Sola Pool, ed., 189–240. Urbana: University of Illinois Press.

Spiegelberg, H. 1980. Phenomenology. *Encyclopaedia Brittanica*, 15th ed., Vol. 14. Chicago: Encyclopaedia Brittanica, Inc.

Spiggle, S. 1994. Analysis and interpretation of qualitative data in consumer research. *Journal of Consumer Research* 21:491–503.

Spradley, J. P. 1972. *Culture and Cognition: Rules, Maps, and Plans*. New York: Chandler Publishing Company.

Spradley, J. P. 1979. *The Ethnographic Interview*. New York: Holt, Rinehart and Winston.

Spradley, J. P. 1980. *Participant Observation*. New York: Holt, Rinehart and Winston.

Staats, S. K. 2008. Poetic lines in mathematics discourse: A method from linguistic anthropology. *For the Learning of Mathematics* 28:26–32

Staudigl, M., and G. Berguno, eds. 2013. *Schutzian Phenomenology and Hermeneutic Traditions*. Dordrecht, Netherlands: Springer.

Stavros, C., M. D. Meng, K. Westberg, and F. Farrelly. 2014. Understanding fan motivation for interacting on social media. *Sport Management Review* 17:455–69.

Stefflre, V. J. 1972. Some applications of multidimensional scaling to social science problems. In *Multidimensional Scaling: Theory and Applications in the Behavioral Sciences*, Vol. 2, A. K. Romney, R. N. Shepard, and S. B. Nerlove, eds., 211–43. New York: Seminar Press.

Steger, T. 2007. The stories metaphors tell: Metaphors as a tool to decipher tacit aspects in narratives. *Field Methods* 19:3–23.

Stein, R. H. 1987. *The Synoptic Problem*. Grand Rapids, MI: Baker Book House.

Stepchenkova, S., and F. Z. Zhan. 2013. Visual destination images of Peru: Comparative content analysis of DMO and user-generated photography. *Tourism Management* 36:590–601.

Stewart, D. W., and P. N. Shamdasani. 1990. *Focus Groups: Theory and Practice*. Newbury Park, CA: Sage.

Stewart, P. J., and A. Strathern. 2002. *Gender, Song, and Sensibility. Folktales and Folksongs in the Highlands of New Guinea*. Westport, CT: Praeger.

Stigler, J. W., P. A. Gonzales, T. Kawanka, S. Knoll, and A. Serrano. 1999. *The TIMSS Videotape Classroom Study: Methods and Findings from an Exploratory Research Project on Eighth-grade Mathematics Instruction in Germany, Japan, and the United States*. National Center for Education Statistics. NCES 99-074. Washington, DC: U.S. Government Printing Office. http://nces.ed.gov/pubs99/1999074.pdf (accessed September 7, 2013).

Stock, W. A. 1994. Systematic coding for research synthesis. In *The Handbook of Research Synthesis*, H. Cooper and L. V. Hedges, eds., 125–38. New York: Russell Sage Foundation.

Stokes, J., and G. Schmidt. 2012. Child protection decision making: A factorial analysis using case vignettes. *Social Work* 57:83–90.

Stone, P. J., R. F. Bales, J. Z. Namenwirth, and D. M. Ogilvie. 1962. The General Inquirer: A computer system for content analysis and retrieval based on the sentence as a unit of information. *Behavioral Science* 7:484–98.

Stone, P. J., D. C. Dunphy, M. S. Smith, and D. M. Ogilvie, eds. 1966. *The General Inquirer: A Computer Approach to Content Analysis*. Cambridge, MA: MIT Press.

Strauss, A. 1987. *Qualitative Analysis for Social Scientists*. Cambridge: Cambridge University Press.

Strauss, A., and J. Corbin. 1990. *Basics of Qualitative Research: Grounded Theory Procedures and Techniques*. Newbury Park, CA: Sage.

Strauss, A., and J. Corbin, eds. 1997. *Grounded Theory in Practice*. Thousand Oaks, CA: Sage.

Strauss, A., and J. Corbin. 1998. *Basics of Qualitative Research: Grounded Theory Procedures and Techniques*, 2d ed. Thousand Oaks, CA: Sage.

Strauss, C. 1992. What makes Tony run? Schemas as motive reconsideration. In *Human Motives and Cultural Models*, R. D'Andrade and C. Strauss, eds., 191–224. Cambridge: Cambridge University Press.

Strauss, C. 1997. Research on cultural discontinuities. In *A Cognitive Theory of Cultural Meaning*, C. Strauss and N. Quinn, eds., 210–51. Cambridge: Cambridge University Press.

Strauss, C., and N. Quinn. 1997. *A Cognitive Theory of Cultural Meaning*. Cambridge: Cambridge University Press.

Sudman, S. 1976. *Applied Sampling*. New York: Academic Press.

Sudman, S., and N. M. Bradburn. 1974. *Response Effects in Surveys: Review and Synthesis*. Chicago: Aldine.

Sudman, S., and N. M. Bradburn. 1982. *Asking Questions*. San Francisco: Jossey-Bass.

Sudman, S., and G. Kalton. 1986. New developments in the sampling of special populations. *Annual Review of Sociology* 12:401–29.

Sutrop, U. 2001. List task and a cognitive salience index. *Field Methods* 13:263–76.

Suttles, G. D. 1968. *The Social Order of the Slum: Ethnicity and Territory in the Inner City*. Chicago: University of Chicago Press.

Swora, M. G. 2003. Using cultural consensus analysis to study sexual risk perception: A report on a pilot study. *Culture, Health, and Sexuality* 5:339–52.

Táboas-Pais, M. I., and A. Rey-Cao. 2012. Gender differences in physical education textbooks in Spain: A content analysis of photographs. *Sex Roles* 67:389–402.

Tacq, J. 2007. Znaniecki's analytical induction as a method of sociological research. *Polish Sociological Review* 2:187–208.

Taietz, P. 1962. Conflicting group norms and the "third" person in the interview. *American Journal of Sociology* 68:97–104.

Tan, K. P. 2007. Singapore's National Day rally speech: A site of ideological negotiation. *Journal of Contemporary Asia* 37:292–308.

Tang, E., and H. Nesi. 2003. Teaching vocabulary in two Chinese classrooms: Schoolchildren's exposure to English words in Hong Kong and Guangzhou. *Language Teaching Research* 7:65–97.

Tang, Z., L. Weavwind, J. Mazabob, E. Thomas, M. Chu-Weininger, and M. Ying. 2007. Workflow in intensive care unit remote monitoring: A time-and-motion study. *Critical Care Medicine* 35:2057–63.

Tannen, D. 1984. *Conversational Style: Analyzing Talk among Friends*. Norwood, NJ: Ablex.

Tannen, D. 1994. *Gender and Discourse*. New York: Oxford University Press.

Tannen, D. 2012. Turn-taking and intercultural discourse and communication. In *The Handbook of Intercultural Discourse and Communication*, C. B. Paulston, S. F. Kiesling, and E. R. Rangel, eds., 135–57. Chichester, UK: John Wiley & Sons.

Tanur, J. M. 1992. *Questions about Questions: Inquiries into the Cognitive Bases of Surveys*. New York: Russell Sage Foundation.

Tashakkori, A., and C. Teddlie. 1998. *Mixed Methodology: Combining Qualitative and Quantitative Approaches*. Thousand Oaks, CA: Sage.

Tashakkori, A., and C. Teddlie, eds. 2010. *Sage Handbook of Mixed Methods in Social and Behavioral Research*, 2d ed. Thousand Oaks, CA: Sage.

Tausczik, Y. R., and J. W. Pennebaker. 2010. The psychological meaning of words: LWIC and computerized text analysis methods. *Journal of Language and Social Psychology* 29:24–54.

Taylor, C. 2014. Investigating the representation of migrants in the UK and Italian press. *International Journal of Corpus Linguistics* 19:368–400.

Taylor, P. M. 1995. Collecting icons of power and identity: Transformation of Indonesian material culture in the museum context. *Cultural Dynamics* 7:101–24.

Taylor, W. K., L. Magnussen, and M. J. Amundon. 2001. The lived experience of battered women. *Violence Against Women* 7:563–85.

ten Have, P. 1991. Talk and institution: A reconsideration of the "asymmetry" of doctor–patient interaction. In *Talk and Social Structure. Studies in Ethnomethodology and Conversation Analysis*, D. Boden and Z. H. Zimmerman, eds., 138–63. Berkeley: University of California Press.

ten Have, P. 1999. *Doing Conversation Analysis: A Practical Guide*. Thousand Oaks, CA: Sage.

Tenam-Zemach, M. Kirchgessner, J. Pecore, L. Lai, and S. Hecht. 2014. Development of an innovative method for analyzing the presence of environmental sustainability themes and an ecological paradigm in science content standards. *Studies in Educational Evaluation* 41:133–42.

Tesch, R. 1990. *Qualitative Research: Analysis Types and Software Tools*. New York: The Falmer Press.

Thiem, A., and A. Duşa. 2013a. QCA: A package for Qualitative Comparative Analysis. *The R Journal* 5:87–97.

Thiem, A., and A. Duşa. 2013b. Boolean minimization in social science research: A review of current software for qualitative comparative analysis (QCA). *Social Science Computer Review* 31:505–21.

Thomson, D., A. Kaka, L. Pronk, and C. Alalouch. 2012. The use of freelisting to elicit stakeholder understanding of the benefits sought from healthcare buildings. *Construction Management and Economics* 30:309–23.

Thompson, C. 1999. Qualitative research into nurse decision making: Factors for consideration in theoretical sampling. *Qualitative Health Research* 9:815–28.

Thompson, E. C., and Z. Juan. 2006. Comparative cultural salience: Measures using free-list data. *Field Methods* 18:398–412.

Thompson, S. 1932–1936. *Motif-index of Folk-literature. A Classification of Narrative Elements in Folktales, Ballads, Myths, Fables, Mediaeval Romances, Exempla, Fabliaux, Jest-Books, and Local Legends.* Bloomington: Indiana University Press.

Thornberg, R. 2008. "It's not fair!"—Voicing pupils' criticisms of school rules. *Children and Society* 22:418–28.

Timm, J. R., ed. 1992. *Texts in Context. Traditional Hermeneutics in South Asia.* Albany: State University of New York Press.

Tirella, L. G., W. Chan, S. A. Cermak, A. Litvinova, K. C. Salas, and L. C. Miller. 2007. Time use in Russian baby homes. *Child: Care, Health and Development* 34:77–86.

To, S. 2013. Understanding sheng nu ("leftover women"): The phenomenon of late marriage among Chinese professional women. *Symbolic Interaction* 36:1–20.

Tourangeau, R., and N. M. Bradburn. 2010. The psychology of survey response. In *Handbook of Survey Research*, 2d ed., P. D. Marsden and J. D. Wright, eds., 315–46. Bingley, UK: Emerald Group Publishing.

Tourangeau, R., and T. Yan. 2007. Sensitive questions in surveys. *Psychological Bulletin* 133:859–83.

Toyokawa, N. 2006. The function of the social network formed by Japanese sojourners' wives in the United States. *International Journal of Intercultural Relations* 30:185–93.

Tremblay, M.-A. 1957. The key informant technique: A nonethnographic application. *American Anthropologist* 59:688–701.

Tribble, C. 2010. What are concordances and how are they used? In *The Routledge Handbook of Corpus Linguistics*, A. O'Keefe and M. McCarthy, eds, 167–83. New York: Routledge.

Trotter, R. T., III, and J. M. Potter. 1993. Pile sorts, a cognitive anthropological model of drug and AIDS risks for Navajo teenagers: Assessment of a new evaluation tool. *Drugs and Society* 7:23–39.

Trow, M. 1957. Comment on "Participant Observation and Interviewing: A Comparison." *Human Organization* 16:33–35.

Tsang, W. K., and M. Wong. 2004. Constructing a shared "Hong Kong identity" in comic discourses. *Discourse and Society* 15:767–85.

Tufte, E. R. 1997. *Visual Explanations: Images and Quantities, Evidence and Narrative.* Cheshire, CT: Graphics Press.

Turner, L. H., and R. Shuter. 2004. African American and European American women's visions of workplace conflict: A metaphorical analysis. *The Howard Journal of Communications* 15:169–83.

Turner, R. 1953. The quest for universals in sociological research. *American Sociological Review* 18:604–11.

Umezaki, M., T. Yamauchi, and R. Ohtsukatime. 2002. Time allocation to subsistence activities among the Huli in rural and urban Papua New Guinea. *Journal of Biosocial Science* 34:133–37.

United States v. Pelley; Same v. Brown; Same v. Fellowship Press, Inc. 1942. Nos. 8086-8088. United States Court of Appeals for the Seventh Circuit. 132 F.2d 170; 1942 U.S. App. LEXIS 2559. December 17, 1942.

Van Boeschoten, R. 2006. Code-switching, linguistic jokes and ethnic identity: Reading hidden transcripts in a cross-cultural context. *Journal of Modern Greek Studies* 24:347–77.

van den Hoonaard, W. C., ed. 2002. *Walking the Tightrope: Ethical Issues for Qualitative Researchers*. Toronto: University of Toronto Press.

van der Vaart, W., and T. Glasner. 2007. Applying a timeline as a recall aid in a telephone survey: A record check study. *Applied Cognitive Psychology* 21:227–38.

van der Vaart, W., and T. Glasner. 2011. Personal landmarks as recall aids in survey interviews. *Field Methods* 23:37–56.

van der Vaart, Y., A. Ongena, and W. Dijkstra. 2006. Do interviewers' voice characteristics influence cooperation rates in telephone surveys? *International Journal of Public Opinion Research* 18:488–99.

Van Holt, T., J. C. Johnson, K. M. Carley, J. Brinkley, and J. Diesner. 2013. Rapid ethnographic assessment for cultural mapping. *Poetics* 41:366–83.

Van Leeuwen, T., and C. Jewitt, eds. 2001. *Handbook of Visual Analysis*. London: Sage.

Van Maanen, J., M. Miller, and J. C. Johnson. 1982. An occupation in transition: Traditional and modern forms of commercial fishing. *Work and Occupations* 9:193–216.

van Manen, M. 1990. *Researching Lived Experience. Human Science for an Action Sensitive Pedagogy*. Albany: State University of New York Press.

Varangis, E., N. Lanzieri, T. Hildebrandt, and M. Feldman. 2012. Gay male attraction toward muscular men: Does mating context matter? *Body Image* 9:270–78.

Vaughn, S., J. S. Schumm, and J. M. Sinagub. 1996. *Focus Group Interviews in Education and Psychology*. Thousand Oaks, CA: Sage.

Verma, R. K., G. Rangaiyan, R. Singh, S. Sharma, and P. J. Pelto. 2001. A study of male sexual health problems in a Mumbai slum population. *Culture, Health and Sexuality* 3:339–52.

Wagholikar, K. B., K. L. MacLaughlin, M. R. Henry, R. A. Greenes, R. A. Hankey, H. Liu, and R. Chaudhry. 2012. Clinical decision support with automated text processing for cervical cancer screening. *Journal of the American Medical Informatics Association* 19:833–39.

Waitzkin, H., T. Britt, and C. Williams. 1994. Narratives of aging and social problems in medical encounters with older persons. *Journal of Health and Social Behavior* 35:322–48.

Wansink, B., K. v. Ittersum, and J. E. Painter. 2006. Ice cream illusions: Bowls, spoons, and self-served portion sizes. *American Journal of Preventive Medicine* 31:240–42.

Ward, W., and D. Spennemann. 2000. Meeting local needs? Case study of a communication project in the Pacific islands. *Public Administration and Development* 20:185–95.

Warwick, D. P., and C. A. Lininger. 1975. *The Sample Survey: Theory and Practice*. New York: McGraw-Hill.

Watts, L. K., and S. E. Gutierres. 1997. A Native American–based cultural model of substance dependency and recovery. *Human Organization* 56:9–18.

Weaver, A. D., A. D. Menard, C. Cabrera, and A. Taylor. 2015. Embodying the moral code? Thirty years of final girls in slasher films. *Psychology of Popular Media Culture* 4:31–46.

Weaver, S. E., and M. Coleman. 2005. A mothering but not a mother role: A grounded theory study of the nonresidential stepmother role. *Journal of Social and Personal Relationships* 22:477–97.

Weber, R. P. 1990. *Basic Content Analysis*, 2d ed. Newbury Park, CA: Sage.

Wei, L., and L. Milroy. 1995. Conversational code-switching in a Chinese community in Britain: A sequential analysis. *Journal of Pragmatics* 23:281–99.

Weigl, M., A. Müller, A. Zupanc, and P. Angerer. 2009. Participant observation of time allocation, direct patient contact and simultaneous activities in hospital physicians. *BMC Health Services Research* 9:110–19.

Weine, S., K. Knafl, S. Feetham, Y. Kulauzovic, A. Klebic, S. Sclove, S. Besic, A. Mujagic, J. Muzurovic, and D. Spahovic. 2005. A mixed methods study of refugee families engaging in multiple-family groups. *Family Relations* 54:558–68.

Weisner, T. S. 2002. Ecocultural understanding of children's developmental pathways. *Human Development* 45:275–81.

Weisner, T. S. 2008. Well being and sustainability of the daily routine of life. In *The Good Life: Well-being in Anthropological Perspective*, G. Mathews and C. Izquerdo, eds., 349–81. New York: Berghahn Press.

Weisner, T. S., L. Beizer, and L. Stolze. 1991. Religion and families of children with developmental delays. *American Journal of Mental Retardation* 95:647–62.

Weisner, T. S., and H. Gamier. 1992. Nonconventional family life-styles and school achievement: A 12-year longitudinal study. *American Educational Research Journal* 29:605–32.

Weisstub, D. N., ed. 1998. *Research on Human Subjects: Ethics, Law, and Social Policy*. Kidlington, Oxford, UK: Pergamon.

Weisstub, D. N., and G. Diaz Pintos, eds. 2007. *Autonomy and Human Rights in Health Care: An International Perspective*. New York: Springer.

Weller, S. C. 2007. The cultural consensus model. *Field Methods* 19:339–68.

Weller, S. C. 2014. Structured interviewing and questionnaire construction. In *Handbook of Methods in Cultural Anthropology*, 2d ed., H. R. Bernard and C. C. Gravlee, eds., 343–90. Lanham, MD: Rowman and Littlefield.

Weller, S. C., and A. K. Romney. 1988. *Systematic Data Collection*. Newbury Park, CA: Sage.

Weller, S. C., T. K. Ruebush, II, and R. E. Klein. 1997. Predicting treatment-seeking behavior in Guatemala: A comparison of the health services research and decision-theoretic approaches. *Medical Anthropology Quarterly* 11:224–45.

Wells, K. 2011. A narrative analysis of one mother's story of child custody loss and regain. *Children and Youth Services Review* 33:439–47.

Wennerstrom, A. 2001a. *The Music of Everyday Speech. Prosody and Discourse Analysis*. New York: Oxford University Press.

Wennerstrom, A. 2001b. Intonation and evaluation in oral narratives. *Journal of Pragmatics* 33:1183–206.

Wentland, E. J., and K. W. Smith. 1993. *Survey Responses: An Evaluation of Their Validity*. San Diego: Academic Press.

Werner, O. 1992. How to record activities. *Cultural Anthropology Methods Journal* 4(2):1–3.

Werner, O., and H. R. Bernard. 1994. Short take 13: Ethnographic sampling 1. *Cultural Anthropology Methods Journal* 6(2):7–9.

West, C. 1984. *Routine Complications: Troubles with Talk between Doctors and Patients*. Bloomington: University of Indiana Press.

West, C. 1995. Women's competence in conversation. *Discourse and Society* 6:107–31.

West, C., and D. Zimmerman. 1983. Small insults: A study of interruptions in cross-sex conversations between unacquainted persons. In *Language, Gender, and Society*, B. Thorne, C. Kramarae, and N. Henley, eds., 102–17. Rowley, MA: Newbury House Publishers.

West, E. 2010. A taste for greeting cards: Distinction within a denigrated cultural form. *Journal of Consumer Culture* 10:362–82.

Westbrook, J. I., E. Coiera, W. T. Dunsmuir, B. M. Brown, N. Kelk, R.Paoloni, and C. Tran. 2010. The impact of interruptions on clinical task completion. *Quality and Safety in Health Care* 19:284–89.

Weston, C., T. Gandell, J. Beauchamp, L. McAlpine, C. Wiseman, and C. Beauchamp. 2001. Analyzing interview data: The development and evolution of a coding system. *Qualitative Sociology* 24:381–400.

White, D. D., A. Wutich, K. L. Larson, P. Gober, T. Lant, and C. Senneville. 2010. Credibility, salience, and legitimacy of boundary objects: Water managers' assessment of a simulation model in an immersive decision theater. *Science and Public Policy* 37:219–32.

White, S. B. 2006. Telling the story: Kansas City mayor and United Methodist pastor Emmanuel Cleaver's use of storytelling to transcend racial barriers. *Journal of African American Studies* 9:32–44.

Whiting, B. W., J. W. M. Whiting (with R. Longabaugh). 1975. *Children of Six Cultures: A Psycho–Cultural Analysis*. Cambridge, MA: Harvard University Press

Whiting, J. B., and R. E. Lee. 2003. Voices from the system: A qualitative study of foster children's stories. *Family Relations* 52:288–95.

Whorf, B. L. 1945. Grammatical categories. *Language* 21:1–11.

Whyte, W. F. 1960. Interviewing in field research. In *Human Organization Research*, R. W. Adams and J. J. Preiss, eds., 299–314. Homewood, IL: Dorsey.

Whyte, W. F. 1981 [1943]. *Street Corner Society: The Social Structure of an Italian Slum*, 3d ed. Chicago: University of Chicago.

Whyte, W. F. 1984. *Learning from the Field: A Guide from Experience*. Newbury Park, CA: Sage.

Whyte, W. F. 1996a. Qualitative sociology and deconstructionism. *Qualitative Inquiry* 2:220–26.

Whyte, W. F. 1996b. Facts, interpretations, and ethics in qualitative inquiry. *Qualitative Inquiry* 2:242–44.

Whyte, W. F., and K. A. Whyte. 1984. *Learning from the Field: A Guide from Experience*. Beverly Hills, CA: Sage.

Wickens, C. M., D. L. Wiesenthal, A. Hall, and J. E. W. Roseborough. 2013. Driver anger on the information superhighway: A content analysis of online complaints of offensive driver behaviour. *Accident Analysis and Prevention* 51:84–92.

Wiederman, M. 1993. Evolved gender differences in mate preferences: Evidence from personal advertisements. *Ethology and Sociobiology* 14:331–51.

Wiederman, M., D. Weis, and E. Algeier. 1994. The effect of question preface on response rates in a telephone survey of sexual experience. *Archives of Sexual Behavior* 23:203–15.

Wierzbicka, A. 2004. The English expression good boy and good girl and cultural models of child rearing. *Culture and Psychology* 10:251–78.

Wilcox, F. D. 1900. The American newspaper: A study in social psychology. *Annals of the American Academy of Political and Social Science* 16:56–92.

Williams, L. M., and R. A. Farrell. 1990. Legal responses to child sexual abuse in day care. *Criminal Justice and Behavior* 17:284–302.

Willis, F. N., and R. A. Carlson. 1993. Singles ads: Gender, social class, and time. *Sex Roles* 29:387–404.

Wilson, H. S., S. A. Hutchinson, and W. H. Holzemer. 2002. Reconciling incompatibilities: A grounded theory of HIV medication adherence and symptom management. *Qualitative Health Research* 12:1309–22.

Winchatz, M. R. 2010. Participant observation and the nonnative ethnographer: Implications of positioning on discourse-centered fieldwork. *Field Methods* 22:340–56.

Windsor, L. C. 2013. Using concept mapping in community-based participatory research: A mixed methods approach. *Journal of Mixed Methods Research* 7:274–93.

Witavaara, B., B. Lundman, M. Barnekow-Bergkvist, and C. Brulin. 2007. Striking a balance— health experience of male ambulance personnel with musculoskeletal symptoms: A grounded theory. *International Journal of Nursing Studies* 44:770–79.

Wodak, R. 2006. Medical discourse: Doctor–patient communication. In *Encyclopedia of Language and Linguistics*, 2d ed., K. Brown, ed. 681–87. San Diego: Elsevier.

Wodak, R., and M. Meyer, eds. 2011. *Methods of Critical Discourse Analysis*. London: Sage.

Wodak, R., and M. Reisigl. 1999. *Discourse and Discrimination. The Rhetoic of Racism and Antisemitism*. London: Routledge.

Wolcott, H. F. 1992. Posturing in qualitative inquiry. In *The Handbook of Qualitative Research in Education*. M. D. LeCompte, W. L. Millroy, and J. Preissle, eds., 3–52. New York: Academic Press.

Wolcott, H. F. 2005. *The Art of Fieldwork*, 2d ed. Walnut Creek, CA: AltaMira.

Wolcott, H. F. 2008. *Ethnography. A Way of Seeing*, 2d ed. Lanham, MD: AltaMira.

Wondergem, T. R., and M. Friedlmeier. 2012. Gender and ethnic differences in smiling: A year-book photographs analysis from kindergarten through 12th grade. *Sex Roles*: 67:403–11.

Woodward, J. L., and R. Franzen. 1948. A study of coding reliability. *Public Opinion Quarterly* 12:253–57.

Woofit, R. 2005. *Conversation Analysis and Discourse Analysis: A Comparative and Critical Introduction*. Thousand Oaks, CA: Sage.

Wright, J. 1997. Deconstructing development theory: Feminism, the public/private dichotomy, and the Mexican maquiladoras. *Canadian Journal of Sociology and Anthropology* 34:71–91.

Wu-Tso, P., I. L. Yeh, and C. F. Tam. 1995. Comparisons of dietary intake in young and old Asian Americans: A two-generation study. *Nutrition Research* 15:1445–62.

Wutich, A., T. Lant, D. D. White, K. L. Larson, and M. Gartin. 2009. Comparing focus group and individual responses on sensitive topics: A study of water decision-makers in a desert city. *Field Methods* 21:49–68.

Wutich, A., R. Stotts, J. Rice, A. Brewis, M. du Bray, J. Maupin, and D. White. 2015. The 2013 global ethnohydrology study: Cross-cultural perspectives on wastewater treatment. Unpublished report.

Wysoker, A. 2002. A conceptual model of weight loss and weight regain: An intervention for change. *Journal of the American Psychiatric Nurses Association* 8:168–73.

Yaghoubi-Notash, M., and M. Janghi-Golezani. 2013. From frequency to instructional order: Insights from a narrow-angle corpus of psychology RA introductions. *Theory and Practice in Language Studies* 3:1034–39.

Yakali-Çamoglu, D. 2007. Turkish family narratives: The relationships between mothers- and daughters-in-law. *Journal of Family History* 32:161–78.

Yamaguchi, M. 2012. Finding culture in "poetic" structures: The case of a "racially-mixed" Japanese/New Zealander. *Journal of Multicultural Discourses* 7:99–117.

Yancey G. A., and S. W. Yancey. 1997. Black–white differences in the use of personal advertisements for individuals seeking interracial relationships. *Journal of f Studies* 27:650–67.

Yang, Y. 2001. Sex and language proficiency level in color naming performance: An ESL/EFL perspective. *International Journal of Applied Linguistics* 11:238–56.

Yasumoto, S., and R. LaRossa. 2010 The culture of fatherhood in Japanese comic strips: A historical analysis. *Journal of Comparative Family Studies* 41:611. http://tinyurl.com/mhj6qas (accessed September 7, 2013).

Yeh, C. J., and A. G. Inman. 2007. Qualitative data analysis and interpretation in counseling psychology: Strategies for best practices. *Counseling Psychologist* 35:369–403.

Yin, R. K. 2008. *Case Study Research: Design and Methods*, 4th ed. Thousand Oaks, CA: Sage.

Yin, R. K. 2014. *Case Study Research: Design and Methods*, 5th ed. London: Sage.

Yodanis, C. 2006. *Journal of Contemporary Ethnography*. 35:341–66.

Yoder, P. S. 1995. Examining ethnomedical diagnoses and treatment choices for diarrheal disorders in Lubumbashi Swahili. *Medical Anthropology* 16:211–48.

Young, J. C. 1981. Non-use of physicians: Methodological approaches, policy implications, and the utility of decision models. *Social Science and Medicine* 15:499–507.

Young, J. C., and L. C. Garro. 1994 [1981]. *Medical Choice in a Mexican Village*. Prospect Heights, IL: Waveland.

Yule, G. U. 1968 [1944]. *The Statistical Study of Literary Vocabulary*. Hamden, CT: Archon.

Zakrzewski, R. F., and M. A. Hector. 2004. The lived experiences of alcohol addiction: Men of alcoholics anaonymous. *Issues in Mental Health Nursing* 25:61–77.

Zeitlyn, D. 2004. The gift of the gab: Anthropology and conversation analysis. *Anthropos* 99:452–68.

Zeoli, A. M., E. A. Rivera, C. M. Sullivan, and S. Kubiak. 2013. Post-separation abuse of women and their children: Boundary-setting and family court utilization among victimized mothers. *Journal of Family Violence* 28:547–60.

Zieziula, F. F., and K. Meadows. 1992. The experience of loss and grief among late-deafened people: A report on research and theory. In *Facing Deafness*, S. Larew, K. Saura, and D. Watson, eds., 58–63. DeKalb, IL: Northern Illinois University Research and Training Center on Traditionally Underserved Persons Who Are Deaf.

Zimmerman, D. H., and C. West. 1983 [1975]. Sex roles, interruptions, and silences in conversation. In *Language and Sex: Difference and Dominance*, B. Thorne and N. Henley, eds., 105–29. Rowley, MA: Newbury House.

Zipp, J. F., and J. Toth. 2002. She said, he said, they said: The impact of spousal presence in survey research. *Public Opinion Quarterly* 66:177–208.

Znaniecki, F. 1934. *The Method of Sociology*. New York: Farrar and Rinehart.

Author Index